THE SWINDON BOOK

The
SWINDON
Book

A Companion
to the History of
Swindon

Mark Child

First published in the United Kingdom in 2013

by The Hobnob Press, 30c Deverill Road Trading Estate, Sutton Veny, Warminster BA12 7BZ
www.hobnobpress.co.uk

British Library Cataloguing in Publication Data
A catalogue record for this book is available from the British Library

ISBN 978-1-906978-28-0

Typeset in Octavian and Franklin Gothic Heavy 10.5/12 pt. Typesetting and origination by John Chandler

Printed by Lightning Source

PREFACE

This book originated in the 1960s, when I was a reference librarian. It was then that I began to jot down on record cards occasional facts that I came across relating to the history of Swindon. These were of contemporary occurrences: ('Regent Street: Anstiss gutted by fire, 29 January 1965'; 'High Street: King of Prussia inn demolished 1981') or retrospective: ('Regent Circus: One-way traffic operated from 5 December 1932'). The criterion was that they might be of interest at some point in the future, when someone asked the question but no-one knew where to find the answer. The information on the cards was gradually fleshed out, and they built up over the years as I undertook original research into Swindon's history and wrote specific monographs on aspects of its people and its past.

Swindon has history in its landscape, in every building that has ever been there, in each person who lived in the town, and in all the organisations that have made it what it is. History is being made at every moment, so any book on the subject can only ever be a companion to what has gone before.

I would like to thank those people who witnessed events and places mentioned in these pages, and who so willingly and generously described them to me, or answered my queries on specific points. People of our time are herein recorded for their important contributions to the town, who, without exception, acceded to my request for interviews and biographical details. I am particularly grateful to them. My greatest thanks are to my wife Lorraine, who shares in all that I do, and whose proofreading skills have made this book much more readable than it would otherwise have been.

MARK CHILD
April 2013

THE SWINDON BOOK

Adastrians Drama Club, The In the 1930s, Joan Parsons trained at the London Academy of Music and Drama and was a student at the British Drama League, where she specialised in Shakespeare and modern playwrights. She also acted in plays, produced by her mother for the Swindon Women's Fellowship Council, and she became an elocution teacher in Swindon. In 1934, Joan and her cousin Grace Keene founded the Swindon Junior Drama Society, which gave performances in the Scouts' Hall, Dowling Street for the YMCA Red Triangle Boys' Club (the Swindon branch of which was founded in 1923 in Fleet Street). The Drama Society disbanded when war broke out, and Joan spent hostilities working at the YMCA. In 1943, she began to plan for a theatrical school, and this became the Lyndhurst School of Drama.

In 1945, she founded the Adastrians Drama Club, which quickly became established as a major theatrical force in the town. Its name was taken from *per ardua ad astra*, 'through adversity to the stars', the motto of the Royal Air Force, in which her husband was serving when he was killed in the conflict just one week after their marriage. The company's first production was *The Camel's Back*, put on in the Recreation Centre, Faringdon Road. The Adastrians soon relocated to the town's Arts Centre, and although their performances were well received and well patronised, by the mid-1950s internal difficulties had occurred and few of the originators remained. In order to keep The Adastrians alive, David Wainwright and his wife Vera (Bennett), and Stuart Macpherson and his wife Barbara invited members of all Swindon theatrical societies to a meeting at the Oxford Hotel in 1957. At this, the organisation was hauled back from the brink of closure with an injection of fresh talent that re-established it in pole position.

The society remained at the Arts Centre until 1972 when they opened at the Wyvern Theatre with a production of *The Miracle Worker* by William Gibson. Thereafter, they performed in the Wyvern's main theatre, in the Joliffe Studio, and at the Arts Centre, and they also produced musicals at the Playhouse Theatre in the Mechanics' Institute, Emlyn Square. The Club's most high profile president was the poet and writer John Betjeman, and he was succeeded in 1975 by the actor Nigel Stock. The Club disbanded in the 1980s. Former members have met bi-monthly at the Goddard Arms since 2008.

Affleck, William (1816-94) There are still many pieces of street ironmongery and street furniture in Swindon (principally covering what would otherwise be holes in the ground) that variously bear the names of Affleck and his Prospect Works. Born at Gateshead, and the son of an engineer, Affleck was firstly apprenticed to Hawks & Sons at their Gateshead Iron Works, and then worked for Maudsley & Field, mechanical engineers and marine engine specialists at Lambeth, London. He came to Swindon in the 1840s and at first worked as a GWR employee, but was sufficiently experienced to be given contract works in the Swindon Works, building iron trolleys. He married Maria Phillips (b. Godalming, Surrey, 1827) and the couple lived at 10 Faringdon Street, when the 1851 census recorded him as an 'engineer erector'. During the 1850s, he established his Prospect Works, off Eastcott Hill. There, he styled himself 'engineer, millwright, machinist, iron and brass founder, boilermaker, etc', and specialised in a wide variety of agricultural implements, which he displayed and sold on the large site between South Street and King William Street. By 1861, he was living at Prospect Place and employing seventeen men and three boys; the number had increased to twenty-five men and five boys by 1871 and Affleck was a 'practical engineer'. From 1860, he was a member of the Old Swindon Local Board, and he became a director of the Swindon Central Market Company when it was formed in 1864. When the Old Town cattle market was laid out in 1887, the Prospect Works supplied most of the cast iron pens. William Affleck died at Manor Farm, Ashbury.

Agriculture There is evidence that arable farming took place on the lighter soils around the downland areas, and on those rises in terrain associated with chalk and flint that were more free-draining. However, the area occupied by Swindon is generally too poor for a strong agriculture industry ever to have established there. The free-draining Cotswolds, to the north, historically supported sheep rearing and the production of foodstuffs necessary for the animals' welfare. The downland immediately to the south of Swindon was also sheep-rearing country, more recently given over to cattle and arable farming. The vale immediately to the north of Swindon hill is composed of heavy clays, and is consequently poorly drained. As prehistoric farmers cleared the scrub that grew there, the land was used for rearing cattle. Archaeology in the 1970s revealed an Iron Age farm, self-sufficient in crops, pigs and sheep, in the lowlands immediately to the north of Swindon hill. From the 5th century, the Saxons farmed the land and made cloth on and around the hill. We know that the town's name is derived from this period, and is supposed to reflect the pig-keeping that went on hereabouts, although this has often been disputed. (See also Geology.)

Akers Way, Moredon Akers Way was named after Francis Elliott Akers, Mayor of Swindon 1949-50, and was opened in 1949. It was built to run west from Cheney Manor Road and formed the southern boundary (although was not itself residential) of a small council estate that was being built at the same time on former farmland and which was accessed from Moredon Road to the north. The River Ray runs parallel immediately to the south, and part of the land between this and Akers Way was developed as the Moredon Golf Course, which opened in 1975.

Akers Way tragedy One of the roads built off Akers Way in 1949 was Bourne Road. On 13 September 1991, a group of children were playing on and around a seat on open ground at the end of Bourne Road, when they were ploughed into by an out-of-control car, allegedly travelling at more than 80 mph. The speed restriction on the road at the time was 40 mph. Five of the children, Ian Lilley aged 7, Sheree Lear aged 8, Paula Barnes aged 15, Paul Carr aged 16, and Belinda Brown aged 19 were killed, and others were injured. The vehicle that struck them sideways-on, and which finished upside-down in an adjacent hedge, was driven by Shaun Gooch of Burbage Road, Penhill.

It emerged at the subsequent trial at Gloucester Crown Court that Gooch had been racing along the road in competition with a car driven by Anthony Gallagher of Beech Avenue, Pinehurst. Gooch was attempting to overtake Gallagher's car when the latter pulled out to overtake a third vehicle travelling in the same direction, within the speed limit, and in so doing clipped the rear of Gooch's car as it went past. On 30 September 1992, Gooch was convicted of causing death by reckless driving, and was sentenced to five years in prison by Judge Gabriel Hutton. Gallagher was found guilty of driving without due care and attention. Following the tragedy, the bench on which some of the children had been sitting was removed, a permanent memorial to those who died was set up on Akers Way, and the speed limited was changed to 30 mph. A local Anglican minister, Geoffrey Crees, who counselled the bereaved, responded by writing the book *Where Was God Last Friday?* and this was published by Hodder & Stoughton Religious Books in 1995.

Albert Street In 1840, Queen Victoria married Albert, Prince of Saxe-Coburg and Gotha. Shortly afterwards, development began on a track leading across a field to the east of Victoria Street, and parallel to it, known as Back Lane and already with a few low, thatched cottages along it, at what had been called Home Ground by 1643. This was named Albert Street in commemoration of the royal wedding. By 1848, this had become a street of small cottages and stone-built terraces, initially housing independent tradespeople of some respectability. Here there were several milliners and dressmakers: the misses Martha and Emma Butler, Ann Hayward, Ann Keylock, and Sarah Rudman; and straw bonnet maker Sarah Mulcock was of their company. William Hayward was the Albert Street carpenter, John Wheeler was the baker in residence, and from here Reuben and William Horsell ran their business as slaters and plasterers. Laurence Lawrence lived there too, a seller of 'patent medicines'. Throughout the 1840s, the street was respectable, and it continued to attract a wide variety of businessmen and professional people, craftspersons, and artisans. Yet Albert Street was also part of the red-light district of its time, the haunt of prostitutes and thieves; its hostelries were patronised by the lowest type of labourer, and by the navvies who were associated with the railway in the new town.

Here, as the 1840s progressed, was established William Waller as a beer retailer; here, dressmaker Lucy Rogers also began to brew; and Joseph Patchett (her son-in-law) opened his shooting salon. One of these beer houses became the 'Heart in Hand', later named 'The Rising Sun', but long known as the 'Roaring Donkey'. Lucy Rogers's brewhouse became 'The Rhinoceros', the

most notorious public house in the town. Albert Street remained a backwater. By 1880, most of the cottages were purely residential. Edward King the coach builder had his premises on the corner with Wood Street, and almost next door was Martha Scapelhorn's bakery. Daniel White had a shop nearby, and wheelwright William Bizley also lived there. The properties in Albert Street thereafter gradually deteriorated, and the last of them was pulled down in the 1960s. (See also Little London; Rhinoceros; Vitti, Angelo.)

Alfred Williams Heritage Society The Alfred Williams Heritage Society was founded by newspaper columnist Graham Carter, consultant obstretician and gynaecological surgeon Dr John Cullimore, and Caroline Ockwell, and was launched at Swindon Central Library on 8 December, 2009. It held its first Alfred Williams Heritage Festival at Swindon's Steam Museum in 2010. In his book *A Wiltshire Village*, Williams described the Swindon & Highworth Union Workhouse that was situated in Highworth Road at Stratton St Margaret, and which latterly became a general geriatric hospital . In 2012, the Society obtained a grant from the Heritage Lottery Fund to help its research into the hospital's history. (See also Hammerman, The; Williams, Alfred)

All Saints' church, Southbrook Street The church opened on 17 September 1938 as the successor to a 'temporary building' of 1907-8 (which was originally intended as a future schoolroom). Prior to that, services had been held in a local school hall. The first church was a mission offshoot of St Mark's and remained as such until the area it served became an autonomous parish

in 1930. The designer of the 1938 building was Percival Hartland Thomas (1879-1960), architect and Bristol Diocesan surveyor, who specialised in churches, particularly around Bristol and Gloucestershire. All Saints' was an uncompromisingly stark design, partly for the use of white bricks throughout, and partly because of the tall, narrow appearance of the buildings, their box-like arrangement, and the tall, thin square-headed windows that are a feature of the elevation. The east window is a roundel, high in the wall and just below a plain, abbreviated shoulder gable. The church was built with chancel, nave, Lady Chapel and vestry; the font, choir stalls, and organ came from the previous building.

Allen, Gordon (b.1925) Gordon Allen is arguably best known in Swindon for his association with the second-generation Golden Lion sculpture. Born in Great Bowden, Leicestershire, he came to Swindon in 1953 after reading a newspaper report that skilled people could obtain a council house there within five weeks. An acute housing shortage in the Midlands meant that he was living, at the time, with his wife and their first child, in the home of his wife's parents. He was given a property on the newly built Penhill estate and, being a skilled toolmaker, a position soon followed with Vickers-Armstrong at South Marston, where he earned £12 per week. There, he was active in the trade union movement, trying to bring stability at a time of considerable unrest in the factory. He took up sculpture in the early 1960s whilst on sick leave and wanting to do something creative, and made a bust out of the blue clay being dug out of a trench. He then devised a means of making pots from cement. Proceeds from this, and his work as a project engineer and a production controller

for Vickers, enabled the family to move from Penhill to a bungalow on The Lawns, and then to a house in Goddard Avenue. He joined the Swindon Artists Society and was for a time its chairman, and he exhibited at a number of Royal Academy summer exhibitions.

Much of his work was carried out in either aluminium or steel; it devolved on his skill as an engineer and his interest in abstraction. Ironically, since he is an agnostic, a considerable amount of his sculpture in the Swindon area has been done for churches, and this includes a piece in the parish church at Wroughton. Many of his pieces are based on the design of a crucifix; 'The First Good Friday' is one, created in 1972, and several of his larger works, made using scrap pieces of aircraft components, are on a similar theme. In 1974, he left Swindon for Stow-on-the-Wold, where he rebuilt a cottage from the ground up and included a studio. In 1998, he relocated to St Ives, Cornwall, where he firstly had a studio at Carn Brae in premises occupied by his architect son, and latterly in the converted ticket office of the former railway station at St Erth. From 2010, he worked only in a studio area with turntable in his flat at St Ives. (See also Golden Lion.)

Ancillary Societies In 1943, the Swindon public library service sponsored its first ancillary societies: forerunners of the numerous clubs and associations that would become allied to the library and museums service over the next few years, many of which would be designated under the umbrella of 'public library extension activities'. The first one to register was the Gramophone Society. By 1947, there were six more 'official' public library societies: the Art Discussion Society, Ballet Society, Debating Society, Film Society, Play Reading Society,

and Poetry Society. In the 1960s, when gatherings of various sorts were at their peak, more than three hundred associations of one sort or another had registered with the library service. (See also Phoenix Players.)

Anderson's Almshouses Alexander Anderson (born in Scotland in 1808), died a Swindon resident in 1874, leaving a bequest that was used to build almshouses beside the churchyard at Christ Church. Some very old thatched cottages were demolished for the purpose; William Henry Read of Swindon was the architect of what originally comprised four almshouses known as Anderson's Hostel; and the work was carried out by builder Thomas Barrett of Newport Street in 1877. Anderson's intention was to provide accommodation for widowed or single people, who could be male or female, aged over sixty and finding themselves in seriously reduced circumstances. They had to have resided in Swindon for at least three years. The dwellings are of four bays and were originally designed as a single storey and attic, in Gothic style, with braced decorative bargeboards to the gables, grouped triple lancet mullioned windows above and square-headed lights below, and iron casements, set in ashlar dressings. There is an inset plaque to Cricklade Street that gives brief details of the bequest. In 1897, the original endowment was augmented by a bequest under the will of John Chandler, the Wood Street draper. The buildings were Grade II listed in 1970. In 1993, the four almshouses were remodelled internally into self-contained flats for the elderly, winning a Thamesdown Borough Council's Conservation and Design Award.

Anstiss Department Store John Ernest Anstiss was born at Aylesbury,

Buckinghamshire in 1878; he was the son of Charles Anstiss, a clerk and sometime 'mineral water carman', and his wife Sarah Elizabeth (née Summers). John was an assistant draper at Aylesbury by 1901. In c.1908, he came to Swindon and set up at 74 Regent Street as 'a baby linen warehouse' and later as a milliner. This business quickly developed into the large drapers store that bore his name, and he married Winifred, a Swindon girl, in 1910. John Anstiss Limited, a two-storey building, stood at 73a, 74 and 75 Regent Street, on a large corner site with Havelock Street, opposite McIlroy's store, which was, in many respects, its chief competitor. Its early advertisements promised 'seven windows full of good things', and it called itself 'The Small Profit Draper'. In fact, the whole of the ground floor elevation was glazed, as were all of the window returns into the doorways, and were all packed with goods for sale .

The premises were much damaged by fire on 21 December, 1948, when flames raced through the first floor of the shop where the firm's Father Christmas, Mr J. Webb, saw a blue flash just before his 'inflammable' costume caught fire! The shop was latterly a rather municipal-looking, two-storey, art-deco-style premises, whose demise was no architectural loss. This occurred on 29 January 1965, when the building was then entirely gutted by fire. Despite hopes of a rebuild, the company continued to trade out of two smaller adjacent premises in Regent Street, and nothing was done to the original site, other than to level it. It was eventually sold and redeveloped into other retail premises.

Applause Sculpture When the revamped Swindon Arts Centre in Devizes Road was opened in 2003, its forecourt included the 2.5- metre-tall sculpture called 'Applause' – a pair of clapping hands – by local sculpture and mural painter Mark Amis. The surface of the piece is a veneered skin of laminated aircraft-grade woven fibre, and this covers a frame made of welded steel. Amis studied at Swindon School of Art & Design. He specialises in lavish murals, trompe l'oeil, and fine art canvases. (See also Arts Centres.)

Apsley House This large town house of c.1830, was built in Bath Road, probably for the surgeon Charles James Fox Axford ; it later accommodated his colleague Frederick Henry Morris. It was also the home, from 1862, of coal and coke merchant Richard Tarrant; from 1870, this was the home of his great business rival John Toomer. It was almost certainly Toomer who named the property, because he was born at Apsley in Hampshire. The collections that formed Swindon's natural history museum relocated there from Regent Circus in 1930, and that is where the town's main general museum is still to be found. Apsley House is built of Bath stone, and has a rusticated ground floor front elevation with string course, and flat pilasters. It features a small Greek Doric portico with full-height, round-headed windows at ground level on either side to the north, and the cornice and parapet complete a fine façade. Inside, the high rooms, with plasterwork, were a fine setting for the increasing number of artefacts.

Arcadia cinema The 1,000-seat Arcadia was opened in Regent Street in 1912; it was so named after the shopping arcade that was demolished to make way for it. This was the only Swindon cinema to be initially owned

and operated by a local company, and had its own orchestra. The children's matinees held there were known as the 'Penny Rush'. The Arcadia became the Classic Cinema, run by Classic Repertory Cinemas of 100 Baker Street, London in the 1950s, then the Classic Cartoon Cinema after a period when it showed avant garde and foreign films as an art house, and finally the Vogue Bingo Hall. It was demolished in 1974.

Archers Brewery The Great Western Railway erected its weigh house – part of 'A' shop – in red and black brick in 1906, in an area that was already packed with railway sidings and which was usually full of rolling stock. Locomotives were brought into this building along a single track, to be weighed and balanced. A few years later, the building was extended in breeze blocks, and the interior was refurbished in the 1920s. Photographs taken there in the next decade show balancing machines that were all named and dated 'Henry Pooley & Sons, Birmingham and London, 1930. In 1995, Archers Brewery took over the disused building, refurbished it, and enlarged the property in order to extend its range of ales. Archers was founded in 1979 by former RAF pilot Mark Archer Wallington and his wife Wendy, setting up in an industrial unit made out of the one-time GWR carriage and wagon works in London Street. In 1999 it relocated into the former weigh house on what became Penzance Drive when the whole area underwent residential redevelopment. Archers Brewery was modernised in 2001 – the year Mark Wallington retired – when a considerable amount of equipment was bought, and it was allegedly producing 190 different ales. Its award-winning products supplied the independent pubs sector; it

had a conservative acquisitions policy, but developed a country-wide clientele for its products. The brewery went into administration in 2007, but was saved by businessman John Williams. It went into liquidation in 2009, and the company name was bought by Simon Buckley, owner of Evan Evans Brewery of Llandeilo, Wales's oldest family brewer, in business since 1767. They thereafter brewed Archers beers in Llandeilo and sold them country-wide. In 2010, Swindon Borough Council granted planning permission for the building to be turned into a pub/restaurant and micro brewery. The site was bought by Anthony and Allyson Windle, owners of the Three Crowns at Brinkworth, and in 2011 the refurbished site (at a cost of £2 million) opened as The Weighbridge Brewhouse. Mark Wallington came out of retirement to look after the micro brewery on the site.

Arkell, John (1802-81) Farmer, brewer and innkeeper John Arkell was born at Kempsford, Gloucestershire, the son of farmer Thomas Arkell and his wife Sarah (née Iles). At the age of twenty-nine, John emigrated to Canada with his cousin Thomas, where they founded Arkell Town in Southern Ontario. He took with him Elizabeth Hewer, also of Kempsford, but the North American climate did not suit her, and she made it clear that if they were to marry, she wished to return to England. The couple returned to Stratton St Margaret, near Swindon. John and Elizabeth married in 1833, and settled at the house in Swindon Road that would be John's home for the rest of his life. Meanwhile, under the Beerhouse Act 1830, home brews could be sold through cottage outlets without official licensing approval. John grew barley on his own farm, made his own home brew, and

sold it to the local cottage beer houses. In 1843, he built his own brewery in Swindon Road, Stratton St Margaret. Between 1835 and 1850, John and Elizabeth had nine children, of which the eldest son Thomas and the youngest son James followed their father in the family business. Another son, Richard Iles Arkell, was named after John's mother's family; another was called William Cobbett Arkell. The other boys were Henry and John. A daughter, Anne Hewer Arkell took her mother's maiden name; the other daughters were Susan and Martha. Elizabeth Arkell died in 1858 and, in 1860, John married Frances Weatherstone of Windrush, Gloucestershire. She came with her son John aged twelve and daughter Fanny aged ten. The Arkell family had servants at Stratton, and also housed various lodgers, who were mostly employed as maltsters. John was widely known as 'Honest John' Arkell. (See also Arkell's Brewery.)

Arkell's Brewery, Kingsdown
Although the brewery is situated just outside Swindon, Arkell's is claimed as the town's oldest extant business; it has been inextricably linked with the history of the place, and has many of its estate's public houses within the borough. In 1843, the farmhouse at Kingsdown, which was later to be the head brewer's house, became 'The Kingsdown', the first public house in the Arkell's estate and it gained its first full licence in 1847. The brewery was built behind 'The Kingsdown' by John Arkell in 1861, and was extended in 1867. In order to better facilitate the brewery side of the business, new premises that were then built on the opposite side of the road became 'The Kingsdown', and the old public house became the brewery offices, of which they are

still a part today. Close by, John Arkell built a row of 'model houses' for his employees and, throughout the last decade of his life, undertook a programme of new public house building in Swindon. In 1877, large maltings were added to the Kingsdown site. At the time of John's death, in 1881, the Arkell estate numbered thirty houses. Arkell's beer and its outlets had, to that point in time, supplied the navvies who built the Great Western Railway Company's line through Swindon, the builders of New Swindon, the builders of the railway Works, and the huge number of men who went to work 'inside'. Thereafter, an Arkell followed an Arkell into the business, one generation handing on to the next, even to the seventh generation at the present day. The estate built up steadily, and in 1927 became J. Arkell & Sons Ltd., with all its shares being taken up by the family. In 1937, the brewery's landmark chimney was built, ninety feet tall, which had to be camouflaged with green paint during the Second World War. The estate currently comprises more than one hundred houses.

It is worth mentioning Arkell's philosophy, as explained in 2003 by chairman Peter Arkell (1923-2011): 'Just as we are a family firm running from one generation to the next, so, in many instances, does our workforce also run from one generation to the next, and everyone at the brewery is treated as an 'honorary' Arkell. I have always taken the view that this is the right way to run a company. If you expect people to work for you from nine to five every day, then you are obliged to make their working lives as congenial as possible. In my view, if you don't like the thought of coming to work, there's something wrong with the management.' Peter Arkell's 80th birthday was celebrated by an Arkell's beer named

'Moonlight', created by head brewer Don Bracher and brewed in secret. It was also a tribute to Peter's wartime experiences, flying low-level sorties over France in 1943, and picking up agents by the light of the moon.

Arkell's Mural, County Road The brewery was approached by the owners of 11 County Road, a prominent end-terrace property, suggesting that Arkell's might care to 'rent' the wall for advertising purposes. An offer was accepted, and the Borough of Thamesdown proposed 'co-ordination of a scene based upon the brewery artwork by a local school or technical college through the sponsorship of the Arts & Recreation Department'. In May 1985, the muralist Sarah Faulkner was appointed, who had recently executed similar work on the Lambeth Walk shopping area in London. Her design for the Arkell's Mural, which is extant, shows the exterior elevation of the brewing house, surrounded by cameos of the brewing process being carried out by the likenesses of real employees at the time. The piece is surmounted by the legend ARKELL'S BREWERY 1843. She was aided in its execution by sixth-form college students, some unemployed people, and youngsters from the East Street Day Centre.

Arms of Swindon Swindon became a borough by Charter of Incorporation granted in 1900. A competition was put immediately into place to design a coat of arms. The twelve submissions were considered by a committee on 18 March 1901, and two designs were chosen. The winner was H.W. Reynolds, whose quartered shield depicted a bishop's mitre to signify William the Conqueror's gift of the manor of Swindon to Odo, Bishop of Bayeux; three crescents representing the

Goddard family, lords of the manor; three castles representing the Vilett family, lords of another Swindon manor; and a locomotive wheel representing the prominent industry on which Swindon was built. Above all, an arm, holding a hammer, symbolised strength through industry. The arms included the words 'Salubritas et Industria'. Donald Dodson, the runner-up, submitted a much more florid design surmounted by a winged wheel, and had a shield that included a railway locomotive, and a wild boar to signify the place's historical association with swine. The College of Arms incorporated elements from both, and this was accepted by the committee on 27 June 1901. The motto was fixed by them as Salubritas et Industria, meaning 'Health and Industry', and the arms were granted on 21 September, 1901.

The shield was quartered alternately red and blue, symbolising the former Old Swindon and New Swindon, which were joined by the Charter. Three red crescents in the first quarter were reminders of the Goddard family, Lords of the Manor of Swindon from 1562, whose own coat of arms featured 'gules a chevron vair between three crescents argent'. Effectively, the Goddards represented the old town; the new town was represented by the three castles in the second quarter, taken from the arms of the Vilett family, on whose lands parts of New Swindon was built. A golden mitre in the third quarter recalls Odo, Bishop of Bayeux, Earl of Kent and half-brother of William the Conqueror, who was granted a five hide estate at Domesday, which is most probably the part that became the medieval manor of Swindon (alias Over and Nether or West and East Swindon). The winged wheel in the fourth quarter represented speed of travel, a reference to the railway. The further reference

to New Swindon's past was the locomotive, on a silver background on the upper third of the shield, said to be of 'White Horse', 4-2-2 class No. 3029, built in 1891 and withdrawn in 1909. The shield was surmounted by a crest that, in the original, had a bent, muscular arm holding crossed, golden hammers: an illustration of the motto.

These arms were used until 1974 when local government reorganisation included Swindon in the Borough of Thamesdown, the arms of which included no direct image of the railway, and were surmounted by a white swan, signifying the River Thames, with a collar (circlet) derived from the Warneford family of Highworth's crest. Other elements in the Highworth coat of arms (of 1968-74, which was also incorporated into the Borough of Thamesdown) that would subsequently be re-used included the hammer. This, in the Highworth arms, combined a representation of strength and industry with Alfred Williams, the area's 'hammerman poet', who worked in the GWR Works; and also castles which denoted the ancient hillforts of Liddington hill and Barbury Castle. Much of it was green in colour, including two horses breathing fire: 'iron horses' that were said to be symbolic of railway locomotives.

On 1 April 1997, the Borough Council of Swindon became a Unitary Authority and decided to redraw its coat of arms. Robert Noel, Bluemantle Pursuivant of the College of Arms, was commissioned to provide it. He incorporated elements of the original Swindon coat of arms, those of the former Borough of Thamesdown, and those of Highworth. The blazon is: Quarterly per fess Azure and Gules in the first and fourth quarters, a Mural Crown Argent enfiled by two Hammers in saltire Or and in the second and third quarters a Garb Or on a Chief Argent, a representation of the 'George V' Locomotive proper. Upon a Helm with a Wreath Argent and Azure upon a Mount Vert within a Crown Vallary or a Swan rising Argent legged and beaked proper collared per fess embattled Sable and Or supporting with the dexter claw an automobile Wheel proper Mantled Azure doubled Argent. Supporters: on either side a Pegasus Argent maned and unglued Or breathing flames proper about their necks a collar Gules pendant there from a chain Gules Crest Azure. Motto: 'Salubritas et Industria'.

In the new Swindon arms, the swan now clutches a motor wheel, symbolic generally of the town's post-railway industrial regeneration, and specifically of the motor industry that took over from the railway Works as the town's major employer. Indeed, the new arms were sponsored by Honda of the UK Manufacturing Limited. The hill, beneath the swan and inside a crown, represents the downland hereabouts and the 'high north' settlement. The winged horses on either side breathe out flames of knowledge, and are thereby symbols of wisdom, ingenuity and industry – the new areas of expertise in Swindon. Around their necks hang the Goddard family crescent. Only the motto has remained unchanged through each era.

Armstrong, Joseph (1816-1877)
Widely regarded as the architect of Swindon's community development, he was the GWR's Locomotive Carriage & Wagon Superintendent , 1864-77. Armstrong lived at Newburn House, a piece of fanciful Victorian gothic in three storeys, topped by a riot of gables with decorative barge-boards, and tall chimneys. It was built for him opposite the railway works in 1873, and

was named after his birthplace of Newburn-on-Tyne, Northumberland. The house was demolished in 1937 and is remembered in the name Newburn Crescent, which is built roughly where it stood. Armstrong was a Wesleyan Methodist circuit preacher, one-time chairman of the New Swindon Local Board, and a director of the Swindon Water Company. Under Armstrong, workforce in Swindon's railway workshops reached 13,000, and the 'Sir Daniel' and 'Queen' class locomotives were introduced. The GWR park in Faringdon Road was largely his creation. When he died, the railway company built a temporary platform for the use of mourners; his funeral brought the town to a standstill, and he was buried in the churchyard at St Mark's, where there is a mounted, granite obelisk to his memory. Armstrong Street, built in 1899, was named after him.

Art, Swindon Collection of In 1943, Swindon Corporation began to exhibit collections of paintings to the general public, in a corridor at McIlroy's store, Regent Street, and in otherwise empty rooms within the old town hall, Regent Circus. The local authority bought a few paintings, and then F.C. Phelps, a retired pastry chef, occasionally donated very traditional pictures from his personal collection. In 1945, H.J.P. Bomford, art-appreciating Aldbourne farmer, leant some valuable art – including works by L.S. Lowry, Henry Moore, Paul Nash, and Graham Sutherland. When the arts centre was opened in 1946, it became possible to display permanently some of this work, whereupon Bomford converted his loans to a gift to the town. In 1947, a Private Act of Parliament allowed the Swindon Corporation to establish an arts fund whereby any money left over from

the annual allocation of funds for buying paintings could be held over in a deposit fund instead of being returned to the rates. From the same year, the Contemporary Arts Society donated works, initially including paintings by John Nash and Wilson Steer. In 1951, Phelps left £2000 in his will to the Swindon arts fund and, later, S.B. Cole, the Swindon outfitter, left £300.

The collection ceased to be adequately displayed from 1956 when the lease expired on the first arts centre, and its replacement, a former dance hall in Devizes Road, had less space. The town got over this problem by selecting what were considered to be the best elements of its collection, and sending them on an extended tour of the West Country, followed, in 1959, by an even more extended national tour of twenty cities and towns. Both tours were seen as an answer to the lack of hanging space in Swindon. When the pictures came back, they were put into store.

In 1964, an L-shaped gallery extension to the Bath Road museum was opened, and the Borough resumed the purchase of paintings, albeit with limited resources. The idea was to buy contemporary painters before their work became too expensive, mostly done with the advice of staff at the Tate Gallery in London. The collection was supplemented by pictures on loan from the Arts Council.

Art Deco building, 21 Regent Circus The Swindon Corporation Art Deco electricity showroom, built in 1933 by Richard James Leighfield on the site of the Roman Catholic church and some cottages in Regent Circus, was opened by Cllr. W.H. Bickham on 19 April 1934. The building had public toilets attached. The electricity showrooms were later the premises of the Islington Furnishing Company. In the 1950s,

the building was remodelled internally, and opened as Long John's café, predominantly a pancake parlour owned by a catering company from Oxford. In 1968 the premises were taken over by Paul Notton, renamed Nottons, and has been associated with him ever since.

Paul came from a catering family. His grandfather ran the George Inn Restaurant, Marlborough, where he also had a bakehouse in Angel Yard. His father operated a bakehouse in Buckland, and in 1955 came to Swindon where he opened Nottons Café on the corner of County Road and Manchester Road. The family opened a transport café at Ogbourne St George and, in 1963, a café in Beechcroft Road, Upper Stratton, close to the Moonraker's public house. They supplied many of the local working men's clubs, and carried out the catering at the Town Gardens and Coate Water leisure park. Twenty years after he took over the Regent Circus premises, Paul Notton repositioned the business as a wine bar and restaurant, specialising in British and Spanish cuisine, and renamed it Rudi's. In 2000, he bought the lease of the adjacent and long defunct public toilets building from the Borough of Swindon for £2,500, thereby facilitating extra capacity for the business. Inside, the main building retains its original 1930s' lift in full working order.

Art Gallery Swindon's L-shaped art gallery was opened in 1964, next to the museum in Bath Road, by Sir Philip Morris, Vice-chancellor of Bristol University. It was designed by J. Loring Morgan, then the Borough Architect, and was said to be 'a temporary home for the Swindon Collection'. The site was at the time a car park, and had previously been that of the Bath Road

Congregational Church. The art gallery cost £45,000 and was built by R.J. Leighfield & Sons of Swindon. By then, the Swindon Collection amounted to about 130 pictures. The building featured the ability to maintain the air temperature at 68°F, and had an African Muhuhu hardwood block floor.

Arts Centres In November 1946, the Mayor of Swindon, C.R. Palmer, opened Swindon's first Arts Centre, which was also the first municipal arts centre in the country. This was a culmination of the Library Committee's early support for the arts in the town, and a patronage by which it had acquired works of art either by purchase, received as gifts, or on loan. The arts centre was opened, with a piano recital by Joan Baker, and a play, in a former Primitive Methodist schoolroom, which had been taken by Swindon Corporation on a ten-year lease, off Regent Street. This arts centre had a 1,800 square foot hall with a gallery that could seat a total of 300 people; its stage was 30 feet wide by 20 feet deep; and there were alcoves along its length wherein was displayed the art collection. It included two smaller halls, dressing rooms, offices, cloakroom, and a kitchen. The architect for the reordering of the building was T. Burrington; the work was carried out by the building firm of R. J. Leighfield and cost about £7,000.

The job of steward was given to Stanley Jarman, a long-time producer of amateur theatricals, and himself a performer – making his first stage appearance in 'The Farmer's Wife' in 1930. He was also a pioneer of the Swindon & District Amateur Theatre Guild. When Jarman left school in 1917, he started work in the library of the Mechanics' Institute and had been a founder member of the GWR Photographic Society. When he

left the Institute in 1945, he was the library's chief assistant. He would remain at his arts centre post until his death in 1952.

In that year, he was succeeded by Walter (Wally) Webb, a native of Swindon, who first came to public notice in 1947 when he was involved in the Ballet Club. He acted on the amateur stage in the town from that time, and also distinguished himself as a notable producer. His work encompassed the annual Swindon Guild one-act drama festivals, a drama group at the Ferndale Youth Centre, and latterly at Westcott Youth Centre.

When the lease on the former Methodist premises expired, the Library Committee decided to adapt the Bradford Hall in Devizes Road. This was a council-owned property that was built in 1900, when it was named after J.E.G. Bradford, a Swindon solicitor, who owned the site on which it stands, together with the stables and cottages that were demolished to make way for it. Originally used for meetings, the Bradford Hall had been privately owned between the end of the First World War and 1945, during which period it became one of the town's venues for dances, and was much favoured by servicemen – principally American forces stationed locally – during the Second World War. The venue was particularly associated with Swindon's Harry Smith and his band; the bands played on the balcony at the rear, and the dancers performed below them. The hall was then acquired by the Borough of Swindon, which continued to let it for public dances until 1955. The building was then internally remodelled, but retained the sprung wooden dance floor that remains beneath the auditorium to this day. It was given a theatre that seated 240 people on former cinema seats; it also had offices, committee rooms, a meeting room, a club room, workshops, and a store, and was opened by mayor Norman Toze in 1956. It was refurbished in 1967 when raked seating was put in, but continued largely as a venue for local societies' meetings, occasional concerts, and amateur theatrical productions until 1994 when the decision was taken to expand the programme of professional entertainment and cultural events. Over seven months during 2002, the building was redeveloped inside and out, and extended at a cost of £665,000. The poet Pam Ayres was the guest of honour when it was re-opened on 27 January 2003, and in 2010 it became the venue of the Old Town library. The Arts Centre is said to be haunted by the spectre of a woman in a brown dress (who has also been seen in other places around Old Swindon), who is known among the Centre's staff as 'Mrs B'. (See also Applause Sculpture; Bradford, J.E.G.)

Astill's printing works Astill's printing works was situated at 3 Victoria Street, and was previously the premises of Abbott Dore, who, in the 1840s, was the town's only printer, and also the proprietor of a circulating library. Dore began his printing works in order to produce posters and catalogues for the Dore family of auctioneers, land surveyors, house agents and appraisers. From 1863, he was also the publisher of a *Swindon Almanac*. In 1877, Dore's business and premises were acquired by printer Robert Astill (1837-1915), originally from Coventry. Formerly living in Swindon at 5 Bath Terrace, Astill and his family moved into the fine, stone-built, three-storey house adjacent to Dore's business (separated only by a garden) in 1866. Formerly, and despite its proximity to Wood Street, the address of this residence was The Sands; by the time of

Astill's occupancy, it had become 1 Victoria Street. He became the publisher of *Astill's Swindon Almanac* from 1867 to 1888. Mrs Margaret Astill established her millinery business in the house, also specialising as a 'dress and mantle maker' and an exponent of 'ladies' under clothing neatly executed'. The junction of Victoria Street and Bath Road became known as 'Astill's Corner'.

Astill used both premises not only for his own business, but they were also sub-let to other traders. The house and works were offered for sale in 1903, when they were described as being suitable for 'any large business or office'. The premises could be entered from either street and, internally on the ground floor, comprised drawing room, reception room, breakfast room, kitchen, scullery, coal house and greenhouse. In 1903, Walter Henry Bush, hairdresser, occupied the drawing room and reception room. The breakfast room was where Astill had his stationery and fancy goods business. On the first floor were the dining room, three bedrooms and dressing rooms; the second floor comprised four large bedrooms and a linen closet. One of the three cellars was a wine store. A carriage entrance stood adjacent to Victoria Street, admitting to the yard and stables (then let to a William Greenaway, boot and shoe maker), with a coach house beyond, above which slept the servants (the Astills had several). The property also had other outbuildings, and gardens.

Attwood, Harry Carleton (1908-1985) Always profoundly deaf, and apparently uncommunicative because he insisted on keeping his hearing aid turned off, Carleton Attwood was nonetheless a sculptor of national standing. He was born in Bath Road, and took up pottery at the age of ten, using clay that he dug out of the garden of the home in Goddard Avenue that he shared with his mother and sisters, to whom he was always known as 'Boy'. He worked in the cellar and made larger pieces in the greenhouse. Work that did not come up to standard was thrown in the garden pond. In the 1920s, influenced by the work of Eric Gill, he trained in the Art Department of Swindon College, where he won prizes for his carving. Whilst there, he modelled from life the well-known plaster bust of Swindon benefactor Reuben George. He also made busts of Richard Jefferies, Alfred Williams, and the Swindon footballer Harold Fleming.

Attwood was better known elsewhere, before he received recognition in Swindon, making carvings in 1935 for Stephen Courtauld's house in London at the request of architects Seely & Paget, and designing a sundial for A.A. Milne that featured the author's famous characters Christopher Robin and friends. He also made sculptures for Eltham Hall in Kent. An exhibition of his sculpture and other works was held in the Swindon arts centre in 1948.

During the war, he worked in Garrard's on munitions. In 1958, he cast in aluminium a portrait roundel of his friend, the poet Paul Weir, and around the same time made a series of numbered aluminium masks. He painted numerous frescos and experimented with smaller metal items very much in the spirit of the Arts & Crafts movement, in which Eric Gill had been a participant. For a while in the mid-1960s, Attwood taught nude drawing at Swindon College. When Thamesdown Community Arts opened the town hall studios in the 1970s, he became a fixture there. In 1979, he painted the mural 'Nature — Mother of the Arts' over an

upstairs doorway in the town hall.

His best-known work in Swindon is arguably the second-generation Golden Lion on Canal Walk. He also made small, scale replicas of this, as he did also of 'The Watchers', the pyramidal group of guardians of Toothill, made of ferroconcrete in the town hall studios in 1982. This was one of his last pieces, inspired by the way he saw a family huddled together and draped in a cape against the rain, whilst he was running the line at a rugby match. The original terracotta version of this went to Australia. Exactly what the watchers are watching, Attwood always enigmatically said was in the mind of the beholder, although he did maintain that the child represented 'curiosity', the woman 'introspection', and 'comprehension' was attributed to the man. The dog at their feet was not described.

Carleton Attwood is represented in *The Swindon Review*, where two photographs of his pottery pieces appear. These are 'David' (No.2, 1945) and the erotic 'Orpheus and Eurydice' (No.7, 1955). He lived in Goddard Avenue. (See also Golden Lion.)

Ausden, Kenneth Rupert (1924-2009) Born at 26 Graham Street, Ken Ausden was the son of (also Swindon-born) Rupert Stanley Ausden and his wife Francis Doris (née Kent) of Rugeley, Staffordshire, where she was in service before their marriage. R.S. Ausden, a frail man as the result of being gassed during the First World War, worked as a clerk in the railway Works. Ken was the eldest of his three children and went to Sanford Street School and Commonweal Grammar School in Swindon, and St Paul's College, Cheltenham, where, being the youngest in his year, he was known as 'Babe'. He served in the Royal Artillery during the Second World War, and was in Italy 1944-46. During the 1940s and 1950s, he achieved some recognition for ornamental gardening, winning – variously between 1956 and 1966 – several *Amateur Gardening* and *Popular Gardening* medallions and certificates for his roses and chrysanthemums. In 1960, he won *The Smallholder* Championship Medal.

His teaching career began at Gorse Hill Junior School, where he was in charge of the school football team in the Junior League, which produced a number of lads who later played professional football. Ken Ausden was the first deputy head of Lawn Junior School, and then of Penhill Junior School; in 1961, he was appointed headmaster of Even Swindon Junior School, where he remained until he took early retirement in 1983. He was a strong union member (Swindon secretary of the NUT), and was responsible for the junior school fixtures in the Swindon Schools' Football Association. He was also a lifelong follower of Swindon Town F.C., and for eight years broadcasted match commentaries on their games. Ken was married to Aida (née Henderson), whose family lived in Carfax Street, and she described herself as 'a frustrated actress'. The couple, who had no children, lived latterly at 9 The Quarries, Old Town.

As a playwright, Ken Ausden's published work includes two radio plays. *Full Time* (1970) was about the private lives of professional footballers, and was broadcast by the BBC; this was followed by *A Town Grows Up*, which was written for the BBC School's History series. In 1972, his stage play, *Full Head of Steam*, which had a Swindon and a railway bias, was performed at the newly opened Wyvern Theatre, running from 19-29 April. He was the author of two books, both of which were set in Swindon; they were heavily biographical but

slightly fictionalised accounts in short story form of his boyhood with his friends growing up in the town in the 1930s. These were *Up The Crossing* (BBC Books, 1981), which was serialised on BBC Woman's Hour, and *Further Up The Crossing* (Golden Lion Books, 1987).

Aylesbury Dairy Building, Station Road In the late 1860s, G. Mander Allender, a Buckinghamshire farmer who owned prize Berkshire pigs and a fine herd of Alderney cows, established the Aylesbury Dairy Company. In 1876, W.H. Read, the Swindon architect, designed for him a strange building in two adjacent blocks, on the corner of Station Road and Aylesbury Street, to be used as a milk processing plant. It was built in just twelve weeks by George Wiltshire, and the machinery inside was supplied by Swindon engineer William Affleck of the Prospect Works. Allender's company took milk from the dairy farms around Swindon, upwards of 3,000 gallons each day, and processed it in pans some 400 square feet in area. Around 1,000 pints of cream were made each day in a dairy measuring 2,400 square feet; three tons of cheese per week were produced from skimmed milk in a separate dairy of comparable size. Whey, decanted into a whey tank, and other waste products from its processes were pipe-fed by a steam injector process to the company's pigs, which were kept in a field about 300 yards distant, on the north side of the railway line. (On the opposite side of the road to the dairy building is an incline towards the railway station, known as the 'milk bank', as a result of this process.) Allender was very proud of the dairy, to which he freely admitted visitors, and the model and economic lines on which he supplied and ran his piggeries. The building was remodelled in 1891 when it was taken over by the Southern Laundry. The property, of brick with Bath stone dressings, comprises two adjacent blocks that are built with corner piers (one has a ball finial) almost as if the architect intended them to look like separate, if related, pieces. Each is gabled to the Station Road elevation, and each gable has a plain moulded, triangular panel bearing a central oculus of which the eastern one is keyed. One front is a single storey of four bays, the other also of four bays but of two storeys. The Aylesbury Street elevation is of eleven bays. The windows have segmental heads, and beneath each is a rectangular panel with chamfered mouldings.

Backhouse, David William (1933-2001) In 1984, David Backhouse published *Home Brewed, A History of Breweries and Public Houses in the Swindon Area*. A revised edition came out in 1992. It was the result of years of original research that included working on the sometimes centuries-old deeds to many of the properties in and around the town that have at some time been licensed to sell alcohol. It added immeasurably to the town's local history, and is the work for which he is best remembered. He also founded the Swindon branch of CAMRA, the Campaign for Real Ale, was secretary for that organisation in the West of England, and wrote three of their publications: *Wiltshire, the Pub Guide*; *Wiltshire, the Pub Guide 1991*; and *Wiltshire, the Pub Guide 1994*. He originated and organised the annual Swindon Beer Festival, which was established at the Mechanics' Institute in Emlyn Square in 1976; it then transferred to the Drill Hall in Church Place and continued for several years.

The Backhouse family removed from Kent to Ashford Road, Swindon in the early 1940s, when David's father was employed at RAF Yatesbury on secret radar development. David went to Commonweal School, and afterwards became a road manager employed by the Cana Variety Agency specifically to accompany touring British and American traditional jazz bands from the early 1950s onwards. It was during this period that he developed the liking for local British ales that resulted, much later, in his involvement with CAMRA. In the capacity of touring manager, he was involved – as a passenger with Mike Cotton's Jazz Band – in a road accident after a late-night gig. It put him in hospital for more than a year and left him paralysed for the rest of his life. The compensation payment was the largest to that point in time for such an injury, and it enabled him to adapt his home at Foxhill to facilitate his disabilities, and also paid for the services of a housekeeper. After he recovered sufficiently, he continued to work as a tour manager for Cana artistes.

Dave Backhouse was always interested in transport, particularly the railways. He frequently visited the depot of the Bristol Omnibus Company in Regent Circus, where he took numerous photographs. Many of his photographs of Great Western Railway steam locomotives and Bristol Omnibus Company vehicles were reproduced in early relevant titles published by Ian Allen Limited. He died leaving a very large collection of railway books, many of which went into the STEAM archive in Swindon. All of his research material on Swindon's public houses is in the County Records Office at Chippenham.

Backsword Playing This ancient sport, otherwise known as single-stick, became popular during the 16th century. William Morris devoted several pages to it in *Swindon Fifty Years Ago*, which he published in 1885. He described the two classes of players ('Old Gamesters' and 'Young Gamesters') and the two styles of playing ('rough' and 'smooth'). 'As recently as forty years ago,' he wrote, 'there were men living in and around Swindon who enjoyed the repute of being among the best Backsword players in England'. He described how, constrained by tape that secured thigh to thumb so that their reach was limited, the combatants set about each other with sticks made of ash wood. Their aim was to cause blood to run one inch from a crack on the head of an opponent, whilst successfully warding off his attacks. Morris tells us that backsword playing was common in and around the town, usually on stages or rings set up in open fields, and that Swindon butcher Robert Blackford was a renowned player in the 1780s. This Robert's son, also Robert, and his grandsons Robert, John and Joseph, all became butchers in the town. In 1845, the son of the backsword player was leased newly built premises on the corner of Wood Street and Cricklade Street, and a slaughterhouse a little to the north in the latter, and these became the main site for the Blackford family's butchery business. The slaughterhouse was leased to John in 1863.

Morris also records that the last backsword bout in the Old Town market square was in 1808, and that 'the last great Bout at Backsword in Swindon' took place in 1840 or 1841. It was arranged by James and Thomas Edwards who also provided the prizes, allegedly as a dual celebration: the opening of the Great Western Railway Company's line to Swindon, and their acquisition of fields in the Regent Street and

Bridge Street area of the new town. It was on part of this land that James Edwards, a coal merchant, almost immediately built the Golden Lion public house close to the Wilts & Berks Canal. The landlord of the hostelry in 1851 was Thomas Edwards, and he stayed until the Golden Lion was sold out of the family seven years later.

Baily, Revd Henry George (1816-1900) The last vicar at Holy Rood church was certainly the driving force behind the subscriptions that were raised in order to build its successor in the Old Town, Christ Church. The latter was dedicated in 1851; the former was partially demolished the following year. Baily was born in Calne, came to Swindon in 1843, and was vicar of the parish from 1847. His forceful pleading letter to potential subscribers in 1849 raised nearly £3,000 towards the cost of the new church, of which he subscribed £500 of his own money. Christ Church was designed by Sir Giles Gilbert Scott. Revd Baily was there when the foundation stone was laid in June 1850, and at the church's consecration in November 1851, when he became its first minister. He was, among numerous other appointments, a director of the Swindon Water Company when it was formed in 1857 to bring a supply of drinking water to the town. Guardian of the parish of Swindon in the Swindon and Highworth Union, and president of most of the local ecclesiastical societies and associations, he also took an active part in the movement, in 1864, to set up the two Local Boards (one for Old Swindon and another for New Swindon), and became chairman of the Old Swindon Local Board at its inception. In 1871, he built a church school in King William Street. In 1885, he became rector of Lydiard Tregoze, where he spent

the next fifteen years. He is buried in the churchyard at Christ Church.

Baker, Orlando (1834-1912) The architect and cartographer is best remembered for his map of Swindon that was reproduced in the 1883 issue of the *North Wilts Directory*. It showed the point in time at which the two settlements of Old Town and New Swindon were about to join physically, and is important for depicting the topography of the area just before this happened. His maps of 1887 and 1889 showed the area filling up with streets. Baker was born at Brimscombe, Gloucestershire, the son of stone mason William Baker and his wife Jane. He lived in a small family community of masons and carpenters, although his sister Caroline taught at the local infant school. By 1851, Orlando was a carpenter's apprentice, and in 1858, when he was a builder's clerk, he married Louisa Antill (b. 1834, Chalford) at Stroud. In 1870, the family (six children had by then been born to them) relocated from Brimscombe to 23 North Street, Swindon, when Orlando Baker was described as a builder's clerk and draughtsman.

He immediately studied 'the theory of music and musical composition' for Society of Arts certification by means of evening classes at the Swindon Mechanics Institution, was successful in this and in obtaining qualifications from the Department of Science and Art. Thereafter for most of the 1870s, he taught music at the Institute, and was also organist at the Congregational church in Bath Road. He went into partnership, early in that decade, with James Hinton, forming the short-lived firm of Baker and Hinton, Auctioneers, Valuers, Architects, Surveyors, House Estate

and General Agents. This partnership was dissolved on 31 December, 1875, and Baker continued to practise on his own in the town until 1890 when the family moved to Tasmania where, in 1902, he designed the Hobart Customs House. He retired in 1911, and died the following year.

Baker's Arms, Emlyn Square Built as business premises on the corner with Bath Road (renamed Bathampton Street in 1901), c.1846, this was immediately leased to land agent Richard Perris. It quickly developed into flour factor and baker Richard Philpott Perris's baker's shop, with a bakery at the rear and a beer house on the side. The premises were taken over in 1848 by Richard Allnatt, who continued in both trades for over three decades. Allnatt relocated the bakery side of the business into nearby Taunton Street, from where he delivered around New Swindon on a horse and cart that he accommodated at the rear of the premises. This established the public house in a rather plain (at one time gabled) street-corner, three-storey building of coursed limestone with ashlar quoins; three bays to Bath Road, and a single bay on the Square. The second and third storey windows are square-headed with hood mouldings and labels.

Bampton Brothers Edwin ('Ted') and Reginald Bampton were apprentice coachbuilders in the 1920s who, in 1932, decided to create their own business. They invested £120 in one acre of land beside Stratton Road, Swindon where, in May 1933, they launched their car body works company in makeshift sheds. (During the 1960s, they bought more adjacent land that they mostly covered with workshops.) Soon they were designing and building small expanding caravans, one of which they displayed in the car park opposite Olympia in London during the 1934 Motor Show, thereby attracting the attention of the proprietor of Welfords Caravans, through whom they subsequently sold many vehicles. Production of these stopped in 1939 for the duration of the Second World War, during which time they worked on War Department contracts, principally building ambulances, and on the repair and refurbishment of the omnibuses belonging to the Bristol Tramways & Carriage Company. After the war, they resumed caravan production, but of larger vehicles. In 1976, Bampton's specialist body workshop was sold outright to Dillmay Limited, and the business ceased in 2003. Three years later, one of the former workshops, by then derelict, was set on fire. Attempts were made, from 2008, to turn the site into a residential development.

Bampton, Daphne (1922-2005) In 1947, Ted Bampton of Bampton Brothers married Daphne Dorothy M. Beale at Poole, Dorset. She was a cashier at Lloyds Bank who, in 1955, became company secretary of her husband's firm. By the 1960s, she had become founder (and treasurer) of the local branch of the Vehicle Builders and Repairers Association, and was secretary of the Swindon Business and Professional Women's Club. Daphne Bampton was the author of *Bampton's 1933-1979: a history in the evolution of the coachbuilding and repairing industry.* Latterly, she became a public moral conscience of Swindon, and was sometimes to be seen picketing (with a placard) outside some entertainment in the town that she considered to be dubious. Her objections to the film 'Last Tango in Paris', were vociferously displayed outside the cinema showing it.

Banking in Swindon, Origins of

In 1800, James Strange, draper and mercer, lived in two cottages in High Street, on the north side of the entrance to the Goddard estate. Immediately on the south side, was an ale house and then Richard Strange's grocer's shop. These Strange brothers also operated as coal merchants on the Wilts & Berks Canal, and their elder brother Thomas dealt in coal and salt out of Swindon wharf. In 1807, Richard and James leased part of an old house immediately next to James's cottages, then owned by Thomas Coventry, lived in by his family since the 1600s, and which was at the time occupied by the surgeons John and Joseph Gay, who relocated. In this building, they then established Swindon's first bank – Strange, Garrett, Strange & Cook. This became James & Richard Strange & Co., and when James died in 1826, Thomas took over his drapery business and banking interests; the bank became Thomas & Richard Strange & Co., and the brothers continued to trade in coal and salt on the Wilts & Berks Canal. In 1818, a group of Swindon tradespeople formed the 'savings bank' in Victoria Street, in opposition to the Stranges' enterprise. Its president was the Earl of Shaftesbury. The savings bank closed in 1895.

The Wilts & Dorset Banking Company opened in 1835 in a one-room office in William Scotford's high street tailor's shop, and closed down almost at once. The North Wilts Banking Company saw an opportunity to fill its place and in 1836 opened in a house in Wood Street belonging to Henry Tarrant. It remained there until 1845. In 1842, the Strange brothers' bank was taken over by the County of Gloucester Banking Company, and Thomas and Richard remained as managers. Thomas Coventry sold his old family home to Thomas Strange in 1846 and this was rebuilt by Thomas Barrett of Newport Street as the County of Gloucester Bank's main building.

At about the same time, the North Wilts Banking Company moved in next door. The builder Thomas Barrett retained his connection with the County of Gloucester Banking Company. They commissioned him to provide bank fittings in mahogany when they built a New Swindon branch in Fleet Street in 1874. This was a vaguely Italianate building, designed by W.H. Read on two floors, built by George Wiltshire, also of Swindon, with carvings by Chapman & Stillman of Bath.

The Wilts & Dorset Banking Company came back to Swindon in 1876, buying surgeon John Gay's cottage on the corner of Wood Street and Cricklade Street, which had Richard Tarrant's bootmakers shop at street level. The bank rebuilt these premises and opened there in 1885. Meanwhile, the North Wilts became the Hampshire and North Wilts Banking Co., then the Capital & Counties Bank in 1880. Lloyds Bank took over the County of Gloucester Bank in 1897; they took over the Wilts & Gloucester in 1915; and added the Capital and Counties Bank in 1918, although the last-named continued to trade under its own name until 1927. The Strange brothers' original double-gabled bank premises were demolished by Lloyds Bank in 1899. The fine limestone Lloyds Bank building in present-day High Street is built on the site of the former Capital and Counties Bank building to the north, and the County of Gloucester Bank building to the south. It is Grade II listed. (See also Lloyds Bank, High Street; Wilts and Dorset Bank Building.)

Baptist Chapel, Cambria Place

(See Cambria Baptist Chapel.)

Baptist Church, Gorse Hill In 1878, members of Revd Richard Breeze's congregation at the Fleet Street, Swindon, Baptist Church, having taken on missionary work in the Gorse Hill area, built a chapel there on what became the corner with Ferndale Road (when this road was built up in the late 1880s, and then named). Beatrice Street was built and named at about the same time as Ferndale Road, and a replacement Baptist church was erected there, 1903-4, on its corner with Gorse Hill. The foundation stone was laid by retired bank manager William Brewer Wearing (1818-1912), who then lived at 3 Gloucester Villas, Bath Road. Until 1913, Baptism in Gorse Hill was dependent upon firstly the Fleet Street church, and then the Baptist Tabernacle in Regent Street, Swindon, after the Fleet Street congregation relocated there in 1886. (See also Wearing, W.B.)

Baptist Church, Fleet Street Custom-built in Italianate style in 1848, on the corner of Fleet Street and Bridge Street, this was the Old Swindon community of Baptists' means of gaining a foothold in New Town. The necessary funds were raised by Revd. Richard Breeze, who owned the house next door, to the west; the architect of the church was Sir Samuel Morton Peto, entrepreneur, designer and high-profile Baptist; the builder was Thomas Barrett of Newport Street. It opened on 4 January 1849. Those who came to it from Old Town had to approach along a track through fields and allotment gardens, and had to cross the Wilts & Berks Canal, which made them vulnerable to attack and verbal abuse. The new premises had an apsidal north end separated from the body of the church by a tall, round arch; the hall was galleried on

short pillars, and could seat 530. The church had five bays to Fleet Street and seven to Bridge Street, each divided externally by flat pilasters. In 1861, the church bought Revd. Breeze's house, which later became a shop. All that remains of the Fleet Street Baptist church is the north wall, and the former schoolroom that was built adjacent in Bridge Street in 1868, designed by Thomas S. Lansdown of Brunswick Terrace, Bath Road. The congregation moved to the Baptist Tabernacle in Regent Circus in 1886. The following year the Fleet Street premises were partially demolished, and the site was converted into four shops.

Baptist Tabernacle, Regent Street In 2004, some 260 tons of Swindon's former stone-built Baptist Tabernacle, which once stood adjacent to Regent Circus, were discovered on wooden pallets in a field in Northamptonshire. Demolition of the building in 1978, amidst a furore of public anger, was widely regarded as the epitome of all that is wrong in the town's attitude to conservation. John Betjeman compared the building with the architecture of St Martins in the Fields, London, and Nikolaus Pevsner said it was 'remarkably purely classical'.

When the Baptists bought the site in 1885, it was in a fairly isolated spot, although since Regent Street was then being built up, and the site was more or less where the roadways between Old Town and New Swindon met, it had much potential. Behind it, to the south, lay only fields and to the south-west there were fields and allotment gardens before the break in the landscape that was the Wilts & Berks Canal. The Tabernacle was designed in ancient Roman style by W. H. Read, and built of Bath stone in 1886 at a cost of £6,000. It was surrounded

by iron railings in front of the steps, and had high panelled plinths carrying Grecian torch-style lamps. The interior was a hall that could accommodate 1,000 people, with a gallery that had an ornamental front on three sides and was supported on iron columns. The whole site occupied 3,589 square feet, with an additional 2,000 square feet of schoolroom. The entrance was behind an impressive colonnade of six Tuscan columns beneath a large pediment, enhanced by a flight of stone steps that ran the entire width of the front.

When it all came down, sections were held for a time in the grounds of Abbey Nursery at Malmesbury. The portico was bought by artist Stanley Frost, who thereafter failed to get planning permission to set it up at Bell Farm, Brokenborough, where he lived. In 2002, he sold it to Neil Taylor, the owner of a business park, who similarly failed in his plans to re-erect the columns, bases, façade wall and door frames, and window surrounds into his new country home. In 2006, Swindon Borough Council entered into negotiations to buy back the remains, with the prospect of rebuilding them into some future regeneration project in the town. They were eventually brought back to the town in September 2007, at a cost of £360,000. Pending future use, they were stored at the Science Museum, Wroughton.

Barracks, Emlyn Square In order to house its increasing workforce, particularly the great number of young, single men coming to the Works from the north of England, the GWR decided to use its own labour to build a large tenement in High Street (Emlyn Square). The architect of this model lodging house was said to be Isambard Kingdom Brunel, who planned a three-storey, nine-bay building in 17th-century Cotswold style, but this was not as eventually built. It was begun, however, and had reached the first floor when the railway went into recession, many men were laid off, and much of the machinery at the Works was silenced, greased for protection whilst idle, and effectively mothballed. The Barracks remained in this unfinished state and uninhabitable for some years, until the GWR's fortunes revived and the company spent about £10,000 on completing the lodging house to a different design.

The Barracks (so named in 1861, although until then known as 'the lodging house') was erected of ashlar limestone and constructed in a 'u' shape; it had a west front with north and south wings. The main entrance, opening on to Emlyn Square and given a gabled porch in 1869, was set in a three-storey, gabled elevation. At each end, was a four-storey, buttressed tower, each with a parapet and corbel table. Throughout, the lights at each stage were paired or in threes, either trefoil-headed or shouldered, and those at the ground floor had transoms. The elevations to Faringdon Road and Reading Street were also three-storey, and similar to the gabled linking block to Emlyn Square, except that each had a central gable that was larger than the others.

The premises had one hundred cell-like bedrooms, each just large enough to have a bed, a chest of drawers, and a chair. There were large day rooms, communal cooking arrangements, a bakery and a laundry. Some of this was occupied sporadically during the early 1850s, but it remained substantially empty (partly due to another recession at the Works, and partly because people simply did not want to live there) until 1855 when a speculative landlord, Joseph Robinson,

leased the premises from the GWR and attempted in vain to sub-let. The Barracks did not find favour with its occupants, who quickly moved elsewhere, and the building then stayed empty until 1861 when it was converted internally to accommodate Welsh ironworkers and their families who had come to Swindon to establish the rolling mills.

In 1863, the GWR Medical Fund Society transferred sixteen Turkish baths from the Mechanics' Institute, added a slipper bath and showers, and set them up just behind the Barracks, with general wash houses in an area that had been intended for a bakery. The Welsh families relocated to Cambria Place from 1864, and very soon the Barracks was again empty. It remained so until 1868 when, largely through the good offices of Joseph Armstrong, the building was acquired by the Wesleyan Methodists. (See also Wesleyan Methodist Chapel, Faringdon Road.)

Barrett, Thomas (1816-1898) Few Victorian tradesmen were as enduring as the builder Thomas Barrett. His advertisements were all encompassing: 'Builder, carpenter, appraiser, and undertaker. Plate-glass fronts put in complete. Conservatories and hot houses of all kinds. Every description of shop fittings executed at the shortest notice. Paper and bell hanger. All kinds of jobbing work neatly executed. Plumbing in all its branches. Painting and graining. Always on sale, dry boards and plank of every description. Mahogany, oak and fancy veneers. Oak and deal laths. Cement and plaster. Drain pipes and chimney pots'. Barrett always lived in, and worked from, Newport Street. In 1842, he built the County of Gloucestershire bank in High Street; in 1863, he rebuilt The Barracks in New Swindon for the Wesleyan Methodists; and in 1864, he built nearby

Blunsdon Abbey, which was destroyed by fire on 22 April, 1904. In 1877, he built Anderson's Hostel, the almshouses beside the churchyard at Christ Church.

In 1851, he was employing six men; this had risen to twenty by 1861. He married twice, although the sources for his wives are not sound. It is likely that his first wife was Rebecca née Davis (b. Eastcombe, Devon, 1816). The couple had three sons: John, b.1839; William, b.1844; and Richard, b.1849. John was to take up the trade of builder and carpenter. Rebecca died in the 1860s, and Thomas remarried in 1865. It is believed that his second wife was Harriet née Chappel (b. Bristol, 1837). They had no children of their own, but they brought up Thomas's granddaughter Lilian (who would grow up to be a school teacher), initially with the help of a governess, and always with one servant. Thomas was still working as a builder in his mid-seventies.

Bath Road From the early 1800s, the course of this narrow roadway between the old town and Kings Hill was known as 'The Sands', a reference to the sandy deposits to be found thereabouts that were associated with the Portland stone quarries that lay immediately to the south. Houses began to be built alongside it in the 1830s, and by 1840 the town's gentry were beginning to establish a select community; there were eleven residencies on the Sands at considerable distances apart. It housed, in the 1840s, solicitors, auctioneers, surgeons, the town's registrar, and a private school. One of the best buildings was the Georgian Apsley House, across the road from which the town's post office was established in the 1840s. By 1854, additional small, but very attractive, villas had been erected on the

south side, close to the junction with Victoria Street. Then, men who were at that time influential in commerce and trade built larger and individually designed villas at regular intervals along its length. Unofficially, the section leading west from Wood Street was called Bath Road from the 1850s, probably because the earliest residencies there were built of Bath stone. By the 1860s, traders had begun to creep along it from the Wood Street end. Between 1860 and 1880, further architecturally designed villas of character, if sometimes of dubious taste, were put up at intervals as monuments to their owners' affluence. Residencies had names like Alexandra Villas, Auckland House, Bellavista Villa, Clyde Villas, Devonshire Villas, Dorchester Villas, Eversely, Fairfield, Fairview, Highfield House, Ightham Villa, Kingshill House, Longford Villa, Oxford House, Sandown Villa, Summerville, Walton House, The Willows, and Yucca Villa. (Plurals in each case were a pair of semi-detached residencies.) Brunswick Terrace and Gloucester Terrace were built close to Prospect Place and Victoria Street, marking the business end of Bath Road, and were occupied by professional men and their families. By the 1880s, the Old Town fire station stood on Bath Road, almost opposite Eastcott Lane, and further to the west were the offices of the Swindon Waterworks. Otherwise, Bath Road was then at its residential and fashionable peak. The name was officially changed from The Sands to Bath Road in 1904, by which time it had become the most fashionable residential street in the town.

Bath Road Terrace In c.1835, a terrace of three modest town houses with cellars was built on the north side of the road, beginning

Swindon's residential expansion immediately to the west of the hilltop. These were two-storey, three-bay, double-fronted properties of brick, laid in Flemish bond, with lunette attic windows in the slate roof, and chimney stacks on each side of the shared walls. These properties remain, although they are now in commercial use rather than residential, and are distinguished by small lead-covered canopies at the front entrances above square, decorative wrought-iron openwork porches. Inside, the staircases are placed centrally, and the properties are two rooms deep.

Bath Road Villa Number 68 Bath Road was a substantial villa of two bays and five storeys with a central pediment and fine stone dressings. It was pulled down in the 1960s.

Bathampton Street Built in terraces in 1842-6, Bathampton Street (named Bath Street until 1901 when it was changed to avoid confusion with Bath Road in Old Swindon, whose name had recently been changed from The Sands) ran between High Street (renamed Emlyn Square in 1901) and the GWR park (formerly the cricket field). It was one of the earliest developments in the railway village. On the south side of the street is a fine terrace of twenty-one two-storey cottages, now in double and single units, and two rooms deep. They are built of coursed, rough-faced limestone with ashlar dressings; they have deep, inset doorways and casement windows, and rear yards with brick walls.

Baths, Public In 1851, the GWR opened its lodging house for young, unmarried GWR workers (known as 'The Barracks') in Faringdon Street. In 1860, the GWR

Medical Fund Society put Turkish baths into the Mechanics' Institute and, in 1863, transferred them to an area at the rear of The Barracks, adding a slipper bath. They were let privately, and were opened to men for two hours on Wednesday and Saturday evenings, and for four hours each Sunday morning, and to women for four hours on Wednesday afternoons. In 1868, a series of penny readings began at the Institute, with the purpose of raising money to fund better public baths. These were constructed in 1869 in a small building on the north side of the railway line, and there were a number of showers in Taunton Street. The Society opened its brick-built baths complex on the corner with Milton Road in 1892. It had two swimming baths: the smaller, of 1,500 square feet, was for women and children; the men's bath was larger, at 3,330 square feet. A wash-house was added to deal with the increasing amount of laundry from the GWR cottage (accident) hospital. In 1898, washing baths were added, followed in 1899 by Turkish and Russian baths. Gradually, in the 20th century, other services were added, such as a hairdresser, who had gone by the end of the First World War; between then and the mid-1940s, eight consulting rooms were added, as were a dental surgery, a psychological clinic, a dispensary, an ophthalmic practice, a chiropodist, a physiotherapist, a paediatric clinic, a skin clinic and a masseur.

The baths were refurbished and updated in 1937. During the Second World War, they were covered over and the rooms used as a temporary hospital. In 1948, the medical side became an NHS health centre under the National Health Service Act, 1946, but retained many of the former services. At the same time, Swindon Borough Council acquired ownership of the building. In the 1950s, the main bath was covered over during the winter, when it became a roller skating area and was also used for concerts, sales and meetings

The whole building was latterly known as the Health Centre and Milton Road Baths, and the Swindon Hydro (a Swindon Borough Council initiative); it is still used as a public swimming bath. Its facilities as a health centre were transferred to a new Health Centre that opened in Carfax Street in 1986. The iron rings in the outside east wall were used by former visitors to tether their horses. (See also GWR Medical Fund Society; Majestic Ballroom.)

Beaney, Albert George (1913-2009) Albert Beaney is best known as a photographer of children, although he left some 40,000 black and white photographs of Swindon people of all ages, taken between the 1940s and 1970s. Several generations of this line of the Beaney family lived in Kent, where Albert George's grandfather, George Fullagar Beaney (1838-1883) was born at Woodchurch. He was a general labourer who became a foreman in a chain printing works. He married tailoress Mary Ann Elizabeth Cruse, and the couple settled in Limehouse, London, where they had seven children. After George's death, his widow and some of her children relocated to Mile End, where two of the boys, Walter and Thomas, also went into the printing business, starting as a printer's porter and a lithographer's boy respectively. The fourth child of this marriage was Albert Henry Beaney (1875-1931), who came to Swindon c.1900 to work as a French polisher in the Great Western Railway Carriage and Wagon Works, lodging with the family of a GWR engine driver, Frederick Fairthorne, at 28 Harding Street. In 1912, Albert Henry

Beaney married Alice Jane Richings in Swindon, and the pair settled in 50 Beatrice Street, and his younger sister Mary Ann also lived with them.

In 1904, a Men's Adult School and a Women's Adult School were formed as separate entities in Swindon, and in 1906 they were combined as Swindon Adult School Union. Albert Henry became secretary of this umbrella organisation until 1909, and his sister Mary Ann was secretary of the Gorse Hill branch. The purpose of the Union was to give bible lessons and discuss topics of general interest, and to organise good works; Mary Ann had at her disposal a savings bank, the coal club, an outing fund, and an old people's tea fund. Between 1911 and 1920, Albert Henry was also district secretary of the International Order of Good Templars and local secretary of its Swindon United Lodge.

Albert George Beaney, Albert Henry and Alice's son, was born at 50 Beatrice Street and educated at Gorse Hill and Ferndale Schools. His interest in photography began as a child, and his first images were taken using a pinhole camera constructed out of a cornflakes box. After leaving school, he was employed as a French polisher in the GWR Carriage and Wagon Works, which he left to serve in the RAF during the Second World War. Whilst based in Lincolnshire during hostilities, he met Joan Newmarch from Barton-on-Humber. The pair were married at Scunthorpe in 1946, and came to live in the Beaney family home in Beatrice Street. Once demobbed, Albert George joined the Post Office and was a postman until he retired in 1973, and he spent the next five years as a cleaner working for Square D. In his spare time, he cycled around the town, speculatively photographing groups of people, and individuals working and playing. He used his front room window to display his work, and kept a box of photographs within, from which people could select images, pay for them, and take them away. In 1953, he moved to Moredon, where he lived in Fernham Road and Pembroke Gardens. Interest in Beaney was re-kindled in 2011 when Swindon's art initiative Create Studios mounted an exhibition of his work, and four schools in the town – Jennings Street, Churchfields, Sevenfields, and Commonweal – set about digitalizing the thousands of examples of his work that remain. His images are valuable on a number of levels: mostly of people, they therefore show the clothes of the age and the spirit of innocence that exude from the posers; the backgrounds, although most often incidental, include areas of Swindon as they were in the mid-20th century. In 2012, at the suggestion of the Swindon Society, a newly built roadway in Moredon was named Beaney View to commemorate the photographer.

Beard, Edward William (1878-1982) E.W. Beard began his working life in 1892, and in 1897 he founded the building firm that still bears his name. He was still at his desk in the mornings when he reached his centenary. This presented difficulties for those of his sons who had followed him into the firm and who, despite being past retirement age, felt morally obliged to continue working. As the head of the firm, E.W. Beard was at one time known as 'the man who built Swindon', such was the wide-ranging E.W. Beard & Sons' residential and commercial portfolio as the town expanded throughout the first half of the 20th century. E.W. gave up driving a motor car in his nineties when, during one of his annual

driving appraisals (he had never taken a formal driving test), the old man was told his reactions were a little slower than they had been. He parked on the side of the road, declared he would not drive again, walked back to his home in Belmont Crescent, and despatched one of his sons to collect the car.

Beatles in Swindon Few people in Swindon had heard of the Liverpool band when John Lennon, Paul McCartney, George Harrison and Pete Best were booked to play McIlroy's ballroom for a fee of £27.10s (£27.50). The engagement was for Jaybee Clubs' 'Top of the Pops' Tuesday night series of promotions, run by Bill Reid and Dave Backhouse, which brought top bands of the day to the town. The Beatles were promoted as 'the fabulous beat group from Liverpool' and 'the most popular group in the north', and would appear at a venue that could comfortably hold (and sometimes did for its Thursday night jazz clubs) some 1,800 patrons. The Beatles, who had played at the Cavern in Liverpool the day before, and would return to it the following day, made their appearance in Swindon on 17 July 1962 to just 360 of the largely disinterested but diehard 'Top of the Pops' club faithful. They played two hour-long sessions between 8.00 p.m. and 11.00 p.m. Within a month, Pete Best had been replaced on drums by Ringo Starr, but the group was never to return to Swindon.

Beatrice Street boating lake see Whitehead, George.

Bell and Shoulder of Mutton Public House, Marlborough Road Built in 1895, this was a very attractive brick building with stone dressings, decorated keystones and hood mouldings, moulded string courses, exceptional corner mouldings, pilasters, and knop and pendant finials. It was closed in 1968, and was demolished for no good reason in 1969.

Bell Inn, High Street An inn called 'The Lapwinge' stood on this site until sometime in the mid-17th century, when its name was changed to 'The Bell'. The hostelry is said to have originated in 1515, when it was established by Flemish wine and spirit merchants, and under its earlier name it was conveyed by lord of the manor Richard Goddard to Samuel Haggard in 1649. This may have been when it was renamed, and it appears as the 'signe of the Bell in Swindon' in a document of 1666. Early in the 19th century, (the date of the front elevation as it is today), Charles Rose operated it as an inn and posting house. He took the latter business, as a post office, to Bath Road in c1845, and left The Bell to John Woodroffe. In the days of travel by coach and horses, it was the stopping-off place for the York House passenger coach that ran between Bath and Oxford, and was a terminus for the post coach between Swindon and London. Frederick Edwin and James Franklin were the landlords in 1855; William Godwin by 1864. The hotel was re-fronted in the late 1870s. The building is of three bays and three storeys; there is a central canopied entrance between two bays, and a carriage entrance through the third into what was a galleried stable yard (some of the timber framing remains) at the rear. The windows to ground floor and first floor are square-headed type in canted bays with carving between. A cornice of paired modillions runs the width of the front elevation. For many years, a canopy crossed the pavement from the front door;

the position is now distinguished by a large, gilded bell. The premises closed in 2011, following licensing problems; it changed hands, was refurbished, and reopened in 2012. (See also Belmont Steam Brewery.)

Belmont Steam Brewery, Devizes Road

The chimney, brewhouse tower, and tunhouse are all that remain of the Belmont Brewery complex, off Devizes Road. Since the premises ceased to be a brewery in the 1930s, they became a builder's store and, later, a cabinet makers; the property fell into disrepair and was frequented by tramps and other homeless people. In the later 1990s, the premises were gutted and refurbished, leaving some of the internal supporting pillars. Beneath the main building is a very deep well, from which the brewery drew its water, supplied by one of the many natural springs thereabouts. Thus it has remained.

In c1870, William Godwin of the Bell Inn, High Street (where he had a brewhouse), built a small brewery on this site, probably in competition with Richard Bowly's much larger North Wiltshire Brewery (now demolished), which was erected in that year just a few yards to the north by builder John Phillips of Devizes Road. Three years later, Godwin, who lived at Belmont House, Quarry Road, obtained Kinsey & Merritt of London to design more substantial premises, and commissioned John Phillips to build them. The brewery remained in the family after the death of its founder in 1877, and became known as Godwin Brothers' Brewery, although its principals latterly had little interest in developing it. Wadworth's bought the premises in 1938. The building is distinguished as a landmark in Old Town by its polychromatic exterior in rubblestone and red brick, with blue brick and ashlar dressings, and its blank arcading of four-centred arches on pilasters.

After falling into disrepair, it was opened as Mission nightclub in 1998, then became Studio, a similar establishment, which closed in 2005. The building remained empty until August 2012 when refurbished, it opened as Tiger Bills night club. This closed three months later.

Betjeman, Sir John (1906-84)

The man who was knighted in 1969 and appointed poet laureate in 1972 knew Swindon well and wrote about aspects of it on many occasions. Notably, in one of his *Town Tours*, broadcast in 1937, he was less than kind, calling the place 'a blot on the earth', but he later ameliorated his words. His poem 'On hearing the full peal of ten bells from Christ Church, Swindon' appeared in *New Bats in Old Belfries*, published in 1945. In the same year, Betjeman opened the Bomford Collection of French Paintings exhibition in the town hall with the words: 'Do not look at a picture first to see what it is about. Look at it primarily as a juxtaposition of colours, textures and volumes.' In 1948, he was less scathing than hitherto about Swindon, in his broadcast on St Mark's Church (also mentioning a few others in the town). Betjeman wrote a paper on Swindon, 1952, in the British Towns & Cities series of articles in *History Today*. He contributed the chapter on architecture in Swindon Borough Council's 1950 publication *Studies in the History of Swindon*, in which he famously said: 'There is very little architecture in Swindon and a great deal of building.' In the 1960s, he campaigned to save the Railway Village from redevelopment, and in the 1970s spearheaded a successful fund-raising appeal to stop Swindon Borough Council — which

since 1926 has owned Coate Farmhouse, the home of writer Richard Jefferies – from pulling down an associated barn and some pigsties.

Bevan, Frances (b.1953) Born in London, Frances Bevan came to Swindon in 1987. She is a direct descendant of George Thomas Joseph Ruthven (1792-1844), who joined the Bow Street Runners at the age of seventeen and became their principal officer. It was Ruthven who stormed the Cato Street stable where conspirators were plotting to assassinate members of the government, and who afterwards tracked down their leader, Arthur Thistlewood. It was said that Ruthven was a government spy, and when he retired in 1839 he was awarded a pension by the British government, as well as by those of Prussia and Russia for his work in detecting forged currencies. This detective work clearly found its way into Frances's genes who, between 2008 and 2011, carried out a wide-ranging programme of research into aspects of local and family history in Swindon; she presented the results to the town three times each week through the popular 'Remember When' column that ran in the *Swindon Advertiser*. Arguably, she did more than anyone else to popularise Swindon's history and make it available to the average reader. She also won a Millennium Award to fund research, writing, and production of a local history project for West Swindon schools, focusing on farms in the area. Frances Bevan was instrumental in establishing the Friends of Radnor Street Cemetery in 2011. This group copied the registers for burials at Radnor Street, otherwise held in bound volumes at Kingsdown Crematorium, and regularly made the information available to family history researchers in the cemetery chapel. Under their auspices, the chapel was also used for displays by local history groups, and as a meeting place for the Friends' guided walks of the grounds, often conducted by Frances. She is also the author of *A Tale of Two Parishes*, the story of Lydiard Tregoze and Lydiard Millicent. (See also Radnor Street Cemetery.)

Bickle, William (1819-1909) The engineer whose claim to fame was a miniature working model of non-condensing steam engines displayed at the Great Exhibition of 1851, lived twice in Swindon. He was born at Phillack, Cornwall, the third of five sons born to engineer Thomas Bickle (b. 1796) and his wife Mary (b. 1791), and began his working life as a blacksmith. Three of his brothers were similarly employed, and the fourth started out as an apprentice draughtsman. William Bickle was initially employed by Harvey & Co., blacksmiths, engineers and iron founders of Hayle in Cornwall, but he came to Swindon during the 1840s to work on the railway as an engine fitter. In 1847, he married Elizabeth Perris (b 1822, Seagry, near Sutton Benger), of a family of drapers and tailors, and the couple set up home at 18 Reading Street, Swindon, in what was then a brand new cottage in the railway village. Their first three children were born there, and this was still their address when William's working model appeared in the Great Exhibition. The official catalogue described it as standing 'within the compass of a shilling, and weighs three drachms; made, with the exception of the piston rods, of a fine white metal'.

By 1861, the family were living at 24 Victoria Street, Masbrough, Yorkshire, where their fourth child was born in 1865, after which they relocated to 3 Viceroy

Terrace, Lambeth, London. William became a foreman engine fitter. He was still working as such, aged seventy-two, when the family moved to Oldfield Road, Hampton, Middlesex. Following the death of his wife, William returned to Swindon during the 1890s to live at 4 Oriel Street with his son Jebus (b.1852, Swindon), a steam engine fitter, his wife Sarah (b.1851, Malmesbury), and their son Frederick, whose first job was as an apprentice mechanical engineer. In 1981, the *Swindon Evening Advertiser* printed a reference to William Bickle at Oriel Street, given by a man who, as a teenager, had visited him there. He recalled that he was 'an outstanding engineer who made at least two microscopes, a gyroscope, and his own geometric lathe which enabled him to produce many other pieces'.

Binyon, Brightwen (1846-1905) Binyon was a painter, and an architect of national standing, whose offices were in Ipswich from 1873, in which town he mostly lived, and whose clients included Queen Victoria and the Empress of Russia. The son of a Manchester Quaker sugar refiner and tea dealer, for four years he was an assistant to the architectural practice of the Gothic Revivalist Alfred Waterhouse (1830-1905), who is best known for the Natural History Museum building in South Kensington. Binyon became a competent designer of municipal and public buildings, schools, and domestic properties throughout the country, and of furniture, doing so in a wide range of styles. He started to practise in Ipswich in 1871. Binyon married Rachel Mary (née Cudworth) in 1879; their daughter Mary (b.1882) became a painter and an art potter, and their son Basil (b.1885) was a research engineer with strong military connections.

Binyon was particularly active in Suffolk, although he designed the most architecturally satisfying building in New Swindon – the town hall (1891) – and enlarged, 1892-3, the most iconic – Robert Roberts's Mechanics' Institute of 1854. His estimate for the town hall at Swindon was £7,760-£8,000. He also designed board schools in the town, most noteworthy being Gilbert's Hill school in Dixon Street, Queenstown School, Sanford Street School, and Westcott School in Birch Street. He retired from practice in 1897.

Bird, Denis (1923-2001) This is 'the man who photographed Swindon in black and white', and whose images, particularly those taken in the 1960s and 1970s, recorded so many of the town's ordinary buildings just before they were swept away under road-widening and general redevelopment schemes. He was born in Glamorgan, took up photography in 1937, and relocated to Swindon in 1940. Following war service with the army in the Middle East and Malta, he became a clerk in the GWR railway works, where he remained for over four decades. Denis began to photograph the town almost as soon as he arrived. He was a member of Swindon Camera Club (formed 1898), a founder member of The Swindon Society in 1972, and much of his work appeared in the *Swindon In Old Photographs* series of books. His particular interest was the old Holy Rood church on the former Lawn estate, about which he published *The Story of Holy Rood* in 1975, and around whose ruins he conducted tours in the summer. He also co-authored *A History of Christ Church* (with Rosemary Stephens) in 1969.

Denis never married, and lived alone in Drove Road. Following his retirement, he voluntarily taught photography for fifteen

years to children at Holy Rood Junior Roman Catholic School in Upham Road. He left his photographic collection to Brian Bridgeman of the Swindon Society.

Bishops of Swindon Malmesbury was established as a suffragan bishopric in 1927. In Church of England terms, a suffragan bishop is subordinate to, and supportive of, a diocesan bishop – in this case, the Bishop of Bristol – in a place that does not itself have a cathedral. There were six bishops of Malmesbury between 1927 and 1994. Then Rt. Revd Barry Rogerson, (Bishop of Bristol 1985-2002), changed the title to Bishop of Swindon. The first holder of this was Rt. Revd Michael David Doe (b.1947), who held office between 1994 and 2005. He was followed in 2005 by Rt. Revd Dr Lee Stephen Rayfield (b.1955).

Blind House The Humphris (sometimes spelled Humphries) family were associated with the Swindon quarries from the 1600s, through Thomas Humphris and then his son William, who both lived in Wroughton. In 1696, stonecutter William Humphris went into partnership with Richard Hopkins of Swindon, also a stonecutter and a member of a family that also had long associations with the quarries. Together, they rented a half-acre of the quarry site. In the early 1750s, William Humphris, 'quarryman and stonecutter' was charged by the parish with providing the stone to build a lock-up or 'blind house', paid for out of the Poor Rate, for the temporary incarceration of prisoners (before being brought before magistrates), drunks, general nuisances, etc. The Swindon blind house was built c.1752, and stood at the western end of Newport Street, most probably on the north side. In 1804, it was described as being in a wet state and thereby dangerous to the health of prisoners, and the suggestion that its arched roof needed repairing gives the only first-hand indication of its actual appearance. However, William Morris, editor of *Swindon Advertiser*, writing from memory in the late 1880s, said that the building was about eight feet square with a stone floor, and a door into which was set an iron grating, some eight inches square, through which came the only light to illuminate the interior. Inside, there was just a wooden bench, which was fastened to the wall. (The lock-up extant at Trowbridge seems generally to fit this description, with perhaps a door set in the wall like the one at Box.) The Swindon blind house was demolished c.1853.

Bluebird Toys One of the iconic children's toys of the 1980s was a big plastic yellow teapot, called by that name, and so famous that its maker, Bluebird Toys of Swindon, was often addressed on envelopes as The Big Yellow Teapot Company. Bluebird was begun in premises in Kembrey Street in 1981 'with a handful of willing workers and a very large prayer mat'. Its founder was entrepreneur Torquil Norman (six feet eight inches tall), whose enterprise was in response to the fact that fifty per cent of all children's toys then being sold in Britain were made in other countries. Instead of licensing the teapot as was his initial intention, he decided instead to set up his own production company. Bluebird made the teapot, children's lunch boxes and flasks, and a handful of other items. In 1983, the company was voted British Toy Producer of the Year by the Toy Retailers Association, and Norman became chairman of the British Tot & Hobby Association. In 1984, the company relocated its offices and shop to

Cheney Manor industrial estate, retaining a warehouse at its former home. That year, it launched its other great iconic toy, A La Carte Kitchen, and followed up in 1985 with the 'Clix' pre-school system of interlocking building bricks. The company was declared 'Toymaker of the Year' in 1984, and from the mid-1980s it had a substantial worldwide market. The Polly Pockets doll, made of plastic and less than one inch tall, was launched in 1989 by Bluebird; the company had bought the product from designer Chris Wiggs, whose prototype for his own daughter Kate had a home in a powder compact. Polly was to become a huge worldwide success (she was joined by Mighty Max in 1992) until about 1996, by which time her popularity was on the wane. Nonetheless, Polly Pockets was to become Bluebird's legacy, although the company ceased to manufacture toys in 1990, when the Swindon operation, still with Norman at the head (until 1996), became wholly administrative. In 1998, the company was taken over by Mattel. They re-formatted the Polly Pockets line, and closed down the Bluebird site in Swindon.

Book Club Associates In 1964, W.H. Smith entered the direct mail book club business, when it established its Direct Book Service in London. In 1965, it linked up with Doubleday Inc. of America and formed the Cookery Book Club. The following year, it bought The Reprint Society of Aldershot (which Doubleday of America also wanted to buy at the time), the publishers of World Books since 1939. This operation was established on the top floor of its multi-storey office block at Greenbridge, Swindon (opened in 1967), providing space for book club stock in the warehouse. This arm of the company was called Book Club Associates

which, over the subsequent decades, was to establish a good many different niche and general book clubs, as well as record clubs and the offering of general home and garden catalogues. BCA eventually relocated: first to the newly built WHS offices (Bridge House) on the corner of Farnsby Street and Faringdon Road; then to Princes House in Princes Street (now a hotel); and then to its own multi-storey offices (Guild House) next to the WHS building in Farnsby Street. At its height, the company was operating twenty-six book clubs from its offices and warehouses in Swindon. In 1980, BCA opened (at a ceremony performed by WHS chairman Peter Bennett, and John Sargent, chairman of Doubleday) its own custom-built warehouse and distribution centre on the Groundwell Farm industrial estate. Doubleday, which for much of the time had held a half-interest in BCA, was bought by the German publishing giant Bertelsmann in 1986; the following year, W.H. Smith sold its own half-share to the German company, which continued to control the organisation until 2009. By then, it had become largely a telephone customer service and telemarketing organisation, both of which were outsourced from 2004 when the lease on Guild House expired and was not renewed. The customer service/call centre went to India. In 2009, Bertelsmann sold BCA to Aurelius AG of Munich, who reorganised the company, restructured it, and introduced new IT systems. They sold it on to the Webb Group in 2011, and all that remained of BCA at Swindon was immediately relocated to Burton-on-Trent. A comprehensive history of the company was chronicled in *Book Club Associates at Swindon in the History of the British Book Clubs Movement*, a monograph by Mark Child for Swindon Local Studies.

Bowly's Brewery see North Wilts Brewery

Bowmaker House, Wood Street
This typical Georgian town house of c.1780 is at the west end of Wood Street, where it would have been the most imposing private building in Wood Street before this began to be developed for trade towards the end of the 19th century. Bowmaker House has four bays, with the doorway in the third bay, and is of two storeys, with a concealed roof of slate. The doorway was formerly in the first bay to the west. It is shallow and has a triangular pediment above plain shafts. The windows have flat, stone architraves with keystones.

Bradford, James Edward Goddard (1828-1912) J.E.G. Bradford was a third generation of Swindon-born solicitors. He was admitted in 1851, and became a partner in the High Street, Swindon firm of Bradford & Foote. (William Foote, who was admitted in 1844, lived in Bath Road.) J.E.G. Bradford's father was James Bradford (1795-1861) and his mother was Annica Werden, née Goddard (1803-1881), born at Clyffe Pypard. The family lived in High Street, where they had several servants. In 1852, J.E.G. Bradford was a director of the Swindon Market Company, and served on a number of local authority committees and utility committees. He remained a bachelor, using his money to acquire land and property (he would eventually be described as a 'landed proprietor'), until 1885 when he married Charlotte Beatrice Tyndale Ripley (1841-1934), the daughter of the Revd Thomas Hyde Ripley (1782-1865), of Wootton Bassett, and his wife Caroline Augusta, née Tyndale (1772-1855). The marriage took place in St George's church, Hanover Square, London. He retired in 1891, and he and Charlotte went to live in Bath, firstly at 8 Queen's Parade, and latterly at 16 Marlborough Buildings, whilst retaining land and properties at Broad Town. The couple kept five servants: lady's maid, housemaid, parlour maid, kitchen maid, and cook. When he died, J.E.G. Bradford left almost £50,000. The couple are buried at Christ Church, Swindon. The Arts Centre in Old Town is in the former Bradford Hall, named after the man who owned the properties where it now stands. (See also Arts Centres.)

Bradford Hall see Arts Centres

Bradley, Thomas Frederick 'Trigger' (b.1943) In 2010, Tom Bradley was given a Gold Badge Award for his contribution to the music industry by the British Academy of Singers and Songwriters Composers and Authors in Association with the Performing Rights Society for Music. His mother Joyce lived near Highworth; his father Thomas Bradley came from Pontefract, Yorkshire and it was there that the couple married and Trigger was born. During the war, he and his mother lived with her parents, and his grandfather gave him the nickname by which he was always afterwards known, based on hand actions he assumed as a baby. Released from the war, his father became a shunter with the GWR in Swindon. In 1949, the young family moved into Westdown Drive in the Ministry of Aircraft Production (MAP) bungalows at Upper Stratton. Tom went to Headlands grammar school. The family later moved to Ruskin Avenue, Meadowcroft.

Influenced musically by his grandfather, who played concertina, piano accordion,

and banjo, Trig learnt to play the guitar. At sixteen, he left school and took up a commercial apprenticeship with Pressed Steel at Stratton, a company that would later enable him to take an HND Business Studies on full pay. In 1960, he joined The Satellites, a Swindon group that included Justin Hayward (later of the Moody Blues). In 1961, he was a founder member, with other musicians from The Satellites, of The Sapphires, also known as Trig and the Sapphires. In 1964, he joined The Misc. He married Mary Nichols in 1967, and the following year formed the band Rookery Nook, which played together in the Aylesbury area until 1973.

Tom Bradley qualified as an accountant in 1972, which led to a career in financial and general management in the music industry, wherein he became financial controller of George Martin's AIR studios. He went on to become general manager of Magnet Records, and was at A&M Records for three years before joining its publishing section in 1983. He was deputy managing director of EMI Music Publishing, for whom he worked 1995-2003, then he left and formed his own publishing company, Quiet Man Music. In 1992, he became chief operating officer of the Mechanical Copyright Protection Society Ltd, and was elected its chairman in 2004; he was appointed chairman of the Copyright Licensing Agency in 2010. Mary died in 1996, and he later met Rachel, who was to become his second wife. (See also Sapphires, The.)

Braid, Alexander James (1814-1899) In 1844, the Great Western Railway Company's school opened in Bristol Street. Braid was appointed as its headmaster and moved with his family into the adjacent school house. He was born in Hastings,

Kent, where he was also to be at the time of his death. His wife Jane (1812-1874), who was born at Brigstock, Northamptonshire, was a schoolmistress at the Isle of Thanet Union Workhouse in 1841, and the couple already had three children of their own. Braid is not only notable as the first headmaster of the first school in New Swindon; in 1844, he also became the first secretary of the New Swindon Mechanics' Institution and was a tireless worker in establishing its educational classes, to include 'improving' leisure activities that the institution set up for the benefit of the Company's workforce and their families. He was also the first secretary of the group, established in 1850, that brought the principles and approach of the 'Rochdale Pioneers' to co-operative retailing in Swindon. Braid also helped to set up the Institution's series of 'People's Penny Readings', himself reciting at the inaugural event in 1865. He is thought to have retired in 1874, possibly following the death of his wife, and coincidentally at the time when the Company-built College Street School had superseded the one in Bristol Street. Braid retired to a home for widowed and elderly single men in Saltash, Cornwall, but by 1891 he had returned to Kent, where he was living at Brunswick Terrace, Tunbridge Wells and being looked after by a widowed housekeeper.

Brick and Tile Works Established during the early 1870s, the Swindon Brick and Tile Works were located immediately south of the Medgbury Road section of the Wilts & Berks Canal, a little to the east of the road (later called Princes Street) that linked York Place (Regent Circus) with the Whale Bridge over the canal. The company had offices at 42 Cricklade Street. The works

were situated on the Kimmeridge clay of the lowlands beneath Swindon hill, the clay providing the raw material for its products. Several kilns operated in the works, the most important being the Friedrich Hoffmann's patent brick kiln, which had been invented in 1858, and for which the company had negotiated the sole rights of use in the neighbourhood. It took three million bricks to build it at Swindon, and all of these, except for the fire bricks that lined it, were made on site. The Hoffmann kiln was circular, had twelve chambers — each of which could hold up to fourteen thousand bricks — and its prime benefit, according to the brick and tile company, was that it enabled them to save six hundredweight of coal on every thousand bricks baked. As it had an upper floor for use as a drying shed, it meant that the company did not, as hitherto, have to dry the product outside, subject to the vagaries of the weather. Other kilns on the site were used for making pottery, roofing tiles and fancy tiles, flooring tiles, drain pipes and garden flower pots. The process involved transporting the clay in trucks and putting it into a machine for pressing, working, shaping and cutting bricks, or a clay crushing machine for pottery and tiles. By 1875, Swindon was expanding so rapidly that the works were unable to keep up with the requirement for bricks.

Bridge Street In the 1840s, a few cottages were built just south of the GWR's railway line, a little to the west of Bullen's Bridge over the North Wilts Canal. They were called Sheppard's Cottages, named after John Henry Harding Sheppard, a brewer, on whose land (Sheppard's Field) the cottages stood, adjacent to the north-east of the area that would become the GWR model village. (Sheppard Street, built c.1873 on the same property, was also named after him.) These cottages were at the northern end of what became Bridge Street, a thoroughfare which would eventually connect the railway village with Old Town, via Regent Street and Victoria Street.

Bridge Street developed in two sections. One ran south-west from the railway line to the point where it was crossed by Fleetway. This was an ancient trackway, recorded as *le flet* in the early 17th century, and in the 18th as 'the Fleetway track'. This ran along the line of the present-day Westcott Place, Faringdon Road, and Fleet Street. The other section continued from this point to the Golden Lion bridge over the Wilts & Berks Canal. This part lay alongside the trackway that ran between Fleetway and Upper Eastcott Farm (which was in the vicinity of the present-day Regent Circus). Before the 1850s, any properties north of the Wilts & Berks Canal were described as being in Eastcott.

By 1855, this roadway had been designated as Bridge Street (or Bridge Road). The properties in the street were built of red brick. The whole stretch ran between the Golden Lion public house to the south-east and the Union Railway Hotel (built 1841 and demolished 1958) to the north-west, at the junction between Sheppard Street and Station Road. From c.1854, until it was demolished in the 1930s, a two-storey public house stood on the corner of Bridge Street and Fleetway. Originally named the Jolly Tar, it became The Volunteer in the 1860s, and The Oxford following some remodelling to the façade, 1911-12, when the previously plain parapet was also improved and it was given some decorative pediments in keeping with the aspirations of the area.

Bridge Street grew up from the 1850s as a community of tradespeople who had an eye

towards the needs of the railway workforce. During the 1860s, it became the first road in New Swindon outside the railway village to be lit by gaslight, and that was paid for by public subscription. There were then seven beer retailers and public houses there; a chandler, a grocer, and a baker were already established; and the Methodists and the Roman Catholics built places of worship there, as did the Free Christian Church. Within a decade, Bridge Street was full of tradespeople, living over their places of work, and it thereby became the first real shopping centre for New Swindon. By the 1870s, about two-thirds of the street was in trade. As the street began to advance beyond the Golden Lion and the Wilts & Berks Canal, this extension was also called Bridge Street until about 1865, when the whole of the roadway between the Golden Lion and York Place (which became Regent Circus) became known as Regent Street. By the end of the 19th century, one could find here, within a few yards of each other, a cycle repair shop, shoe repairer, barber, tobacconist, pork butcher, faggot and peas shop, grocer, sweet shop and a restaurant. Its most enduring business, Samuel Gray's cottage bakery, opened there in 1919. Bridge Street maintained its retail independence as Regent Street developed, but gradually became less of a shopping source from about the second decade of the 20th century. (See also Regent Street.)

Bridgeman, Brian (1936-2003) Born in Station Road, Swindon, he was a pupil at Lethbridge Road and Sanford Street schools, and Headlands grammar school. After school, he took up an aircraft engineering apprenticeship with Vickers Armstrong at South Marston, became a chartered mechanical and production engineer, and was employed by Square D Limited from 1967 to 1997. Brian was a founder member of The Swindon Society and the author of several books. He was also the principal author and editor for the Society's series of *Swindon In Old Photographs* books. He was particularly interested in the history of the Midland & South Western Junction Railway, whose Swindon station was off Newport Street, and co-authored three books about it. His book (co-authored with Theresa Squires) *The Old Lady On The Hill*, the story of Christ Church from its establishment in 1851 and the Swindon community it supported, was published in 2001. *The Flyers* was the true story of mercenary pilots in the Spanish Civil War. He was a consultant for the Time Life USA-published series, *Epic of Flight*. His last book was *Swindon Living Memories*, published by Frith in 2003.

Bristol buses The Bristol Tramways Company Limited was established in 1874, initially to operate under lease a tramway line that Bristol Corporation had been building for a whole year between Colston Street and Blackboy Hill. The local authority retained the right, under the Tramway Company Act 1870, to acquire the undertaking, although this was never done. The Company's service began in Bristol with three horse-drawn trams built at Leamington Spa. In 1886, the Bristol Cab Company Limited was formed, and the following year both organisations were incorporated as the Bristol Tramways & Carriage Company Limited. This organisation operated its first electric tram, in Bristol, in 1895. In 1904, the Swindon Corporation electric tramway opened in Swindon, operating its fleet of trams only within the borough. The Bristol company introduced its first motor bus service in 1906,

in Bristol. It eventually saw that the potential existed to provide motor transport to the peripheral areas of Swindon and, in 1921, opened there with a single omnibus.

The company's offices and waiting rooms were on the east side of Regent Circus, in premises that had formerly housed The Picture House, an early Swindon cinema that was operational c.1910-13. As the company's routes increased (although it could deposit passengers at the Corporation's fare stage stops, it would never be allowed to pick up fares within the borough), each one began and ended at a different point around the Circus. The Company moved its offices to the south side of Regent Circus, on the corner with Rolleston Street, and, in 1957, changed its name from the Bristol Tramways & Carriage Company Limited to the Bristol Omnibus Company Limited. The Company continued working out of Regent Circus until 1967, when it transferred to the town's temporary custom-built bus station at Wellington Street. This was rebuilt as a permanent site, and opened in 1984.

In 1983, the Bristol Omnibus Company was chopped in two, and the Swindon services became part of the organisation renamed as Cheltenham & Gloucester Omnibus Company. This was subject to a management buy-out three years later, and in 1993 was sold to Stagecoach.

Bristol Street This earliest part of the railway village was mostly built variously between 1842 and 1846 by J.D and C. Rigby. The street is notable for the GWR water tower (1870) and the high rock-faced walls with ashlar quoins and flat pilasters that once separated the residential side from the sawmills and carriage works of the GWR Works. The cottages were arranged internally as 'one up, one down' dwellings, with a small rear yard and virtually non-existent facilities. Yet the external elevation presented towards the railway line, the double front doors masqueraded as a single entrance, and imposing gabled sections were built symmetrically to add visual width to the street scene; it was all done for show and gave a false impression that here was more fulsome accommodation than in actuality. When complete, Bristol Street mainly comprised a terrace of twenty-two properties. (See also Water Tower.)

Britannia, Devizes Road In 1849, an alehouse was built for James Howe on the corner with Britannia Place; it was kept by home-brewer Richard Stagg (described as a beer retailer in 1851) from the outset, and first appears named as the Britannia Inn, 'Short-hedge', in 1853. Stagg stayed there until 1867, after which he is described as a 'beer retailer of Newport Street'; The Britannia was thereafter occupied by Caroline Watmore, (born at Avebury), her son Francis William, her uncle Isaac Rickett, and a servant. Watmore stayed until the public house was put up for sale in 1870. Then, it had four public rooms and four bedrooms. It was bought by the North Wilts Brewery (a nearby competitor of the Belmont).They installed George Daniels (born Purton), and redeveloped the premises and extended them as they currently present: two blocks, each of two storeys and three bays, of stucco with stone quoins. The entrance occupies the left-hand bay of the southern block, which slightly projects out on rounded, recessed corners. It is an attractive façade. The ground-floor windows have segmental

heads and moulded sills, and are tied together by a continuous string course that is pointed above each window to admit decoration in the spandrels. The windows of the upper storey are square-headed, with pretty, bracketed sills, and have decoratively moulded architraves and embellishments in the spandrels. The northern wall is gabled; there is a plain parapet with moulded cornice, and a west-facing gable with scroll brackets flanking a fountain in relief. Bowly's, owners of the North Wilts Brewery, re-named it The Fountain in 1870, which name remained for more than 120 years, before it had several changes, and is currently The Pig on the Hill. When the Swindon Town Football Club played at The Croft, this hostelry was advertised as being the players' dressing room. (See also Britannia Place.)

Britannia Place This was a narrow lane leading off from Devizes Road, and which initially cut into a number of long gardens that were attached to properties in High Street. In 1810, before Devizes Road began to be built up, some small, thatched cottages were built along the north side of this lane. In the late 1840s, the way was given a dog-leg extension close to a brewery (it became the Belmont Brewery), for which it also provided access, and was named Britannia Place. A terrace of red brick cottages was erected here, with front and rear gardens. By 1858, there were twenty-three houses in Britannia Place, and a larger residence called 'Britannia Cottage'. They all accessed, for their water supply, the 'Britannia Pump' on adjacent land owned by Charles Anthony Wheeler. Before piped water was brought into Swindon, this was one of only four public sources of supply in Old Town. (See also The Hermitage).

Brockhill The point at which Cricklade Street, the old coaching road at the northern end of High Street, suddenly dropped down was commonly known as Brockhill (variously Brock Hill, Brockle Hill, Brockwell or Brockwell Hill) until the end of the 19th century. Horse-drawn coaches struggled up this sharp incline and, when weather conditions were particularly adverse, had sometimes to detour through Albert Street to reach the stable yards of the Old Town inns. The name is popularly thought to derive from badger setts that were once common there. However, a map of 1763 calls this Brookhill, and shows Brookhill Cottages built at right angles to it. Early directory entries and manorial documents frequently make Brockhill and Cricklade Street synonymous, and sometimes combine them. Until the mid-1800s, a natural spring debouched at Brockhill where, as Holy Well, it was a source of water for the townspeople. Here too, was the site of the Swindon gasworks, built in 1841. In 1885, lord of the manor Ambrose Lethbridge Goddard leased seven acres of land at Brockhill to the Revd Maurice J.G. Ponsonby, vicar of St Mark's church, for use as a cricket field. Otherwise, it was the way off Swindon hill that eventually connected with a lane to Stratton St Margaret, a village some three miles distant that, in the 20th century, would join up with the town.

Brown, Alexander James (1892-1977) and Louise Francis (1892-1989) In 1908, Alex Brown's father, James, a one-time stage manager at Drury Lane theatre, London, relocated his family from Brighton to Swindon, where he became licensee of the bars at the Empire Theatre. In 1911, his occupation was listed as barman and cellarman, and young Alex was

described as being 'out of work'. This was not strictly true; he had become call-boy at the theatre almost by default, progressed to electrician, and then became chief electrician and gained experience in stage management. During the First World War he performed as a member of The Imps Concert Party. Meanwhile, Louise Francis Barker, born in Swindon, was a member of a juvenile theatrical group in Wales, where her family lived before returning to Swindon. Alex and Louise met when they both joined the Swindon Young Conservative League, and the couple married in 1920.

Alex and Louise Brown became arguably the best-known couple of their time in the amateur theatre in Swindon, and were particularly associated with The Western Players, which they joined in 1945. Prior to that, Alex formed the Optimist Concert Party which, throughout the Second World War, gave shows under contract to the Ministry of Labour for service personnel stationed around Swindon, employees in the workplace, and hospital staff. Near the end of hostilities, he became stage manager for the Western Players, a position he held for the next fifteen years, built scenery, and also took on a number of cameo acting parts. He also became stage manager for The Poetry Players and The Adastrians, and stage director for the annual drama festivals held under the auspices of the Swindon Theatre Guild. Louise swopped juvenile monologues for Shakespeare and character acting, in which she was particularly successful, and with which she had a long and distinguished career on the amateur stage, right into a considerable old age.

Bruce the Collecting Dog Between 1905 and 1914, T.A. Beale of Nelson Street, who was employed in the machine shop at the GWR Works, used his dog Bruce to collect money for charity. When the animal was eight years old, a postcard was issued that depicted the very hairy Bruce with his collecting box, hasped with a lock, strapped to his back, and with an array of medals about his neck. The caption read: 'I am Bruce of Swindon, the famous Collecting Dog of nearly £500 for Charity. I have travelled over 10,000 miles by rail. A solid Silver Collar, 16 Gold and Silver Medals have been Presented to me for my noble work. I am also a member of the Brotherhood of Hero Dogs London.' Other postcards followed, depicting Bruce. One of Beale and Bruce's favourite fund-raising causes in Swindon was the Victoria Hospital, and a certificate presented to them in 1911 recorded the £140 or so raised in the previous three years. The dog was also successfully active following the Titanic disaster in 1912. His collecting box went into the stock of the Swindon museum but, although extant, it is no longer on display. A likeness of Bruce (sitting in a shop doorway) was painted by Ken White in 1979 in his 'Famous Swindonians' end-wall mural at the end of Union Street in Prospect Place.

Bruddel Wood, Old Town A four-acre strip of ancient woodland, once part of the more extensive Lawn Woods, lies south of the Lawn estate, adjacent to Marlborough Road, south-east of Old Town. There is documentary evidence from 1600 for part of the present-day extent, and the name is said to derive from 'fludwell', a description of the way in which water disposed itself from the natural springs hereabouts. The area has been designated 'Upper Wood' (the oldest part), 'Middle Wood', and 'Lower Wood', each having its own characteristics, and

is managed by Swindon Borough Council to encourage wildlife and facilitate species of flora. The area includes an end-to-end pathway for walkers, and there are two lateral cycle ways between residential roads, adjacent on each side.

Brunel, Isambard Kingdom (1806-59) The first engineer of the Great Western Railway Company is credited as the originator of the railway works at Swindon. Brunel famously travelled the proposed routes of the railway line in a four-wheeled, horse-drawn brougham that included a desk, seating with red cushions, and a bed. According to legend, he arrived in this contraption one day in 1840 to a site of marshy ground in the vale to the north of Old Swindon, accompanied by Daniel Gooch, his Locomotive Superintendent. It is said that Brunel threw a sandwich out of the carriage window, declaring that where it fell he would build his railway works. Swindon station opened in 1842, and the railway works began operating in 1843; residential New Swindon and the necessary social and economic infrastructures were established to accommodate the needs of the GWR.

Brunel Centre The 12.5-acre site on which the shopping mall is built was once occupied by 126 residences, some retail premises and several offices. It was divided into two parts by the line of the former Wilts & Berks Canal, by then filled in. The centre was named after Brunel Street, which it displaced, and which formerly ran diagonally between Cromwell Street and Havelock Street, and which in its turn had been named after Isambard Kingdom Brunel. It was the town's first indoor mixed retail shopping complex.

The original proposals were discussed by public enquiry in 1961, and in 1962 the minister for housing and local government approved the scheme. Swindon Borough Council incorporated the details into its Development Plan, which the council approved in 1964. Compulsory purchase orders for the required land were made in the mid-1960s when a detailed scheme was published. Another public enquiry took place in 1967, and the minister approved the proposals in 1968, at the same time agreeing that the Borough of Swindon could finance the scheme out of its own capital, to the exclusion of private developers. In that way, the local authority would be able to control the development, and any profits would benefit the town. The architects were Douglas Stephen & Partners; Victor Behrens, Sandhurst & Company were the commercial consultants and letting agents. The whole project cost £13.9 million.

Tenders were invited for the first contracts in mid-1970. Temporary shops were made available for each trader who had been displaced by the development, and they were offered the chance of a new permanent shop in close proximity to their former premises. Three traders took up the offer of new premises when the first shops were ready for handing over in the autumn of 1972. Regent Street traders affected by the development continued to operate until April of that year. The rest of the properties became available in 1973. The first stage of the Brunel Plaza, the two-level arcade of shops and the covered market, was opened on 29 March 1973 by Sir James Jones, Permanent Secretary at the Department of the Environment. It was fully operational by July 1974. The following year a 'moving pavement' was installed in the complex. The whole complex was not

finished until February 1977. The Brunel Centre's barrel-shaped roof glazed in bronze-tinted polycarbonate sheet, and curved canopy design, with a framework encased in stainless steel and designed by Aluminium Alloy Fabrications Limited of Woking, was intended to echo grand Victorian covered railway station engineering. There was also an integral 17,000 square-foot Brunel ballroom, wherein the party was held for the dignitaries on opening day. Some remodelling of the area took place 1995-97, at a cost of £20 million, when the site of the market became a department store. In 2004, the complex was put up for sale by the developers, Westfield, and was bought the following year by the Capital & Investment Trust Group. In 2011, by which time the value of a long-term loan considerably exceeded the value of the buildings, the owners, Brunel Unit Trust, placed the Centre in receivership.

Brunel Statue, Havelock Square

The bronze resin statue of Isambard Kingdom Brunel that stands beside the east entrance to the Brunel shopping mall was unveiled on 29 March 1973 by Sir James Jones, Permanent Secretary at the Department of the Environment. He did so by pulling off a gold cloth in which the piece had been draped. The statue was cast from one of the engineer that was created by Baron Carlo Marochetti RA (1805-68), and erected in 1877 on the Victoria Embankment in London. The Swindon statue stands on a podium that is eight feet high and which, from 2003, emitted classical music in a bid to dissuade vandalism; the thinking behind this idea being that any prospective vandals would either be positively affected by the music, or would dislike it so much that they would not go near the statue anyway.

Bryan, Tim (b.1959) Born at Bristol, and a graduate of the University College of Wales, Aberystwyth, Tim Bryan came to Swindon in 1983 as a museum's assistant at the Great Western Railway Museum in Faringdon Road. There, he wrote and lectured on railway history, worked with television and film companies who were covering related topics, and was instrumental in the discussions that eventually led to the establishment of the STEAM museum. As a member of its curatorial team, he was responsible for choosing objects and pictures for the new displays, and writing about them. He became Collections Manager at STEAM, then took the post of General Manager before leaving in 2004 to become Head of Collections at the Heritage Motor Centre, Gaydon, Warwickshire. His published works are:

North Star (Thamesdown Borough Council, 1989)

Return to Swindon (Avon Anglia Publications, 1990)

Swindon's Finest: A GWR Locomotive Album (Thamesdown Borough Council, 1990)

The Golden Age of the Great Western Railway 1892-1914 (PSL, 1991)

Great Western At War (PSL, 1995)

Great Western Swindon (Chalford Books, 1995)

Railway Heritage: Paddington (Silver Link, 1977)

Brunel, the Great Engineer (Ian Allen, 1999)

Swindon and the GWR (History Press, 2003)

All In A Day's Work: Life on the GWR (Ian Allen, 2004)

The Great Western: A Celebration (Ian Allen, 2010)

The Great Western Railway (Shire, 2010)

Railways In Wartime (Shire, 2010)

Railway Workshops (Shire 2012)

Buffalo Bill's Wild West The world-famous American military scout, Col. William Frederick Cody (1846-1917), better known as 'Buffalo Bill', brought his 'Wild West and Congress of Rough Riders of the World' to Swindon on 29 June 1903. The town was one location in his 1902-03 whistle-stop tour of nearly one hundred towns, cities, and principal railway centres of England. The whole show, including 800 people and 500 horses, was packed into four train-loads of 75-foot-long painted boxcars, sleepers and diners, and it was met the day before at Swindon station by a welcome party of civic dignitaries. The two performances, each of about two hours duration, had been advertised to take place at Beechfield, off Marlborough Road, a site that was declared too small at the eleventh hour. The venue was shifted to Corpe's Field, beside the Wootton Bassett Road, where an arena of 382,500 square feet was laid out, enclosed in canvas walls and with a canvas canopy covering three of the sides. Some 20,000 spectators paid 1/-, 2/-, 3/- or 4/- (the more affluent could buy box seats at 5/- and 7/6d) to view the show. It was a continuous programme of events, carried out by American cowboys, 100 Red Indians, Royal English Lancers, Bedouin Arabs, Russian Cossacks, South American Gauchos, Cubans and Mexicans. Cody performed feats of dexterity with firearms, and the performances ended with a re-enactment of the Battle of San Juan Hill.

Building Societies Much of the finance for residential building in New Swindon outside of the railway village, and not associated with private speculative builders, devolved on a number of building societies. These set up in the town from the late 1860s, purchasing from local landowners, and gradually covered the area with houses. The earliest, Swindon Permanent Benefit Building & Investment Society, was formed in 1868, and its president was Daniel Gooch. The society's offices were in the Mechanics' Institute and it built for the 'artisans and craftspeople of the town', then advanced them loans against monthly repayments for between five and twenty-one years to buy the properties. In 1869, this society began to lay down streets in areas close to the North Wilts Canal, and then built upwards of 300 houses during the 1870s, starting with Cheltenham Street, Gloucester Street and Wellington Street. It was said that their 'security is unquestionable, being on freehold houses and land'. Also that 'the impetus given to the building trade, and the large number of houses built upon the excellent sites of the society since its formation, are the best evidence of the success attending its operations'. From 1877, when it was incorporated under the Building Societies' Act 1847, it was named New Swindon Permanent Building Society.

Soon, other building societies also began to take up tracts of land outside the railway village. Principal among these were Oxford Building & Investment Company, which acquired land adjacent to the railway line and built on it. Between 1873 and 1876, it erected Carfax, Merton, Oriel and Turl Streets; Dover Street was its project for 1876; in 1890, it put in Iffley Road; and laid out Cobden Road and Harcourt Road at the beginning of the 20th century. Other building societies who were similarly active in Swindon between the 1860s and the 1880s included Albion Building Society (which built Albion Street), Cheltenham & Gloucester Building Society (which built the two streets named after it), Reading

Building Society, Ramsbury Building Society, Wilts & Western Building Society, Berkshire Perpetual Benefit Building Society of Reading, and Albion Mutual Permanent Benefit Building Society of Bristol.

Carr, Catherine, Farnsby, and Villet Streets were built to the south of Faringdon Street in the mid-1870s by the United Kingdom Land & Building Association Limited. It had also built shops in these streets, and had built premises in Fleet Street and Faringdon Street. This organisation had its own brick and tile works at Cowleaze, mid-way between the old and new towns and close to the canal, and advertised its 'large Fosters Patent Tramway Kiln in which the bricks are burnt on iron wagons, which pass on a tramway through the kiln'. The organisation specialised in 'common building bricks, hand-pressed facing bricks, ornamental bricks of various descriptions, roofing and garden tiles, drain pipes, flooring and ornamental squares, etc.'. The Trowbridge Building Society built Medgbury Road in 1878. In the early 1880s, a group of people who had interests in either the Wilts & Berks Canal or the brickworks in Swindon formed the New Swindon & Southern Counties Permanent Mutual Benefit Building Society, operating out of Queen Anne's Buildings, Faringdon Street. As a result of all this, a commentator in the mid-1880s was able to write: 'We venture to say that there is no place in the kingdom where the ratio of dwellers in their own houses is greater than at New Swindon'; and all the credit was given to the operations of the building societies.

Bull baiting The sport of baiting bulls with dogs was popular nationally from the middle of the 17th century. The only local reference to it taking place in Swindon was made by William Morris in *Swindon Fifty Years Ago*, published in 1885. Morris described how a wooden post was set up in the Old Town market square, and an iron ring was thrown over it to which the bull was secured by a chain. This limited its movements to within a described circle. Thus chained, it was set upon by dogs, one at a time, whose objective was to secure their jaws on the nose of the beast whilst avoiding being gored by its horns. Morris suggested that the spectacle was revived here (he does not intimate when, or even if, it had previously been popular in Swindon) for the enjoyment of the navvies when they passed through in 1804 whilst building the Wilts & Berks Canal, and it then lingered on until about 1812. Morris was born in 1826, but recalled seeing some kind of wooden socket in the Old Town market square in which, he was later told, the post had been inserted whenever a bull was to be tethered and attacked by dogs. The pastime was outlawed under the Cruelty to Animals Act, 1835.

Butt, Raymond Osborne (b.1941)
One person who has been influential in keeping jazz music alive in the town is Ray Butt. Born in London into a musical family, Ray comes from a direct line of classical and dance band musicians that can be traced as such to at least the early 1800s. His grandmother was a cellist with Sir Thomas Beecham; her father played before royalty; and Ray's father was an accomplished musician, playing saxophone and clarinet in top London ballroom dancing hotspots, in bands such as the internationally famous *Squadronaires*. Ray's introduction to music was through his grandmother, who paid him 6d a time to practise on the piano. Mainly

as a result of his father's influence and encouragement, the teenage Ray studied violin and sat his grades, and entered various competitions. Family musical evenings were a way of life, particularly before tea on Sunday afternoons. Ray then met up with the sons of his father's fellow musicians, and they formed their version of 'The Hot Club De Paris' band ... à la Stéphane Grappelli and Django Reinhardt. Soon, he started to sit in on gigs with his father and, after obtaining a clarinet and a bit of fatherly coaching, eventually deputised for him when his father was otherwise engaged.

In the early 1960s, after relocating to AERE Harwell, Ray started to infiltrate the local jazz scene by attending jazz jam sessions at The Bricklayer's Arms, Newbury. This led to bookings by various bands in the Newbury and Basingstoke area. In the early 1970s, his musical interest changed direction; by then, he was playing clarinet, saxophone, and keyboards ... and if he could find a guitar, he would play a bit on that, too! He joined *The Goodtymes*, who were then the most popular show band operating around the Oxford area, and he expanded their repertoire. The band auditioned for Hughie Green's Opportunity Knocks and, after five years with the band, Ray left to explore his keyboard talent. Following a period playing solo and duo gigs, he formed *Nitelife*, a band that performed at various functions in the south of England. In 1979, he relocated to Swindon with his day job and, still playing keyboard, joined with John Lewis, a local drummer, to play as the resident band at The Magnolia Rooms, Wootton Bassett.

Ray's saxophone and clarinet had been cased for twenty years, when he received a call from an old musical acquaintance who offered him a gig on saxophone. The instruments proved to be green with mildew, and Ray's embouchure was out of condition. He declined the offer, but it was the moment that sparked him to pick up playing the instruments again and it wasn't long before he was out doing gigs in his new home county. His mercurial attitude led him to become a gig fixer as well as a performer, and Ray soon formed Fretless & Friends, a name which he adopted as his band name and one which he gave to his very successful musical entertainment agency.

Ray really began to influence the jazz scene in the Swindon area in the late 1990s when he organised highly successful jazz nights and weekend jazz bonanzas at the Ghost Train, Purton, and at a number of other hostelries in the area. He was also successful in organising monthly jazz evenings at Swindon Town Football Club, where bands featured included artistes such as Mr Acker Bilk and other nationally renowned musicians, The Pete Allen Jazz Band, The Temperance Seven, and many others. (See also Cullum, Jamie; Jazz Festival.)

Cambria Baptist Chapel Many of the Welsh ironworkers who came to Swindon in the 1860s were Baptists and they initially held their services, in the Welsh language, in a schoolroom attached to the Free Christian Church in Bridge Street. In 1864, Ambrose Lethbridge Goddard leased to them some land beside the Wilts & Berks Canal, specifically in order that they could build their own chapel. The conveyance stated that the land was not to be used for an inn, public house, or alehouse and, furthermore, the chapel was to be painted every four years, and the interior painted or papered every seven. The 'founder' of the chapel, or principal mover for its existence, was Ebenezer Evans.

The earliest deeds for this building are dated 1864; the chapel was built but not quite finished by the autumn of 1865 and the date stone on the north front is inscribed 1866. It was named 'Britannia Chapel', and was said to be for 'Particular or Calvinistic Baptists'. It was leased to a number of people who lived in Glamorgan and Monmouthshire, and its original trustees worked at the GWR Works, all of whom lived virtually in its shadow.

The chapel was built of rock-faced limestone with Bath stone ashlar dressings. On the gabled north front, the small doorway – with pilasters, archivolt with keystone, and flat pediment – is flanked on each side by a round-headed window. There are flat pilaster buttresses on each end of the front elevation, and three recessed, round-headed windows down each side of the building. An office and a schoolroom were added to the rear of the chapel in 1902. Internally, the chapel could seat about 150 people and was equipped with a little gallery on two slender cast-iron columns. At the south end, there was a raised area, sectioned off by a balustrade. The chapel was taken over by the Baptist Tabernacle in Regent Circus in 1883, and was renovated and redecorated in 1949, and redecorated in 1963. It was closed for worship in 1986, remodelled internally, and became residential. In 1996, when the foundations of the office and schoolroom were dug up, the body of a murder victim was revealed, together with the weapon. Forensic tests revealed that the murder had been committed about a century earlier. (See also Cambria Place.)

Cambria Bridge Mural The vertical surfaces around the point at which Cambria Bridge crosses the filled-in bed of the former Wilts & Berks Canal have long been a site for official and unofficial graffiti artists, and

more conventional painters. In 1980, Ken White painted beneath the bridge a mural of Swindon confectioner W. Nash's shop, showing a Victorian-style window full of sweets and chocolates, and the two Misses Nash in the shop doorway.

Cambria Place In 1861, the GWR established rolling mills at the Swindon Works and immediately brought Welsh ironworkers to make the rails. To begin with, these workers lived at The Barracks in Faringdon Road, which had been erected as a communal dwelling for single men and later remodelled internally to accommodate the Welsh families. In 1863, Thomas Ellis, the manager of the rolling mills, turned speculative builder and acquired an area of Ambrose Lethbridge Goddard's land called Kingsdown Close, situated opposite the GWR cricket field, on which to build what was essentially the second railway cottage estate. Cambria Place was built there between 1864 and 1869, on the north side of the Wilts & Berks Canal, and was named after the Roman word for Wales. Goddard may have financed the project, and it is likely that the building work was carried out by GWR tradesmen. Here, four terraces were built between Westcott Street and the Wilts & Berks Canal, so that the married Welsh workers could move in together with their families. The cottages were built in stone from the Swindon quarries, with Bath stone dressings. To begin with, two smaller blocks, numbers 1-9 and 22-30, looked out on the cricket ground (with their gardens at the rear), and numbers 10-21 and 31-42 were behind them, facing the canal (with their gardens in front of the properties). Ultimately, the estate comprised some forty-eight stone-fronted cottages. Thomas Ellis connected his estate

to a nearby natural spring by means of iron pipes and, in so doing, was the first person to supply water directly to residential houses in Swindon. The occupants of Cambria Place were known as the 'Welsh Colony', many of whom only spoke their native tongue. Of the two public houses that seem to be part of this development, The Greyhound was built c.1848 in order to service nearby Westcott Place, which had then just been completed. The Grapes, operational from about 1863, was clearly coeval with the building of the Cambria estate. Cambria Bridge was built over the canal, next to the estate, in 1877. In recent years, it has been a focus for community arts projects. (See also Cambria Baptist Chapel.)

Candle and Lantern Markets
During the 18th and 19th centuries, candle and lantern markets took place once a month on a Monday morning in High Street. Sometimes they overflowed into Wood Street and Cricklade Street. Butchers and dealers who frequently travelled considerable distances to attend arrived during the previous day and stayed overnight at the town's inns. At three o'clock on Monday morning, cattle were lined up on each side of the street with their back feet in the roadway. They were inspected under the light of candles and lanterns; the deals were made, and the whole market was over before breakfast time. In 1864, a bull that was being led by two handlers to the Monday market broke loose, knocking down and seriously injuring one handler. It was eventually shot, whilst on a rampage, by Mr Stroud, butcher of Wroughton.

Canford House, Devizes Road
This two-storey, three-bay house, with a wrought-iron openwork porch, was built in the 1830s as a private house in Horsefair, to be re-named Devizes Road from the late 1850s. In 1852, the premises became the town's first police house and police station. Police superintendent Joseph Hall was its first resident representative of the law, and he was succeeded by superintendent Henry Haynes, who was also, from 1857, a founder director of the Swindon Water Company. He was followed at Canford House by superintendent George North, who was called upon to read the civil Riot Act from the Town Hall, Old Swindon, following the formation of an angry mob there at the time of the local elections in 1880. During his occupancy, it also accommodated police inspector Joseph Millard and his wife Jane, and two police constables. Canford House continued to be the gaol until 1873 (rings in the cellar wall for the purpose of restraining felons were still in situ in the 1960s) when a new police station was opened on Eastcott Hill. The house became the residence of William A. Godwin, owner of the nearby Belmont Steam Brewery. Later, it was divided into upstairs and downstairs flats by a Swindon solicitor who administered the premises on behalf of his elderly mother, who used the rents as her income, and latterly it was converted to offices.

Carriage and Wagon Works, GWR Works Some wagons were made in the GWR locomotive works almost from the moment they were established at Swindon, and by 1846 there were proposals to develop carriage works there. In the event, these were authorised in 1867 and were built featuring cast-iron pillars and vaulted brickwork in 1868-72, to the design of T.G. Clayton. They were not fully operational until 1875, by

which time they comprised about two dozen shops. Their purpose was to make the wooden frames and iron superstructures, build the coaches, and finish the interiors. There was an integral sawmill, and the workmen there included several kinds of fitters, painters, plumbers, metal smiths, general mechanics, carpenters and cabinet makers, painters, fabric makers and upholsterers. There was a carriage trimmers section, which was a large area where women were employed to deal with the soft furnishings. The shops also included a disinfecting plant. Initially, the department was known as the Carriage Manufacturing Department, which had a paint shop connected to it. By 1872, some forty wagons and four passenger coaches were being made there each week. Associated wagon repair shops were opened in 1877, and the department was extended in the 1950s to facilitate the needs of diesel carriages. The carriage and wagon works ceased to be an independent entity in 1964 when they were combined with the locomotive works. The frontage of the carriage and wagon department eventually occupied the whole of Bristol Street and London Street, where they are extant, although parts of the buildings are divided into small industrial units. (See also Locomotive Works; Rolling Mills.)

Carroll, Tim (b.1959) A native of Wallasey, Merseyside, Tim and his family moved to Swindon in 1969, on the day that Swindon Town beat Arsenal at Wembley in the League Cup Final. He went to St Joseph's comprehensive school, and in 1982 achieved a BA in Fine Art from Leeds University. Well known locally for his refurbishment of the town's Great Blondinis statue in 2009, he also has work dotted about the town, and three ceramic plaques on the theme of insects have been installed on the cycle track at the Cotswold Country Park. Tim is part of Artsite, the artists' collective that is based in the former post office in Theatre Square, which, in 2007, was involved in creating the mural in Queen's Park. He and fellow artist Gordon Dickinson installed two coin-operated machines that, since 2004, have been dispensing original artwork at £1 each. In 2009, Tim was also commissioned to visually document the installation of the light sculpture by Icelandic artist Gudrun Haraldsdottir on the side of the Wyvern Theatre. Otherwise, he exhibits regularly in arts venues around the town, and has been instrumental in opening up new ones.

Carron, Arthur (1900-67) Born Arthur Cox, he was later to become a world-renowned operatic tenor under the stage name of Carron. In 1900, the family lived at 19 Milton Road. Arthur's father, Ernest E. Cox, had previously farmed Walcot Farm, but was now a dairyman, grocer and shopkeeper. His mother, Emily Martha (née Balch) was the daughter of a Somerset farming family, and she married Ernest Cox in 1886. Arthur began to give public performances in 1917, particularly during the Sunday concerts then being held at the Methodist Central Hall in Clarence Street. For a while, in the early 1930s, he sang with the Cardiff Grand Opera Company. Later, he relocated to London, where his voice was professionally trained before he joined what became, in 1934, Sadler's Wells at Covent Garden. That year, Arthur successfully auditioned for Metropolitan Opera, New York, where he debuted in 1936, playing Canio in *Pagliaci*. There followed tours of North and South America, lasting several years, before he returned to Covent Garden

as a considerable international opera star, by then (and during the next decade) also much heard on gramophone records. In 1952, after singing in a performance of *Salome*, Arthur Carron retired from the professional stage. At the time, he lived in Bath Road, and it was in his premises that the Swindon Amateur Light Operatic Society's early meetings were held following its formation in 1952.

Casimir-Mrowczynski, Paul André (1922-1962)

The poet Paul Casimir (the contracted name that he assumed) was born in Jersey, where he became secretary to the headmaster of Victoria College, which he had previously attended as a pupil. Subsequently, he ran a second-hand bookshop on the island. During the war, he was forced to serve with Polish troops in the German army, but was later sufficiently active with the Jersey Loyalists' movement during the Second World War to be on the German occupiers' hit list. The Loyalists planned an anti-Nazi offensive, for May 1945. After the war, he relocated to live with his sister and brother-in-law in Watford, where he joined the library service and eventually became the town's reference librarian. In 1952, he was appointed reference librarian in Swindon, the successor to J.T. Lea. Two years later, he married Hazel, who had been a librarian in Chelsea and, for the previous two years, was reference librarian in Purley. She became Swindon's hospital librarian, covering the Victoria Hospital in Victoria Road, the maternity hospital on Kingshill, the isolation hospital in Gorse Hill, and the hospital at Stratton St Margaret. Paul left Swindon reference library in 1959 and took up a position as tutor librarian at Dacorum College, Hemel Hempstead.

Most of Paul Casimir's poetry was written during his time at Watford and Swindon; it regularly appeared in anthologies and in publications such as *Time and Tide* and *The Listener*. His first book of poems, *Company of Two*, was published in London in 1955 by Derek Maggs. He was represented in *The Swindon Review*: an essay on Edward Thomas in No.6, 1953, which also published two of his poems, 'Elegy for Miners' and 'Guinevere'; 'To a Roman Briton' and 'Old Man' were in No.7, 1955; in No.8, 1956 were 'Song at Evening' and 'Lyric'; and his essay 'Romantic Stourhead' appeared in No.9, 1957. Also in 1957, he was published by Macdonald in *Peninsular*, an anthology of verse from the West Country, edited by Charles Causley. He was also posthumously selected by the poet Maurice Carpenter for the 1963 Elegreba Press anthology *Walking For Joy*. During his life, Paul Casimir gave numerous talks to literary groups, and was well informed about Richard Jefferies (q.v.), although he remained ambivalent about Jefferies's writing. He was also much in demand by various groups to speak on his experiences in occupied Jersey.

In 1959, Paul Casimir was succeeded as reference librarian at Swindon by thirty-two-year-old Keith E. Hardy, previously reference librarian at Torquay, where he was a member of the Malcolm Russell Consort, and the Torquay Group of Singers. Also a member of the Torquay Operatic Society, he took leading tenor roles in their productions. In 1960 in Swindon, he and Colin Ockwell, a local baritone and teacher at The Lawn Junior School, co-founded Swindon Opera. The first production, held in 1960, was John Gay's *The Beggar's Opera*, which ran for two nights at the Arts Centre. Hardy left Swindon in 1964 (he would return in 1966 and take up

his former post) to become reference librarian at Fulham, and was replaced as reference librarian in Swindon by Jim Davies, who came to Swindon in 1959 and had served as branch librarian at Penhill and, latterly, at Park.

Castle Combe Mural The famous view of Castle Combe taken from the bridge and showing the main street with the church and wooded slopes in the background was painted in 1976 on an end wall in Cricklade Road. Funding was provided by Thamesdown Community Arts, and the work was carried out by the 17th Swindon (St Barnabas) Scout Troop and bore symbols of the scout movement. It was obliterated in 1985.

Catalogue Houses, Drove Road The pair of gabled, brick-built, so-called 'catalogue' houses that fronted Thomas Turner's brickworks were built in 1871, when they were known as Pottery Cottages. He built two more in the same thoroughfare in 1889. They were designed as an advertisement for the bricks, range of finials, mouldings, roofing tiles and other decorative terracotta motifs and fancy brickwork that came out of his business, the Swindon Tile & Pottery Works. This was situated behind the cottages in what is now Queen's Park. On his cottages, Turner showed not only the decorative motifs that might be used on domestic architecture, but how structures such as pillars might be constructed and then decorated using terracotta and glazed tiles. He showcased his ability with mouldings and string courses, and detailed elements of polychromy that could be successfully built into elevations to make them more attractive. (See also Turner, Thomas.)

Cattle Market Gatehouse, Marlborough Road Built in the 19th century, this was a distinctive brick-built gatehouse with stone dressings and quoins, pointed window with decorative labels, and carved label stops with sheep's and cows' heads. It was demolished in 1970.

Cellular Clothing Company This business opened in Morris Street, on the corner with Rose Street, Swindon in 1901, and was part of the London firm Aertex Limited (founded 1888). It employed female labour to make shirts, underwear, pyjamas and sportswear, the raw materials for which were obtained from mills in the north of England. The factory closed during a slump in the 1920s, and reopened in 1934. The Ministry of Works acquired the factory during the Second World War. Latterly, the materials, and the garments subsequently made from them at Swindon (from the 1950s these were mostly shirts), were stored at a warehouse in Nottingham. Production stopped in the 1960s and, after a period as a storage facility, the premises in Morris Street were demolished during the 1980s, making way for a residential housing development.

Cenotaph The first memorial to Swindon's fallen in World War I was a wooden cross, erected by the local authority. This was considered to be quite inadequate, infuriated public opinion, and was burnt down. It was replaced by the town's first cenotaph – a short obelisk with a chamfered pyramidal cap – built of wood and painted white by carpenter and joiner George Bathe, who lived in Western Street and who was at the time employed by Swindon Corporation. This memorial was erected in 1916 in Regent Circus, close to the post office that stood on the corner with

Princes Street. Mr Bathe's son, also George, a one-time player with the Swindon Town junior football team, had been killed in the trenches at Kemmel, in February 1915. Bathe senior previously worked for the builder Williams of Bath Road. His wooden cenotaph remained in situ until it was replaced in 1920 by the stone structure erected near the Regent Street entrance of Regent Circus. The cost of this was raised through public subscription, supported by a *Swindon Advertiser* 'shilling fund' campaign that aimed to encourage readers to donate at least that amount.

A peace flagpole, set up in 1918 beside the town hall in Regent Circus, was burnt down by a group of young men who had volunteered to go to war in 1914. They were protesting against the low rate of pay in the army (1/- to 1/6d per day), the paucity of the gratuity given by the government (£17) when they were demobbed after four years' active service, and the low-key welcome home (a free cup of beer each). There was also no guarantee they could have their old jobs back (mostly at the Great Western Railway works). So one day they congregated angrily at the town hall, stopped several passing motorists, appropriated their spare cans of petrol, and burnt down the peace flag.

The local authority, anticipating trouble, had stationed the town's fire brigade in nearby Temple Street, with hoses at the ready. However, as the pole fell, the flag was caught by a policeman; rioters took over the pole and paraded it along Regent Street. A rhyme was written about the incident: *A flagpole was erected/by some misguided chappie/now they've burned the blighter down/the Swindon folk are happy*.

Central Club and Institute Built in 1897, beside the bridge over the Wilts & Berks Canal where Commercial Road and Milton Road meet, and adjacent to Cromwell Street Wharf, this imposing three-storey, five-bay by three-bay building was designed in neo-Dutch renaissance style by R.J. Beswick. It cost £6,500 to construct in red brick with Bath stone dressings, and had a covered access adjacent to the waterway. The building featured a round-headed, scalloped and moulded shoulder pediment to the south front, and acorn finials; the round-headed windows on each level were tied together by a string course that followed their shape, between tall and narrow keystones. The levels were separated by wide string courses. It also had a stone-built porch to the east bay of the south front, with a triangular pediment that was set, almost with the appearance of an afterthought, above the doorway. Inside, there was a reading room, concert hall, billiard room, and double skittle alley. The place became a discotheque during the 1960s and 1970s, when the porch was picked out in coloured lights. The building was demolished in 1982.

Central Electric Cinema This picture house was opened in Regent Street in 1911, and closed in 1930. It became Peacock's Stores.

Central Library Arguably, the first part of Swindon's intended 21st-century regeneration to take place began in 2004 when the Borough Council signed up to the central library concept. In January 2007, the last of the fifty-eight-year succession of 'temporary' central library buildings beside the town hall in Regent Circus was demolished. The new four-storey library building was opened on 20 October 2008, when it had already won a British Research

Establishment environmental award. It was designed by architects Nic Newland and Tony Currivan, cost £10,214,930, including renovations to the old town hall, and was a triumph of powerful contemporary design, great use of building materials, and clean lines throughout. Three of the floors, some 1,909 square metres, were public areas. Some 71,405 bricks were used to build it, topped with 18,415 roof tiles. It had 559 square metres of insulating glass; 2,230 square metres of insulating tiles; 125 square metres of lino flooring and 82 square metres of stone flooring. (See also Library Services.)

Chamber of Commerce Swindon Chamber of Commerce & Industry was formed in 1893 as The Swindon Chamber, and changed its name to Swindon Chamber of Commerce in 1903. The first president was Hubert Deacon, second generation of the well-known Swindon firm of jewellers, and watch and clock makers. In 2006, the Swindon Chamber had around 1,000 members, and went into liquidation the same year with debts of about £500,000. The interests of this organisation's members were then taken up by the Thames Valley Chambers of Commerce, based in Slough, which remotely set up a Swindon Branch.

Chandler, John (1819-1902) Even at the end of the 20th century, older people in Swindon still referred to the intersection of Wood Street and Devizes Road as 'Chandler's Corner', although the man after whom it was so named had been dead for a century. John Chandler was born at Pewsey, and by 1841, designated as draper, he was living in High Street, Old Town, with several other people engaged in the trade. These were possibly some of the journeymen employed by master tailor Nehemiah Lea (1811-62), whose premises were in Wood Street. In 1844, John Chandler married Susannah Hoystrop at Wootton Bassett, and at some point between 1845 and 1847, Lea and Chandler went into partnership as tailors. By 1851, the Chandlers were living over the retail premises at 35 Wood Street, and Susannah gave birth to their eleven children between 1845 and 1865. By 1861, Chandler was designated master draper, and had sixteen apprentices.

Susannah Chandler died in 1867, and John Chandler did not marry again. With the help of a governess and two domestic servants, his two elder daughters were of sufficient age to look after not only him, but also the younger children, and the draper's assistant who lived with the family. In 1876, Susannah, the eldest daughter, married the architect William Henry Read, who lived two doors away at number 31 Wood Street, and they went to live in Bath Road. When the Read's former house in Wood Street came up for sale in 1880, Chandler bought it and moved in with his son Frank, also a draper, a housekeeper, a nursemaid, a general servant, and three assistant drapers, who were not family members. Over the next decade, they all left except for Beatrice, his last but one child, and a cook/domestic servant. At the time of his death, just a housekeeper and one domestic servant were living with John Chandler at 31 Wood Street.

John Chandler was a member of the Old Swindon Local Board and, in 1865, chairman of the Swindon Water Company. When it opened in 1888, Chandler was the first president of the Victoria Hospital. In 1897, he set up a trust to provide a pension for one of the poor people accommodated in the almshouses. At his substantial 'linen

and woollen drapery' in Wood Street, he advertised that 'family mourning attire is a speciality'. He put up a carpet warehouse, and developed showrooms on the corner, which for so long bore his name.

Cheltenham & Great Western Union Railway Almost as soon as Parliament had authorised the Great Western Railway Company's line through Swindon in 1835, a meeting was held in Cheltenham with a view to forming a company that might establish a line between these two places. This new company was the Cheltenham & Great Western Union Railway, whose intentions were authorised by Parliament in 1836. The main opponents were the Thames & Severn Canal Company, which envisaged a damaging effect on its trade, and Squire Gordon of Kemble House, Kemble. Both were persuaded by considerable payments that ameliorated their positions, although Gordon remained unmoved on some restrictions regarding his estate, and required the line to be hidden from view. In 1840, the Company opened a line between Cheltenham and Gloucester, and the following year began to run its train service between Swindon and Cirencester, with stations between at Purton, Minety and Ashton Keynes. In 1843, the Cheltenham & Great Western Union Railway sold its section between Swindon and Cirencester to the Great Western Railway, and under the Great Western Act, 1844, the C&GWUR was amalgamated with the Great Western. The following year, the first train ran between Swindon and Gloucester.

Cheney Manor This part of Swindon lies to the north of the town centre, and is immediately north-west of Rodbourne. It is situated between Pinehurst and Moredon, two suburbs connected by Beech Avenue, a residential area that was developed from the mid-1920s. The name Cheney is derived from that of Ralph le Chanu, who held the manor of Rodbourne Cheney in the 13th century. Cheney Manor Road runs north and south of Rodbourne Cheney church, and is effectively a continuation of Rodbourne Road; it was so named in 1928, after the one-time lord of the manor. Its line was previously made up of Telford Road, which began immediately beyond the Rodbourne Road bridge over the North Wilts Canal; Swindon Road, Church Road, and The Green. Immediately after the Second World War, in 1946, Swindon Corporation laid out Mulberry Grove to the east of Cheney Manor Road, and in 1947 completed a small but spacious residential development of houses, whose half dozen streets were named after trees (as in the earlier Pinehurst model). It was built immediately to the north of Beech Avenue; opposite, in 1947, a slightly larger area of streets was built up, all named after high-ranking wartime military personnel.

To the west of Cheney Manor Road is the former 16th-century manor house. The Cheney Manor trading estate was developed, 1955-58, when it was the second of its kind in Swindon, after Okus, in the early 1950s. It had individually designed and custom-built premises for specific organisations that were establishing in the town to take advantage of the increasing labour force. (See also Rodbourne.)

Children's Story Wall Mural The walls of a small boiler house beside the playground at Lethbridge Road School were painted in 1977 by Ken White, with scenes and fantasy characters suggested

by books then being read by the infant classes. The work was sponsored by the insurance company then named Hambro Life. It was repainted in 1987 by Ken White (his daughter Laura was then a pupil at the school), who updated it with scenes from the school's most recent Fun Day, and included a picture of Richard Branson's Virgin Atlantic hot air balloon.

Christ Church, Cricklade Street

The idea to build a successor to Holy Rood church on the Goddard estate came about in the 1840s, when it was intended to finance the scheme by a special public rate over a number of years. In a vestry meeting in 1848, when matters were well advanced, representatives of the Great Western Railway overturned the idea of a rate levy. The alternative was to pay for the work by public subscription, and this was immediately put in hand. Ambrose Goddard, the lord of the manor, donated the site and gave £1,000, and £50 was the contribution from the driving force behind the scheme, Revd Henry George Baily (who had come to Swindon in 1843 and was to raise £3,000 for the project by 1849).

The foundation stone was laid in June 1850. The church was built in sandstone with Bath stone dressings in early Decorated style from designs by Sir Gilbert Scott, at a cost of £8,000, and the building was consecrated in November 1851. The church consists of a nave of three bays with octagonal columns, chancel (which was remodelled in 1883 at a cost of £500), clerestory, north and south aisles and transepts, and south porch (of 1916). The three-stage west tower has a broach spire (on which a light was installed that 'guided aeroplanes towards RAF Lyneham') and lucarnes on each face. The bells from the demolished Holy Rood

church were relocated there, and these were refurbished and augmented by two more in 1924; the belfry has two-light belfry openings. Most of the church's tracery is Geometric, cusped, and with trefoils and quatrefoils, and the lower stage of the tower has three quatrefoils in a roundel. Beneath this, is a western gabled porch flanked by heavy buttresses that rise through the lower two stages of the tower. The glass in the pointed windows, mostly of two or three lights, with 14th-century-style tracery in the heads (four lights in the transepts and five lights in the east window of the chancel), is mostly mid-19th-century.

In 1881, a brass eagle lectern was added and, in 1892, the Goddard family gave a reredos of marble and alabaster, and an altar and altar steps; in 1905, they gave an alabaster font, and followed in 1906 with a pulpit. The Goddard-financed north transept window in memory of Fitzroy Pleydell Goddard was designed by church craftsman Martin Travers (1886-1948), and erected in 1927. It includes a view of the family home of 'The Lawn', the Goddard coat of arms, and the arms of Christ Church, Oxford, where he went to university. Harold Brakspear designed a Lady Chapel in 1935. In 2001, Bernard Oxborrow restored the wrought-iron font cover, some six feet high, which had been in store since the 1970s. The spire was restored in 2005.

Chronicle of Swindon The *Swindon Advertiser's* copiously illustrated survey of Swindon's history was published as a supplement in twenty-five weekly parts on Saturdays between 27 May and 11 November in 2006. The page size was 370mm by 285mm, portrait format. It began by describing archaeological finds

from the earliest occupation of the area around 4000BC, and continued to the year of publication at the rate of one page a year for most years after 1840. It was researched, written, designed and edited by John Carter, journalist and historian, with the help of The Swindon Society and with reference to some 120 published works. *Chronicle of Swindon* was a brilliant concept that engaged many people on several levels and described not only the momentous events in the town's story but also minor or quirky incidents of interest, and was put together with great skill. Information came from the *Swindon Advertiser*'s own archive, dating from 6 February 1854. Historians and collectors provided artefacts and ephemera, which were photographed and the pictures included, thereby illustrating much that had never before been pictured elsewhere. (See also Swindon Heritage.)

Church Mill, Goddard Estate The medieval church of Holy Rood stood next to 'The Lawn', the manor house of the Goddard family, and immediately beyond its churchyard wall was a pond and an old mill. There is no evidence to suggest that this was one of the Domesday mills of Swindon, although historians have suggested this might have been the case. Documentary evidence for church mill begins in 1757 when lord of the manor Thomas Goddard leased it to William Kemble, the son of a Newport Street baker. In the early 1770s, it was leased to John Morris. Writing in 1826, John Britton said that this mill was 'remarkable for the largeness of its water wheel (historian William Morris said that it was over thirty feet high, and was thought to be the largest overshot wheel in England) and for its proximity to the spring head'. He

continued: 'The water is conveyed in pipes to the overshot wheel, the periphery of which is about one hundred feet, and falling into buckets or troughs, gives it a slow, but regular rotatory motion. Though apparently slow in its revolutions of the interior machinery, it is as effective, and almost as rapid, as other river mills.'

A Mr Garlick assumed occupancy in the early 1820s. It was subsequently occupied by John Jefferies until about 1847, and William Morris mentioned that the building was demolished by 1850. He also said that 'the machinery could be put in motion independent of the wheel, the motion being obtained by the pressure of a column of water contained in a hollow perpendicular shaft, at the bottom of which were two arms, having a small orifice in each, and out of this the water rushed with sufficient force to turn the columns on its pivot and with it the machinery of the mill'. A right of way ran across open ground between the mill and the south side of the market square in Old Town, and which disappeared beneath the market house, built 1852/53.

Church Place The GWR's cricket ground and park were immediately to the west of the growing railway village when, beginning in the 1850s, some larger houses were built for the Company's management and their families. These faced away from the village (and thereby away from the lower-class workers and their families in the smaller terraces), and westwards towards the view of the park. It was a fine example of the hierarchical structure that pervaded the Swindon Works being applied outside its gates. This road, which curled around the park, was initially called Park Road, but the section at right angles to Faringdon Road

was soon changed to Church Place (a name with more quality) after St Mark's church, which lay immediately to the north. Most of the residential properties in Church Place were built after the mid-1880s. The terraces feature shoulder gables, in one instance to give prominence to a mid-way alley entrance and also as means of giving balance to the block, thus making the façade work visually as a homogeneous whole. (See also Park House.)

Churchward, George Jackson (1857-1933) Churchward was born in Stoke Gabriel, Devon. In 1877, at the age of twenty, he took a position in the GWR's drawing office at Swindon, after serving an apprenticeship in the South Devon Railway Works. He rapidly acquired management positions, and was appointed manager of the locomotive and carriage works in 1896. In 1902, William Dean retired as Locomotive, Carriage & Wagon Superintendent, and Churchward took over. The position was re-titled Chief Mechanical Engineer in 1916. At the end of the 19th century, he was chairman of the New Swindon Urban District Council, a primary advocate of amalgamation with the Old Swindon UDC, and a strong supporter of borough status for the combined town. When this took place in 1900, Churchward was the town's first mayor; he was also made a freeman of the Borough. His period at the helm in the railway works at Swindon saw the introduction of the 'City' and 'County' class locomotives, and he designed many new locomotives in these and the 'Star' and 'Saint' classes. His 'Pacific' locomotive, 'The Great Bear' No.111, was built at Swindon, and he was famed for having designed the City of Truro locomotive – which was built in the Swindon works in 1903. Allegedly, in

1904, it became unofficially the first steam locomotive to travel at more than 100 mph, reaching 102.3 mph between Plymouth and Paddington. Churchward retired in 1921. He became increasingly deaf, and was killed on a misty day when he was hit by one of his own locomotives whilst crossing the railway line between Newburn House, where he lived, and the railway works. He was buried in the churchyard at Christ Church.

Cinemas Lantern slide shows – images projected onto a screen – were shown at the Mechanics' Institute before 1900. The same were also featured at the Corn Exchange in the old town, and in the Regent Arcade in Regent Street. The slide shows were followed by black and white newsreels, shown at the same venues, and the first moving picture to be shown in Swindon was at the Mechanics' Institute. In 1908, an open-air café set up a screen in Regent Circus and began showing silent films. (See Arcadia; Central Cinema; Central Electric Pavilion; County Electric Theatre; Electra Palace; Empire Cinema; Greenbridge Cinema; Palladium Picture House; Picture House; Rink Cinema; Regent Cinema; Shaw Ridge Cinema.)

City Status for Swindon In 1992, the Swindon Partnership Initiative, called Swindon: City for the Twenty-First Century, was launched by the Borough of Thamesdown and the Swindon Chamber of Commerce & Industry. The residents of Swindon were generally incredulous that the town should consider itself in any way suited to city status (although two applications were officially, but unsuccessfully, made in 2000 and 2002). Residents need not have concerned themselves; the 'city' aspect was a red herring – effectively only a sprat to catch

a mackerel, in PR terms. The 'partners' were less than enamoured with each other, and neither of them seriously thought that the campaign would enhance the town's status in the long-term, or help towards city status.

This was a trade campaign, designed to encourage inward investment and company relocation into the town. It was, however, the biggest-ever promotion for Swindon, aimed at enhancing trading opportunities worldwide. Local PR company OATS Limited created the campaign's publicity literature and, in September 1993, organised a three-day trade exhibition at Senator House, Queen Victoria Street, London. Just forty-three Swindon businesses and other organisations took part. The exhibition was opened by Sir Derek Hornby, then chairman of the British Overseas Trade Board.

The Borough of Thamesdown was replaced in 1997, and Swindon Chamber of Commerce & Industry was disbanded in 2006. There are books that help to explain the various difficulties facing Swindon in its quest for city status; the most important are *Swindon, An Awkward Size For A Town* by Kenneth Hudson (David & Charles, 1967); *Swindon, A Town In Transition* by Michael Harloe (Heinemann Educational Books, 1975); *Swindon, A Legacy of a Railway Town* by John Cattell and Keith Falconer (HMSO, 1995); and *City For The 21st Century* by Martin Boddy and others (Policy Press, 1997).

Civic insignia The civic insignia used in Swindon comprises: Mace. Hallmarked 'London 1935', this was presented to the Borough in 1936 by William Ewart Morse, who was mayor 1914-16. It is of silver gilt and four feet long, with an open arched crown surmounted by an orb and cross, and bearing a replica of the Royal Arms. The mace head has a coronet of four fleurs-de-lis and four crosses. One of the arches contains the initials E VIII R crowned, interestingly the royal cipher of the king who was never crowned and who abdicated in 1936. The other arches contain the three coats of arms (with some slight alterations) relating to the Borough since 1900 (see Arms of Swindon). There are four oak leaves and acorn brackets beneath the head of the mace; the staff is divided into three sections by two ornamental spheres, and ends in a decorated foot knob divided into six compartments. The mace was re-gilded in 1997.

Mayor's Chain of Office. Two chains were given to the Borough of Thamesdown by Burmah Oil Company. The larger, made in yellow gold, was presented in 1974 and has fifteen oval links, each engraved with a mayor's name and year of office, sixteen lozenge-shaped spacing links, and a centre link from which the appropriate badge is suspended. The smaller chain, of nineteen lozenges, was presented in 1989.

Mayor's Badge was presented by Burmah Oil Company, and was made in 9ct gold by Deacon & Son of Swindon in 1997.

Mayoress's Chain was made in 9ct gold, is thirty-six inches in length and was presented by Hambro Life Assurance in 1979. It comprises thirty decorative, saw-pierced oval links, and a centre link engraved with the word Mayoress.

Mayoress's Badge, by Deacon & Son of Swindon, was made in 9ct gold in 1997 and presented by Burmah Castrol plc. It has a box back and painted coat of arms.

Deputy Mayor's Chain of seventeen links in silver gilt was made by Deacon & Son of Swindon in 1997 and presented by Mondex UK.

Deputy Mayor's Badge was made by Deacon & Son of Swindon in 1997 and presented by Mondex UK. It is of silver gilt, with a box back and painted coat of arms.

Deputy Mayoress's Chain was made by Thomas Fattorini of Birmingham and presented to the Borough of Thamesdown in 1983 by Hambro Life Assurance. It was re-gilded in 1997 for the Borough of Swindon.

Deputy Mayoress's Badge was made by Deacon & Son of Swindon in 1997 and presented by Mondex UK. It is of silver gilt, with a box back and painted coat of arms.

Robes worn by the Mayors of Swindon are in scarlet trimmed with ermine, and were presented in 1927 by William Ewart Morse. For ceremonial occasions, the mayor also has a black hat (a tricorn for a lady mayor) and white jabot (shirt ruffle or frill).

Civic Offices, Euclid Street By the 1930s, the Borough of Swindon's administration departments had outgrown the 'town hall', the former New Swindon Local Board offices of 1890-91 in Regent Circus, and were also in other locations around the town. Plans were formulated to build on the Regent Circus site, but were abandoned when it was thought this might preclude future expansion. In 1934, the council approved the Euclid Street alternative, on the site of a recreation ground, as a better means of bringing all its departments back under one roof. The architects of the building were Bertram, Bertram & Rice of 36 St Giles, Oxford, who won the national competition (as adjudged by Arthur Bedford Knapp-Fisher, then Professor of Architecture at the Royal College of Art, who had been retained for the purpose) that also attracted sixty-seven other designers.

The foundation stone of the Civic Offices was laid by the Marquis of Bath and the mayor, May George, in 1937. The place was built on two floors by H. R. Spackman & Sons of Swindon, using two-inch handmade bricks by the Basildon Brick Company of Pangbourne, and Portland stone for plinths, facings, architraves and other details from Bath & Portland Stone Firms Limited. The Borough Council's Art Deco-style offices were opened in 1938 by the Duke of Gloucester. Inside, there were around 100 rooms, including the mayor's parlour, and several areas featured French walnut panelling by John P. White & Sons of Bedford, and Samuel Elliott and Sons of Reading, by which the interior is still distinguished. The total cost was about £70,000. The gardens of the Civic Offices were designed by J.B.L. Thompson, borough surveyor, who was also responsible for the pergola and rose arbour that still stand today. Over the years since, the Borough Council has expanded into other properties, notably the almost adjacent former Clarence Street school. In 2011, following refurbishment and re-modelling for the purpose by Capita Symonds, the Swindon register office was relocated from Aspen House, Temple Street to a suite of rooms on the ground floor of the Civic Offices.

Clappen's Corner The town hall clock and the clock on the McIlroy's building in Regent Street were both well used, and there was another timepiece above a shop front at the tram centre, where Bridge Street meets Faringdon Road. This was the location from where, before there was any form of motor transport, Gillings ran a brake and two horses 'penny-all-the-way' passenger service between central Swindon and 'The Duke' public house in Gorse Hill, and in the opposite direction to what became the tram terminus in Rodbourne.

William Clappen (1855-1920) was born in Cirencester, where he started his working life as an apprentice in the family tailoring firm. He set up his corner shop tailor and outfitter business in Swindon c.1881, probably at the time of his marriage to Hannah Prior (1857-1928), who was born at Ashton Keynes. The landmark clock was installed later in the same decade. (Clappen's retail premises in New Swindon were later to become Stead and Simpson's shoe shop.) Gillings timed the departure of their brakes by this clock, as would the trams between 1904, when the original three-and-a-half-miles of track was laid, and 1929, when the last tram ran. The clock was initially powered by batteries that were said to last for up to twelve years, and Clappen's ran their own clock inside the shop from the same source. The company capitalised on this association by advertising itself as being 'At the Tram Centre and Wood Street, Swindon'. The latter was where the family lived, at number 14.

Because of its importance in ensuring the trams left on time, the owners in the 1920s arranged for the outside clock to be serviced by Swindon Corporation, whilst agreeing to provide the bulbs that illuminated the face at night. The clock was converted to electric power in 1938.

Clark Report to General Board of Health (See Sanitary Conditions.)

Coate Farmhouse The farmhouse at Coate was built of stone with a thatched roof in the 1600s, and came into the hands of the Jefferies family around the end of the 18th century when Richard Jefferies (great-grandfather of the writer), bought the property, together with thirty-six acres of land, for £1,100. His son, John Jefferies,

and his grandson, James Luckett Jefferies were farmers and bakers in Swindon. In c.1825, the old farmhouse was extended by John Jefferies, who built what was effectively a new house of three storeys and three bays at right angles to it and facing the roadway, and further extensions took place during the later 1800s. Here, in 1848, (John) Richard Jefferies was born, who was later to become a journalist and gain national acclaim in his lifetime as a writer of note. In 1915, it was bought by Job Lawrence, the man who turned Coate reservoir into a pleasure ground (see Coate Water), and there he spent his retirement. The farmhouse was bought by Swindon Corporation in 1926; in 1960, part of it was let as residential accommodation, and a couple of rooms were sparsely furnished and opened to the public, in Jefferies's memory. Later, further rooms were opened, and the place was presented as it would have been in the 19th century, complete with a cheese room, and it became a museum to Jefferies and to Alfred Williams. In 2011, a pathway was opened linking Coate Water with Coate Farmhouse.

Coate Water In 1820, the Wilts & Berks Canal Company planned to build a reservoir as a header tank some two miles to the east (it would remain outside the Borough of Swindon until 1928) of the Old Town market square to replace water that was lost on the locks. The water of the River Cole was diverted, two miles of feeder ditch were constructed between the reservoir site and the canal, and the seventy-acre lake opened in 1822. This was stocked with fish, boats were put on the water, and a small boathouse was built. The reservoir keeper levied fees for angling, and hiring the rowing boats and punts. The lake was surrounded by woodland, so the whole

area was marketed for its leisure potential, with horse-drawn brakes running between the reservoir and the market square. Almost from the outset, wealthy landowners and other gentry in the area maintained pleasure craft on the lake, and financed public events and entertainments on and around it. The Wilts & Berks Canal Company leased the leisure activities at Coate to Job Lawrence in 1874. He gradually refurbished the area, turning it into a boating lake and pleasure park, and also set his own rates for entry. In 1884, Coate Water was included within the Swindon boundary. Until the 1920s, there were only a handful of buildings between Lower Town and the little thatched hamlet of Coate. On Sundays, this was a favourite walk for families and courting couples, regularly attracting hundreds of people; this weekly event was known locally as 'The Monkey Walk'.

In 1914, after the failure of the canal system in Swindon, some eighty acres of land, including the lake at Coate, were bought by Swindon Corporation. The local authority laid down the driveway, added wrought-iron gates to the entrance, developed access paths on site, put up a wooden diving frame and changing huts, and encouraged swimming. A second wooden diving stage was erected in 1922, and a third one was put up in 1932; this was replaced in 1935 by a three-stage, Art Deco-style diving board of masonry, its top level being thirty-three feet from the water. It was built to the design of the Borough Surveyor, J.B.L. Thompson, who had in mind international diving and swimming competitions (which took place there in subsequent years), and was opened by the Mayor of Swindon, F.T. Hobbs. On opening day, several divers gave displays, including Cicely Cousens, who was the 1935 Ladies National Diving Champion.

The lake continued to be used for swimming until 1958, when it was closed in response to a poliomyelitis scare. Allied to the lake was a paddling pool, which was built in the early 1930s and converted to a sandpit fifty years later, and an open-air swimming pool, built in 1936 and remaining as a pool until 1979. Public boating on the lake ceased in the 1990s, although private clubs continued to use it, but the regattas and various other public events that had begun at the start of the 20th century carried on.

What was officially to become Wiltshire's first local nature reserve was created at Coate Water in 1975, centred on a flood storage lagoon, and the area became a Site of Special Scientific Interest in the same year. Together with an arboretum that began to be established on the western side of the park in 1982, and which was formerly opened in 1998, the whole area is now known as Coate Water Country Park. A specially designated country walk around the park takes in Burderop Woods and Hodson.

Cockbill, Trevor William (1930-1999) This man had great prescience of the sheer folly of a local authority that allowed Swindon's build heritage to fall into developers' hands, principally between 1950 and 1980. Architecturally interesting buildings of merit were replaced by ugly structures that are aesthetically impoverished and in every way inferior to the earlier designs and fabric. Trevor was a fourth-generation Swindonian, born in the old GWR hospital and schooled at Gilbert's Hill, Clifton Street and Commonweal. He grew up in Dixon Street, took a job as a clerk at the GWR Works, and was later employed by Vickers Armstrong at South Marston. He became a printer, writer and

campaigner; and was a tutor to the U3A Swindon History Group. Trevor specialised in researching the people and the events that shaped New Swindon as a result of the arrival of the railway. He was the man who researched and published the documents relating to the history and architecture of the town's Mechanics' Institute building, by which English Heritage and the government enhanced its listing to Grade II* in 1998. *This Is Our Heritage* (1997) was the magnificent result of his research into the history of the Mechanics' Institute, published the year after he was a founder member of The New Mechanics' Institution Preservation Trust Limited. His other publications include *Finest Thing Out* – the story of the old institution's first thirty years; *Our Swindon 1939-41* – about his own childhood; *A Drift Of Steam*, and *The Quill Press*. The last named was the printing arm of the stationery business he ran from various locations around the railway village: notably East Street, Wellington Street and, latterly, in Faringdon Road. This was STADS, short for Swindon Typewriting and Duplicating Studio.

Coffee houses In the 1840s, in High Street (Emlyn Square), New Swindon there was an establishment called the Railway Dining and Coffee Rooms, proprietor Edward Frankis. Swindon's first dedicated coffee house was run by The Swindon Coffee Palace Company, which was formed in 1880 to 'give the public the option of obtaining refreshments disassociated from intoxicants'. In that year, it opened The Three Cups in Regent Street, where it offered a bar (for coffee), club room, smoking room, ladies' room, and lavatory; newspapers were provided, as were board games, to be enjoyed by patrons. Its directors were

mainly well-known Methodists of the time, including William Brewer Wearing, manager of the County of Gloucester Bank, and the GWR's Joseph Armstrong, who were also the Company's bankers. Within a few years, it had also become the office of the Starr Bowkett Building Society, of which there were, by 1886, two branches in Swindon. The Three Cups was also the meeting place for the town's United Temperance Board, composed of representatives of local bands of hope and other temperance organisations. The Coffee Palace Company immediately had a competitor in the Kooloo Coffee House Company, which opened its coffee bar and ladies' room (with a separate entrance) at 36 Bridge Street, and followed it with a branch at 23 Wood Street in the old town. The Kooloo's advertisements pointed out that hot dinners could also be had in their establishments on market days, and they specialised in 'Tebbut's celebrated Melton Mowbray pies'. Daily and weekly newspapers were available for customers to read, as were magazines such as *Illustrated London News* and *Punch*. These coffee emporia were soon followed by the Gorse Hill Coffee House in Cricklade Road, which included what was described as the Gorse Hill Reading and Recreation Room. By the mid-1880s, the trend for coffee houses had taken hold in Swindon, and private individuals had opened others around the town. The Great Western Coffee Tavern Company set up in High Street (Emlyn Square), and Samuel Fosse started coffee houses in Newport Street and Regent Street. William Frederick Vincent ran one at 78 Bridge Street, on the corner with Sheppard Street, in competition with Charles Fluck's British Workman Coffee House at No.4. Alfred George May had the Rodbourne

Road coffee tavern, and another was opened by Samuel Tarrant in Wellington Street.

Cole, Jean Audrey (1926-2005)

Born in Swindon, where she lived all her life, Jean was widely known for her questions and answers column that ran in *Family Tree* magazine from 1986 until the year of her death. In 2005 she was elected a Fellow of the Society of Genealogists. Among her publications was *Tracing Your Family Tree*, which sold more than 40,000 copies in its original Thorson edition. She was well known for her untiring ability to research and transcribe material, for her work with the Wiltshire Family History Society and the Wroughton Family History Group, her numerous articles on genealogy, her nationwide lectures on the subject, and her sessions on local radio. She also taught family history at night-school classes.

Cole, Leslie J. (1910-76)

Born in Swindon, Leslie Cole studied at Swindon Art School, specialised in murals and fabric decoration, and had a number of local exhibitions of his work. He later trained at the Royal College of Arts, in London, and then taught in Birmingham and, from 1937, at Hull College of Art. Turned down for active service at the outbreak of the Second World War, he applied to the War Artists Advisory Committee to become an officially salaried war artist. He was successful at the second attempt in 1942, having sent examples of his work that included depictions of the effects of war on the people of Swindon. In this capacity, he worked for the next four years in Europe and the Far East. After the war, he taught at the Central School and Brighton College of Art. A number of Leslie Cole's lithographs were bought for the Swindon art collection in the 1940s, and in 1952 the Borough Council bought *Seated Figure*. This was his first painting to be hung in the Royal Academy, and was at the time on view in Burlington House, London. The Swindon Collection includes several of his pictures painted in oil on canvas, and rather more lithographs – a medium which he favoured after successfully completing a diploma course as a young man at the Royal College of Art. His picture 'Boy With Bird' can be seen in *The Swindon Review* No.7, 1955.

College, The (See Technical College.)

Collett, Charles Benjamin (1871-1952)

A Londoner living close to Paddington during his childhood, Collett entered the drawing office in the Swindon railway works as a junior draughtsman in 1893. Five years later, he became an assistant to the chief draughtsman, and thereafter his rise continued; he was made manager of the Works in 1912 and, seven years later, promoted to Deputy Chief Mechanical Engineer under G.J. Churchward. Collett succeeded to the premier post in 1922, and retired in 1941. In 1924, he dismantled Churchward's 'Great Bear' and re-used its parts. After Armstrong's death in 1933, he was offered Newburn House as his residence, a move that might have saved it from demolition four years later; he declined and instead was domiciled in a more modest, two-storey house with bow windows and shoulder gables at the junction of Church Place with Park Road. Collett appears to have had an ambivalent relationship with his staff, from whom he was more remote than his predecessors had been. Although he was a magistrate during most of the 1920s, he was very little concerned with

those social and economic aspects of the new town that had so interested Armstrong and Churchward. It is alleged that under his fairly austere command, the new locomotives lacked the lustre of earlier years. Castle Class locomotives were built during his time.

Commercial Road Originally intended as Swindon's main shopping street, Commercial Road was built up from 1888 as a spine through the former Rolleston estate. After most of this area of former farmland came on the market in 1885, builders were able to put in Commercial Road, followed by a number of streets at right angles towards the north, linking with Regent Street, and some others up the sides of the hill to the south towards Old Town. In 1885, only Cromwell Street and Havelock Street ran off Regent Street, both built about twenty years previously, and both ending abruptly where they met Rolleston land. By 1899, Havelock Street had been extended to meet Commercial Road; Market Street, Davis Street, Granville Street, and Morley Street had been built linking Regent Street with Commercial Road.

On the northern side of the new spine road, Deacon Street, Morse Street, Newhall Street, Stanier Street, Dowling Street, and Whitney Street were also laid out during the 1890s. The whole area was built to a grid pattern, and had street-long single terraces in red brick, with some brick or terracotta ornamentation and limestone dressings. These streets devolved on Commercial Road, which had Regent Circus with the brand new and impressive New Swindon Local Board offices at its east end, and the provisions and commodities market (from 1892) at its west end. Commercial Road was laid out as six terraces of between nine and sixteen

properties on either side. It never reached its potential as a shopping street, being mostly residential and less readily converted to trade than Regent Street. A number of small shops did go in, however, mostly on the northern side, and these tended to be of independent traders; family-owned restaurants also established in Commercial Road. It retained this mix of late 19th-century terraced houses, offices, and small retail businesses until the 1970s. By then, banks and estate agents had moved in. Most of the remaining residential properties were bought up during the last two decades of the 20th century, and were remodelled or rebuilt, primarily in the service of commerce. Almost all of the retail shops disappeared at that time.

Crombey Street was built parallel to Commercial Road, to the south, in 1891 and was named after its speculative builder. It was crossed by those streets running southwards from Commercial Road but, unlike the latter, was only terraced on its south side.

Compton's Clothing Factory John Compton's first clothing factory was built in Aldgate, London, in 1848. The company came to Swindon in 1871, where it opened with ten workers in a cottage in Sheppard Street. This was where it made corduroy uniforms under contract to the Great Western Railway Company, and clothing for the War Office, the Admiralty, the Post Office, and governments overseas. Architect John J. Smith was retained to design the company's clothing factory, which was built on the site of the cottage, cost £3,000, and opened in 1876. Its main workroom covered 3,420 square feet and housed the machinery needed for sewing, riveting and hot pressing; also in the building was a

packing room, and an employees' dining room with cooking facilities, of which the company was very proud. Compton's (later to be named Compton, Sons & Webb) was the first company to take on large numbers of female workers in Swindon, the majority of whom were outworkers, employed to make the garments at home on piecework. At one time, it also inhabited the premises of a one-time sweet factory in Manchester Road. Within two years of opening, Compton's had 300 women on its payroll, and an employee base of more than 1,000 by the beginning of the 20th century. The workforce expanded during each World War, as Compton's also made military uniforms using supplied cloth. During the Second World War, it opened a temporary sub-factory in Old Town. The main factory in Sheppard Street was enlarged or extended in 1895, 1903, 1932, and 1938. In 1958, the company bought the nearby Union Tavern, closed it down and demolished it, in order to again expand its main site.

Congregational Chapel, Sanford Street A chapel was built in Sanford Street in 1877, attendant upon the church in Bath Road. The chapel was built externally of iron, internally of wooden boards on top of a thick layer of felt, and measured 86ft by 46ft, with a small vestry at the rear. It had a nave with a gallery facing the pulpit; aisles, a clerestory, and a small turret with a spirelet. An adjacent Sunday schoolroom was put up in 1888. In 1894, T.B. Silcock of Bath designed a ghastly neo-Jacobean-meets-Decorated, Gothic-style permanent replacement in red brick with Bath stone dressings. It had a two-stage stubby tower with spire and open cupola on its south-west corner, and a huge wheel window to the south elevation. It cost £3,000, and was demolished in 1977.

Congregational Church, Bath Road This church (originally called the Victoria Chapel), which was built on the corner of Bath Road and Victoria Street in 1866, is one of the great 'lost' buildings of Swindon. The brainchild of Revd G.J. Pillgrem, previously minister of the independent chapel (established 1804) in Newport Street, the Congregational church was designed by William Jervis Stent of Warminster, and built by John Ponton of Warminster and John Phillips of Swindon. The cost, which came to £3,569, was paid by public subscription. The Revd J. H. Snell was its first minister. It was a Lombardic-style, neo-Romanesque design with a 48-foot-wide south frontage to Bath Road, and a 120-foot-long elevation to Victoria Street. The latter featured a run of particularly tall, two-light, round-headed windows tied together by continuous hoods and a string course. A three-stage tower rose to 56 feet on the south-east corner, and each stage was treated differently. It was originally intended to have a spire. The south face featured a dominant wheel window above the recessed Corinthian porch. All of the windows were round-headed and recessed with keystones. The interior comprised a preaching hall with a central aisle, and there was a gallery at the south end. The successor to this building (later to be called the United Reform Church) was built in Upham Road, 1937-39, and the intention was to then pull down the Congregational Church, partly to facilitate road widening at the top of Victoria Road. This scheme was partially carried out by demolishing premises on the other side of the road, but the Second World War intervened and the Congregational Church building was not pulled down until 1949.

Cook, Hubert (1901-1966) Hubert Cook was born at The Pitchens, Wroughton, although the family relocated to Rodbourne Cheney in 1911, where his father ran a market garden. His brother, Arthur Henry Cook, became Chief Warder at the Tower of London, and wrote an account of the prisoners who had therein been incarcerated throughout history. Hubert is best known for his lithographs, an art form that he took up in the late 1930s, and in particular for those depicting life in the Swindon railway works. He was apprenticed there as a young man, and in 1918 was apprenticed as a shaping machine operator in the locomotive department. He married Ivy Lester in 1924, and continued to work as a machinist until 1944. In 1927, he enrolled at the Swindon School of Art and, throughout the 1930s, when he was at his most prolific, he exhibited widely –winning a string of awards for his work and receiving numerous commissions for his portraiture. 'A Welder in a Boiler Shop' (1938) was a representative lithograph that the War Artists Advisory Committee bought in 1943, following its appearance at the Royal Academy. Some of his other scenes inside the Works, and his non-railway pictures were painted in oil on canvas. An exhibition of his paintings and drawings was held at Swindon Arts Centre in 1947.

He had three compositions published in *The Swindon Review*, each representative of some aspect of railway life. His 'Hot Metal Sawing' (No.1, 1945) is a study in fire, heat and sparks in a railway hot shop, through which the three men working there are hardly visible. 'Boiler Shop Furnace' (No.4, 1948) shows three men at a single gaping furnace; and there are again three men 'Unloading Wagons at a Railway Siding' (No.6, 1953). He is well represented in the Swindon Collection,

which has the original of the last mentioned work and which won a bronze medal for lithography at the Paris Salon in 1959. 'The Late Chief Warder A.H. Cook, DCM, MM' (the artist's brother, 1934); 'Moulding Hands in an Iron Foundry' (1943); 'Electric Welder' (1943); 'Rogers Lido, Knaresborough' (1945); and 'The Lawn' (the former home of the Goddard family at Swindon, 1945) are all in the collection. Hubert Cook was the author of two books: *The Technical Illustrator* (Chapman & Hall, 1961) and *Freehand Technical Sketching* (Methuen, 1965).

After leaving Swindon, Cook went to the Portsmouth College of Art as an evening class teacher, and had pictures hung in the Paris Salon.

Co-operative Movement in Swindon In 1850, some six years after the co-operative principle was pioneered at Toad Lane, Rochdale, a group of Swindon men decided to try the approach in Swindon. They began with a box of herrings, bought from a supplier and sold between themselves on the consumer co-operation system from a small room in the Barracks, the GWR's lodging house. The possibility of expanding the scheme was realised when they changed to supplying flour and bread. Then, in 1853, the group registered themselves as the Swindon Co-operative Provident Society Limited. Its office was in Henry Street; its first outlet was at No.4 High Street (Emlyn Square, New Town), and the Society soon added a bakery in Church Place. However, the principals were unable to agree over the direction to take with commodities – the Provident Society wishing to remain and publicise itself as 'bakers and flour dealers'.

In 1861, some members formed (and registered) the breakaway New Swindon

Co-operative Provident Society, which later became the New Swindon Industrial Co-operative Society. Almost at once, they rented stall space in the covered market adjacent to the Mechanics' Institute, and ultimately had three stalls there. Both societies moved into premises in East Place (East Street), where they established stores. During the 1870s, The Industrial Co-operative also diversified into grocery items, boots and shoes, and drapery. By 1875, all was not going to plan. 'It must, however, be confessed that the co-operative principle has not accomplished at Swindon what might have been expected in a community almost entirely of working men in possession of weekly paid wages, and consequently able to pay cash and gain the advantage of the dividend (then typically five per cent) arising from co-operation.' Whilst the older Society continued to 'supply bread and flour upon the co-operative system', the Industrial Co-operative stated that it existed 'to supply unadulterated articles of food, drapery, etc. direct from the wholesale merchant, the profits being annually divided'. In 1877, the Swindon Co-operative Provident Society, which had continued to concentrate on selling flour and bread, bought a bread-making machine, and was able to report that its business possessed 'a large and convenient bakery, a dwelling house for the manager, and other premises'. It also 'supplies grocery, drapery, boots etc., direct from wholesale houses'. Had it moved earlier in this direction, it might not have been in competition with the New Swindon Industrial Society Limited, which by the late 1870s 'dealt in grocery, drapery, provisions, boots and shoes, sewing machines, wringing and mangling machines, bedsteads, filters, ironmongery, crockery, and other household articles'. The Swindon Co-operative

Provident Society installed new ovens in 1892. Its premises in Henry Street went over to making confectionery when it established a bakery in Station Road in 1923. This was demolished in the 1970s.

In 1880, the Kingshill Co-operative Society was formed in competition. Its premises were at 54 Radnor Street, where it opened a three-storey bakery in 1906. The three societies continued to operate in competition until the middle of the 20th century, when economic conditions proved insufficient to sustain them. The Swindon Co-operative Provident Society, centred on Henry Street, ceased to exist in 1951, as did the Kingshill Co-operative Society in 1953. The New Swindon Industrial Co-operative Society continued alone. It became the Swindon & District Co-operative Society, and amalgamated with its Oxford counterpart (founded 1872) in 1969 to form the Oxford & Swindon Co-operative Society Limited. This became the Oxford Swindon & Gloucester Co-operative Society, which merged with the West Midlands Co-operative Society in 2005 to form Midcounties Co-operative Limited.

Corn Exchange, Grand Opening of The corn exchange was opened in 1866 amid riotous celebrations. Females were admitted only to the gallery, where they were served cakes. The men were provided with free champagne by wine merchants Brown & Nephew, and there were numerous toasts, including some to 'the ladies'. Such was the din, the band, which was booked only until six o'clock, thought the proceedings had ended, played the national anthem and left the building. Consequently, the chairman of the organising committee, and all its

members, came to the same conclusion, and also went home. The opening ceremony was followed by a ball with dancing to a Hanoverian band supplied by Milsom & Son of Bath. Harry Sidney, a humorous music hall entertainer, performed a song of his own composition called *In A Quiet Sort of Way*:

Of the corn exchange at Swindon
I should like to say a word
Of the energy which raised it
All now present oft have heard.
Some say the room is much too long
But I hope to see the day
When you'll find it filled with dealers
In a quiet sort of way.

Wilcox of Bath the architect
This building ably planned,
A proof we'd find in this how well
His work he'd understand.
John Phillips carried out his work
Most ably all must say,
Though he once went through his business*
In a quiet sort of way.

I was pleased to hear a short time back
What Joseph Reynolds said
'Bout agriculture's prospects,
He was not at all afraid.
He said that with their industry,
Integrity, fair play,
Its interest would flourish,
In a quiet sort of way.

When Sir George Jenkinson arose
To speak to neighbours here
I was very much delighted
To hear that hearty cheer.
Defeated in his contest he may be
But I know they

Respect him for behaving
In his quiet sort of way.

I've been to many dinners
And great meetings in my time.
I've introduced a lot of funny subjects
Too in rhyme,
But never in my life did I observe
Until today,
Such a moving style of acting,
In a quiet sort of way.

* A reference to the builder's accident (see Corn Exchange.)

Corn Exchange, Old Town

Businessmen had long been agitating for a corn exchange in Swindon when a committee of local tradesmen was formed in 1863, led by lord of the manor Ambrose Lethbridge Goddard, to consider the matter. They found that Goddard was unwilling to give up any of his property, and land was too expensive to buy. The Swindon Central Market Company (see Town Hall, Old Town) was having similar problems, in pursuing the same matter. They were successful in getting Goddard to agree to eject the occupants of two old cottages adjacent to the town hall, so that these could be pulled down and a corn exchange built on the site.

Wilson & Wilcox (James Wilson and William John Willcox) of 1 Belmont, Bath were the architects of the corn exchange, and John Phillips of Devizes Road, Swindon was the builder. During construction, Phillips fell from the roof of the building into the cellar, and was seriously injured. The corn exchange was put up on a triangular site between The Planks and the Market Square. It was described as being 'of Grecian architecture', surmounted by an eighty-foot,

four-stage tower, initially with spaces for a clock face on each side. This was a tour-de-force for Swindon: an ornate structure with open Venetian windows, Corinthian pilasters at the corners, a cornice, a part open balustrade with corner finials, and a square dome with ironwork cresting. The building was opened on 9 April, 1866, and George Deacon provided the clock and its four-foot-wide faces in 1867. It was illuminated by gas, supplied by the Swindon Gas Company. The entrance was through a vestibule below the tower, beneath the legend 'Blessed be the Lord who daily loadeth us with benefits'.

Initially, a rounded corner masked a series of windows that opened into a triangular market house with a fountain in the centre, the whole surmounted by a glass dome. There was also a hall that measured 110 feet by 50 feet, and was 26 feet to the underside of the roof, rising to a ridge that was 34½ feet from the floor. Twenty-three large windows and a skylight ran along the length of the roof. There were folding doors between the lobby and two ante-rooms, and before the great hall, and 100 people could be accommodated in a gallery. A door was put in between the corn exchange and the town hall so that rooms in the latter would be available for eating in, when a ball or some other entertainment was going on in the former.

From the beginning, Brown & Nephew, wine merchants, leased the cellars beneath the corn exchange as wine stores. In 1887, they took office accommodation above. By 1880, dressing rooms and a 1,000-seat auditorium had been provided, and the large hall had been licensed for stage plays. It became a roller skating venue for several years at the start of the 20th century, and was a cinema between 1919 and 1949, named 'The Rink Cinema'. Initially, it screened silent films accompanied by a trio of musicians. In 1951, it became a Grade II listed building. Thereafter, refurbished and redecorated, it incorporated the Locarno Dance Hall, then a venue for wrestling promotions and pop concerts, and latterly a bingo hall. This closed in the 1970s, and the building embarked on a long period of decay and gradual disintegration. In 1999, the structure and the site were bought by Gael Mackenzie, although a planning application to redevelop the site as an entertainment and hospitality venue was rejected. The following year, Swindon Council suggested that the plans might be acceptable if they included the adjacent car park and The Planks. By 2002, there were other plans in place to redevelop the area, initially by Countryside Properties. The building was damaged by fire in May 2003, and again in May 2004. In 2006, Bach Homes, now the preferred developer in the place of Countryside Properties and run by Steve Rosier, submitted plans for residential and hospitality use, the first of which proved to be unviable in the subsequent recessionary economic climate. The second was rejected by the town council, which also cancelled an agreement that would have allowed the developer to include its adjacent land (a car park) as part of the redevelopment. The parties having thus arrived at stalemate, another of Swindon's historic buildings continues to decline.

Cossons, Neil (b.1939) Son of a Beeston, Nottinghamshire headmaster and local historian, Cossons was educated at the Henry Mellish grammar school in Nottingham, and at Liverpool University. He was a twenty-three-year-old museums assistant of some sixteen months' service with Leicester City Museum, possessed

of a Bachelor of Arts degree when, on 3 December 1962, he succeeded to the post of Assistant Curator for Swindon. He listed his interests as industrial technology, 19th-century industrial history, and railways; and his hobbies as geography and rifle shooting. At the time, Swindon's official Museums Curator was Harold Jolliffe, otherwise the borough's Chief Librarian, who received an extra £100 per year in his salary for his 'museums duties'. Cossons succeeded Morna MacGregor, a University of Edinburgh graduate with honours in prehistoric archaeology. She left to marry Derek Simpson – a worker in Devizes Museum whom she met whilst studying at Edinburgh – and, coincidentally, to move with him to Leicester. While in Swindon, Cossons lived at 10 Okus Road. He helped to run the Great Western Railway Museum, which was opened in Faringdon Road on 22 June 1962, organised a new geology room at the general museum in Bath Road, and published a pamphlet on *The Old Great Railways*.

At the beginning of 1964, he left to become curator of the Bristol Museum Department of Technology, saying that he 'liked the town very much, and their scheme for the development of their museum is very adventurous', adding, 'I am glad to be in on the beginning of it'. In 1971, he became the first director of Ironbridge Museum; in 1983, he joined Greenwich Maritime Museum; from 1986 to 2000 he was Director of the Science Museum, London. Knighted in 1994, he was a commissioner for English Heritage in 1999, and chairman of that organisation, 2000-07.

Country Markets, Swindon (See Women's Institute markets.)

County Electric Pavilion In 1910, this picture house was opened in Regent Street by the mayor, William Henry Lawson, and was later designated at number 24. From the earliest time, the management tried to bring variety to the experience by linking the silent films with gramophone records. The property was double-fronted but open at street level, and had its name on a fascia board picked out in letters that were reminiscent of those on fairground rides. The entrance was through a central doorway. The cinema closed in the 1930s, and the site was taken over by F. W. Woolworth & Company's store, which continued there (expanded as 23-25 Regent Street) until 2008 when the company collapsed.

County Ground In 1891, the Wiltshire County Ground Company Limited bought twenty-six acres of land off Drove Road, about one-third of a mile to the east of New Swindon, which then more or less stopped where Regent Circus is now. They put in a football ground, a cricket ground with a pavilion, and a peripheral, circular bicycle track of three laps to a mile, and facilities for a horse racecourse and polo ground. The complex opened in May 1893 as the Wiltshire County Ground. Swindon Town Football Club moved to the County Ground in 1896, and has since remained there. A twelve-and-a-half-acre extension was added to the area in 1930, opened on 5 February by the mayor, Alderman G.H. Hunt.

Court, Terence Roy (b. 1943) A native of Swindon, one-time primary school teacher, and teacher of art at Ferndale Secondary School, and a youth leader, Terry Court was appointed in 1974 as the first Arts Officer for the Borough of Thamesdown, and

he was the Head of Cultural Policy, 1983-93. Arguably, no-one did more to further such a wide range of artistic endeavour in the town. He was initially responsible for the Arts Centre, developing the cultural activities at the town hall that were part-sponsored and which attracted commercial commissions, and the annual Swindon Festival. He established Thamesdown Community Arts in 1974, with a £300 grant from the Borough of Thamesdown. Funds accruing from their events were used to finance murals in the town, street theatre, and the community arts theatre in the town hall, after the Borough had given rent-free accommodation there to the project in 1976. In 1977, he established Thamesdown Dance Studio in the town hall with Marie McClusky, and the Visual Arts Studio in the same venue in 1979. Here were arts and crafts-style studios, run by volunteers until 1978, offering a mixture of courses and a workplace for professional craftspeople who needed to make their work pay. Funds also came in from the Gulbenkian Foundation and, later, Southern Arts.

Under Terry's direction, Public Arts and Percent for Art were established in 1982, which led to various arts residencies, street festivals, and public sculptures. The following year, he became responsible for the then council-controlled Wyvern Theatre, and in 1983 he set up the Magic Roundabout Theatre Company, together with the Manpower Services Commission. Appointed head of cultural policy for Swindon in 1983, he was part of an arts sub-committee (which continued until 1992). In 1984, he began the annual poets-in-residence series that ran for four years, and designed and built the Link Arts Studios – a multi-purpose theatre in the round with adjoining visual arts studio and darkroom.

One of his most successful creations was Thamesdown Foundation for the Arts, established in 1986, which brought together private and public resources, with the interest on investments used to grant-aid arts projects. In the same year, he became responsible for the Swindon Collection of British Art, and in 1988 he assumed overall responsibility for the Council's entire museum division, including the museum and art gallery in Bath Road, the railway museum in Faringdon Road, Lydiard House at the peripheral Lydiard Park, and the Richard Jefferies Museum at Coate. Terry took early retirement to run the Goddard Arms at Clyffe Pypard, where he also held art and sculpture exhibitions, Celtic and other music festivals, and theatre performances. He later moved to Cornwall to continue the parallel career of painter, which he had pursued since attending Swindon College of Art in 1962. Some of his work is in the STEAM Museum.

Court Leet The court leet was the means whereby domestic problems, misdemeanours, common nuisances, matters pertaining to the fabric of the place and of public health were dealt with locally. The court leet for the manor of Swindon was held at The Crown in High Street between c.1650 and c.1835, when it ceased to take place annually but lingered on for the next two decades, being held every four years. (Nationally, some courts leet survive to this day.) Accused persons were summoned before juries of freehold tenants, and the leet also appointed a number of officers such as surveyor, constable, and ale tester.

Courts of Justice, Princes Street The courts were designed by J. Loring Morgan, and built in granite, marble and

Portland stone by Clark Brothers (Swindon) Ltd. The commemorative stone was laid on 12 July, 1963, and the building was opened by Rt. Hon. Lord Devlin on 21 April 1965. The exterior bears the royal coat of arms. The ground floor has a spacious entrance hall, two courtrooms, committee room, accommodation for barristers and court officials, and ancillary rooms. Juvenile and matrimonial courtrooms were placed on the first floor, together with office accommodation for the magistrate's clerk and staff. A covered entrance was erected through which prisoners might be conducted to the cells. The premises were refurbished in 1990.

Cow sculpture, Great Western Hospital

In 1987, sculptor Tom Gleeson's grazing cow, made of welded sheet steel, was installed on a rise, beside an ornamental flower bed outside Princess Margaret Hospital at Okus. When the hospital was demolished, the sculpture was weatherproofed by Wroughton artist David Morse, and relocated next to a link road beside the town's Great Western Hospital at Commonhead. (See also Gorilla sculpture.)

Cricket, Origins of in Swindon

Cricket was played in Swindon from the 1820s. In 1844, the Swindon Cricket Club was founded by a group of Swindon's gentry and businessmen, and it remained the pastime of this level of successful men for several decades. The earliest surviving record is the Treasurer's Book of 1854. The team played in Drove Road, and later at The Sands, on part of what had been Okus Farm, where in 1867 the club's name was changed to the Old Swindon Cricket Club. Five years later, a cricket pavilion with a thatched roof

was built at The Sands, and in 1874 the club was once more renamed, becoming the Swindon Rangers Cricket Club. It is thought that in 1881 this cricket club played a game of football with the lads of St Mark's Young Men's Friendly Society. As soon as it was over, the two decided to join forces, at the suggestion of Revd William Pitt, and became the Swindon Town Football Club. In 1885, A.L. Goddard, lord of the manor, leased a piece of land off Cricklade Street to, among others, Revd Maurice Ponsonby of St Mark's church, for use as a cricket field.

Cricket Pavilion, off County Road

The magnificent pavilion was designed by W.H. Read and Henry Pritchett, and was built in 1893 at a cost of £850. Built of wood and brick with a weather-boarded upper elevation, it is an elaborate two-storey, nine-bay structure with a seven-bay, cast-iron arcade with small caps and lacework spandrels between gabled rooms at each end. The balcony to the upper floor spectator area is constructed of bellied iron brackets with a central stairway leading to the ground. Each of the gabled rooms has a central doorway flanked by square-headed sash windows; there is ornamental braced timber framing in the gables above the weather-boarding, and the bargeboards have billet decoration. Competitors' changing rooms were put up opposite the pavilion at a cost of £450; a further £250 was spent on the lodge house at the entrance to the grounds.

Cricketers Arms, Emlyn Square

The Cricketers was built as a public house on a corner site between Emlyn Square and Exeter Street, and was named after the activity on the nearby GWR cricket field. Built of coursed rough limestone with ashlar

quoins, on the corner with Exeter Street, it is of three storeys, gabled, with three bays to Exeter Street, one to Emlyn Square, and a corner splay with the original entrance between. The Cricketers was the first of the Emlyn Square public houses to be licensed, and was opened in 1847. In the 1850s, Edward Jeffcoate was the landlord; Samuel Dixon was there by 1858, and Martha Dixon after 1865; Richard Skerton took over in 1868. The building has been Grade II listed since 1970.

Cricklade Street Cricklade Street began at the junction of High Street and Wood Street, where it led down the steep gradient off the hill, before Drove Road was built up and so named in the mid-19th century. The gradient where it now passes Christ Church was once several feet higher. This thoroughfare is also named on old documents as Cricklett Street and Creeklade Street, the oldest reference being of 1645 and referring to a lease of a tenement there by Richard Goddard, then lord of the manor. Goddard also leased pasture land in Cricklade Street variously over the following few years, and there were certainly a number of cottages changing hands along it by the 1660s. Stonecutter, silkweaver, baker, clerk and cordwainer are all trades associated with this street in the later 1600s and, in the 18th century, maltster, joiner and labourer.

Here too, in the early years of the 18th century, was The Dog inn, which may have originated early in the 1600s. The Dog was situated opposite the White Horse; the latter was a one-time beer house that had not been in use for some years, and which had become two adjoining houses by the time they were sold to the merchant William Vilett

in 1728. In 1731, he leased from Hannah Spencer, widow, two adjacent properties across the road, one of which had formerly been The Dog. Thereafter, the number of beer houses in Cricklade Street rapidly built up. One of these was the Saracen's Head, in one of two adjoining properties acquired in 1825 by Reuben Horsell. An unpleasant character, Horsell was a slater or tiler, and plasterer, born at Wootton Bassett in 1792, living at 17 Albert Street, where he also had two properties. In 1854, he was fined for punching his neighbour, Mary Ann Gibbs, in the face; she also charged him with breaking her windows, throwing water into her house, and collecting mobs of people to intimidate her. His public house was part of the red-light district, and there were frequent brawls there, and he was charged with accommodating prostitutes. The Saracen's Head existed until the 1850s.

Other brewhouses and licensed premises in Cricklade Street included the Plume of Feathers, which was designated as such in the mid-1700s, later became known as the Oddfellows Arms, and which was incorporated into a 21st-century residential redevelopment. There was also the Carriers Arms of 1847, opened next to the Saracen's Head; it became the Lord Raglan, and closed in 1907.

Cricklade Street is also associated with the Blackford brothers, John and Joseph, butchers in Old Town and New Swindon, and famed as exponents of dangerous and painful sports. In 1845, lord of the manor, Ambrose Goddard leased a property on the corner of Wood Street and Cricklade Street to their father, butcher Robert Blackford. This was said to have been 'newly built', and the same lease also got him a dairy and brewhouse in High Street, and a slaughterhouse at

Brockhill. These premises were leased to farmer George Reynolds of Eastcott in 1848, and were subsequently inhabited by a boot and shoe maker, and then the surgeon John Gay. Then, in 1884, the fine Wilts & Dorset bank building was erected on the site.

Cricklade Street, No. 42 This fine property is now apartments incorporated into a 21st-century residential development called The Old Quarter. Niklaus Pevsner called it 'the best house in Swindon by far'; and 'one of the most distinguished town houses in Wiltshire' was John Betjeman's appraisal. Brick-built apsidal-style ends were added c.1800. The main property was built in 1729, either for William Harding or other members of the Harding family, on the site of a cottage and a one-time inn called The White Horse. The extensive brick-built, vaulted cellars beneath the building attest to its use as an inn. As a family residence, it was called The Hall; a Robert Harding (1721-70) and his wife Mary (née Tubb) lived there. The house is of two storeys and five bays, built of brick with stone dressings, and the front elevation is flanked by flat pilasters with Composite caps. Its symmetrical façade is exceptionally busy, having decorative motifs such as stepped keystones with faces, moulded dressings and cornices. There is a pediment above the three central bays, and a plain parapet behind is pierced with balusters on each side of the pediment. A Venetian window is set above the elaborate ground-floor entrance. Internally, the most distinguishing feature is an early 18th-century staircase with turned balusters, ascending through three levels. In the redevelopment, the property has been renamed Vilett's House, after the family who owned it from about 1770.

Croft, The Otherwise known as Croft House, this mansion was built for solicitor James Copleston Townsend in the mid-19th century, and was acquired by the Morse family of drapers from Townsend's son in 1896. The house stood, foursquare on a rise and in extensive grounds, at the end of a curving driveway to the east of the road to Wroughton, just south of Devizes Road, where it was gradually encroached upon as Old Town expanded south. It was of two storeys and five bays to each elevation, and with a projecting double-height porch. The general appearance was mildly polychromatic, and had a mixture of Romanesque and Gothic elements; semi-circular hoods to the windows, pointed arch to the porch, with a proliferation of shafts with moulded caps and bases dividing the double lights in the windows and in the jambs of the porch. The rooms were very large and, on the ground floor at least, were a mass of decorated plasterwork and panelling. Associated with the estate were two quaint lodge houses, one of which was restored following a fire in 1988. The Croft fell into disrepair but lingered into the mid-1950s, when it was acquired by Swindon Corporation and demolished to make way for the Hesketh Crescent development of 1957. (See also Morse, Levi Lapper.)

Crowdy, Solicitors William Morse Crowdy (1792-1875) and Alfred Southby Crowdy (1806-1883) were brothers, born in Swindon. They were two of the children of solicitor James Crowdy (d.1808) and his wife Elizabeth Henrietta (née Morse). By the time he was in his early twenties, William had taken up his late father's practice in the town, and worked on his own until c.1828, when Alfred joined him. At that time, they

both lived in Newport Street and had their offices in High Street. In 1836, when the North Wilts Bank opened in Swindon, they both became its managers, and held the posts until 1858. In 1831, Alfred married Anna Sheppard (b.1809, Swindon), and they had several children. William married Sarah Vaughan (b. 1811, Marston, Kent) in Bath in 1839, and the couple lived at Chiseldon, with three servants. They never had children of their own.

What happened to Anna Crowdy is not known but, c.1852, Alfred married Emma Eliza Townsend (b. 1829, Seaton, Devon). In the same year, both brothers became directors of the Swindon Market Company. Significantly, 1852 was also the year in which solicitor James Copleston Townsend, Emma's elder brother, joined the firm of Crowdy and Crowdy, which, by 1855, was known as Crowdy & Townsend; by 1857, it was Crowdy Townsend & Ormond. Alfred was the first to leave the firm, and by 1861 he was living with Emma, two of his four children by Anna (née Sheppard), his five children with Emma, a nurse and four other servants at Shaw-cum-Donnington, Berkshire. William retired c.1858, and he and Sarah removed to Paragon Buildings, Bath, and latterly to Macauley Buildings in the same city, employing two servants at each address. By 1871, Alfred and Emma had relocated to Torquay with an extended family that required seven servants to look after them. William Morse Crowdy died at his brother's house in Torquay; Alfred Southby Crowdy died at Timsbury, Somerset.

Crown, The Situated in Marlborough Road (and not to be confused with the Goddard Arms, High Street, which was named The Crown before about 1810), this ancient hostelry was almost at the junction with Newport Street. It had the distinction of being the last thatched public house in Swindon when it was demolished in 1964, having been closed as licensed premises for the previous nine years. It is thought that the building dated from the late 17th century, and that it had begun as a beer house some time in the 1830s. During the Second World War it was a favourite of American service personnel, particularly those domiciled nearby at The Lawn, which had been requisitioned for the purpose, thereby attracting (then and in the decade that followed) sufficient prostitute activity to have it condemned, and then closed, as a place of ill repute.

Crumpled Water Walls, Regent Street Two undulating and ribbed stainless-steel forms with water running over them were officially activated on 19 May 2010 at the junction of Regent Street and Canal Walk. The feature cost £240,000. It was designed by Walter Jack and Paul Channing of the Walter Jack Studio in Bristol, which in 2008 had won a contract offered by the New Swindon Company. The brief suggested only that as there had once been a canal there, some sort of water feature would be nice. The Walter Jack Studio specialises in creating forms that 'are beautiful and playable' and which 'make public spaces more enjoyable, and fun to be in'. The crumpled water walls are two similar forms set side by side. The larger is about three metres square and three tonnes in weight; the smaller weighs about one tonne, and measures about three metres by one metre. The pieces were constructed by Richard Stump and John Hall – specialist project makers who have worked with Damien Hirst – using approximately 1,000

pieces of laser-cut stainless steel. They were designed so that the pumped, filtered, and recycled water should not flow over them in an orderly fashion. The complicated curves and the ribbed surface means that in some places the water simply runs down, in others it appears to cling, splash, or oscillate. When light and shadow play upon the surface in particular juxtaposition, it is possible to discern the shapes of naked bodies, as it were in a shower, in the undulations of the pieces. Within hours of the water feature being switched on, someone added a foaming agent to the water, resulting in a clean-up operation.

Cube Waterfall In 1966, a cube waterfall sculpture was unveiled on The Parade. It was received by the general public with almost universal condemnation. Swindon has never been noted for its appreciation of the avant-garde; only a few years before, the town had been given – on 'permanent loan' to its art collection – two Picasso paintings. The Arts Committee believed that in a working- class town these were unlikely to be understood, and would be met with considerable distaste by the viewing public. The pictures were quite literally kept in a cupboard and never displayed, inaction that so upset the donor, he eventually took them back. Clearly, Swindon was not ready for The Cube, a £3,500 sculpture by the well-known and well-respected London sculptor, painter and designer of the abstract, Geoffrey Wickham (1919-2005). It did not help that he described it inexplicably as 'a revealed aggregate sculpture'. He was also sure that it met two of Swindon Borough Council's criteria when commissioning it: that the finished work would be 'indestructible and vandal-proof'. Most people were extremely sorry that he

seemed to have achieved the first; but in the second, it failed rather spectacularly. Vandalism takes many forms.

The cube weighed 17 tonnes, was 7 feet square and stood on a base in a 24-foot-square shallow tank of water. It was made of square and rectangular blocks of masonry, occasionally hollowed out to admit strange shapes, and otherwise had square- or rectangular-shaped hollows between the blocks. The structure might have been described as Stonehenge meets Troika pottery. Water was pumped through it, trickling out from spaces between the blocks, and it was lit from inside. Almost immediately, it became a rubbish tip; ink was put into the water; detergent made it frothy; and children paddled in or fell into the tank. Des Morgan (then a fifteen-year old, but in 2013 a well-respected presenter on Swindon 105.5, the community radio station) was, on his own admission, responsible for tipping Lux soap flakes into the cube and enjoying the soapy result. In one television interview, a local resident complained: 'and every morning, there's knickers in it'. The complaints became so numerous that the Borough Council discussed its removal as early as 1968. In the event, it was quietly decommissioned and, waterless, allowed to weather until the late 1970s, when it was equally quietly taken away.

Cullum, Jamie (b.1979) In 1997, a seventeen-year old, born in Romford, Essex but then living in Hullavington, turned up at the Fox and Hounds public house, Colerne, to listen to the jazz. He was encouraged by Ray Butt to play a solo interval slot, while the resident trio, led by Ray on clarinet and saxophone, took their brief half-time interlude. The young lad was Jamie Cullum.

Now, he is an internationally renowned pianist, singer and recording artist; then, he was a student, taking a year out and filling in time to develop his music before going to Reading University to study English. Ray gave him the weekly interval spot at Colerne, and Jamie became a favourite with all the patrons of Fox's Den, as it became known during the Fretless and Friends' sessions. He also inked Jamie to a simple contract, inviting him to play with the band, and promised to help promote his talent wherever possible. Ray organised a recording studio session and promptly circulated the recordings to whoever would listen ... radio stations, record companies, and contacts in the music business. He was in no doubt that Jamie would one day become a household name but, despite a fair amount of exposure, the great talent of this young man failed to be recognised at that time by the movers and shakers in the industry. Jamie entered the 1997 Young Jazz Musician of the Year competition and he won through to the Wales and South-West finals. Jools Holland compered the finals night in Cardiff and seemed convinced that Jamie would be declared the winner to go on to the grand final in London, but the judges thought differently. Jamie also auditioned for an ITV talent show and was asked to appear on TV, but by this time he was too busy to appear.

Playing with Fretless and Friends frequently brought Jamie Cullum into Swindon, sometimes playing at Long's Bar, Victoria Road, and he often joined Ray at his jazz evenings in Pizza Express, Bath Road. Whilst at university, Jamie undertook gigs around the Reading area and in London, and gradually became well known. In 1999, his first album, *Heard It All Before*, was issued.

The following year, he performed at the King's Arms, Wood Street, during the first Swindon Jazz Festival. In 2003, he returned to Swindon for a session in The Apartment, and played at that year's jazz festival.

Dammas Lane This was a short roadway of cottages, small houses, high walls and agricultural buildings, roughly constructed in stone and brick, and often a combination of both, which extended north-east from the market square in Old Town towards the Goddard estate. A path led directly from its east end into the estate, through a gate in the boundary wall. It is supposed that this lane (formerly the name was spelled 'Damas') once led towards a standing of damson trees on the lord of the manor's estate, and was therefore so named after the vernacular pronunciation of the fruit. There is no documentary evidence of the trees, but there is of the name being used since 1684. It had a good source of water because it followed the line of several natural springs which also fed the church well on the Goddard estate. Most of the buildings in Dammas Lane were of two storeys and of either two or three bays. A particularly fine house (latterly number five) was tall and narrow with a mansard roof and dormer windows. Most of Dammas Lane was pulled down during the 1960s.

Dave and Amos In a stage career that began in the early 1950s and ended when the pair retired in 2010, Swindon-born Dave and Amos, gentle cross-talking comedians, played most of the provincial theatres in Britain, and travelled the world with their brand of hilarious one-liner comedy, playing civilian venues and also entertaining British troops in places of conflict. William Brian Newson (1931–2013) was Amos, a nickname

he acquired as a child at Sanford Street School, and took the surname of Brown. David Frederick Wilson (also b.1931) was Dave, although his Equity card was made out in the name of Frederick Wilson because the organisation already had a Dave Wilson. Amos worked at Wills cigarette factory and at Pressed Steel; Dave was employed by Wills. In the 1950s, the pair began their career in entertainment by writing sketches for others to perform. By 1956, they had become an amateur double act initially called Ali Bad and Ali Worse, and were working their own highly individual brand of comedy. In 1975 they turned professional, were auditioned for the first Wheeltappers and Shunters Social Club television programme, and thereafter had a successful television and stage career. In their act, they purported to be musicians; Amos carried a mandolin on stage and Dave had a violin, but the instruments were never played (although Dave could play guitar). The pair were exceptionally good at comic timing and derived much of their comedy from each other's facial reactions to something the other had just said. Although significant performers in their own right, Dave and Amos wrote for many other comedians, and also played variety bills with some of the great British and American artistes of the twentieth century. They also appeared on television with Swindon's Diana Dors. After retirement the pair continued to live in Swindon.

Davies, (Richard) Rick (b.1944)
The keyboard-playing founder and member of the rock band Supertramp, vocalist and composer of many of its hits, was born at 43 Eastcott Hill, the son of Richard C.H. Davies and his wife Elizabeth (née White). He was educated at Sanford Street School,

and later worked for Square D as a welder before embarking on a musical career. For a couple of years, he shared a flat in London with Swindon artist Ken White and both were great friends with pianist-songwriter 'Gilbert' (Raymond) O'Sullivan from Ireland, who had been brought up in Swindon. Davies and White met at Swindon College of Art where the former, who had already played with the British Rail Staff Association Band, established a group called 'Rick's Blues', which for a while included O'Sullivan. Davies's mother was a hairdresser with her own business, Anne's Hairdressers, an occupation she pursued in Regent Circus until 1979.

Deacon, Thomas Hooper (1836-1915) Deacon was the great horse seller of Swindon. He was born in Faringdon, the son of Cornelius Floyd Deacon and his wife Ann, and lived in Highworth as a young married man with his wife, Jane, and their son. She died in 1866, and two years later, he married twenty-two-year-old Elizabeth Kempster Sainsbury from Poulton. In Swindon, the family lived at 18 Newport Street. In 1871, he and business partner Thomas Edmund Liddiard established the Vale of the White Horse (also known as Messrs Deacon & Liddiard's) Horse & Carriage Repository, opposite the market square. Their premises fronted on to High Street and, between the date of its establishment and 1874, the pair gradually bought up adjacent properties and lands there and in Newport Street, thus extending their facilities. These included stabling for up to 120 horses, standings for 50 carriages, and an adjoining paddock where hunters intended for sale could first be tried over the fences. They principally sold horses from England, Ireland, France, Poland and

Belgium, and held sales of saddlery on Mondays.

By 1875, Deacon and Liddiard's auctions were disposing of more horses in two weeks than had previously changed hands in a year in Swindon under the old open sale system. (These had historically taken place in Devizes Road, which had been called Horsefair.) In the same year, the pair began to diversify at the VWH Repository, firstly into sales of wool from flocks in the neighbourhood (by 1914, some 15,000 fleeces were being sold there at a time). In 1877, fortnightly sales of cattle began at the yard, and, in 1889, monthly sales of cheese. Deacon also had philanthropic, political, sporting, and business interests outside his Repository. He was a committee member of the Victoria Hospital from the time it opened in 1888, and became Mayor of Swindon in 1908. Once again widowed, he lived for several years at Kingshill House, Bath Road, with his two daughters, a grandchild, one servant and a cook; he died at 58 Newport Street and is buried with his second wife at Christ Church.

Deacon's Corn Stores, High Street The landmark, four storey, single bay building to High Street, with a three bay return into Market Square, Old Town, was built early in the 19th century on the site of two cottages. It is still distinguished by the words 'A.W. Deacon's Corn Stores' high on the northern elevation. Its brickwork is Flemish bond; it has stone corner pilasters, and flat, wide string courses. The windows are all square-headed: those to High Street have stone lintels with flat canopies above, and flat sills beneath, all bracketed out; those to Market Place have similar sills, but brick arches to the windows; the eaves have pairs

of modillions. This all has the 'feel' of the agricultural building it was, and it is believed that Wiltshire cheese was made there in the 19th century, in cheese lofts on the second floor. The premises were originally owned by Phillip Pavey, miller of Elcombe Hall, Wroughton, who established there a corn, manure, and agricultural dealership. A.W. Deacon took over the business, and remained there until 1850, when he sold out to John Toomer, who had come to Swindon in 1849 and was already a coal, coke, lime, salt, and hay merchant of Victoria Street, also operating out of a depot at Swindon station. Toomer was a director of the Swindon Central Market Company, who were ultimately responsible for building the corn exchange on the opposite side of Market Square. The building went through several hands, but it was occupied by a corn, seed, and forage merchant until the 1990s. After this various businesses went in at street level, with offices and residential accommodation above.

Deacon's jewellers, Wood Street
By about 1836, George Deacon (1822-1872), the son of a Westbury farmer, was apprenticed to Thomas Howse, a clockmaker with premises in the high street at Marlborough. (The Deacon family have the small, cottage thirteen-hour long-case clock that was George's apprentice piece; it is dated 1838, and signed by him on the back of the dial.) George saved £100, borrowed £600 from his father, and used the money to buy, from the Old Swindon landowning Bradford family, a house in Wood Street, Swindon that was built in 1738. There, in what would become 13 Wood Street, he opened his own business as a clockmaker and watchmaker on 3 March 1848. This was in direct competition to the by then well-established Charles

Haines, also a clockmaker and watchmaker of Wood Street, who continued in business until 1863. Deacon's business prospered and, in 1853, George made the second- best and therefore unsuccessful bid for the Great Western Railway timing contract. However, the London-based contract winner could not cope on his own, so sub-contracted George, who thereafter made numerous clocks for the GWR.

In 1856, George acquired the adjacent premises of 11 Wood Street. Although he was married, he had no children of his own, so, in 1861, he took as apprentices his nephews, Joshua and Hubert. The former eventually set up his own business in The Shambles at Bradford-on-Avon. In 1866, George Deacon made the clock with four-foot-wide illuminated dials for the Corn Exchange, Old Town. It struck the hours on a 2 cwt. bell, and the quarters on two smaller bells.

Hubert John Deacon (1845-1927) successfully bid with his uncle for the timing contract on the Midland & South West Junction Railway, between Andover and Birmingham. Railway timing was then the catalyst for the business, and its lifeblood, with all the timepieces being made in Wood Street. Under Hubert's ownership, the business continued to expand, and in 1881 he was able to buy part of the Rolleston estate, on which he built the 122 terraced houses of Deacon Street. He founded the Swindon Building Society (which became the Stroud & Swindon Building Society), whose early meetings were held on Deacon's premises in Wood Street, enabling the society to loan money to people buying his Deacon Street properties. Hubert had two sons, one of whom died aged four, and eight daughters, who all lived very comfortably on the income from the houses in Deacon Street. Hubert

established a branch of Deacon's in Fleet Street, New Town, selling china and glass. He supplied the clock for the local authority offices in New Town (the town hall) in 1891. Hubert had additional business interests, being chairman of both the Southern Laundry Company, and the Swindon Plate Glass Company.

George Godfrey Deacon (1874-1913), Hubert's son, inherited the business, but had little impact before he died of tuberculosis. His widow Mildred (1883-1938) née Pakeman, of the well-known family of High Street tailors, carried Deacon's through the difficult trading times of the First World War, initially with the help of her father-in-law, who came out of retirement. During this time, she had to re-mortgage the premises three times to keep the business going. The Fleet Street shop was closed down, and Mildred continued to run Deacon's from Wood Street until one of her three children, Henry John ('Jack') Deacon (1905-1988) was old enough to take over. Jack did his apprenticeship at Johnson's of Devizes, and gained experience with Butt & Co. of Chester. He took over Deacon's in time to experience the trading difficulties presented by the Second World War and the depression in its aftermath. In 1958, he was joined by his son Michael.

Michael Henry Deacon (1935-1998) and his father opened a branch in Marlborough, which the latter operated autonomously. Michael, a dedicated horologist who had inherited his great-grandfather's entrepreneurialism, opened branches at Highworth (1971), Wootton Bassett (1974), Faringdon (1976), and Tetbury (1981). The business also bought the former wool shop, next door in Wood Street, and established it as the china and gifts department. Until 1979, limited edition clocks were

manufactured in Wood Street for the American market, under contracts to Cartier in New York, and Neiman Marcus of Dallas. Workshops were built at Wood Street during Michael Deacon's tenure, and subsequently developed by his son as a comprehensive mixture of traditional and state-of-the-art technology.

Richard Deacon (b.1965) took over the company in 1998. In 2002, he re-opened a branch in Marlborough, and a branch was added in Newbury in 2011. The north elevation of Deacon's Wood Street premises is of ashlar limestone, probably a re-building by George Deacon in the mid-1800s. The roof trusses of the early Georgian building are of stripped Scotch pine. The front features bracketed cornices with leaf moulding, and a blind parapet. (See also Aylesbury Dairy building.)

Deacon's Mill A corn mill was built at Swindon Wharf, on the north side of the Wilts & Berks Canal, and most probably by the canal company, at some point between 1805 and 1812. It was known as Deacon's Mill, and was demolished during the 1880s.

Dean, William (1840-1905) In 1855, when Joseph Armstrong was at Wolverhampton, Dean entered his service as an apprentice, becoming his assistant in 1863. Five years later, Armstrong, having by then been appointed to the senior post at Swindon, employed Dean as his chief assistant. It was obvious that when the older man succumbed to a heart attack in 1877, he would be succeeded as Chief Locomotive Engineer by his protégé. Dean was a Justice of the Peace, as were the three men who followed him in succession in charge of the GWR's operations in Swindon. He

designed the 'Duke' and the 'Bulldog' class of locomotives, and retired in 1902.

Dearden, Harold (1882-1962) Born in Rochdale, Harold Dearden attended Rochdale School of Art 1905-10. Following a period at the Royal College of Art, he obtained his ARCA in 1914, was appointed Principal of Swindon Art College in 1920 and remained in that post up to 1950. Until 1929, he lived at 45 Eastcott Road, and thereafter at Fairhaven, 58 Westlecot Road. An excellent draughtsman in ink and wash, he also painted in watercolour and oils. Dearden founded the Swindon Artists' Society in 1934 and was its president, and exhibited widely in London and at provincial galleries. He was also the mentor of Hubert Cook, the railwayman artist, and was instrumental in organising the portrait that Cook painted of William Henry Bickham in his mayoral year. He contributed a number of drawings to *The Swindon Review*. These included '*Youth and Age*' (No.1, 1945), which depicted an old horse standing with some distain above a young one that is rolling about on its back; and a study of three horses – '*Horses*' – in No.2, 1945. In No.4, 1948, there is '*Unloading Cattle*' in which the beasts are being taken from a truck at Swindon's cattle market, against a backdrop of the corn exchange; and his '*Hauling Lobster Pots*' (No.5, 1949) shows two men pulling a pile of these on a cart, with a fishing boat in the background, set against the outline of Penzance. Dearden was a Christadelphian, and also had an international reputation as a writer and dramatist. He is represented in the Swindon Collection by three pieces: *Central Library, Swindon*, completed c.1960, shows the first 'temporary' library huts put up in Regent Circus in the 1950s; *Mevagissey*, painted in

1944, and *Log Cutting* from the following year.

Designer Outlet Village The Swindon railway Works closed down in 1986. The following year, Tarmac bought part of the site, and within six months had announced its plans to develop an ambitious residential, commercial, and industrial complex there. In 1996, work began to convert part of the site into a retail shopping mall. It took 300 construction workers just over a year to complete the project, and cost £40 million. The walls of the Grade II listed former industrial buildings were constructed of bricks, made on site in the 19th century by the GWR Company from clay obtained six to eight feet beneath the ground on which they actually stand. The shopping mall conversion included the original wagon paint shop of 1846; the former boiler shop and tender shop of 1876; the brass foundry; and shops, mainly of the 1870s, that were associated with the coppersmiths, toolmakers, brass finishers, machinists, and tank makers; also the pattern makers' shop of 1924. The McArthur Glen Designer Village was opened on 13 March 1997 by Lord Inglewood, Parliamentary under-Secretary of State for the Department of National Heritage; the United States' Ambassador, Admiral William Crowe; and Swindon's Labour Leader of the Thamesdown Council, Cllr Sue Bates. The mall incorporated more than one hundred top-named stores, and was then Europe's largest covered outlet centre.

Devizes Road In the latter years of the 18th century, and during the early years of the 19th century, a sale of horses was held in the lane that led off the Old Town hill towards Wroughton. This lane was flanked by hawthorn bushes, and these defined the point at which the horses stood, facing the foliage, with their back legs in the road. Thereby, the sales took place at 'short hedge', sometimes contracted to 'shortedge'. The track continued in a northwards direction (more or less along the line of the present-day Devizes Road), eventually meeting one that ran down the western side of the hill towards Kings Hill. Around this intersection in the early years of the 19th century were a few cottages associated with quarry workers. The section that ran over the hill was called 'horsefair' or 'horsefair street' because it gave direct access to the horse sales at short hedge. These names remained in common usage until c.1853, by which time the police house had been built (c.1840), and a few cottages had appeared along its length (one included Thomas Greenaway's blacksmith's forge). Devizes Road was built up very slowly. Sarah Tuck, a lady of independent means, had a house there by 1848, and one of the cottages was home to carpenter Thomas Weeks. Thomas Rose, a Swindon builder, leased a plot of land at Short Hedge for the purpose of developing it residentially, and this resulted in Bath Buildings and Bath Cottages.

Of the mid-19th-century residencies extant in Devizes Road, two pairs of semi-detached properties are interesting. One pair comprises Frampton Villa and Albion Villa, now both in commercial use, made of squared ashlar blocks, each of two storeys and two bays, with hipped roof and attic. The bay windows have a cornice. The property was made to look as one by placing the doorways centrally next to each other and running a single hood on scroll brackets across both. In the 1870s, Frampton Villa was the home of William Edwin Morris, eldest son of the

founder of the *Swindon Advertiser*, who worked with his father and later became surveyor to the Old Swindon Local Board and the New Swindon Local Board. At the same time, Albion Villas belonged to Charles L. Bowley, the wine and spirit merchant.

Next door are Clarendon House and Belmont House, the former now with a shop front at street level. It is another aspirational property meant to be viewed as a whole, when it presents three storeys with cellar, of four bays to the ground and second floors and three bays in between. The second floor has four segmental-headed windows; there are triple round-headed lights to the first floor with hood mouldings on acanthus leaf brackets, and here the large central window has been blocked to admit the boundary wall between the two properties. There is a plain dentil moulding between the first and second storeys, with a plain cornice above. The doorways have plain lunettes. A church and Bible Institute was built in Devizes Road in 1923. (See also Britannia, and Canford House.)

Domesday, Medieval, and Later Manors In 1086, Swindon measured 21¾ hides, divided into five holdings. Odin the Chamberlain had, at 12 hides, the largest portion and this eventually formed the nucleus of the medieval manor of High Swindon. This was held by the de Valence family in the 13th century, and it was William de Valence who apparently established the place as a market town. Ulric had a smaller portion at Domesday, whose 2-hide estate most probably became the medieval manor of West Swindon, and accords today with Old Town. In the 16th century, these two Domesday holdings were joined, becoming Over and Nether Swindon or West and

East Swindon. At Domesday, too, Ulward had a small holding, and Alvred (Alfred) of Marlborough had 1½ hides. Odo, Bishop of Bayeux, Earl of Kent, and half-brother to King William had 5 hides, later to become Nethercott and, in the 1400s, to be split into Eastcott and Westcott. Eastcott was acquired by the Vilett family early in the 1700s, and by the Goddards later in the same century. In the early medieval period, there were also manors at Even Swindon and Broome; when they were established is not known, but they were eventually incorporated, with Walcot, into Nethercott.

Dore, William (1812-1877) For more than eighty years, the livestock and commodity markets in Swindon were dominated by the same family. In about 1780, a carrier named William Dore became an auctioneer, selling cattle in High Street. He also established a printing company in the town, mainly to produce his own auction bills, catalogues and posters. In 1795, his son, also William Dore, a maltster, similarly began to run sales of cattle. This William's brother, Alfred Rogers Dore, was put in charge of the family printing business. William's son, yet another William Dore, entered the business as carrier and auctioneer in the late 1820s, when the firm was named William Dore & Son. It is the son of this title who was to change the face of the town's livestock sales.

William Dore (the third) sold anything vaguely agricultural: beasts of all kinds, lands, and even rights to keep the streets clean of excrement came under his hammer. He established sale yards around Old Town and, after the railway was established, in New Town as well. In 1871, he bought the land in Marlborough Road that effectively became Swindon's famous cattle market, and

there built sufficient pens for 1,500 sheep, 200 head of cattle, and up to 500 pigs. It opened with great ceremony in 1873, during which the local vicar presented William Dore with a solid gold hammer. The market's increasing success gradually eclipsed the sales that had traditionally been held on certain roadways about the old town.

Dore's firm expanded without him, but kept the name of its founder. William died just after he had engaged Henry Smith as a partner. Smith took on William Radway; the firm of Dore (posthumous), Smith & Radway was born. Later, it became Dore, Radway & Titmas; by the turn of the century, it was Dore, Fielder & Matthews; the originator's name continued in the title until 1914, thirty-seven years after his death. The family printing business was acquired, in 1877, by Robert Astill, who had published his annual *Swindon Almanack* since 1863. His premises, which were on the corner of Victoria Road and Bath Road, were demolished in 1904 to facilitate road widening needed for the new tram service.

Dors, Diana (1931-1984) Diana Mary Fluck was born at the Haven Nursing Home in Kent Road, Swindon. Her parents, who married in 1918, lived at 210 Marlborough Road. Her mother's name was Winifred Maud Mary (née Payne, later Padget), and her father, Albert Edward Sidney Fluck, worked in the offices of the Great Western Railway's works and was sometime also a part-time pianist in the orchestra at the Empire Theatre. Diana took her grandmother's maiden name and appeared, aged fifteen, in the film *The Shop at Sly Corner*, after which her suggestive style of preening and pouting glamour was much favoured in such as *Dancing with Crime, Good-time Girl, Holiday Camp,* and *A Boy, a Girl, and a Bike.* Her early career as a celluloid sex symbol mirrored a personal life that was to a degree orchestrated by her ambitious mother. Men who wished to date her had to apply to Mrs Fluck, who wrote their details into a note book.

The Flucks, mother and daughter, accompanied each other to wartime dances in Swindon and district, and Diana achieved considerable notoriety for the manner and execution of her jive, and for her stamina. In later years, she was to portray blowsy females, and was latterly given a number of character parts, in which she excelled. Diana was included on Peter Blake's cover for the Beatles' 1968 album *Sgt. Pepper's Lonely Hearts Club Band.* In 1981, she appeared in the video for 'Prince Charming', a chart-topping pop song by Adam and the Ants. Diana famously disliked the town of her birth. Because of this, production was temporarily halted on a mural by Ken White that included her likeness, whilst councillors argued over whether she should be included on the wall of a walkway leading to the lower arcade in Swindon's Brunel Shopping Centre. A bronze bust of a young Diana Dors, by sculptor Enid Mitchell, was bought for the Wyvern Theatre in 1989; in 1991, John Clinch's full-length statue of the actress at her most celluloid seductive was unveiled outside a multi-screen cinema at Shaw Ridge.

Dunsford, Henry Lyde (1823-1891) and **Dunsford, William Besley (1798-1845)** These two men, son and father respectively, were both born in Swindon, where they became carriers on the Wilts & Berks Canal, principally importing slate, coal and stone, and exporting Swindon

stone and gravel from the quarries in Old Town, some leaving the town by the North Wilts Canal. W.B. Dunsford established a coal yard at Swindon Wharf, which was later used by other local coal dealers, and lived in the nearby Wharf House, which the canal company built for its senior manager in the area. In 1817, he married Elizabeth Lyde, and he subsequently became Superintendent of the Wilts & Berks Canal at Swindon. Canal records show that he brought coal into Swindon from the Forest of Dean, as well as from coalfields in Staffordshire and other Midlands areas.

H.L. Dunsford took up civil engineering but also assisted in his father's business from the age of twelve. After William's death, Henry succeeded him in the position of Superintendent. In 1847, he married Susanna Baden Choules (b.1825) from Badbury, and the couple had five children before she died in 1867. By then, Henry had long been designated Superintendent of the Wilts & Berks Canal Company, and in this capacity became a well-respected businessman in the town, and an advisor to several of the undertakings of the day. He was a particular thorn in the side of the Great Western Railway Company, whom he accused of polluting the canal, and of the two Local Boards, demanding that they clean out the sewage that was continually flowing into the water. His wife died in 1867, and in 1869 he married Elizabeth Plummer (b. 1815) from Great Somerford. The couple retired to Axbridge, Somerset, where they lived with two servants. Henry died in 1891, and Elizabeth in 1911, at the age of ninety-six.

Eastcott The hamlet of Eastcott was situated about a mile and a half to the north-west of the town on the hill. It has been identified with Nether Swindon, one of the manors at Domesday. It was called Estcote in 1276; in 1366, it was Eastcote; and there are many references to leases and land transactions associated with Eastcott Down, Marsh, or Mead, in manorial documents after the manor passed to the Goddard family. It was 'Eastcott or Estcot' on Andrews' & Dury's map of Wiltshire 1773. Eastcott was made up of farms and associated clusters of cottages. Upper Eastcott Farm stood approximately where Regent Circus does now; Lower Eastcott Farm was north of it; and the hamlet of Eastcott was around the present-day Corporation Street area. Most of these had been taken over by the emerging new town of Swindon by the 1850s.

Prior to that, the hamlet of Eastcott stood among a number of trackways. One of these connected it directly with Swindon on the hill, and from c.1841, when it was built, the canalside and track-side Golden Lion public house was designated as Eastcott. This track led away to the south-west of the settlement and then ascended the hill to a point where it joined the road running to the west out of Old Town, towards Kingshill, as it was then spelt. There were only isolated dwellings beside this track, and small groups of cottages at intervals, and it became known as Eastcott Lane.

Among the traders listed here in the 1840s were George Bishop, beer retailer and cowkeeper; William Smith, beer retailer and carpenter; and beer retailer John Page. Henry Tarrant the builder lived at Eastcott; Charles Sharp had his chandler's shop there; and other occupants included Henry Baker the tailor; horse and cattle dealer Thomas Cooker, baker John Cullern, James Morgan the bootmaker, and grocer George Selby. At one time, this lane may have been developed

as the main thoroughfare between New Swindon and the old town, and certainly a rather tortuous route had begun to be built up along its path by 1850. During the 1850s, Eastcott Hill was terraced on both sides, almost up to present-day Crombey Street.

The thoroughfare was officially named Eastcott Road in 1891 (and is also called Eastcott Hill). The main business associated with Eastcott Road in the 19th century was William Affleck's Prospect Works, where he made agricultural implements and machinery. Hereabouts, too, was the conservatively Italianate police station of 1873, which remained operative for a century. The name also continued in Eastcott Terrace, built at the Regent Circus end of Princes Street, but now demolished.

Edwards, William Vaughan (1822-1884) His is the story of a blacksmith who diversified at an early age, and made good. Born in Brecon, and living in Prospect Place, Swindon by the mid-1840s, Edwards had aspired to being a blacksmith and ironmonger in Wood Street by 1848, where the company was named Edwards & Thompson. It advertised itself as 'wholesale, retail and general furnishing, bar iron and glass merchants'. Edwards was a Methodist, and lived alone with a servant. By 1851, he had a full-blown ironmongery business and was employing twelve males as apprentice smiths. In 1852, he became a director of the Swindon Market Company, and married Jemima Wansbrough (b.1821) in Bristol, her home town. Soon afterwards, the couple settled for a while at Beaufort Cottages, Walcot, in Bath. By 1871, they were back at 2 Prospect, Swindon, and Edwards leased land at the quarries, described as having 'a powder magazine' standing on it, from the lord of the manor. The firm of Edwards & Thompson was by then employing nineteen men and four boys. The couple had no issue and continued to live with one servant, later relocating to Gloucester Villas, Old Town. When Edwards died, his estate was valued at just over £5,500. Jemima went back to Bristol, where she died in 1899.

Electra Palace This cinema opened in 1914 in Gorse Hill. It had 860 seats and gave a discount on the seat price to anyone who proved – by showing their tram ticket – that they had travelled some distance to see the film. The cinema was well known locally for its Saturday afternoon 'two-penny rush' performances of cartoons, westerns, and blood-and-thunder serials aimed at children. It became known as 'The Palace'. The cinema closed in the 1960s and became a motor cycle retailer, then a Mecca Bingo Hall, which closed in 1998. The building was demolished in 2003 to make way for the Thomas Edward Coard Building, residential apartments and retail shops.

Electricity in Swindon Electricity came to Swindon under the Swindon New Town Electric Lighting Order, 1895. The local authority bought Lower Eastcott Farm, with a view to establishing its electricity generating station on the site, and engaged the services of electrical consultants Lacey, Clirehugh & Sillar of Westminster, London, who advised on the electrification of tramways. They were the architects, and Swindon's A.J Colbourne was awarded the building contract. The electricity works opened in 1903, proving to be an austere structure with a 150-foot landmark chimney and a cooling tower (which would later be relocated to Moredon). The initial plant comprised three Lancashire

boilers, and three 200 kW direct current dynamos driven by reciprocating engines. These were added to in 1908 and, in 1913, were further augmented by a steam turbine driven 500 kW direct current generator. The GWR produced its own electricity on its Works site until 1925, when the company agreed to take it from the local authority's source. Buildings and plant on the original site continued to increase to capacity, and the electricity commissioners agreed in 1926 that a new power station could be built at Moredon. This was designed by consulting engineers Preece, Cardew & Rider. The location took advantage of its proximity to the Midland & South West Junction railway, and access for services afforded by the line of the disused North Wilts Canal. The power station opened in 1929, when it also sold its product to the Wessex Electricity Supply Company for use in the wider area. The station came under the control of the Central Electricity Board in 1935, was extended in 1942, and remained in use until 1972. Much of the property was demolished in 1979, and the area was redeveloped as residential. The original electricity works in Corporation Street were vacated by Southern Electricity in 1978, when they became solely the Swindon Corporation bus depot. They were substantially demolished in 2006. (See also Art Deco; and Tramways)

Emlyn Square Between 1842 and 1849, buildings were erected on the west and east sides of an open space at the centre of the developing, symmetrical railway village in New Swindon. The open space was a large rectangle of grass, planted with trees and railed off; the adjacent buildings were put up specifically for trade, and as the area was conceived as the High Street, it was

so named. In 1855, part of this open space was given up to the Mechanics' Institute, opened that year, and the octagonal covered market adjacent, which followed almost immediately. A much smaller area, also railed off, was then made on the north side of the Institute building. Some eight new shops, and public houses, were established on either side of the Institute and market, and some of the old town businesses took the opportunity to open branches in the new high street, to serve the railway families. Here, in the early days, were James Copeland, butcher; Edward Frankis and his Railway Dining and Coffee Rooms; J. H. Mason, grocer and tea dealer; Richard Philpott Perris, baker; James Praed, hairdresser; James Trego, chemist and druggist, who shared, with the Post Office, the corner with London Street; William Warner, linen draper; and Edmund Webb, grocer.

The area of High Street immediately to the south of the Mechanics' Institute and the octagonal market gradually became the location for travelling vendors, livestock sales, cheapjacks, and quack doctors. For a while, it became known as Market Square. High Street, New Swindon was renamed Emlyn Square in 1901, in recognition of Frederick Archibald Vaughan Campbell (1847-1911), Viscount Emlyn, and later 4th Earl Cawdor, who was Chairman of the GWR Board 1895-1905.

Empire Cinema Immediately the Regent opened in 1929, the management of the Empire Theatre realised that the theatre was in trouble. There had been a sustained fall-off of audiences, although the live performances had been of good quality, whilst cinema audiences were dramatically increasing. At the end of 1930, the lease of the theatre

was taken over by Swindon Entertainments Limited, who immediately converted the building into a cinema, named it 'The Empire Perfect Talkie Theatre', and opened on 26 January 1931 with a showing of *All Quiet on the Western Front*. It then remained a cinema for the next sixteen years, except for the occasional amateur production, some combined film and live show offerings, pantomimes and some Sunday concerts, with the exception of 1937, when it reverted to live shows for most of that year. Afterwards, it was re-launched as a 'Super Cinema', and continued as such until 1947, when it once again became a live performance venue. It closed in 1955, and was demolished four years later. (See Empire Theatre.)

Empire Theatre Architects R. Milverton Drake and John M. Pizey of Baldwin Street, Bristol, designed the 1,600-seat theatre that was built on the corner of Victoria Road and Groundwell Road, Swindon 1897-98, at a cost of £10,000. They described the exterior as being in 'a free Renaissance style', and said that the interior 'pursued the Italian Renaissance that had a very chaste and pleasing effect'. The work was carried out for Ernest Carpenter, designated 'proprietor and manager', who was also proprietor of the Old Theatre Royal, King Street, Bristol; the builder was Charles Williams of Regent Street, Swindon. It took just thirty weeks to build on the 10,350 square-foot, corner site, in red brick with cream freestone dressings, flat string courses, and pediments. The building featured corner turrets, pinnacles, drop pediments, and a large central pediment with columns above the main entrance. It was a very imposing building, indeed.

The intention was to erect an architecturally inspirational property, com-mensurate with the aspirations for the developing Swindon, and one that would underline the trend set a few years earlier with the New Swindon town hall. Both were on prominent sites. A steel roof was put over the theatre's auditorium, over a domed and richly plastered ceiling some forty feet in diameter above the grand circle. The interior was picked out in cream and gold, and the soft furnishings were in old gold and blue, and comprised stalls, dress circle, and upper circle, above which were a few rows of seats known as 'the gods'. There were bars on each level; twelve doors, which all opened outwards, provided entry and exit from the building; nine led from the auditorium, and three from the stage area close to the dressing rooms on either side. The stage was fifty-five feet wide and thirty-five feet deep, with a proscenium opening of twenty-nine feet by twenty-six feet. It was famed for its succession of attractive safety curtains, packed with advertisements.

On the day it opened, 7 February 1898, the Swindon theatre was called The New Queen's. Jack Gladwin was the 'acting manager', soon to be replaced by Claude Jullion. The inaugural performance was of Dick Wittington, an extravaganza by George Phillips and his performers, which had 'a powerful company of over forty people', including what were described as 'star artistes' by way of acrobats, dancers, etc. The first night audience would have been relieved to know that 'all available precautions have been taken against panic or the results of panic'. This included a curtain of water that could 'be utilised at a moment's notice' between the proscenium and the audience, in case of fire. In 1906, the theatre's name was changed to The Empire.

In 1931, The Empire became a cinema and thus it remained for the next eighteen

years, the only stage show during this period being the annual pantomime. In 1947, it reverted to live variety shows, musical and theatrical performances, and pantomimes, and continued in this way until 24 January, 1955, when the pantomime Robinson Crusoe was called off mid-run over a wages dispute. Aladdin, the pantomime that should have followed it, stayed away for the same reason, and the theatre did not re-open. The last manager was W.S. Bobby. The theatre was demolished in 1959, to be replaced in 1960 by Empire House, a characterless block of offices and shops.

Empire Theatre Artistes The Empire Theatre was generally on the 'B' circuit for provincial theatres, but nonetheless did attract some top-flight performers of the day. These were almost exclusively booked through the Bernard Delfont agency in London. Some top-of-the-bill variety acts (with their catch phrases or epithets) who appeared there when at the height of their popularity in the 1940s and 1950s included:

Max Bacon, comedian 'Radio's heavyweight champion of humour'
Ivy Benson and her All-girl Band 'Radio's orchestra of charm'
Issy Bonn, comedian 'Oh! Get in there, Morton'
Peter Brough, ventriloquist, and Archie Andrews, doll
Peter Cavanagh, impressionist 'The voice of them all'
Leon Cortez, comedian 'Don't be higgerent'
Sam Costa, comedian 'Was there something?'
Billy Cotton and his Band 'Wakey Wakey!'
Phyllis Dixey, erotic dancer. 'Peek-a-boo'
Percy Edwards, impressionist 'The ace mimic'

George Formby, ukulele entertainer 'Turned out nice again'
Nat Gonella and his Georgians
Henry Hall & his Band 'Here's to the next time'
Frankie Howerd, comedian 'Ooo, missus'
Allan Jones, Hollywood singing star
Hetty King, male impersonator 'England's finest'
Primo Scala and his Accordian Band
Turner Layton, entertainer 'My piano and me'
Vera Lynn, singer 'The forces sweetheart'
Marie Lloyd Jnr, singer
Felix Mendelssohn and his Hawaiian Serenaders
Max Miller, comedian 'There'll never be another'
Sid Millward and his Nitwits, comedy band
Richard Murdoch, comedian 'Much Binding in the Marsh'
Tessie O'Shea, banjo comedienne 'Ten ton Tessie'
Vic Oliver, comedian
Sandy Powell, comedian 'Can you hear me, mother?'
Martha Raye, Hollywood film comedienne
Old Mother Riley (Arthur Lucan) and Kitty McShane
Derek Roy, comedian
Tommy Trinder, comedian 'You lucky people!'
Troise and his Mandoliers, band
Elsie & Doris Walters, entertainers
Wilson, Keppel & Betty, sand dancers
Rob Wilton, comedy character actor 'Mr Muddlecombe'
Norman Wisdom, comedian
Wee Georgie Wood, comedian
Arthur Worsley, ventriloquist 'The peerless ventriloquist'

Empire Theatre Orchestra The first musical director of the pit orchestra at the Empire Theatre was always referred to in print as 'Herr Klee'. In the 1860s, genuine German bands were popular in England, and it was then that the musical Klee family brought their Rhine brass and string band twice each year to Malvern, where they played in the Winter Gardens. Some of them settled in the Worcestershire town and married there; and it was at Malvern in 1867 that Konrad Klee (the Empire's Herr Klee) was born. His parents, Conrad Klee and Elisabeth (née Reichwein), were both German.

Conrad was one of several musical brothers; Hubert and Joseph both studied at music college, and the latter, one-time organist at Durham Cathedral, lived in Swindon at the same time as Conrad, at 3 North Street, where he practised as a teacher and professor of music. Conrad Klee lived at 38 Kent Road; he was a violin player, and his employment at the Empire Theatre often required him to take to the stage and give solo performances. He later ran the Opera House, Leicester.

Klee's successor was John J. Gale, a native of Swindon, born 1873, and living at 48 Victoria Road, where he was a self-employed teacher and professor of music. He left in 1904, and was replaced by a 'Mr Monk'. The pit orchestra at the time was a twelve-man ensemble, in which Monk played the piano; it included a double bass, two cellos, two violins, a trombone, two clarinets, a saxophone, a trumpet, and a percussionist. Monk's successor, the following year, was Fred H. Lucas. He was followed in 1914 by Fred Stone, and the baton was taken over in 1920 by Oswald Bentley, the Dewsbury, Yorkshire-born son of a carpet weaver, who had been pianist and conductor of the theatre

at Stockton-on-Tees since 1904. He remained in charge at Swindon until 1924.

When the Empire Theatre became a cinema in 1931, the members of the orchestra were dismissed. Its leader at the time was Thomas Coxon, known as 'Tim', who had relocated from Hartlepool to join the Empire's orchestra as leader, pianist and violin player in 1924. Seven years later, he contemplated forming a dance band with his musical colleagues whose employment had been lost at the Empire, but this came to nothing because most of them also had full-time day jobs. Coxon found work as a motor mechanic in the Durham Street workshop of the nearby Victoria Garage. He was renowned for being little affected by electrical currents, and was consequently much in demand as a human circuit maker when work colleagues wanted to ascertain whether wires were live. Another member of the Empire Theatre orchestra who worked by day at the Victoria Garage was John Walker, known as 'Jock', who played saxophones and clarinet, lived at Pinehurst, and kept tropical fish. He had played with most of the Swindon bands between the 1920s and the 1940s.

The Empire continued as a cinema from 1931 until 1947, except for 1937 when, for that year only, it reverted to presenting live stage shows. An orchestra was formed under the leadership of Ivan Barry. It included Tim Coxon, and was frequently presented on stage as Ivan Barry and his Empire Melody Makers.

From 1947, when the Empire resumed as a variety theatre, its pit orchestra was under the musical direction of Albert Dunlop, who was noted for always appearing in full evening dress. During his tenure of the baton, the pit orchestra often appeared on the stage of the Empire as 'Albert Dunlop and his

Gang of Muscle-Bound Musical Athletes'. Dunlop lived as a long-term lodger with Kate Brittain, a theatrical landlady in Islington Street in whose digs stayed a good many of the lesser artistes who played the Empire. Late of the Royal Scots Greys, Dunlop was a very handsome man.

Between 1949 and 1952, the musical director of the twelve-strong pit musicians was again Tim Coxon, who had re-joined the orchestra in 1947 but also kept on his day job at the Victoria Garage. In 1949, he arranged for his brother-in-law, George Lax, to join the Empire's orchestra; Lax had hitherto been playing clarinet and saxophone at the Hippodrome, Darlington. Also from the late 1940s, the Empire pit orchestra included clarinet and saxophone player Charlie Comley, who sometimes deputised for Tim Coxon. As a young man, Comley had played with Swindon's John Prosser and his Rhythmic Revels, at one time ran his own band, and during the 1940s had gone on to become part of the Johnnie Styles Band, which had won many awards. He was also a retailer of musical instruments whose shop, when he joined the Empire Theatre, was just a few yards away in Victoria Road. Comley formally took over the baton in 1952 and remained the musical director until the theatre closed in 1955, his orchestra frequently taking to the stage during the intervals. After the Empire closed, Comley moved his shop to Havelock Street and was the musical director for shows such as *The Quaker Girl*, *Carmen*, *The Merry Widow*, and *Showboat*, all staged at the Playhouse.

Evening Advertiser see Swindon Advertiser

Fairholm see Wharf House

Fairy Castle Mural This gable-end mural, which no longer exists, can best be described as Bavarian castle meets Walt Disney. This was an initiative by Thamesdown Community Arts, painted in Westcott Place in 1976 by youngsters on a job creation scheme, and some volunteers who were not. It showed a chalet cottage, nestling beneath the wooded slopes of a rocky outcrop, on top of which stood a monastery-like building comprising elements of medieval and Moorish.

Falcon Inn, Westcott Place Built of stone c.1849 as part of the Falcon Terrace development, the public house is distinguished in the block by its pediment, and the square bow windows flanking the entrance at street level. Elizabeth Harrill was keeper of The Falcon by 1861, and was soon afterwards followed by Robert Wattleworth, a railway labourer from the Isle of Man, who had previously been lodging in nearby Westcott Place. He gave board at The Falcon to Edward Bell and Charles Priest, chairmakers. The premises were extended in 1869, and altered internally in 1896. The hostelry closed in 2010, and two years later was sold for redevelopment as residential apartments.

Falcon Terrace, Westcott Place This run, initially of eight dwellings and a public house, was erected c.1849 to the west of the railway village. It was one of the first private, speculative developments intended to accommodate the growing GWR workforce, and was allegedly built by the Wilts & Berks Canal Company. The two-storey terrace is of rough Swindon stone with Bath stone dressings, and has, at its centre, The Falcon inn.

The cottages are as attractive as their counterparts in the railway village. Certainly, the earliest known residents seem to have been railway labourers, particularly working in the iron works there, and other Works' employees, such as factory machinists, engine smiths, and carpenters. Each of the cottages was home, variously, to more than one family, several generations of the same family, or else the occupying family also had boarders living with them.

By the 1870s, the name Falcon Terrace had also been applied to further properties that flanked the original cottages, and then numbered 1-27, in one of which lived railway machine man James Harding, with his wife and ten children. There were still GWR workers in the street: notably, striker Henry Summers, whose premises must have been as short of space as were Harding's, for he lived with his wife, seven children, and four lodgers – one of whom was a female seamstress. By this time, Falcon Terrace was no longer occupied solely by railway workers; William Ford the baker lived there; bookmaker Edwin Davis was in residence; the butchers William and Thomas Chapman were there with their widowed mother and their butcher's apprentice; and it was home to plasterer John Spakeman.

Famous Swindonians Mural In 1979, Ken White (with help from some Swindon College students) completed his 'shop front' mural on the end of Union Street, Prospect Place in Old Town, and there it stayed until 1991. The shop front was that of J.H. Jones, umbrella manufacturer, and either peering from its windows or arranged in front of it were: Alf Bown, former mayor; Bruce the Collecting Dog; Isambard Kingdom Brunel, the founder of modern Swindon

through the railway Works; Rick Davies, pop artist; Diana Dors, actress; Harold Fleming, footballer; John Francome, jockey; Justin Hayward, pop star; Richard Jefferies, writer; David Murray John, former town clerk; Desmond Morris, anthropologist, artist and author; William Morris, founder of the *Swindon Advertiser*; Gilbert O'Sullivan, singer songwriter; 'Raggy' Powell, philanthropic rag and bone dealer; Don Rogers, footballer; Alfred Williams, the hammerman poet; and XTC, pop group depicting Barry Andrews, Terry Chambers, Dave Gregory, Colin Moulding and Andy Partridge. Latterly, the wall suffered badly from damp, so the mural had to be sacrificed in order to carry out necessary repairs to the brickwork on which it was painted.

Faringdon Road Park see Park, The

Filtness's Publicity Handout An insight into mid-19th-century everyday living may be had by reading the exhaustive and exhausting catalogue in rhyme, provided in the publicity hand-out that S. Filtness (later Mary E. Filtness), a general dealer of 40 Newport Street, Swindon published in 1840.

Where all may be furnished with goods of the best
Of various articles herein expressed:
Namely, brushes of all sorts, for wet and dry rubbing,
Soft brushes for toilet, and hard ones for scrubbing;
Paint brushes, tooth brushes, hearth brushes, and brooms,
With mops of the best yarns for scrubbing of rooms.
Shoe brushes, horse brushes, curry combs

and tin tacks,
Note paper, envelopes, and good sealing wax.
Smelling bottles, pins for the hair, and bed sacking,
Bread trays, tea trays, glue, and fine japan blacking.
Looking glasses, skimmers, cedar pencils round and square,
And all sorts of glass, china and crockery ware.
Scuttles for coals, or cinders, or ashes,
Hair powder, chalk lines, and pulleys for sashes.
Great choice of nick-nacks, combs, ivory and bone,
The very best mouse traps that ever were known.
Pins papered and loose, hooks and eyes, and carpenters flaskets,
American clocks, nutmeg graters, and fancy baskets.
Fine razors and knives, and razor strops neat,
Pens, penholders, and shaving boxes complete.
Warming pans, handles, and handles for mops,
Hand bowls, copper kettles, and watering pots;
American tubs, fenders, frying pans and pails,
Coffin furniture, lace, white and black nails,
Rummers, tumblers, and cruets for mustard,
Glass cups, china cups, and cups for custard.
Saws, chisels, brad-awls, and hatchets,
Scissors, paper knives, and black lead in packets.
Cotton purses, silk purses, and purses of leather,
Umbrellas to keep out the tempestuous weather.
Braces, belts, fancy pins, and studs for shirts,
French clogs, plain clogs, and pattens to keep

from the dirt.
Tin cups, tin kettles, and coffee cans.
Boilers, saucepans. Door mats, and dripping pans.
Tea caddies, work boxes, and cinder riddles,
Writing desks, jews-harp, whistles and fiddles.
Table knives, carving knives, of the very best steel,
Tapes, ball cotton, and cotton on reel,
Shoe makers knives, rasps, an assortment of rules,
Italian irons, flat irons, and carpenters tools.
Pictures in gilt and plain frame,
And various articles too numerous to name.
To enumerate all that's sold by this general trader
Would exhaust all the patience of writer and reader,
He invites all his friends to visit his store,
Assured they'll be pleased, and a great deal more,
For the goods are so cheap and gain such renown,
There ne'er was before known the like in this town.

Fire Services By the 1850s, Old Swindon's manual fire engine was housed in a Newport Street lock-up. The keys were kept at the police station in Devizes Road, and at the premises of William Read the town's surveyor, in Wood Street. The engine was a horse-drawn Shand-Mason (this London company began in 1774) made of wood, painted in red, and hung with hose and buckets. The Old Swindon Local Board augmented this contraption in 1869 when it bought four lengths of hose and entered into an arrangement with the Swindon Water Company for the emergency use of water, piped from its supply at Wroughton as

necessary, in the case of fire. The fire engine was also available for use outside the parish, on payment of a fee. Persons requiring its services were required to apply to Mr Read, or to Supt. Henry Haynes at the Old Town police station in Devizes Road.

In c.1868, the GWR acquired for its own use in the Works one of the Shand-Mason steam fire engines. Once the fire had been lit, steam could be achieved from cold water in upwards of six minutes, and the machine could pump 300 gallons of water per minute. It was immediately pressed into service, extinguishing fires around New Swindon. By the early 1870s, the GWR Works also had about its premises, some two dozen large fire extinguishers and as many water hydrants.

The eight-man Swindon Volunteer Fire Brigade was formed under Capt. W.E. Morris (son of *Swindon Advertiser* editor William Morris) in 1879, and the old town fire engine was relocated to its new 'fire engine house' at an entrance to the quarries, off Bath Road. (Victoria Road had also been suggested for the site, but this was not taken up.) The public were advised, should they spot a fire, to go round to the house of the secretary of the Swindon Volunteer Fire Brigade, or to that of any of its members (at each of which residencies was kept a key to the fire engine house), and report the matter! The public spirited Robert Astill, writing in his *Swindon Directory* of 1882, suggested that: 'Lists of the members should be placed in the bar of every hotel and public house in Swindon; and it would also be convenient if a small board was placed upon the house of each member intimating that a member resides there.'

In anticipation of the two towns amalgamating, the Swindon Fire Brigade was officially created in 1899, and sites were acquired for new fire stations in Lansdown Road and Cromwell Street. The latter was built in 1901, and housed a Shand-Mason double vertical steam fire engine that had been bought the previous year, a fire escape, and a hose cart. The old manual fire engine, a hose cart, and a large fire escape were kept in the Lansdown Road fire station. The brigade also had an official horse keeper, and an arrangement with the Great Western Hotel, opposite Swindon railway station, to use its horses when necessary. When the Borough of Swindon was formed in 1900, the fire service became the Swindon Corporation Fire Brigade.

Coverage of the town continued slowly. A fire hose box was put up in the Swindon cattle market, Old Town, in 1903. By 1907, there was also a hose cart at the fire depot in Chapel Street, Gorse Hill and the similar establishment in Charles Street, Rodbourne. The Market Square had recently acquired a fire box containing a stand pipe and a hose; and a hose cart and fire escape were kept at the rear of the town hall, Regent Circus. It had originally been intended to incorporate a fire station into the rear of the town hall when it was built 1890-91. In 1908, a hose box was put in at 99 Victoria Road. Hose boxes were installed at the Technical College in Victoria Road in 1914. The GWR bought a Dennis fire engine in 1912, which was housed in a shed on the corner of Church Place and Bristol Street, and was kept in service until 1942. A siren was installed beside the Corporation Electricity Works in Corporation Street in 1918 and used to call the brigade if needed during the daytime. In the same year, the Lansdown Road fire station was taken down, and Cromwell Street was, for the first time, continuously staffed by one day-time and one night-time employee. In 1920, the service

was extended by means of a series of fire-call bells between the town hall and the houses of the brigade. At the same time, the GWR bought a 400-gallon Dennis motor turbine fire engine.

Skurray's garage sold two Dennis pump escapes to the fire service in 1923. Over the years, the Swindon Corporation Fire Brigade continued to acquire vehicles and equipment. By 1941, when the fire service was nationalised, there were already plans in development to remove the Swindon borough brigade from Cromwell Street to a site in Drove Road. This was not realised until 1959, when the Drove Road fire station opened on 14 October. The Cromwell Street fire station stood empty for some time, and was pulled down in 1968.

Fleming, Harold (1887-1955) The only footballer ever to play for his country whilst playing for Swindon Town, Fleming was born at Duck Lane Cottage, Downton, near Salisbury, the son of butcher Frederick Henry Fleming and his wife Jane. When he was a small boy, the family moved to Market Street, Swindon, where his father had a shop. Harold attended Sanford Street school, and played football for the St Mark's church team. Although he considered a career in the church, he was eventually employed in the GWR Works. He joined the town's (then non-league) football club in 1907, then managed by Sam Allen, and helped its entry into the football league in 1920 as a founder member of Division Three. He remained with the club until 1924. Throughout his career, he would not play football on Good Friday or other Christian religious festivals. He married Grace Haskins. At Swindon, he played inside right, was a prolific goal scorer, and was capped for England nine times

between 1909 and 1914. During the First World War, Fleming was a PE instructor. After he retired from active participation in the game, he opened a football boot factory, and established a sports shop that bore his name in Regent Circus. The local sculptor, Carleton Attwood, made a statue of the former football star, which was erected inside the main entrance to the County Ground. Fleming Way in Swindon was named after him.

Flying Pigs Mural see Iffley Road

Folksingers Club The most enduring regular musical gathering in the town is the Swindon Folksingers Club, which was founded in 1960 by Ted Poole and his wife Ivy. Ted was an aircraft fitter at the South Marston works of Vickers Armstrong, where he was particularly active in the trade union movement. The club's first venue was the cellar beneath Swindon's communist party headquarters in Bridge Street, where it initially met fortnightly. During its history, the members and their frequently well-known folksinger guests have met in several venues around the town. These are The Cellar, Bridge Street (1960-63); The Locomotive, Fleet Street (1963); The Greyhound, Faringdon Road (1963-79); The Grapes, Faringdon Road (1979-81); The Prince of Wales, Union Street (1981-96); Pinehurst People's Centre (1996-2000); Penhill Royal British Legion Club (2001); Gorse Hill Working Men's Club (2001); The Cricketers, Emlyn Square (2005); and Milton Road Social Club (from 2005). In 1969, the club celebrated its ninth anniversary and acknowledged folk music's debt to Alfred Williams, by presenting a special occasion of the songs he collected. It also organised,

in the same year, an Alfred Williams' festival and exhibition, and a barn dance in various venues at South Marston. Performing artistes included Dave and Toni Arthur, who specialised in traditional folksongs of the Upper Thames area; Bob Davenport, The Rakes, and the Marsden Rattlers, with dance from Bampton Morris. The club's logo featuring a harp, guitar and violin, which was designed and drawn freehand by Mark Child (the author of this book) in 1976; it was reproduced the same year and issued on lapel badges sold to members. It has ever since appeared in its original form on all of the club's literature and weekly posters, and latterly on the club's website.

Football Pink In 1922, a weekly Saturday evening football paper, the Football Pink (printed on pink stock) was first published by Swindon Press, the proprietors of the *Swindon Evening Advertiser*. It was normally of either four or six broadsheet pages, and its primary purpose was to report on Swindon Town FC's match of the day, and include the football results. It was also enjoyed for the weekly cartoon by Bill Paul. The paper was rushed through the press and usually available for purchase from about 6 p.m. on match days. It ceased publication in 1970.

Forward, Colin Busby (1923-2001) Colin Forward came to the attention of Swindon when, in 1962, he appeared outside the central lending library in Regent Circus with a hand cart, which he had borrowed from the Territorial Army, packed with books. This piece of entrepreneurialism was disapproved of by Harold Jolliffe, the borough librarian, and by the local constabulary, whose emissaries regularly moved him on. Even so, the enterprise was

so successful that he opened a second-hand bookshop in Havelock Street, wherein Avis Lever sold stamps upstairs. In 1966, Mrs Lever relocated to the top of Commercial Road, where she opened Pool of Tears, selling hippy clothes and stamps, and Colin opened Shakespeare & Co elsewhere in the same street, in premises that had previously been the Soo Ling Chinese laundry. Here, his daughter Vieve (Colin had six children) convinced him to sell second-hand records, as well, and he kept 'adult material' under the counter. In a small way, this was Swindon's first sex shop.

Born in South Wales, educated at Pontllanfraith Grammar School and Cardiff School of Art, Colin was a talented artist and life-long illustrator who taught the subject at Pontypridd Grammar School for Boys, Islington Secondary Modern, Malmesbury Grammar School, Swindon College, and Dorcan Secondary Modern School. Mostly, he moved on or was sacked from these because of his inability to keep discipline or motivate pupils. He once described himself as 'an ideas volcano', and was ever frustrated in his failure to become a television director, the only area in which he felt he might satisfy his creative ability. In the event, he had some thirty non-teaching jobs, having an uncanny knack of convincing would-be employers that he was eminently suitable for positions for which he was not at all qualified.

Colin Forward was a most lovable eccentric, and his kindness and generosity was legendary. He often bought unsaleable books and other material from people who needed some money; and he employed, befriended or financed a succession of waifs and strays to whom he sometimes lent any small profits that the shop made. The business failed, and was sold in 1971, after

he stood guarantor for one of his customers to buy a car, and the man decamped. He lived at Malmesbury, where he was a town councillor from 1963.

Fountain public house see Britannia, Devizes Road

Foxies Gentlemen's Club In the late 1960s, Swindon Borough Council refused an application to hire a public room in the town hall, above the reference library, for the purpose of presenting striptease on a regular, if infrequent, basis. During the 1970s, topless go-go dancing and striptease were sometimes presented at weekends in one or two of the town's public houses, but had no lasting success. Swindon was not ready to embrace the sex entertainment industry, and was hardly served by it until Foxies arrived. This was the town's first topless, table-side dancing club.

In 2001, businessman David Broome and one-time Swindon Robins speedway rider John Jefferies formed Foxies Entertainment Limited, financed by the sale of Broome's company, Bee-Line Oils. The pair aimed to acquire the former Electra Palace cinema (opened 1914) in Gorse Hill, and convert it into a topless dancing club. The venue had most recently been a Mecca bingo hall, but had been empty since 1998. It was next to retirement flats, and the possible effects on people who lived in them became the focus of a local campaign against the project. Opposition came from nearby residents, churchmen, and town councillors; most objected to the choice of venue in Gorse Hill, although some were appalled at the concept per se being suggested for anywhere in Swindon. Broome and Jefferies withdrew their application, leaving the property available for a competitor who wanted to turn it into a live music venue. (This also fell through; the cinema building was demolished and residential apartments were built on the site.)

Foxies Entertainment Limited immediately acquired and converted premises, lately vacated by Bar 150, at the Regent Circus end of Victoria Road. The organisation employed professional dancers, some under contract through agencies, and opened in March 2001 with twelve girls working on each shift. In 2002, Foxies obtained a licence for its dancers to strip completely naked, and, two years later, began providing pole dancing classes. The following year, Jefferies sold out to his co-owner and returned to grass track racing, a sport that he had pursued since he was a small boy. In 2006, Foxies relocated to Theatre Square and became Foxies X-treme; the Victoria Road premises were taken over as The Pink Rooms, a club for the town's gay community. An application was made in 2009 for a pole dancing club two doors away from The Pink Rooms, and this was opened that year as The Godfather club. It later became Dream Lounge. Old Swindon had a short-lived topless pole dancing club, Rouge, which ceased business in 2008.

Francome, John (b.1952) Seven times National Hunt Champion Jockey in a horse racing career in which he won 1,138 times, Francome was born in Mulberry Grove, Swindon, the son of Norman J. Francome, a railway fireman, and his wife Lillian (née Purcell). He went to Park Senior High School, and in 1968 was apprenticed to Fred Winter's stable at Lambourn, where he relocated into adjacent lodgings. He was awarded the MBE in 1986, the year that saw the publication of

the first of his series of successful novels. He has also written his autobiography and, following his retirement, has been notable as a trainer, newspaper columnist, and broadcaster.

Free Christian Church Revd Frederick Rowland Young submitted plans to the New Swindon Local Board in 1874 for a new church to be erected in Rolleston Street, which were approved. Whilst the building of what would be designated St John's church took place, Young conducted his Unitarian-style services in an auction yard, by courtesy of its owner, Fred Davis, one of his ardent supporters. He opened his church in August 1875, and suddenly declared, in September, that he had withdrawn from the Unitarian body, and henceforth his church would be non-denominational. The new church was built of brick and random coursed stone, with Bath stone dressings and a slate roof. It was designed in 14th -century style. The front to Regent Circus was gabled and had three pointed windows with geometric tracery in the heads, and a moulded string course running beneath them. The interior measured 1,550 square feet, with a vestry to one side and an organ opposite, and was aisled. The interior walls were of stucco; the altar was raised, with a traceried window behind it; the floor throughout was made of encaustic tiles, and all the woodwork, including the two hundred chairs for the congregation, was of varnished pine. Throughout his career in Swindon, Revd Young and his various interests, particularly those involving spiritualism (he edited his own magazine, *The Christian Spiritualist*), frequently came into conflict with the views of William Morris, who regularly denounced him in the *Swindon Advertiser*. In 1879, Young was

granted permission to build a house next to the church in Rolleston Street, on land that he had enclosed in 1875. In 1879, he suddenly resigned his seat on the Old Swindon Local Board, and gave up his ministry. The Free Christian Church building was bought by the Roman Catholics in 1882, and opened by them in February of the following year. (See also Iron Church; Museums; Young, F.R.)

French, George (1841-1906) Possibly the only 'ordinary' Swindon person to be depicted on a postcard, let alone several, George 'Hooty' French was an unlikely celebrity. He was a typical itinerant labourer, at one time employed as a bricklayer on the furnaces at the Swindon United Gasworks in Gypsy lane, and later in the boiler house of the locomotive department at the GWR factory, with responsibility for blowing the GWR hooter. Dismissed for poor timekeeping and general inattention to work (the hooter failed to be blown if his attention had been diverted elsewhere), he turned to vagrancy and to scraping a meagre living making children's toys. He is known to have taken lodgings for a while at Vitti's boarding house in London Street. It was said that, in his younger days, he had been 'The Champion Walker of Wiltshire'. George obtained his nickname by his ability to imitate the sound of the GWR Works' hooter by blowing through a small piece of pipe. It was alleged that, after he left the GWR's employment, Hooty slept inside the large empty pipes stored around the railway site. This earned him the name 'Hooty-up-a-gas-pipe', which the local children called after him. When they did so, he would whip out a pocket knife and chase after them. He carried his belongings in a home-made trolley, created out of a square, wooden tea chest with wooden

handles attached. The few likenesses of him extant show a spare, lugubrious man, thin faced, sometimes sparsely bearded, wearing clothes that were patched up, ill-fitting and clearly second-hand and, characteristically, boots, and always a cap. Something of an entrepreneur even in reduced circumstances, George French made square-bladed paper windmills on sticks that he exchanged for jam jars, which he then sold on. He also sold matches, and having by some means obtained a hurdy-gurdy, he used it to entertain crowds for money at Swindon events. He is depicted on postcards soliciting for coins, his clothes frayed and patched. This was not the stuff of success, however, and he died in the workhouse. An epitaph was written when he died:

No more you will see his figure or hear his plaintiff [sic] call
With windmills or the organ, well known to one and all
The working match is over, his earthly training done;
And George is gently resting with his latest victory won.
Now doff your hats, you beggars as his bier passes by
When dead we all are equal and all must surely die.
He was always rough and ready; yet beneath his grimy skin
He'd a heart both true and manly and a conscience there within.
And will the Judge despise him in that final reckoning day;
With all his faults He will bid him; wanderer come My way.

Garrard Engineering and Manufacturing Company

The company was formed in 1915, in London, as an offshoot of a family firm that had been crown jewellers from early in the 18th century. In 1919, the engineering arm took over existing premises in Newcastle Street, which was then rebuilt and extended for them by the Swindon builder, E.W. Beard. The company opened, under the direction of S.H. Garrard and Herbert Slade, with just forty workers, who were employed to make gramophone motors that previously had to be imported from continental Europe and America. Garrard became a public company in 1926, and in 1928 they went into full-scale production of complete gramophone turntables. Between then and the late 1950s, it was pre-eminent in turntable technology. During the Second World War, the company made an amount of military equipment. It subsequently developed automatic and multi-function record players; its products were sold in the private and commercial markets, and its export successes were considerable. Perhaps more than any other factory, Garrard was successful in breaking the historic economic dependence of Swindon on the railway Works. At its height, the company operated from its original factory, and outlets at Cheney Manor and Blunsdon. The Newcastle Street premises suffered a fire in 1958, which badly affected the assembly and despatch areas in particular, but the company swiftly recovered. Garrard was sold to the Plessey Company in 1960, but they failed to inject sufficient investment or capitalise on its expertise in precision engineering. The Newcastle Street site was closed down in 1969. In 1971, a fire that was said to have been caused by arson wrecked much of the Cheney Manor site. Plessey's failure to invest left Garrard vulnerable to the advances being made in recorded music product technology elsewhere in the world,

and in 1978, two-thirds of the workforce were made redundant and the Blunsdon site was closed down. The following year, Plessey sold Garrard to Gradiente Electronics of Brazil. Garrard ceased manufacturing in Swindon in 1982. The Newcastle Street building was demolished in 1984, and the Cheney Manor operation, a much reduced development facility, closed in 1995.

Gas in Swindon Those residents of Old Town who could afford to buy it, received their first gas supply in 1841. This was supplied by the Swindon Gas & Coke Company Limited, formed in that year, whose works were on the west side of Brockhill. Gas came early to the street lights in the railway village, courtesy of the Great Western Railway Company, but not to the other houses of New Swindon. In 1863, the New Swindon Gas Company Limited was formed, whose works were near the Golden Lion Bridge. In 1864, it established gas works, south of Queen Street, beside the Wilts & Berks Canal. The first public street lamps outside the railway village to be lit by gas in New Swindon appeared in 1867, and by 1886 the two companies had more or less covered the main roads of the two towns with public gas lamps. Penny-in-the-slot meters were first installed in retail premises, and a few domestic residences, in 1896. In 1893, the New Swindon Gas Company relocated its works to Gypsy Lane, and in 1902 the two firms amalgamated as the Swindon United Gas Company. The gas company treated its employees badly, working conditions were poor, and there was little job security; by the time of the First World War, the Workers' Union was representing the men. The gas company supplied only Swindon until it took over the Wootton Bassett Gas, Coal, Coke

and Fittings Company in 1934. Thereafter, it spent the next decade acquiring smaller gas undertakings in nearby towns and villages, and using the network as a springboard for supplying outlier villages that had not previously obtained gas. During the Second World War, hydrogen balloons and barrage balloons were made at the Swindon gasworks, under the auspices of the Air Ministry. Following nationalisation of the gas industry under The Gas Act, 1948, the Swindon United Gas Company was merged into the South Western Regional Gas Board. The town's gas supply has since followed the various Acts of Parliament by which the gas industry has been restructured and privatised nationally. The late Victorian Gas Works in Gypsy Lane were closed and demolished in 1968, with only the gas holders remaining and in use.

Gateway Beacon Sculptures In 2011, two sculptures, each costing £38,000, were erected in the town as part of the regeneration of the central area, under the auspices of Forward Swindon. One was a six-metre-high structure in College Street, near the junction with Regent Street; the other was installed in Edgeware Road, close to its junction with Regent Street. Both were designed by Arup Engineering working with Nicholas Pearson Associates, and were created in association with the multi-award-winning lighting sculpture and installations artist Peter Freeman of Nancledra, Cornwall. The project was part of the Public Realm Renewal scheme for Regent Street. The sculptures were intended to welcome people along the approach into the main shopping street and draw them in. They were described by Forward Swindon as 'reactive light gateway beacons', were designed as 'setting

off points', such as way markers or standing stones, and their shapes were inspired by the former tram tracks along Regent Street, stylised and twisted into art forms.

One of the sculptures is a vertical curve on a concrete plinth; the other is a twisted structure. Both were made of a brushed stainless- steel cladding over a steel 'backbone'. Each is about six metres in height, and weighs around half a tonne. They are studded with a regular grid of multi-coloured, low-energy LED, motion-sensitive lighting. As people walk past, the sculptures light up in an upwards flow, and also along adjacent pavement lights. These pieces were made by Jordan Manufacturing of Bristol, specialists in steel structures.

Gay, Family of Surgeons William Gay (b.1785), John Gay (1792-1870), and Joseph Gay (1793-1862) were all natives of Swindon, the sons of William and Mary Gay. All three were surgeons, although William seems to have practised in London. Joseph and John worked together in High Street, in part of a property three doors to the north of the drive to The Lawn, leased from the Tuckey family, whose home it had been for generations. This property also accommodated James & Richard Strange & Co's bank (the first bank in Swindon). John moved out in the 1830s and set up a separate practice in a cottage on the corner of Wood Street and Cricklade Street, where he lived with his daughter Mary (b.1817), and his son John (b.1821), who also became a surgeon and went into practice with his father. This cottage had previously been associated with the business premises of John Blackford the Swindon butcher and slaughterhouse keeper, and Richard Tarrant, the boot and shoe maker. (In 1884, the site of this cottage became that of the new Wilts & Dorset Bank building.) The household of the two John Gays had four servants, and the surgeons kept five horses. William Morris, in *Swindon Fifty Years Ago*, says that John Gay 'was entrusted with the keeping of everybody's secrets'.

Joseph Gay continued to practise in High Street, and to live there with his unmarried sisters Jane (b.1784) and Ann (b.1796), until Strange's bank was taken over by the County of Gloucestershire Banking Company in 1842. William Morris recalled that there was a long garden at the rear of this property, on part of which Joseph Gay carried out blood-letting of patients on one day each week, thereby fertilising the soil to the advantage of plants grown there. This story has also been told of the garden at John Gay's cottage in Wood Street, although in that instance probably due more to the former activities of Blackford the slaughterman. The County of Gloucestershire bank rebuilt the premises in High Street that Joseph Gay had continued to lease from the Tuckey family, and the surgeon relocated to Bath Road with his two sisters, who never married; when elder brother William retired, he went to live in this household.

Gay, Frances Josephine (1886-1974) Formidable and energetic, Frances Gay was chairman of the Richard Jefferies Society from its formation in 1950 until 1971. She was also secretary and treasurer of the Swindon Family Planning Clinic, 1950-60.

Frances had been a great admirer of Jefferies' writing since the opening years of the twentieth century, and the success of the Society in his name was almost entirely due to her tireless work over these two decades. She regularly stood in for other officers in times of vacancy, was fearsome in her support for

Richard Jefferies, and highly focused in her attempts to swell membership of the society. This was one of the first organisations in the town to be accepted under the banner of the Swindon Public Libraries, Museums & Art Gallery's family of 'extension activities'.

Frances Matthews was the youngest but one of the sixteen children born to Jessie Matthews (b. 1844, Wootton Bassett), a tailor newsagent, stationer and general shopkeeper of 71 Regent Street, and his wife Maria (née Smith, b. Gloucester, 1843). Maria was the first woman in Swindon to become a Poor Law Guardian. Encouraged by her mother, Frances took up teaching, training at College Street Infant School, and then practised in succession at Lethbridge Road Infant School, Even Swindon School, Euclid Street School, and Sanford Street Boys School. In 1921, she married George Gay and, eleven years later, the family moved to Broome Manor Lane, where Frances remained. She taught at Lyneham, and at Rockley, near Marlborough, and retired from the profession in 1949. Her husband became an Alderman of Swindon, and was town's mayor 1961-62. Frances also contributed occasional childhood memories to the *Evening Advertiser*.

Gaze, Charles Edward (1882-1964) The artist who painted the Hinder's pet shop mural in Commercial Road, and the famous sign for the Angel Inn public house at Purton, was deeply religious. He signed all of his work 'LJC' (standing for 'Lord Jesus Christ', and thereby transferring credit to where he believed it was due for any talent he might have). Gaze was born in Gloucester, the son of William Gaze, a carpenter, and his wife Lucy Susan (née Hodges), who married in 1877. Charles was the fourth of their ten children. The family moved to Bridgwater,

Somerset soon after he was born, and relocated to Swindon in the late 1880s, where they lived at 195 Cricklade Road (and later for a short time at 15 Caulfield Road).

Charles was one of the first students at the newly opened Swindon & North Wiltshire Technical Institution in Victoria Road, where he studied commercial art, and was apprenticed to the signwriting trade by the age of fifteen. At nineteen, he was described as a signwriter 'working on own account'. In 1907, he married Emily Goodship of Bright Street, whose father, William, was an iron moulder. The couple had three sons, and the eldest, Charles William (b.1908), eventually took over the business, which later embraced general decorating and became Charles Gaze & Sons, working out of the premises in Cricklade Road.

As a young man, Gaze was contracted to the Great Western Railway Company as a signwriter on coaches for the Carriage and Wagon Department, and in his spare time he painted scenery at the Empire Theatre. In a long career (he never actually retired), Charles Gaze became a well-known figure in and around Swindon, wearing round spectacles and his trademark Homburg hat, as he painted inn signs, shop fronts, and publicity on commercial buildings and hoardings.

Gazebo, Goddard Estate In c.1850, a gazebo was built on a rise to the east of the house, possibly above an ice house, in Portland stone and using bricks from the tower of the then lately demolished Holy Rood church. The gazebo is said to cover the same ground area as did the church tower. It is square on plan with a pyramidal roof, topped by a square lantern and weathervane, and faces away from the site of the former manor

house. There is a cornice of dentil mouldings beneath the eaves, blocked up doorways, and square-headed sash windows. Beyond the gazebo, are the remains of a ha-ha whereby the estate's cattle were discouraged from straying on to the lawns of the house.

Geology of Swindon Swindon hill, on which the old town was built, is about 450 feet above sea level. Just beneath its surface are beds of Portland stone and Purbeck limestone, which have been quarried at various times but to no great degree. These are Jurassic rocks, some 150 million years old, laid down when the area was a sub-tropical sea. Evidence of this can be seen in the railway cutting at Old Town, now part of a footpath and cycleway. Here, just north of the site of the former Midland & South West Junction Railway's station, there are layers of limestone and sandstones containing fossils, and a board with a timeline explains what can be seen there. The Cotswolds, which lie immediately to the north, are part of the Jurassic system.

Kelly's Directory of Swindon in the late 19th-century described the geology thus: 'Quarries of oolite, well adapted for building, are abundant in the neighbourhood and quantities of fossil and other remains have been found, including remains of an extinct reptile known as the Omosaurus. Fresh water marls and limestones of the Purbeck age are found in the quarries here with bones of the earliest true frog and fossils of fresh water shells.' Immediately to the south-east of the hill is a ridge of greensand and other sands that extends towards a range of chalk and flint uplands known as the Marlborough Downs or the Wiltshire Downs, which have mostly supported arable farming and sheep rearing. Looking north from these chalk

Downs, or from points above Wroughton, extending perhaps westward by way of The Ridgeway, the panoply of landscape presented is composed upon gradually ageing areas of rocks and clays.

The hill is surrounded on all sides other than to the south by a low-lying plain that extends north to the Cotswolds, and north-east through the Vale of the White Horse. This is composed of Kimmeridge clay, with a sandy layer known as Swindon Sands, progressing into Oxfordshire, and large deposits of gravel associated with the River Kennet and Upper Thames areas. The broad band of Oxford clay runs immediately south of Swindon, and this forms the valley of the Bristol Avon and the upper reaches of the Thames valley. There are two nearby ragstone ridges that rise above escarpments and the upper Thames valley; these are between Highworth and Blunsdon and between Purton and Wootton Bassett, and both have been favoured for settlements in antiquity. Corallian limestone is encountered here, younger than the oolitic limestone that runs diagonally through the Cotswolds a little further to the north, which was also laid down in the Jurassic period.

New Swindon is built on the clay vale immediately to the north of Swindon hill. When the Swindon Brick and Tile Works were being laid out in this area in the 1870s, it was reported that: 'During the excavations the remains of two remarkable sea dragons or large reptilian whales, mounted on paddles, were discovered. The first was sent to the British Museum, and was considered to be such an extraordinary curiosity that a special engraving was made of it, and upon receiving notice of another discovery, a curator was sent from London to superintend its removal.'

George, Reuben (1864-1936) Born in Gloucester, in a boot shop in Barton Street, Reuben George was cleaning boots before breakfast by the age of eight. At sixteen, he was employed by the Gloucester Wagon Works where, seven years later, he was involved in an accident that severed parts of several of his fingers. He became an agent for the Wesleyan & General Insurance Company, in which capacity he relocated to Swindon in 1890; was elected councillor to the New Swindon Urban District Council four years later; and became an alderman of the town in 1900. In 1918, he stood, unsuccessfully, as Labour parliamentary candidate for Chippenham.

An idealist by inclination and a lifelong Socialist (the local Wesleyans disassociated themselves from him on the grounds that his views were incompatible with Christianity), he was also a pacifist and opposed to all military action. Twice an alderman, he famously refused to sit in judgement on his fellow men, by refusing his right, during his mayoral year of 1921-22, to sit as an ex-officio magistrate. He did, however, dress up as Father Christmas and visit all of the schools in the town at the end of 1921, and his response to those who complained that it brought such high office into disrepute was to continue to do so until 1934, when he was forced to stop through ill health. He also wrote a weekly column for the *Swindon Advertiser*.

Reuben George is best remembered for his thirty-year association with the Workers Educational Association, the Swindon branch of which he helped to found in 1907. His general contribution to public life there, his unstinting work to make matters better for the people of Swindon through education (which he believed to be the key to social reform) and by an appreciation of nature, was only equalled by his commitment as a Saturday countryside rambler. His philosophies in these respects were outlined in his 1919 publication, *Unconventional Approaches to Adult Education: Our School Among the Hills and Hedgerows*. In 1916, he brought to Swindon the then poet laureate, Robert Bridges, who addressed the Swindon WEA on 'the improvement of the educational condition of the working classes'. During his term of office as mayor, he officially opened a wooden diving board at Coate Water by jumping from it into the lake. He was also instrumental in Swindon Corporation's purchase of Coate farmhouse in 1926. It was said that no man of the time had more friends among the ordinary people or more friends among the great and the good than Reuben George. His funeral cortege 'stopped Swindon', and he was buried in Radnor Street cemetery. The Reuben George Hall was built by Swindon Corporation in Cavendish Square, Park North, and named in his memory in 1963.

Gilbert's Furniture Shop Gilbert's furniture shop has been on the corner of Newport Street and High Street since the early 1870s. William Gilbert (1831-1911) was born at Grafton, near Marlborough, the son of Philip Gilbert, a sawyer by trade, and his wife Sarah (née Chouls), who married in 1828 at Great Bedwyn. By the date of his own marriage at Calne in 1860 to dressmaker Susanna Caroline (née Beaven), William was describing himself as a 'cabinet maker journeyman'; the couple set up home in Blowhorn Street, Marlborough. By 1865, they were in Swindon, living at 12 Belle Vue Road, where William was occupied as a grocer. He continued in this trade at the same

address for the rest of the decade, adding 'upholsterer' in 1867, and 'cabinet maker' in 1869. At some point between 1871 (when he was a 'cabinet maker employing one man' but still at Belle Vue Road) and 1875, the family (there were five children and one more soon to be added) moved to a house and shop on the Newport Street site. There he advertised himself as cabinet maker, sold all manner of furniture, fixtures and fittings for the home, and set up his Furniture Warehouse on the premises, using the land at the rear.

By 1881, William was employing one man and two apprentices; his firstborn, Albert John, had become a cabinet maker, and the couple's second child, Emily, had taken up her mother's former occupation of dressmaker. The shop in Newport Street was rebuilt and remodelled, 1886-87, giving 6,000 square feet of warehousing space, and the family moved just around the corner into Ingleside, 40 Devizes Road. In 1889, the business became William Gilbert & Son. The latter, Albert John (known as John Gilbert), effectively took it over in 1900. Finding his premises a few yards from the Old Town terminus after the introduction of trams in 1904, John suggested in his publicity that customers should just ask the conductor for fares to 'Gilbert Furniture, Please!'. The elder Gilberts were still at Ingleside in 1906 when Susanna died. The following year, William married Rosanna (née Breakwell), who was twenty-three years his junior.

Gin and Water Sales The gin and water sale of corn was the forerunner of the pitched market. Farmers who had in their pockets small samples of the corn they wanted to sell, settled themselves down with a glass and a pipe in their preferred hostelry in Old Town, where prospective dealers and buyers would know where to find them. If a deal could not be made under one roof, the farmers would often go from inn to inn, hoping to attract the attention of other dealers, until they were successful. The amount of alcohol consumed meant that this method was eventually considered to be unsatisfactory, and dealers were wary of the small samples on show.

At Swindon, posts and rails were set up where farmers could stack whole sacks of corn for inspection. Inclement weather often precluded the opening of sacks, however, so both parties then had to return to the days of gin and water sales, or go to other places where the market was held under cover. Over time, the latter was favoured, and Swindon's corn market declined in consequence. By the 1840s, it was 'a tumbledown affair', which harboured rats beneath the boards and stood adjacent to pig pens and sheep folds. The corn took secondary place, the sacks being stacked up against a row of old stables that had warehouses and cheese lofts above them. Afraid that this might weaken the economy of the town, and his own prestige, Ambrose Goddard, lord of the manor, offered to forego all claims to market tolls if the farmers and dealers agreed to return and once again pitch in the market square. The pitched market continued in Swindon until 1866.

Glue Pot, Emlyn Square The three-storey, gabled Glue Pot on the east side of the square, opened as a public house in 1850 on the corner of Oxford Street and Reading Street. Built in the latter half of the 1840s, it was originally intended to be a dwelling house and shop, and by 1848 it was leased to David Dunbar, a sculptor of Pimlico. At one time, it was in the occupancy of a Mr Fidler, whose trade is not known. By 1850, it was William Warner's wool and linen

drapery, which retail premises occupied what is now the public bar, with parlour, kitchen and scullery to the rear. Warner must have converted it to a public house because, by 1857, he was described as a beer retailer there. The premises were added to and remodelled in the 1860s. It has the most pleasing façade of all the former commercial buildings around the square, featuring gables with blind roundels, built at right angles to each other with the impression of being shouldered, and on either side of a splayed corner elevation. All the square-headed windows have hood mouldings with labels, and a continuous string at first-floor level at one and the same time separates out the retail part from the accommodation above, and defines the doorways and the windows below. It was at one time called the London Stout Tavern.

Goddard Arms Hotel, High Street

The Goddard Arms was the most important hostelry in Swindon. It was built at the point where High Street meets Cricklade Street, c.1815, on the site of The Crown. This was a small, thatched alehouse (possibly constructed from more than one cottage) of which the earliest named mention extant is a 16th-century lease by Sir Richard Bridges, then holder of the manor of West Swindon, to a man named Allworth. After Allworth died, his widow married William West, who bought the freehold of The Crown in 1581 from Anthony Bridges, son of the late Sir Richard. In 1621, the property was sold by West to Thomas Goddard of Upham, by then lord of the manor of Swindon. Goddard leased it in 1633 to Francis Kiblewhite, gent, of Windsor, Berkshire. In 1697, the landlord was William Elton. The 'Crowne Inn' was one of the properties released in trust as

settlement in 1776, when Ambrose Goddard married Sarah Williams. It was run by several members of the Gray family in the 1700s, and rebuilt c.1780. It was named after the Goddard family in about 1810.

During the 1800s, The Goddard Arms rapidly became the most important hostelry in the town, where the court leet met, and the magistrate's and county courts were held (in the oak-panelled and later-named Pleydell Room, which the hotel latterly used for conferences), and where most of the traders' associations and public societies of the period held their meetings. It was also a scheduled stop for the passenger coach *The Plough*, on its way to Southampton on Mondays, Wednesdays and Fridays, and on the return journey to Cheltenham on Tuesdays, Thursdays and Saturdays. After 1840, it was the booking office for the railway in New Swindon, and horse-drawn carriages travelled six times daily between the hostelry and the station.

A large assembly hall was built to the rear in 1850, used for balls, public concerts, and other entertainments; at about the same time, a livestock sale yard was established at the rear by auctioneer William Dore – which operated there until well into the 20th century. William Westmacott (1809-1873), born at Shalbourn, was one of the town's best-known tradesmen since he began as a saddler and harness maker in 1832; he leased the hotel from 1857 until 1870, when he retired and the lease was then acquired by Henry Church of Pewsey. Westmacott spent his final years living at 20 Prospect. In 1877, the Goddard Arms was bought by Bowly's brewery. The hotel thereafter had several owners, but having not kept up with the needs of the times became down at heel by the end of the 20th century. In 2005, its

restaurant was renamed the Buccleuch Grill, but the complex closed down in 2007. It was bought by the Barracuda Group, completely refurbished, and opened as a restaurant and bar with rooms in 2009. Private dwellings and apartments were built in the grounds to the rear.

The present building has a long, low frontage of seven bays and two storeys with a mansard roof of stone slates and attic accommodation. The hotel is built of diaper brickwork, and the entrance is through the fifth bay, beneath a fluted Tuscan portico and a late 18th-century arch that was uncovered in 1955, and is inscribed 'licensed to let post horses'. The building has a stone-tiled mansard roof.

People associated with the Goddard Arms include Robert Watkins, who, in 1819, was falsely accused and hanged for a murder to which his father later confessed; Watkins junior allegedly ate his last meal at the hostelry in the company of the hangman. The writer Robert Smith Surtees was there in the 1830s. In 1863, the hotel's boots boy discovered the previously hidden body of a long-dead baby in a lumber room at the hotel. (See also Hunter, Priscilla Francis.)

Golden Lion Swindon's most enduring piece of public art was the recumbent lion, the sculpted beast that originally sat on a base with large scroll brackets, above the central first-floor window of the Golden Lion public house in Bridge Street. It remained in its lofty position until the 1920s, when there were fears that its position might prove not to be in the interests of public safety. William Horsington, licensee at the time, relocated the 'golden lion' on the narrow garden forecourt of the building, behind a wrought-iron fence beside the canal. There it remained until the 1960s, some years after the public house had been demolished, often played on by children. Officially, the lion ended its days frost-cracked and disintegrating beyond repair in a local authority council depot, yet a legend persists that it did not meet its end in this manner, but that it remains in some private collection to this day. Carleton Attwood, a sculptor in stone and cement, working under the umbrella of the Thamesdown Community Arts Project with metal-worker Gordon Allen, who was then the Project chairman, and woodworker Edwin Horne, made a more friendly looking replacement out of concrete reinforced with fibreglass to commemorate the Silver Jubilee of Queen Elizabeth II. The glass fibre was provided by its manufacturer, the Swindon building firm of Edwin H. Bradley. A time box was placed inside the lion's neck, containing, among other ephemera, a priced shopping list of the day, a copy of the *Evening Advertiser*, and a number of photographs. In 1978, with great ceremony and the accompaniment of a jazz band, the replacement lion was placed on wheels, and pulled from the town hall and erected on Canal Walk, near the original site. There, set up facing along the line of Regent Street, it was officially unveiled by Alf Bown, one-time mayor, and then chairman of the development trust. The sculpture was moved in 2000, and rotated to face east along Canal Walk; in 2009, it was returned to Regent Street, parallel with the site of the former pub.

Golden Lion Bridge, Regent Street
An ornate iron lift bridge, built in the GWR Works, was put up in 1870 where Regent Street crossed the Wilts & Berks Canal. It replaced a wooden swing bridge of about twelve feet wide that had been erected on

the same spot in 1803. In 1858, John Toomer was successful in bringing a case against Henry Lyde Dunsford, the clerk and agent of the Wilts & Berks Canal Company, who had 'obstructed the free passage of a bridge passing over the canal ... and running along the street at New Swindon now known as Bridge Street' since mid-1857. Effectively, this was a test case, in which Dunsford was amiably complicit, in order to facilitate a court ruling on whether the bridge constituted a public right of way. Henry Kinneir, solicitor for John Toomer, found a document dated 1657 that ascribed the road for the use of those who lived adjacent to it. The land 'having been bought by the Company in 1806 and a wooden swing bridge being built soon thereafter', the public had ever since passed freely across it. The road on either side had been made up by public subscription in 1845, then opened to the public, and since repaired by the parish. This was an important case, and the adjacent Golden Lion public house (built 1840) had recently given its name locally to the canal-crossing at this point. In 1870, the wooden bridge was replaced by the famous iron lift bridge, and thereafter known as the Golden Lion Bridge. This had a hump-backed walkway, four huge, hollow stanchions, and ball finials, and was operated by means of a complicated system of weights and pulleys, the mechanism for which was below ground level. It was reinforced in 1904 to facilitate the tramway, and the raised footbridges were removed two years later. The bridge was demolished by military personnel in 1919.

Golden Lion Bridge Mural Arguably the best-known, and certainly the most lasting, of Ken White's series of Swindon murals was that of the Golden Lion Bridge, which the artist created on the west end of a terrace in Medgbury Road in 1976. This was carried out as part of a job creation scheme under the auspices of Thamesdown Arts, to commemorate the centenary of the birth of Alfred Williams, Swindon Works' 'hammerman poet'. The mural occupied the whole of the side of a house, and was based on a photograph taken in the early 1900s. It shows the footbridge across the canal, and several people standing facing the camera in the kind of pose that was typical of the day whenever someone turned up with a camera. The piece was repainted in 1983, and was fully restored by the original artist in 2010. (See also White, Ken.)

Golden Lion Public House, Bridge Street Built close to the Wilts & Berks Canal in 1845, the Golden Lion has only achieved posthumous fame because of the history of the lion statues, and the story of the most complex and ornamental bridge at the canal that bore its name. This was, after an extension of the premises in 1875, a two-storey, three-bay public house, with street-level picture windows that had wooden styles and muntins, and were separated by flat pilasters. In its early days, the pub had numerous licensees, but remained in the Horsington family from 1920 until 1951. It was sold in 1952, and demolished in 1958 after which the site was redeveloped as a shop and offices.

Gooch, Daniel (1816-1889) The man who built the railway works at Swindon was the GWR's Locomotive Superintendent from 1837-64. He is credited with designing some 340 locomotives. Allegedly, it was he who pointed out to Brunel that the ideal spot for

the railway works would be on some farmland where the North Wilts Canal met the Wilts & Berks Canal, at a junction of the then uncompleted GWR mainline with the course of the Cheltenham and GW Union Railway. Gooch never lived in Swindon, although he was the first president of the Mechanics Institution — which the Swindon GWR workers established internally in 1843 as a means of self-education and entertainment. In 1859, he famously issued a warning notice stating that he would discharge from the service of the company any man who allowed any member of his family to behave in an unruly or mischievous fashion in New Swindon. The year after he retired, Gooch became MP for Cricklade (which at the time included Swindon), and continued in that capacity until 1885. He was knighted for leading the project by which the first transatlantic cable was laid, then returned to the GWR as its chairman, successfully returning the financially challenged railway company to profitability.

Gorilla sculpture, Queen's Park

Commissioned of sculptor Tom Gleeson by Thamesdown Borough Council, made of welded sheet steel, and officially named 'Sampson' but locally known as 'Kong', the seated, contemplative gorilla was installed in Theatre Square in 1985. There it was vandalised, before being removed and stored by the local authority. At the suggestion of Thamesdown councillor Derek Benfield, an employee of the town's Rover plant, in 1993 Sampson became a restoration project for training instructor Ron Selby and apprentices at the motor manufacturer's apprentice school. It was shot-blasted, welding repairs were carried out, and the sculpture was given a translucent wax skin.

In 1994, it was ceremonially (Mayor Doreen Dart did the honours) relocated in a border beside the lake in Queen's Park. (See also Cow sculpture.)

Gorse Hill

The area was first called Gorse Hill in the early 1880s. Much of it had historically been part of the parish of Stratton St Margaret for centuries, but in 1885 the sections of the latter that were within the auspices of the New Swindon Urban District Council were made a separate ecclesiastical parish. Until the mid-1800s, much of the area had been either farmland or open spaces, although a level crossing marked the point at which the Great Western Railway Company's line crossed the trackway that bisected it. Gorse Hill (together with nearby Rodbourne Cheney) became part of the borough of Swindon in 1890, a decision taken by the Areas & Boundaries Committee of the County Council, in the face of opposition from the New Swindon and Old Swindon Urban District Councils, and the school board for the parish of Swindon. These bodies all felt that the resulting sudden intake of additional children to be educated by the borough would place too great a financial burden on them. As soon as the area became part of Swindon, Avening Street and Chapel Street were built, and Bright Street, begun some years earlier, was extended, although not yet named. Speculative builders, among whom was James Hinton, mayor of Swindon 1903-4, immediately began to lay out streets. Gorse Hill had a public house known as 'The Tabernacle'. By 1870, sufficient houses had been built to warrant an iron church, dedicated to St Barnabas, as a daughter church of St Margaret at Stratton; and then a school at the end of Avening Street (1878), which was at first called School Street.

Gorse Hill Mural In the summer of 2010, some thirty-six students from Swindon College School of Art & Design set about covering a 100-metre by 2-metre stretch of wall beside a residential area of Gorse Hill with a series of linked murals, loosely based on themes of music and dance. The idea came from a police officer Steve Yeates, who noticed how the wall was being vandalised; the project, which was undertaken following discussions with local residents, also took account of other suggestions received during a period of consultation. Each student worked on a 5-metre width of the wall, creating individual visuals in a wide range of artistic styles.

Gosling VC, William (1892-1945) Born at Somerset Farm, Wanborough, Gosling emigrated to farm in Canada in 1909, three years after his father suffered a fatal accident at Wanborough and the family moved to Artis Farm, Wroughton. He returned at the outbreak of the First World War, and joined the Swindon detachment of the Wessex Brigade of the Royal Field Artillery. Prior to emigrating, he had been a volunteer in the same detachment with the rank of corporal. For a short time, he was riding instructor at the riding school attached to the Vale of the White Horse Repository, High Street, Swindon. It was from there that the detachment was mobilised for France in 1914, Gosling having now acquired the rank of sergeant. He earned his Victoria Cross near Arras. The citation, dated 14 June, 1917 read: 'The award of the Order of the Victoria Cross has been made to No. 645112 Sergeant William Gosling, RFA, who, on 5th April, 1917 when in charge of a heavy trench mortar, owing to a faulty cartridge a bomb after discharge, fell ten yards from the mortar, Sergeant Gosling sprang out, lifted the nose of the bomb, which had sunk into the ground, unscrewed the fuse and threw it on the ground where it immediately exploded. The very gallant and prompt action undoubtedly saved the lives of the whole detachment.' The people of Wroughton collected £50, which was presented to the new VC on 2 August 1917 at the village's Oddfellow's Hall, and the following day, at the Empire Theatre, Swindon, the town's mayor presented him with an antique silver tobacco box. Eddie Thomas of the Swindon Advertiser called for a subscription from readers, and on 22 August, Gosling – whose leave had been extended by eight days to the 24th for the purpose – was presented with £130 5s 6d, raised by 257 subscribers. There was a procession from Old Swindon to New Swindon, behind the Wilts National Reserve Band and members of the volunteer training corps. The ceremony took place at the town hall in the presence of the mayors and civic dignitaries of most of the local towns; thousands of people turned out, and Gosling was also given a scroll and a silver salver. The inscription on it read: 'Sergeant William Gosling VC, RFA. Presented in recognition of his gallantry by his admirers in Swindon and District together with £130 War Loan'. The subscription collected had been exchanged for war loan stock. Gosling left the army at the end of the war with the rank of acting battery sergeant major. He married in 1919; was awarded the Coronation Medal in 1937, and served as a captain in the Home Guard during the Second World War. He died at Summerhouse Farm, Wroughton of kidney disease, and is buried in Wroughton churchyard.

Gospel Hall, Regent Place Built as a Christian meeting place in 1899, the

otherwise named 'Regent Hall' was a conservatively polychromatic red brick building of four bays by six bays. The hall had stone dressings, round-headed windows with decorative banding and flat keystones that were separated by a brick pilaster, doorways with lunettes, a circular window in an eccentrically angular stepped gable, and little turrets on the roof. Its architect, and the prime mover to obtain the necessary funds, was William Hooper, the Swindon photographer, a deeply religious man. The hall was demolished in 1972.

Gradwell, Ike (1906-1979) The man who was to become Swindon Communist party branch secretary relocated to Swindon in 1935. He was the son of Septimus Gradwell and his dressmaker wife, Lizzie née Irving. In 1936, Ike joined Swindon Communist Party. During the war, he was an aircraft tool room fitter at Shorts aircraft factory, and was later employed at Marine Mountings. Prior to arriving in the town, Gradwell had allegedly used part of his fee when signing as a professional with Hull Kingston Rovers rugby league club to qualify as a handicrafts teacher through night school. In Swindon, 1 Bridge Street was acquired on mortgage by the Swindon branch of the Communist Party in 1942, and cost £740. Ike Gradwell was to be the president of Swindon Teachers' Association in 1948 and again in 1966. He was instrumental in setting up the Swindon Communist Party's Unity Bookshop in Corporation Street. In 1962, the mortgage on 1 Bridge Street was paid off and Angela Tuckett, who was to become his second wife the following year, wrote a poem about finally acquiring the property. The house was called Edith Stevens House, after the retired Swindon schoolteacher, Communist supporter and activist, who had largely been responsible for ensuring that the mortgage had been kept up.

Granville, Bath Road Built of brick with stone dressings in about 1880 for the physician and surgeon William Powne, Granville, at 16 Bath Road, is a sumptuous Victorian residence. Powne and his wife Marianne lived there with their eight children and three servants until c.1888, when Granville was bought by Levi Lapper Morse (see separate entry), who lived there with his wife Winifred, five children, and four servants. They were there until 1896, when it became the property of Samuel Barrett Cole, one of the town's best-known clothing outfitters. Cole sold it, c.1900, to the surgeon James Carson Rattray. This imposing, but asymmetrical, two-storey building is on three levels, with attic and cellar, and has a square bay to ground and first floors. The left-hand, gabled section has eaves that are bracketed out with a round-headed window with hood moulding at attic level. The façade of Granville is all about its arrangement of narrow, round-headed windows on the south elevation, put up as single, double, or triple lights with singles in the returns, and with hood mouldings as part of a continuous string course at ground-floor level. They all have sills on scroll brackets. The treatment of the windows is more ambitious at first-floor level, where they are arranged in two groups, each beneath a plain, moulded cornice. There are minor decorative motifs throughout the south front, sufficiently understated to give character to this fine building. The original masonry has long been whitewashed, earning it the name 'The White House'.

Gray, Cyril Alfred (1906-2001) When he was ninety-two-years old, Cyril

Gray decided to retire as head of the Swindon bakery business founded by his father, Samuel, just after the First World War, and in which Cyril had worked full-time since 1921. Samuel advertised himself as 'a high-class pastry cook', and his printed publicity always included the words: 'We improve the shining hour/Making nice things out of flour'.

According to the National Association of Master bakers, Cyril had been, since the 1980s, the oldest working baker in Britain. Cyril was born in Newport Street. In 1916, the family returned to Swindon from their home of ten years in the Isle of Wight because they were fearful that Germany was about to invade the island. Three years later, Samuel bought a small bakery in a two-bedroom cottage at 9 Bridge Street for £500, and Gray's Bakery was born. At the time, there were thirty other small bakers operating in the town. Being close to the GWR village, the railway works, and other nearby large factory employers, gave Gray's the edge. From the moment Cyril joined his father, aged thirteen, he was at work before six o'clock every morning. He left school and went to work full-time at the age of fifteen. Although famed for their crusted cottage loaves and a range of cakes, it was Gray's Wiltshire lardy cake that brought fame to the bakery.

Cyril was a lifelong motor cycle enthusiast; secretary of the North Wilts Motor Cycle and Light Car Club, and for five years wrote and edited *Motor Racing* magazine. This had a weekly circulation of 50,000 copies, and although often required to work on it until three o'clock in the morning, Cyril was always back in the bakery, two hours later. At its height, just after the Second World War, the Gray empire included seven shops, eight delivery vans, and 120 employees operating a 24-hour rota system. Each day, the bakery was producing 73,000 uncut loaves of bread, 30,000 rolls, 4,000 soft finger rolls, 1,000 crumpets, 300 French batons, 200 French sticks, and 400 sausage rolls. The company sold its first sliced loaves in the 1950s. In 1976, Cyril closed the business, except for one shop in Devizes Road. This he altered internally, installed an oven, put it in charge of his daughter, and carried on in a small way until the shop finally closed in 1998.

Great Blondinis, The In 1985, Thamesdown Borough Council commissioned sculptor John Ian Howard Clinch (1934-2001) to design a statue of 'The Great Blondinis', for public display in the town. This was something of a misnomer. *Blondini* was the stage name of a local street and circus entertainer whose female assistant, although crucial to the original act, received little recognition. The couple performed high wire, balancing and juggling during the 1920s and 1930s, often appearing at fêtes around the town. Clinch's seventeen-foot-high statue was created at Swindon's railway works, where it was one of the last pieces to be made before the place closed. The whole process, from small models to full-size sculpture, involved around a dozen patternmakers, mould-makers, founders and welders, and was made of aluminium supplied free of charge by British Alcan Aluminium as part of its own centenary celebrations. A local company Metalfast provided the interior stainless-steel reinforcing rods. Southern Arts and Sun Alliance Insurance Company sponsored the work.

The finished piece depicted the great man balancing on a ball and supporting a parasol-

waving female assistant on his shoulders. It was very colourfully painted, and was set up in 1987 amid flowerbeds and walkways on Wharf Green. There, it was regularly defaced, particularly by the addition of genitalia; after numerous cleanings, and then a lengthy period of acceptance of the inevitable, it was taken down in 2005.

It was, however, an important piece by an important artist, and was very representative of his style of work. Eventually, Swindon Borough Council offered £2,000 for its restoration, and the contract was won by Tim Carroll. He had the difficult job of matching the remnants of the original paint, and then giving the piece an anti-graffiti coating. The job was carried out with the help of the Swindon company Holman Paint Specialists, and carried out at the Swindon Borough Council depot where the statue had been languishing in a state of disrepair. It took ten days to complete, and the restored piece was set up, in 2009, in the Beatrice Street recreation ground, off Gorse Hill.

Great Western Community Forest
This public scheme was approved in Parliament in 1990, when Swindon was still part of the Borough of Thamesdown, and is now carried out under the auspices of Swindon Borough Council. This was the government's 'Great Green Initiative', a scheme to plant and maintain urban forests, and create sustainable rural characteristics such as woodlands, lakes, grasslands and other wildlife habitats where they may not have previously existed. Funding is by government grants, European funding, and a variety of sponsorships, with much of the work carried out by local people, and private and voluntary organisations. Associated with this was the 'Greening of Swindon'

document, launched in 1994 by botanist Dr David Bellamy. The GWCF covers some 168 square miles, which lie between Wootton Bassett in the west, eastwards to Faringdon, and from the Wiltshire Downs north towards the line of the River Thames, and its main focus in Swindon is centred on Thamesdown Drive. From here can be accessed the Mouldon Hill Country Park with its lake, within the area of the Community Forest, and also the five-acre Berriman's Wood, which is in the hands of the Woodland Trust, and where broadleaved trees were planted between 1998 and 2000. This is part of a developing 'green corridor' linking Swindon with Cricklade, and is associated with the River Ray, the North Wilts Canal that is being restored, and a line of the Swindon & Cricklade Railway. The railway is building a station at Mouldon Hill as a precursor to eventually establishing a direct link to Swindon for its steam engines and historic rolling stock. Many schools in Swindon have become involved in the GWCF by planting wooded areas in their grounds. Also part of the Community Forest area is the River Ray parkway, a path for cyclists and walkers between Coate Water and Mouldon Hill. (See also Bruddell Wood; Moredon Tree Collection.)

Great Western Hospital Work on a replacement for Swindon's Princess Margaret hospital began at Commonhead in 1999, and the complex officially opened on 3 December, 2002. It had 550,000 square feet over six floors, and cost £132 million. In 2006, The Princess Royal opened its additional £32 million Brunel NHS Treatment Centre.

Great Western Hotel, Station Road The name was far too grand for

what was a drinking house with limited accommodation, albeit one whose façade suggested middle-class affluence. The hotel was designed in Gothic (in this case Early English) style by Thomas Smith Lansdown of Bath Road, and built in 1870. Lansdown's neat building, a two-storey, three times three-bay affair (plus two bays to Wellington Street) of brick with stone dressings, which particularly picked out the upper storey, presented as floor-to-roof canted bay windows with octagonal pitched roofs almost as corner turrets on the elevation facing the station. The range of upper windows is of pointed lights, paired beneath a continuous hood moulding and separated by slender shafts with caps of stiff leaf. With the exception of the pointed arch over the central doorway, the windows at ground-floor level are round-headed, and are also decorated with a continuous hood moulding. Stabling was added in 1872, and the original hotel building was remodelled in 1876 and extended to the east in 1896. This provided a three-storey, two-bay bedroom wing with octagonal pitched roof, and a similarly arranged linking building with gables, and a chimneystack between, to the upper storey. This ruined the symmetry of the north-front elevation, and the whole façade was thrown further out of shape by a projecting porch in the angle of the extension. Although Lansdown's design had moved on in an architectural sense from the Swindon hotels of the 1840s, it was not until the place had been remodelled and extended again in 1905 that its levels of accommodation achieved very much. Since it ceased to offer bedroom accommodation in the 1960s, the Great Western Hotel has gone through several name changes and various roles as restaurant and bars.

Greenbridge Cinema The multiplex at Shaw Ridge was Swindon's first multi-screen cinema; its second was built at Greenbridge, named Cineworld, and opened in 1998. In 2005, Cineworld merged with the French company Union General Cinematographique (UGC), as a result of which the Office of Fair Trading required the organisation to sell seven cinemas, of which the site at Greenbridge was one. It was bought by the Empire Cinema Group formed in 2006 and named after the Empire Theatre, Leicester Square, London, was renamed the Empire Cinema, and reopened as such that year.

Groundwell Farmers This was the name given to a community of street performers, musicians and craft workers who lived in a former farmhouse at the town's northern extremity. They included a silk screen printer, a potter, and a basket maker. The farm was recorded at Domesday. The house in which the community lived had the medieval cellars of two cottages that predated a small manor house that was built on the site in the 16th century, on which the present property was probably based when the manor house was either rebuilt or remodelled the following century, with dairy or brew house at the rear. Groundwell farmhouse was latterly five-bays square, and of two storeys, made of rubblestone with ashlar dressings, and having an attic, and a hipped roof with three dormers to the front and two to the sides. The main doorway, in the centre bay, had a moulded architrave, and a triple keystone, beneath a bracketed triangular pediment. Other features included stone transomed and mullioned ground-floor windows.

The building had long been at the heart of a working farm. It was purchased

in a poor state in the 1940s by Hills, the property developers, and was bought from them, c.1970, by private property developer Ramon Greene. He almost immediately sold part of the portfolio, including the house, to Swindon Borough Council.

In 1975, Action Space, a London fringe theatre organisation, rented Groundwell farmhouse and its immediate environs from Thamesdown Borough Council, the purchasing authority's successor. Action Space set up Groundwell Farm Arts Workshop, forming the initially eleven-strong Groundwell Arts Group, with the aim of bringing community arts, street theatre and other entertainments to the town. Swindon was sceptical but tolerant, and the community worked hard and flourished. The new residents had to refurbish the farmhouse in order to make it reasonably comfortable, which they did using the knowledge of two architects who were among the company, but they still lived in very cold conditions during the winter. Their ethos was all about providing art and creative play, workshops and hands-on opportunities for the local community. This they maintained despite annual rent rises, and a serious cut in their grant under the Conservative government that came to power in 1979. One of their projects resulted in an adventure playground at Penhill.

The group split from the parent company and thereafter became widely known as the Groundwell Farmers. They were apocryphally regarded locally as a hippy commune, although their work ethic and approach to business belied the common definition of the term, and they were self-sufficient in garden produce. The craft- and leisure-based community living ended in 1996 after some members had left, and the farmhouse once more declined in the hands of the local authority. In 2002, the place was bought by Dr Patrick Holmes and remodelled as a dental surgery, which opened in 2007. (See also Stredder, Henry Robert.)

GWR Medical Fund Hospital Much of the hospital was formerly a drill hall and armoury built in 1861 for the use of the XI Wiltshire Volunteer Rifle Corps, which had been formed in the GWR. The rest of it included two adjacent existing cottages. These were all converted for dealing with the results of accidents in the Works (the hospital was not concerned with diseases), and to provide accommodation for nurses. The Medical Fund's cottage hospital, with operating room, opened in 1871. One of the cottages became a separate dispensary. A further ward was added in 1898, raising the number of beds to eighteen. Gradually, more equipment and services were added: accident chairs, invalid wheelchairs, and airbeds; trusses, elastic stockings, and miscellaneous sick room appliances; and a small library for the use of patients. It also offered 'the great boon of ice, in case of illness', and by the turn of the century subscribed to twenty London hospitals and four seaside convalescent homes. In 1927, the garden immediately in front of the cottage hospital was mostly sacrificed to a 'temporary' extension, which enabled the hospital to have forty-two beds, an x-ray department, and run a blood donor service. In 1936, a minor accident and emergency outpatients department was added, with a small operating theatre, which continued to function until 1959. The GWR hospital closed in 1960; the premises became a social club for council workers, and thereafter a community centre. The building can still be seen as part of the GWR

model village complex. Since 1970, part of the original building has been a community centre. (See also Baths, Public.)

GWR Medical Fund Society The Society came into being as the direct result of difficulties experienced by railway workers made redundant by a recession of 1847 in paying for medical care for themselves and their families. For most, there was no work elsewhere, and they had little alternative but to remain in the town in the hope of being re-employed by the GWR. Daniel Gooch, Locomotive, Carriage & Wagon Superintendent at Swindon, persuaded the company's directors to make free accommodation and financial provision for the doctor to attend all employees. He also established the idea of those still in work contributing a proportion of their wages to a fund that would cover medical costs for all. The Society was formed to do this in December 1847. Its contributors were railway workers in employment at the Works, and its president was Archibald Sturrock, the Works Manager. The Society was organised by a committee of three officers and nine members, and these remained the town's only sanitary authority until the local Board of Health was established in 1864. Eleven years later, the GWR Medical Fund was registered as a Friendly Society. The Society set up a dental clinic in 1887, and appointed an undertaker. From then on, it was widely said that the GWR looked after its workers 'from cradle to grave'. In 1948, the Society's services and buildings were transferred to the Swindon & District Hospital Management Committee under the National Health Service Act, 1946, and in 1950 it was fully absorbed into the National Health Service as jointly operated by this Committee and the Oxford Regional Hospitals Board. (See also Baths, Public and GWR Medical Fund Hospital.)

GWR Works Tunnel, London Street The main entrance into the railway workshops was always an approach from High Street (renamed Emlyn Square in 1901) and across the railway lines north of London Street. The Company's Carriage and Wagon Works were built around this point, 1868-72. In 1871, Joseph Armstrong, then the Carriage & Wagon Superintendent at Swindon, decided to limit the potential for accidents to the workers entering and leaving the premises, by building a tunnel that ran beneath the carriage works and the main line. The tunnel was 380 feet long, and was kept open at all times of the day and night to accommodate changing shifts. It was said that the sound of men running through the tunnel at the end of their shift 'was like a stampede of animals', and some of the best historic pictures of railway workers show them bursting out of its entrance opposite the Mechanics' Institute.

It was to a little coal office near the end of this tunnel that retired railway workmen, or family members on their behalf, went to place orders for the railwaymen's subsidised 'allocation' of coal and wood. After the closure of the Works in 1986, the tunnel had periods of disuse. It was for a while the entrance to the Swindon Chamber of Commerce offices and then, around the beginning of the 21st century, to that of the Great Western Business Centre. When part of the railway workshops complex was revamped and opened in 1997 as the retail Designer Outlet Village, the old tunnel became the ten-minute walkway between that area (which now includes the STEAM railway museum, the National Monuments Record, and the National Trust

shop and restaurant) and the Swindon town centre.

In 2012, the tunnel was refurbished, and its north-east wall was illuminated by ten light boxes in laser-cut stainless steel, each measuring two metres by one metre, containing three-dimensional archive images of railway workers photographed over the course of a century. On the opposite wall, spelled out in capital letters 0.5 metres high, was 'Swindon Works'. This piece of public art, entitled 'Railway Workers', otherwise known as 'green metal light sculptures', was the work of Bruce Williams, a specialist artist and muralist based in Brighton. It took eighteen months to develop, and cost £150,000, which was paid for by Central Government and Forward Swindon. Prior to this, in 2008, Williams had completed a series of laser-cut steel panels, galvanised and painted, and also the college sign for Nova Hreod College, Swindon.

Hambro Life Assurance This company was formed in 1970 when, backed by its main shareholder, Hambros Bank, it established its headquarters in Swindon, above Debenham's store on The Parade. Its directors were formerly those of Abbey Life, including that company's founder, who had left Abbey Life after it was taken over by ITT, an American corporation. Hambro Life was importantly the first and most high profile of Swindon's 'service organisations' that have since taken over as major employers from the industrial firms, on which the town's economy was formerly based. In 1970, it set up the Hambro Life Charitable Trust with five trustees who were all directors of Hambro Life, two of whom were based in Swindon. The company also had a non-charitable fund for helping sports projects locally. In 1984,

the company was disposed of by Hambros Bank and, as the major unit holder of Allied Unit Trusts, it changed its name to Allied Hambro. Following its acquisition of the small private bank Dunbar & Company, it changed to Allied Dunbar in 1985. That year, the company was bought by the American BAT (British American Tobacco) Industries, which the previous year had acquired Eagle Star Insurance, and the two organisations were merged. In 1998, the resulting company was sold to Zurich Financial Services, and it remains in Swindon, in 2012, named Zurich.

Hammerman, The Dr John Cullimore, consultant obstetrician and gynaecological surgeon, wrote the music for a stage musical called *The Hammerman*, based on the life of Alfred Williams, with book by John Moorhouse. This was successfully premiered at the STEAM Museum in Swindon in November 2010, with support from the Heritage Lottery Fund. Dr Cullimore has also issued two CDs, *The Other Side of the Knife*, with his former group Under the Knife (2004), which included the material on two previously issued EPs, Railway Town, (2002) and Smooth Operators, (2003) with additional material; and *The Hammerman* (2008).

Harrod, Sheila (b.1944) Best known as the founder, in 1964, and musical director of The Kentwood Choir, Sheila Snook was born to music. On the day she married Chris Harrod in 1967, she conducted the choir, while in her wedding gown. Her father George, an insurance clerk, was born into absolute poverty. He was a naturally gifted musician who had no music lessons but taught himself to play from a theory book, for which he paid 3d. George's principal

instrument was the trumpet, although he was proficient on a range of brass, and also on the piano accordion, of which he wore out three in the course of his musical career. During the Second World War he performed in 'Stars In Battledress', played in the Glen Miller band, and accompanied Dame Anna Neagle, Charlie Chester, and Frank Chacksfield. For sixty-five years, George was the Salvation Army divisional bandmaster for the south and west of England. His wife Annie Olivia (née Matthews) was a Swindon florist, and a well-known singer of her day. The family were involved in concert parties, and carried out an enormous amount of charity work.

Sheila was born in the maternity hospital at Kingshill. She attended Westcott Infants School, and Clifton Street Junior School. Aged seven, she began piano lessons with Ada Fisher, and two years later started singing lessons with Salvationist singing teacher Enid Gunter; she then had training with Doris Parsons, and would later study in London. At eleven, she went to Headlands Grammar School. The corgi puppy with which she was presented for passing the scholarship was named Kentwood after the kennels near Oxford where she was purchased. By fourteen years of age, Sheila had achieved all her music grades for singing and playing. She was a bank cashier with a Diploma in Music when, in 1961, she successfully applied for the position of music teacher at Ridgeway School, Wroughton, which she was to hold for fourteen years. During that time, she was also a speech therapist at Burderop hospital, and began giving private singing tuition to five girls. These became a dozen, and the seeds of The Kentwood Choir were sown. Sheila was of a mind to call them The Snook Singers, but instead decided to name them after

her dog. In 1978, she set up the Kentwood School of Music, now called the Kentwood Voice Studio. There are three choirs in the Kentwood stable, and more than 500 people have belonged at one time or another. At its largest, the main choir had seventy-three singers, and has performed all over the world. In 1993 the choir's junior section performed in *Joseph and the Amazing Technicolour Dreamcoat* at the London Palladium, with Philip Schofield in the title role; it also appeared in the 1993 Royal Variety Performance. Also that year, Sheila Harrod was awarded the British Empire Medal in the New Year's Honours List: the last person to be given one. At the age of fifty-three, in 1997, she studied new ways of teaching singing at the Liverpool Institute.

In her private practice she teaches voice and piano, and tours the country with her voice workshop programmes. The presidents of Swindon's famous Kentwood Choir were the late Sir John Dankworth, and Dame Cleo Laine, who actually had wider family connections with the town. The choir sang at their fiftieth anniversary at the Royal Albert Hall in London.

Hawksworth, Frederick W. (1882-1976) Hawksworth was the only Swindonian to be appointed Chief Mechanical Engineer of the GWR, and the last person to hold that post before the railways were nationalised in 1949, when the position was abolished and he retired. An educational product of Sanford Street School, and the North Wiltshire Technical Institution (which became The College), and influenced in his choice of career by a father who worked in the GWR drawing office, young Hawksworth took an apprenticeship in the Works in 1898. Seven years later he was a

draughtsman; in 1925 he was appointed Chief Draughtsman. This was a man whose huge technical potential might have moved locomotive design at Swindon out of the rut into which it had fallen during the Collett years. However, by the time Hawksworth succeeded to the post of Chief Mechanical Engineer in 1941, the Second World War was well under way. Under him, the 'County' class came to prominence, and 'Hall' class locomotives were modified to improve their performance using coal of poor quality, which was all that was available for domestic use after the war (the best quality was being exported). Some seventy-one 'Halls' were modified between 1944 and 1950.

Hayward (David) Justin (b. 1946)

The lad who was to become best known as the singer and lead guitarist with the pop group The Moody Blues was born in Dean Street. He was the son of Sanford Street School teacher Frederick Hayward, and his wife Gwen. The family moved to Bourton, some eight or so miles distant, and Justin first went to school at nearby Shrivenham, which was also where he had his first music lessons. At the age of three he acquired his grandfather's collection of 1930s' gramophone records. In 1957 the family returned to Swindon, living at 54 The Mall, from where Justin went to the nearby Commonweal Grammar School. The Haywards attended St Saviour's church, Ashford Road, where Frederick was an altar server; it was there that his son's career in music began in a church skiffle group. He later became part of a pop group, The Satellites, which played locally in halls, etc. As a teenager, Justin joined several Swindon bands, notably The Revels, who were later renamed The Offbeats; The Whispers, All Things Bright, and The Shots.

For eighteen months, he worked as a trainee salesman at the Swindon building firm of Edwin H. Bradley. In 1963 he answered an advertisement in *Melody Maker*, which resulted in his becoming one of the Marty Wilde Trio, together with the singer himself and his wife Joyce Baker. At this point in time, he left Swindon for London. Three years later, he joined The Moody Blues, a band that had formed in 1964 and by then needed to replace two members. Justin learnt that he had the job whilst in the Swindon branch of the music shop Duck, Son & Pinker. His first album as The Moody Blues lead singer was *Days of Future Past*, released in 1967. The group's biggest selling song was *Nights in White Satin*. They broke up in 1974, but reunited in 1978 and recorded *Octave*. In 1997 Justin Hayward was the subject of a *This Is Your Life* television programme. He wrote the song *Tuesday Afternoon* in Lydiard Park.

Hemsley, Harry May (1878-1951)

Born in Swindon, Harry was the son of scenic artist William Thompson Hemsley and his wife Fanny (they also had daughters Ivy and Grace Fanny Harriett, who were born in London in 1885 and 1888 respectively). Harry also grew up to be an artist and scenic designer, who married Rose Florence (née Kingwell) at St Paul's church, Battersea in 1907. (The couple had one son, the delightfully if jokingly named Norman Castle Hemsley.) Harry made a career for himself on the stage, at one time as a singer, and then developed an act called 'Childlife' in which, it was written, he 'depicts in truly amazing manner the humorous side of child life, in the relation of familiar fairy stories and natural observations from the child's point of view, at the same time reproducing in life-like similarity the child he is impersonating'. His

private life did not reflect the comedy in his act. Before the First World War, he suffered a nervous breakdown. Although he was called up in 1917, and put into the Army Service Corps Mechanical Transport, he was found to have flat feet, varicose veins in his legs, and a number of other disorders, including a nervous disease. This became apparent when he broke down and sobbed whenever given an order by a superior, and occurred so frequently that within five months of call-up he was discharged as being physically unfit and suffering from neurasthenia. Thereafter, he became a vocal child impersonator, always obscuring his mouth when speaking with a child's voice, and created the imaginary 'Fortune' family. 'It is the perfect child's voice which Mr Hemsley assumes', wrote one critic, 'that is so marvellous.' Harry Hemsley sometimes deployed his skill as an artist in his stage act, and had a very successful career as such on the variety circuits and on radio.

Hemsley, William Thompson (1850-1918) In about 1860, George Storey Hemsley (b.1822), an engine fitter in Gateshead, County Durham, brought his wife Mary (née Hart) and their family to Swindon. George secured employment at the Great Western Railway Company's Works, and the family moved into 6 Westcott Place. Later, they relocated to 22 Reading Street. William Thompson Hemsley was one of at least six children born to the couple, and he later served an apprenticeship as a fitter in the Works. (His brothers James and Henry would become brass moulder and engine fitter there, respectively.) In 1873, William married Fanny Harriett Castle, née May (1852-1923) at St George's, Hanover Square, London. He had been taking evening classes in art at Swindon's Mechanics' Institute, and had begun to design, construct and paint scenery for the productions being put on in the Institute's theatre. In 1887 he was responsible for the generic 'new and appropriate scenery' that was a fixture at the Institute's theatre, and he was described as 'a rising London scenic artist'. This was the start of his professional career in artistic theatrical design, during which he designed scenes for productions at the New Queen's (later Empire) Theatre in Swindon, and for touring shows that played there, and was also scenic artist for productions at several London theatres, including The Adelphi, Covent Garden, Drury Lane, Haymarket, His Majesty's, and the Metropolitan, Edgware Road. Renowned, and highly sought after, Hemsley was considered to have been pre-eminent in his chosen profession.

Hermitage, The This large, part neo-Tudor, part Gothic, linked double-winged house with gables was built just off Market Square, c.1830, by Old Town chemist and druggist – and sometime printer, bookseller, stationer, and cigar dealer – Charles Anthony Wheeler. He also built Redville House in Charlotte Mews and Rose Cottage in Drove Road. The north wing of The Hermitage was part timber- framed with overhang and decorative openwork bargeboards. The rest was in stone, with canted bay windows with stone mullions and transoms, and string courses. The large rectangular porch on the central section was similarly arranged, and the doorway had a depressed Tudor-style arch. Later, the property was the family home of Swindon solicitors Henry Kinneir and, between 1922 and 1960, John L. Calderwood, who was a partner at Townsend's. Then, the house was sold to Swindon Corporation and

in 1964 it became a short-stay nursing home for the elderly, but was latterly neglected and stood vacant before being pulled down in 1994. Excavations on the site uncovered evidence of Anglo-Saxon buildings.

High Street In the 14th century, the hilltop settlement was called Hegherswyndon (High Swindon) because of its location, and it is possible that High Street was also so called because of its position on the hill, rather than the more usual 'main street' usage. The earliest known record of the name here is 1581; it appears in the manorial documents from 1615, and thereafter leases on dwellings in the street regularly change hands. Shops are mentioned from the early 1700s, and Swindon's first named grocers shop was started here by Robert and Margaret Boxwell in 1705. Their premises became part of The Bull inn, which was itself later incorporated into Mason's grocery store. Meanwhile, High Street gradually built up a number of small traders and cottage industries. A bank was established here in 1807, largely to facilitate the needs of market traders, and the street had taken on more trade: by the 1820s it had a baker, basket maker, two blacksmiths, butcher, carpenter, chemist, drapers, dressmakers, hairdressers and an ironmonger. There were professional people too: John and Joseph Gay, the sibling surgeons; Jonah Reeve, the auctioneer; and the postmaster Charles Rose. Because of its proximity to the Goddard estate, whose main entrance was from High Street, it attracted 'gentry' and some prosperous businessmen and their families. The first half of the 19th century saw larger business premises being custom-built here, and some larger residential properties.

By the 1870s, High Street had become the main shopping centre of the town, with virtually all the commodities represented that one might expect to find in a town of its size at that period; the street included four butchers, three grocers, three drapers, tailors and outfitters, fishmonger, ironmonger, confectioner, chemist, wine merchant and hairdresser. It had also become a favoured location for the town's solicitors and auctioneers. As the more traditional businesses shifted away from High Street, so were their premises remodelled and rebuilt, rather more in the service of commerce than trade. The bank buildings, now among the finest 19th century architecture in the town, are good examples of this. They have been retained, although not always, as in the case of the Wilts & Dorset bank of 1884, still in the business. The 20th century saw the destruction of several architecturally and historically important buildings in High Street (they are noted separately in this book) for the purposes of road widening, car parks, or to be replaced with uninspiring mixed business and residential premises. One of these, immediately east of Manchester House, was a three-storey, four-bay, 18th-century property. At street level, it incorporated shop premises; notably, from the late 1800s, those of William Henry Norris, saddler and harness maker, and during the first half of the 20th century it was occupied by Fred Cleverly & Son, antique dealers. It was demolished c.1966.

Hinder's Mural The earliest mural in Swindon was a business advertisement painted in the 1950s on the western wall of Hinder's pet store in Commercial Road, on the corner with Temple Street. The artist was Charles Edward Gaze. Hinder's was best known for its bird seed, which carried the

company's slogan 'Packed Amidst the Pure Air of the Wiltshire Downs', and which was also written on the wall. Gaze's mural had the words 'HINDER'S BIRD SEED' in letters several feet high, made up of logs, against a background of flowers and birds, and topped with a white horse in the gable to underline the Wiltshire connection. The building was demolished when Temple Street was re-built. (See also Gaze, Charles.)

Hodson, Denys Fraser (1928-2013) During his tenure as Director of Arts & Recreation in Swindon, Denys Hodson did more than anyone else has ever done to raise the overall cultural status of the town. He was appointed by Swindon Corporation in 1970 and continued under its successor, the Borough of Thamesdown, until his retirement in 1992. His great contribution to the arts and leisure facilities in Swindon includes the Wyvern Theatre, Thamesdown Community Arts, Swindon Dance in the Town Hall, the Oasis leisure and performance facility, and the golf course at Broome Manor. Of particular value to the town was his work in maintaining the Swindon Collection of 20th-century paintings, in which he always held a considerable interest, and about which he gave talks until the year before his death.

Denys Hodson was born at Northleach, Gloucestershire, the son of Reverend Harold Victor Hodson MC, and his wife Marguerite (née Ritchie) who married in Guildford in 1919. He was educated at Marlborough College, and his own marriage to Julie (née Goodwin) took place in 1954. He came to Swindon after developing a career in advertising, after which his general involvement in the arts brought him into contact with regional and national arts bodies, where his experience was much valued and he became Vice-chairman of the Arts Council for Great Britain. All of this led to his being awarded the CBE for services to arts in 1981. He was Chairman of the Friends of Lydiard Tregoze (where the local authority-owned house at Lydiard Park had been part of his remit). In retirement, he became a Trustee of the Friends of Fairford Church (in which village he lived), leading fund-raising campaigns to preserve its fabric and its nationally important medieval stained-glass windows.

Holland, Leslie (1907-2005) Famed as the cover designer of the first edition of *Brave New World* by Aldous Huxley (Chatto & Windus, 1932), Leslie Holland was also a notable muralist, who in 1986 decorated the site of the former M&SWJ Railway's station in Old Swindon. He was born in Ealing, London, and soon showed a natural gift for pencil drawing and close observation, and advanced to such a degree that he was invited to join both the Slade and the Royal College of Art. He chose the latter, but left before the end of the course, unhappy at what he felt to be the constraints on art when institutionalised. As a commercial artist he produced posters for London Transport, greetings telegrams for the Royal Mail, and book covers for a number of publishers. Leslie Holland spent his life with a sketchpad to hand, and was endlessly drawing.

After spending time in the artistic hotspots of Europe, in 1939 he married Gerty, an Austrian nurse, and the couple travelled around England's West Country. They lived in temporary accommodation such as a gypsy caravan and a cricket pavilion, before settling for a while with a Christian Bruderhof community in Shropshire. Communal work and life suited them, and

the family, by now with six young children, continued this approach in deepest Paraguay. There, he drew everyday community life, and the drawings were later used to illustrate a book about the Bruderhof in Paraguay. By the early 1960s, Leslie Holland and his family were living in Purton, where they remained for the next forty years. He illustrated the village magazine, painted 'The Last Supper' for St Mary's Church, Purton when their original was stolen, and became artist in residence for the Swindon Festival of Literature.

Holy Rood Catholic Church, Groundwell Road In 1851, a chapel was opened for Roman Catholic worshippers in Bridge Street; before this time, a priest said mass once a month at the Greyhound public house. In 1882, the Roman Catholics took over the Gothic-style premises at the northern end of Rolleston Street that had been built as a Free Christian Church in 1875, and the adjacent house. They refurbished this as a church and presbytery, and re-opened it in 1883. Internally, it had a chancel separated from the nave by a rood screen, and a Lady Chapel. The walls included illustrations of the Stations of the Holy Cross, and the altar had niches for six statues. A vestry was added in 1887, and a school two years later. This church remained the Roman Catholic place of worship until 1903, when they took on the corner site in Groundwell Road, building Holy Rood in flint to the Early English-style cruciform design of Edward Doran Webb, at a cost of £4,000. The first marriage ceremony to be held there was on 19 December 1903. It originally had chancel, nave, aisles and transept but was realigned and extended in the 1970s. The Rolleston Street complex was used as a museum, 1920-30.

Holy Rood Church, Goddard Estate The remains of what was probably a Norman foundation, and of which the earliest mention extant is dated 1154, stand in isolation on The Lawn estate in Old Town. It was dedicated to St Mary until the mid-16th century. The route to it from High Street was along the line of The Planks, past the mill pond that existed just to the south of the churchyard wall until the late 19th century. The church was partially restored in 1736 and bell founder Abraham Rudhall of Kendal provided five bells in 1741. Most of the church was demolished in 1852, although both Buckler and John Luckett Jefferies had made drawings of the place. The existence of a photograph taken c.1847, possibly by Nevil Story-Maskelyne, who was a friend of photography pioneer Henry Fox Talbot, confirmed the exterior, and it is possible to reconstruct the interior from the fragments remaining on the ground.

The church consisted of a two-stage tower (which William Morris said was supported on four tree trunks), built of bricks in 1748; chancel, nave, north and south aisles with square-headed windows over which were clerestories with little pointed windows, and a vestry of 1820. The chancel remains, of two orders on 14th-century corbels, and there are a number of repositioned wall memorials. Fragments of the former nave arcade reveal hexagonal pillars, and the floor is paved with 18th- and 19th-century tombstones. There are some table tombs still in the old churchyard.

Swindon Corporation took over the ruin in 1949, kept the chancel locked for several decades, and used it as a groundsman's hut until restoring it in 1970; in the following year the chancel was re-opened as a chapel of unity. The font and the pulpit were rebuilt

by Ronald Packer of Bartlett Brothers, who also renovated some of the wall memorials and re-arranged them. The altar is made from sections of an 18th-century table tomb that was in the churchyard, and has a cross of black marble. The building is occasionally opened to the public.

Honda of the UK Manufacturing In 1985, having previously struck a deal with the nearby Austin Rover car plant to co-operate on building an executive Rover car, Honda bought some 370 acres of the former Vickers Armstrong estate at South Marston. The property included the company's one-time airfield and runways, and Honda began building its Swindon engine and assembly plant there. The engine plant went into production in 1989, making units for Honda and Rover cars. A £300 million car plant with a potential capacity of 150,000 vehicles per year opened there in 1992, and thereafter Honda manufactured complete vehicles at South Marston. Three years later, a second engine assembly line went in; a second car plant, which was built adjacent, 1999-2001, raised the annual total capacity of the site to 250,000 vehicles. In 2011 Honda installed at South Marston the UK's first public hydrogen refuelling station, following its production of the FCX Clarity, the world's first dedicated platform hydrogen vehicle.

Hooper, William (1864-1955) Born in the village of Windrush, Gloucestershire, Hooper began his working life as an estate worker at nearby Sherborne House. He came to Swindon in 1882, lodged in Oxford Street in the railway village, and was employed in one of the locomotive repair shops at the GWR Works. During this time, he took up photography as a hobby. William lost the

lower part of a leg following an accident in B Shop at the Works and, as a result, was later invalided out of railway service. He married Mary Stroud at Swindon's Baptist tabernacle, Regent Street, in 1890; and her sister Alice married Thomas Richards, another GWR employee. The latter's ability to make optical lenses, and his interest in lens construction, would later give an edge to William's photographic work. By the time he set up as a professional photographer, c.1903, there had been photographic studios in Old Town for about forty-five years, and for about two decades in New Swindon. Thomas, also a keen amateur photographer, imparted his knowledge to William and helped to ensure that, above those of all other Swindon photographers of the late 19th and early 20th centuries, the latter's pictures became notable for their clarity and diversity. William Hooper's first studio for portraits was at 2 Market Street, and in 1906 he relocated the business to 6 Cromwell Street. He retired in 1921, leaving a fine legacy of photographs showing Swindon's streets; pictures of his own premises; events that took place in and around the town; himself and his wife and, famously, the motor bicycles on which they travelled. Both are buried in Radnor Street cemetery, Swindon. A monograph *The Life & Times of William Hooper* by Paul A. Williams was published in 2007.

Hooter, The GWR Works' To begin with, the Works summoned its employees by tolling a bell. However, from 1867 the instrument that called time for the railwaymen was the GWR Works' steam-driven hooter. This was erected above 'R' Shop, a new engine house building of 1865, and eventually relocated above the hydraulic

power engine house, which thereafter became known as 'Hooter House'. The hooter was described thus: 'For ten miles round it performs a useful moral work. By its voice, thousands are warned of the approaching hours of labour; men are imbued with habits of regularity, and regularity begets order in the general affairs of life'. An employee was deputed to blow the hooter at the prescribed times, which were several in advance of the early morning shift, and thereafter at the moment each shift could leave the premises; employees pressed hard against the closed doors awaiting its sound. In 1873 Lord Bolingbroke of Lydiard House, a few miles distant, succeeded in a legal action to revoke the hooter's licence to blow, on the grounds that the noise was detrimental to his heart condition when he was resident in his country house (an annual occurrence). A new, even louder, atmospheric hooter was installed nearby. During the Second World War, this was used as an air-raid siren, and it continued to be operated until the Works closed in 1986.

The hooter was twice brought back into service. At the suggestion of one-time railway worker Jack Telling, who had operated the hooter, it was blown three times to mark the 50th anniversary of D-day in 1994. (Coincidentally, the opening day of the National Monuments Record) This was done by means of an air compression unit, taking the place of steam, but the pressure through the whistles was only one-thirtieth of the power formerly used. It blew again when the Designer Outlet Village was opened in 1997.

Horder, Albert (1831-1902) From the late 1800s, Horder's the drapers, ladies' outfitters, and milliners occupied a substantial section of High Street between Lloyds Bank and the entrance to the Goddard estate. These were three-storey, six-bay premises with a carriageway to the south. At street level, when the frontage had been remodelled, there were two entrances into the shop area, with large window displays between; the first floor had six-pane, round-headed windows with Classical hood mouldings and window surrounds; the second-floor windows were square-headed, their sills formed of a continuous string course with brackets beneath. Each bay was topped by a segmental, moulded pediment. Horder's continued to operate until the 1970s, when it was sold and the building destroyed in favour of residential apartments.

Albert Horder, the founder of this business, was born at Donhead St Mary, south Wiltshire, the son of farmer William Horder and his wife Sylvia. Eventually Albert went into the drapery business at Shaftesbury, Dorset. He was in High Street there by 1861, unmarried although employing his spinster sister Mary as housekeeper, keeping young Mary Blandford of Tisbury as a servant, and occupying two draper's assistants and an apprentice in his 'linen and woollen drapers'. In 1865, he married Mary Ellen Jeeves, a farmer's daughter of Bampton, Oxfordshire, and the family lived over the business, having as boarders the three young draper's assistants that he employed in the shop. In 1872, Albert set up his business in High Street, Swindon, in a large residence that had long been in the Coventry family, but lately in that of Strange. The family then had three sons: Edward (b.1868), who would eventually take over the business; Arthur Albert (b.1869) and Thomas (b.1871). At the outset, Albert employed his niece Hannah Baker as a draper's assistant, and also his nephew Gideon Heath; among others

employed was Elizabeth Pond, who was also born at Donhead St Mary. Following his retirement, Albert and Mary lived at 'Wincombe' (named after his father's farm), with one servant, at 88 Devizes Road.

Housing estates The first area of Swindon to be built up as a planned housing estate was Pinehurst, c.1919-36, on the town's north-east boundary with Stratton St Margaret. This was followed from the mid-1930s by a few roads to the east of Drove Road between Old Town and New Town, which became known as Old Walcot. Rodbourne Cheney was the first residential area to be established after the Second World War, on land adjacent to allotments to the west of the thoroughfare between New Swindon and Pinehurst. Between 1951 and 1955, Penhill was developed, essentially for the intake of workers from London, under the Town Development Act, 1952. This pushed Swindon's boundary to the north, beyond Pinehurst, and the roads there were all named after Wiltshire villages. Cheney Manor, north of Rodbourne, was laid out in 1952.

Thereafter, the main thrust of Swindon's residential development took place in the area to the east of Drove Road, bounded in the north by the old road to Marlborough. Here, from 1954, The Lawns residential development was established, named after the Goddard family's former residence, which had stood nearby, and on part of whose estate the roads were laid out. Next to it, and to the east of Old Walcot, came the Walcot estate, which was put up 1956-60. Park South was built to the north-east of The Lawns, 1956-65, and Park North was built next to it during the same period. In 1948, the local authority bought farmland at Moredon

and built a large council estate there during the early part of the 1950s.

Attention then switched east of Walcot, Park North and Park South, and the town's eastern flank between Stratton St Margaret and Wanborough began to be developed residentially. Covingham, Dorcan and Nythe were developed from the mid-1960s, and Eldene from the 1970s. During the next decade, the developers switched to West Swindon, south of Lydiard Tregoze and north of the M4 motorway. Toothill and Freshbrook were built 1980-84, followed from the middle of the decade by Grange Park, which was squeezed in next to Lydiard Park Estate. Eastleaze and The Prinnels followed.

Swindon's expansion into its Northern Development Area, mostly in the parishes of Haydon Wick (which had itself been part of Rodbourne until 1928) and Blunsdon St Andrew, began 1993-97 with the development of the Abbey Meads estate, named after nearby Blunsdon Abbey, which was destroyed by fire in 1904. St Andrew's Ridge, named after Blunsdon St Andrew, was built 1998-99. The northern expansion continued in earnest from 2000, devolving on the northern orbital road that was opened the following year, with the huge Priory Vale development, which opened in 2002. This comprises several 'villages', namely Redhouse, Haydon End, Oakhurst and Taw Hill.

Hudson, Arthur Kenneth (1916-99) Kenneth Hudson was an important industrial archaeologist, archaeological editor, and prolific writer, whose interest in museums occupied much of the latter part of his life. During the mid-1960s, he spent much time in Swindon, particularly in the reference library, researching his seminal urban study

An Awkward Size For A Town: Swindon at the 100,000 Mark (David & Charles, 1967). Despite Hudson's impeccable pedigree, the town and its residents exhibited the inhibiting and narrow-minded social attitudes implied in parts of the study by questioning whether an 'outsider' was qualified to comment on the town. Seemingly eschewing his very positive comments about aspects of the place, many were quick to defend the areas of which he wrote negatively, often countering him in a spirit of churlishness. Hudson was the first to recognise that Swindon was simply too old-fashioned and inward-looking in its outlook for its future good, and that people expected much more by way of amenities than a town of its size could provide. His discussion on the town's character, economic base and post-war development described how Swindon had got to the point it had in the mid-1960s, and then went on to suggest how it might develop to advantage in the future. It did not endear Hudson to already disgruntled Swindonians when the media immediately featured the study, majoring on the negative aspects of Swindon and quoting several of the author's less than complimentary comments. *An Awkward Size For A Town* remains a brilliant historic study of a town already in transition, but too hidebound at the time to realise it.

Hunter, Frances Priscilla (1892-1914)

This sensational murder was remarkable for the degree of public sympathy in favour of the murderer when it was revealed that Frances Hunter had been unfaithful to him with a married man. On 29 April 1914, Walter James White, a painter and decorator of 10 Dover Street, Swindon, killed Frances Hunter at the Goddard Arms Hotel, High Street, where she had been employed for

seven months as a between maid. At the date of the murder, White was employed by house decorator H.C Cook of Wood Street, and had been working at the premises of George H. Pakeman, tailor, of 20 High Street. Frances lived at 14 Holbrook Street, and her father Richard John Hunter was a checker at the GWR Works. White lived at 17 Turner Street, and was the son of Thomas White, a railway labourer.

White and Hunter had been going steady for about six months when the couple left Swindon on 25 September to visit the girl's brothers at Bargoed, Glamorgan, where they tried to find lodgings with a Mrs Blewitt at Commercial Street, Gilfack. The landlady refused to accommodate the girl, and wrote to White, when the couple returned to Swindon, that she had certain information relating to his girlfriend's earlier conduct. White returned to the lodgings in Wales, where he was informed that Frances Hunter had for three months lived as the wife of another woman's husband. This news so adversely affected White that he bought a six-chambered revolver and some ammunition in Bargoed, returned to Swindon and wrote a series of letters, with the assumption that what he planned to do would result in his own death.

He presented himself at the Goddard Arms and was taken by Hunter to the staff room, and thereafter, apparently at her suggestion, to the nearby coal hole, possibly to continue their discussion out of the hearing of Ernest John Walter Looker, the hotel's boots, who was having his tea in the staff room. White alleged that Hunter confessed to the truth of the allegation, agreed that she had disgraced White and hoped that God would forgive her. According to White, he then announced that he was going to kill

her, whereupon Hunter cried out 'for God's sake do it then', and kissed him. White pulled out his revolver and fired two shots, one of which entered the right ear, the other the left-hand side of the neck. Frances Hunter was killed instantly, and White then discharged the remaining rounds into the air and waited to be discovered. He was apprehended by Amos Church, the hotel's manager, put in the charge of police constable Waite, and the girl's body was removed to the mortuary, under the auspices of Dr R.P. Beatty. Frances Priscilla Hunter was interred on 5 May, 1914 at Radnor Street cemetery, following a service at St Mark's church.

Walter White was found guilty of wilful murder and sentenced to death. Yet from the moment in Bargoed when he learnt of Hunter's disgrace, he had been 'dazed and ...in great mental anguish'. The community took him to their hearts as being misguided, but not a real criminal; they felt he had been driven to temporary insanity by Hunter's actions. A petition calling for him to be reprieved was immediately raised in the town, based on his youth and the degree to which he had been provoked. When presented, this had five thousand signatures, and people in Cirencester also added their names to the appeal for mercy. His cause was taken up by Reuben George and Frederick Olsen in Swindon; Richard C. Lambert, MP, who presented the petition to the Home Secretary, also argued vigorously on White's behalf. Home Secretary Reginald McKenna rejected the application', and White was hanged at Winchester prison on 15 June, 1914. (See also O'Callaghan, Sian; and Swinford, Esther.)

Ibberson Jones Trophy for Poetry

In 1959, Mrs E.J. Jones, the widow of a local poet, Wilfred Ibberson Jones, gave a poetry trophy to be awarded annually in his memory. Jones was a Canadian by birth, who served in the Royal Engineers during the First World War and, in the 1920s, established the electrical engineering firm of Teesdale & Jones, at Park Lane in Swindon. He latterly lived at 44 Westlecot Road, Old Town.

The writers who submitted work for the Ibberson Jones Trophy had to live within a twenty-mile radius of Swindon. They were required to submit their own work in no longer than fifty lines of verse, and the winner would be the writer of what was adjudged to be the best poem. Forty-nine poems were submitted in 1959, from which a judging panel selected twenty-one that they considered of sufficient quality to be submitted to an adjudicator for his final judgement. The winners received the trophy and a book token, at a 'private, low key ceremony' that usually involved the mayor of the year, who made the presentation, the adjudicator of the year, and members of the Library Committee. The privacy under which this took place annoyed members of the Poetry Circle, who were at first vociferous in their complaints.

The winners were:

1959 Peter Little, a Swindon College lecturer for his poem *In The Park*, chosen by critic, author and poet Geoffrey Grigson, who lived at Broad Town farmhouse.

1960 Norman E. Passant, for his poem *Term End*, chosen by poet and architectural writer John Betjeman.

1961 Geoffrey Grigson did not consider that any poem submitted came up to standard, so the trophy was not awarded.

1962 Graham Carey of Malmesbury, a teacher at Malmesbury Secondary Modern School and Swindon College lecturer for his poem *Landscapes*, chosen by Charles

Causley, the West of England poet and author.

1963 Marguerite Johansen Deane of Picton House, 100 Bath Road, a former secretary of Swindon Poetry Circle, for her poem *I Have That I Have*, chosen by D. W. Alun Llewellyn, playwright and poet.

1964 Marguerite Johansen Deane, for her poem *The Pool*, chosen by Robert Armstrong, General Secretary of The Poetry Society in London.

1965 Marguerite Johansen Deane, for her poem *High Heeled Boots*, chosen by Mrs Joan Marie Simpson, who had been nominated by The Poetry Society.

1966 Georgina A. Scrivens of 153 Shrivenham Road, Swindon, for her poem *Softly, Carefully*, chosen by Mrs Joan Marie Simpson, who had been nominated by The Poetry Society.

1967 Norman E. Passant, for his poem *Chiff Chaff*, chosen by Peter Robins, who had been nominated by The Poetry Society.

1968 Wes Magee of Bath Road, for his poem *The Windmill Hill People*, chosen by Peter Robins, who had been nominated by The Poetry Society.

1969 Norman E. Passant, for his poem *His Creature*, chosen by Norman Hidden, Chairman of The Poetry Society.

1970 not awarded

1971 not awarded

1972 Brenda Stewart, of Shaftesbury Avenue, Park North, for her poem *Comment On Senility*.

1973 Marguerite Johansen Deane, with her poem *The Well*.

Marguerite Johansen Deane (b. 1907) helped to set up the Swindon Philosophical Society in the 1960s, of which she was eventually made life president. She became a teacher of philosophy to the University of the Third Age in Swindon, and was still teaching when in her nineties. She published many slim volumes of her poetry.

Iffley Road Mural Iffley Road, Rodbourne was speculatively financed by the Oxford Building Society, c. 1882, and was completed by 1890. In 1982, Ken White, with the help of some unemployed people, painted a mural to celebrate 'Fifty Years of Voluntary Effort in Swindon' on the gable end wall of a terrace in Iffley Road. The mural was of a three-storey house of red brick with stone-coloured quoins, lintels, sills and flat string courses, painted as if it was on a triangular site, so that the entrance front and two sides of the property were visible. It was based on the Faringdon House, Faringdon Road, headquarters of the Swindon Council of Social Services, formerly the Citizens Advice Bureau, but at the time it was painted it was known as the Thamesdown Voluntary Service Council. The piece was unveiled by former cabinet minister Richard Marsh and the one-time boss of British Rail, by then Lord Marsh of Mannington, who had been evacuated during the Second World War to live in Redcliffe Street with his grandmother.

The visual complexity of the Iffley Road mural made it one of Ken White's more complicated designs for a domestic scale. It was also slightly surreal, as it featured pigs apparently falling from a third-storey window, and representations of a pig farm in nearby Ferndale Road, which was then owned by Swindon Social Services. For this reason, the wall was known as the 'Flying Pigs Mural'. The piece included the likenesses of the Swindon philanthropist James 'Raggy' Powell, social services staff of the day, a meals on wheels delivery van, a community transport vehicle, a guide dog

for the blind, boy scouts, girl guides, and brownies. The wall also included a number of emblems and badges associated with social organisations, disability, etc. The mural was removed in 1990 when the wall on which it was painted succumbed to damp.

Ing, Edwin Robert (1830-1909)

Ing's ginger beer bottles, distinguished by their crossed battle axes logo, are the finest of all the similar manufacturers in Swindon. The company's proprietor was born in the hamlet of Walton, Buckinghamshire, where his parents lived at Walton Terrace. (Edwin would later give the name 'Walton House' to his own house in The Sands (Bath Road), Swindon.) His parents, George Ing and his wife Ann were recorded as being of independent means. In 1852, Edwin, by now living in Bath Road, Swindon, established himself as a chemist in Wood Street. The business included a young apprentice, Walter Pigott. Edwin married Adelaide (née Baden, b. 1830, Coate) in 1855, and they had three children by 1860, and two female servants. In 1857, he became a founding director of the Swindon Water Company, was a founding director of the Swindon Central Market Company in 1862, and was one of the committee that organised the inaugural ball of the Corn Exchange in 1866. By 1871, the couple had five children and a governess Martha Holmes to look after them, and the family also employed three other female servants. Another child was born in 1874.

E.R. Ing made his own Toothache Pills, Cough Pills, Balsamic Tincture, Stomachic Digestive and Dinner Pills, Aronica Montania Embrocation, and Antiscorbutic Dentifrice, which were used in large quantities in the town. His Farmer's Friend cured colic in horses; cattle, horses and sheep that suffered from 'sprains, cuts, bruises, over-reaches, treads, crashing, swelling, broken knees, and all external inflammation' might get relief from his Superior White Oils; limping sheep could be treated with his Wiltshire Dressing for Footrot in Sheep; and he also made a wide range of cow drinks and other cattle medicines.

By 1880, he had expanded his chemist's business into premises in High Street and was also advertising himself as a manufacturer of soda water at the Wood Street address. In 1882, he sold his chemist's business to John J. Shawyer, and set up his North Wilts Aerated Water Manufactory in Lansdown Road. This operated 'by steam power, bottled under pressure of 300 pounds to the inch', and made a wide range of soft drinks. Following the death of his wife in 1900, Ing relocated to 'The Mount', Devizes Road, where he installed his sister-in-law Elizabeth Baden. His company merged with W. Leese & Son in the mid-20th century, thereby forming Leese, Ing & Co. In 1973, this was taken over by Ace Soft Drinks, a brand that Swindon brewers Arkell's had established in 1939, the name of which was sold on when the company closed its soft drinks plant at Kingsdown in 1962.

Iron Church

In 1861, Revd Frederick Rowland Young opened his Free Christian Church in Regent Street, between the Wilts & Berks Canal and the junction with Cromwell Street. The side walls of his church were ten feet high and had square-headed windows, and the barrel-shaped roof was thirty-two feet from the ground at its highest. It had a similarly shaped entrance porch, made of the same material, with a rectangular window in each side. A single gas lamp lit the entrance. From the roadside, it presented a low brick wall, surmounted by wrought-iron railings of

poppy head design, with a pillar at each end, and a similarly designed gateway. Within a year Revd T. Noble had been employed as assistant minister, and a schoolroom that doubled as a Sunday school and a public meeting place was established next door, with G.J. Davis as schoolmaster. The church began to fail when worshippers complained that the price of sittings was too high, and Revd Noble and Mr Davis both left.

The iron church ceased to be used as a place of worship in 1874. The iron church was sold, although it is not clear to whom, and became a music hall and a skating rink before being taken down. It was then sold to Arkell's brewery at Stratton St Margaret and erected as their barrel store in St Philip's Road, Upper Stratton. It had a spell as a chapel before St Philip's church was built nearby in Beechcroft Road in 1904, when it became the church hall and remained as such until the 1950s when, considered to be unsafe, it was abandoned. The building was demolished in November 1967 by Messrs Wilsons builders, who had bought the site for residential redevelopment. (See also Free Christian Church; Museums; Young, F.R.)

Isolation Hospital, Gorse Hill
Now the Hawthorn Centre, this red-brick building with Bath stone dressings was designed by Henry Joseph Hamp of Victoria Road, Surveyor to the New Swindon Urban District Council, and built in 1892 at a cost of £4,500. The complex was constructed on a system of blocks: one was the isolation section with two wards each for males and females, and rooms for the nurses who administered to them; the other contained the offices, storerooms, disinfecting ovens, mortuary, wash-house, and laundry room. There was also accommodation for a caretaker and the staff, which also provided space for the stores. The hospital was extended in 1903. Over the years, the wards were better separated to reflect the prevalent infectious diseases of the time: two sections dealt with cases of scarlet fever; others contained patients with typhoid and diphtheria; and there was a building, about four hundred yards from the main block, in which were put those who had smallpox.

Jazz Festival In the late 1990s, organiser Ray Butt decided that Swindon should have its own jazz festival and also its own jazz radio station, in order to put Swindon on the national jazz map. The idea to organise a jazz festival in Swindon in 1999 fell on fallow ground; he had been warned that Swindon was a difficult place to introduce new ideas and many people had tried to run jazz festivals before, without sustained success. Ray abandoned his plans when the Borough Council declined to give financial support, and sufficient corporate interest could not be found. There was, however, a grass roots groundswell of support, and during the latter end of 1999 he decided that 'by hook or by crook' a Swindon Jazz Festival would take place in April 2000 under the banner of Fretless and Friends. It centred on the hostelries of Old Town, and featured many of the bands and musicians that Ray associated with during his time in Swindon. He canvassed and cajoled relentlessly in order to obtain funding for the many musicians who would form the dozen or so bands playing during the weekend. The Musicians' Union were so interested in Ray's idea that they offered a considerable sum of money in order to substantiate its success.

The jazz festival was opened by the Pete Allen Jazz Band, which had a strong

local following made even more popular by its jazz fish and chips suppers in Lydiard Millicent Village Hall. The whole festival was an unqualified success, particularly as most of the jazz sessions were free to the public; only three ticketed evening concerts were held, featuring star bands such as The Roger Marks Jazz Band, and Fretless & Friends, which included the very talented young Jamie Cullum (q.v.). The huge crowds that attended made it known that they would be back for more of the same the following year ... if not before! During the following months, Ray's second dream project to put a new radio station into Swindon was gaining momentum. By the autumn of 2000, Ray was beginning to put together plans for the 2001 jazz festival and he suddenly confronted new-found interest from those organisations who had previously eschewed the idea. Thus, with more funding in sight from the Musicians' Union and other companies in Swindon, the Borough Council set up a committee to organise the jazz festival for 2001, featuring many stars from the world of jazz. A new Swindon radio station was introduced in 2001 and co-founder Ray was delighted to be presenting jazz-featured programmes on Swindon FM.

The radio station did not survive; however, the jazz festival continues to feature as one of Swindon's many cultural offerings and is now ably organised by jazz aficionado David Knight. David was a leading light in the Swindon Jazz Society, which was formed in 1962 as one of the 'public library extension activities' that took place in the town's Arts Centre, Devizes Road. Since 2001, its home has been the King's Arms in Wood Street. Ray Butt and Fretless and Friends continue to play at the Swindon Jazz Festival, and he

is also a member of the U3A Dance Band – a group of seasoned amateur musicians who play mainly at monthly tea dances for the benefit of the local ballroom enthusiasts, which in turn raises money for local charities.

Jefferies, Joan May (1908-1998)

As characters go, Joan tipped the balance into eccentric. This is the woman who knitted woollen vests to put on cormorants that became oil-soaked during the Gulf War, and gave boiled sweets to bus drivers. She was psychic, interested in ghosts, and knew much local folklore. Her husband Will was a GWR train driver, and the couple came from Chippenham. They saw their home in Corby Avenue being built, acquired it from new in 1935, and Joan lived there until her death. Here, her garden was famously left to run itself and became a wildlife haven. An avid collector of artefacts and books, she lived her adult life on committees and in support of charities and causes. These frequently necessitated obtaining signatures for petitions, and she would undertake such tasks on behalf of causes in which she believed, no matter how small or hopeless the quest. If she could justify action in her mind, then passionate action was what she took. She was involved in the Townswomen's Guild and the Women's Institute, was a founder member of The Friends of Alfred Williams, and one-time secretary of the Richard Jefferies Society. She joined The Swindon Society, and her literary and artistic interests led her into the Swindon Artists Society, the Swindon Debating Society, and the Swindon Literary Society. Approaching her mid-eighties when Swindon's Bath Road museum suffered cash problems in 1992, she nonetheless threw herself into a petition that helped to save it. She also supported the

local Prospect Hospice, and the Marie Curie Cancer Care charity.

Jefferies, (John) Richard (1848-1887)

Richard Jefferies, naturalist writer and prose poet, was born at Coate farmhouse. In 1866, Jefferies became a journalist on Joshua Henry Piper's *North Wilts Herald*, which was established five years earlier, and also contributed to William Morris's *Swindon Advertiser* (established 1854). Jefferies took lodgings in Victoria Street, close to the *Advertiser's* offices. It was said of him that 'he was naturally indolent and would never have worked but for pressure of necessity'. His first book, *Reporting, editing and authorship: practical hints for beginners in literature*, was published in 1873; he published *The Scarlet Shawl*, his first work of fiction, the following year. Also in 1874, he married Jessie Baden from nearby Dayhouse Farm, Coate, and the couple left Swindon the following year.

Jefferies's essays for the *Pall Mall Gazette* came out in 1878 as *The Gamekeeper At Home*. Unsuccessful with three novels in the later 1870s, he came to prominence with letters to *The Times* on the condition of the agricultural labourer. *Round About A Great Estate*, published in 1880, was based on Burderop Park. *Bevis*, published 1882, was a partly autobiographical account of his boyhood around Coate.

In 1926, the Borough of Swindon bought Coate farmhouse for £2,100. A Richard Jefferies Society was founded in Swindon by Harold E. Adams (also its inaugural chairman) in 1950, at a public meeting held in the town hall. Its first president was Samuel J. Looker; at his death in 1965, the position was taken by Henry Williamson, and then W.J. Keith of Toronto University. In 1951,

as part of the Festival of Britain celebrations, and in Jefferies's memory, the society erected a wooden seat on Liddington Hill, with funds obtained by international subscription. It was made by Swindon craftsman R. H. Gardiner, and cost £60. A one-room Richard Jefferies Museum was opened at Coate Farmhouse ten years later. There is a memorial to members of Richard Jefferies's family, on a chest tomb near the ruins of Holy Rood church on the Lawn estate.

John, David Murray (1908-1974)

Born in Sunderland, David Murray John was the son of David John John, a Baptist minister from Gowerton, Glamorgan in Wales, and his Sunderland-born wife Elizabeth (née Murray). The couple married in June 1907, and shortly after their son's birth they relocated to Great Yarmouth. David Murray John married Elsie (née Rogers) in Sunderland in 1936.

He was appointed deputy town clerk of Swindon on 25 June 1937 and became, on 1 May 1938, the youngest town clerk in the country at the time, a capacity in which he continued until just before his death. He was awarded the OBE in 1942 and, thirty-one years later, was given the freedom of the borough. Swindon's tallest building – the Murray John tower – was posthumously named after him in 1976. He was small in stature, and a life-long chain smoker with a preference for Woodbine cigarettes. It was Murray John who organised Swindon's involvement as an overspill town under the Town Development Act, 1952, thereby starting its large post-war population rise. He is generally credited as the architect of Swindon's retail and business expansion after the Second World War, and the development of its social infrastructure. It was also Murray John who bought

Lydiard Park – the house and 147 acres of surrounding land – for £4,500 of public money in 1943 when much of the grounds was in the hands of the military.

In 1970, following Elsie's death, Murray John moved into the terraced house in South Street where he would remain until the end of his life. When he finished his career in public service he was in ill-health, and severely disenchanted by the local government reorganisation of 1974 under which Swindon was swallowed into the Borough of Thamesdown. His decade-held hopes for Swindon becoming a city – everything which, in his own mind, he had worked towards – had been dashed on the anvil of central government. Although he was a broken man, his own retirement was postponed whilst he oversaw the transition. He died on his sixty-sixth birthday, of an illness that many who knew him said was exacerbated by a broken heart. (See also Murray John Tower.)

Jolliffe, Harold (1914-1969) Until 1942, when Swindon adopted the Public Libraries Act, local people were served by the Mechanics' Institute Library. Swindon's first public library was opened as a single room in McIlroy's department store on 14 August 1943. In the first year, just over twenty-nine per cent of the town's population joined the new library, some ten per cent higher than the national average. Harold Jolliffe was born in Bury, Lancashire, became chief assistant at Leicester City Libraries, and was appointed Chief Librarian at Swindon in 1946. The Swindon Arts Centre was the first local authority arts centre in the country. It opened two years before the Local Government Act, 1948 allowed councils to levy a rate in order to do so.

Jolliffe, who lived in Scotby Avenue, thereafter initiated a programme for developing the arts in the town, and created the means whereby 'ancillary societies' and 'extension activities' could be formed for leisure and learning under the auspices of the libraries department. At its height, there were some 500 such groups operating in the town. Jolliffe became one of the most significant and well-respected figures in the library movement nationally, in 1962 publishing the textbook *Public Library Extension Activities*, the first of its type since 1927. The book was written at the request of The Library Association, which wanted to include the topic in its professional examinations for librarians, and took two-and-a-half years to write. His other book, based on his experiences in Swindon, was called *Arts Centre Adventure*, published in 1968.

Four hundred people, including officials from the Borough Council and luminaries of the library world, attended his funeral, which was conducted at St Mark's church by his long-time friend Canon W. J. Cratchley. In 1971, a concert was held at the Arts Centre, Swindon, under the auspices of The Harold Jolliffe Memorial Foundation, which had been set up in May of that year, in order to raise funds to provide a memorial to his memory. Among performances of words and song by a number of people, poems were read by Walter Webb, the actor manager of the Arts Centre, and reference librarian Keith Hardy, founder of Swindon Opera, sang at the event. In 1971, a plaque was unveiled to him as the 'Pioneer of Arts in Swindon' by his widow Clary Jolliffe, in the then newly opened Wyvern Theatre. There, the Jolliffe Studio was opened in his name, but this would later be renamed Studio One. The first

Jolliffe memorial concert, organised by the Harold Jolliffe Memorial Foundation, took place with pianist Nina Walker in 1973 at the Arts Centre. The annual Harold Jolliffe One-Act Play Festival is also held in his memory.

Harold Jolliffe was succeeded as Borough Librarian by Thomas Sommerville McNeil (d.1999), his long-time deputy. Known as 'Mac', he had been educated at Airdrie Academy in Scotland, joined the town's public library service, and progressed to the post of reference librarian at Chelmsford before relocating to Swindon in 1947 as the senior library assistant. In 1949 he became Swindon's lending librarian, and afterwards the deputy borough librarian.

Jubilee Clock London designer Edwin Wright's eyeball of a clock was commissioned by the Borough Council in 2002 to mark the Golden Jubilee of Queen Elizabeth II. It was made by the Cumbria Clock Company of Dacre in the Lake District, cost £50,000, and inaugurated by HRH The Duke of Edinburgh at the intersection of Canal Walk and Regent Street on 28 February 2003. The clock was a gold-coloured acrylic sphere, 1.5 metres in diameter, with four dials (it was known locally as 'the eye in the sky') that nestled within stainless-steel branches, springing from the top of a slender, ribbed shaft. The tallest branch was twenty-seven feet from the ground. The hands of the clock were made of titanium, set against a dial that glowed blue at night, and incorporated a Westerstrand masterclock system. It chimed the hour and the quarters, and also featured an electric speaker through which tunes could be played, as well as Christmas carols at the appropriate times. In 2008 this timepiece stopped; it was explained that the power had been switched off to facilitate remedial work on the nearby Brunel

Centre. The power was not reconnected and, in 2009, the Jubilee clock was removed into storage, and thereafter returned to its maker for refurbishment, prior to being installed in Swindon's redeveloped station forecourt in 2012.

Juvenile Fete This annual children's extravaganza was organised by the GWR Mechanics Institution, was run by volunteers from the railway's employees, and began in 1868. It took place in the park (then the company's cricket field) in Faringdon Road on either the first or the second Saturday in August. Children under fourteen years of age were admitted free and given a ticket for the roundabouts, and there were also coconut shies, hoopla, Punch and Judy, sideshows, stage performances and swing boats. People danced to music provided by a GWR ensemble. Initially, buns were given out to children attending the event; later, it was cake. Those who wished to take advantage of half-a-pound of fruit cake, which had been carefully cut and wrapped beforehand by an army of adult female volunteers, had to pay 'a small sum'; it was not free. From 1891, a cake-cutting machine, designed and made in the railway Works, saved all the labour by hand. (On one occasion, allegedly, 3½ tons of cake and 1,200 gallons of tea were distributed.) Children who required a mug of tea were expected to provide their own mugs. There was a firework display at dusk. The fête did not take place in the war years, 1914-18, and, after the 1939 fete, did not again take place until 2003, when a new series began, organised by the Swindon Mechanics' Institute Trust.

Kibblewhite, James (1866-1941) Born at Purton, Kibblewhite the runner is

best known as the one-time English and World three-miles record holder, which he achieved at Stamford Bridge, London in a time of two-fifths of a second under 14½ minutes. He was one of seven children born to James, an agricultural labourer, and his wife Caroline; the family lived on Purton Common. James Kibblewhite (the younger) began work as a post office messenger boy, and then joined the GWR Works in Swindon where he was employed as a machinist in 'R' Shop. In 1884, he watched some of his work colleagues compete in a number of races at Cheltenham, determined that he could do better, and began to train hard. It is said, possibly apocryphally, that he ran the six miles each way daily between Purton and the Works in Swindon, but he certainly trained after work, often in the dark, on the GWR cricket field. In May 1884, he easily won his first competitive race, the one-mile handicap on Swindon Sports Day. His dedication and the support of others was such that his colleagues organised a subscription that financed two weeks' training for him, accompanied by a trainer, at Weston-super-Mare.

In 1894, he married Mary Bristowe from Warminster, and the couple had four children. Their daughter Kathleen Mary was killed in 1945 by an express train when she was crossing the railway line. Kibblewhite's running career lasted just eleven seasons, ending in 1895. His successes during that time included winner of the Stourbridge Challenge Cup in 1886; from 1888, he was the outright winner of the Cheltenham Challenge Cup; amateur one-mile champion in 1889; four- and ten-mile champion in 1890; Southern Counties Cross Champion in 1890 and 1891; and National Cross Country Champion in 1891. He also ran for Spartan Harriers, after which he named the cottage in Purton where he lived and died, the building of which he had financed by selling some of his trophies. James Kibblewhite retired from the GWR Works in 1931. A letter addressed to him in 1940 from Salford Harriers (which had been formed in the year Kibblewhite took up competitive running) addressed him as 'Dear Old Champion'.

King Brothers During the first half of the 1800s, Napoleon King was a saddler and harness maker in Victoria Street and High Street. Henry and Edward King were coach builders, established c.1845, with premises in Wood Street (later numbered 30) and at the hamlet of Kingsdown, near Stratton St Margaret. In the latter, they occupied premises at the Boundary House, which was latterly styled 'King Brothers' Napoleon Carriage, Cycle & Motor Works'. Their great competitor in the old town was T.P. Stroud, who had established himself in 1841 as a carriage builder in Marlborough Road. For a while, Henry and Edward also found themselves in competition with another brother, John, who had set up as a coach builder in Newport Street in the mid-1860s, much to their annoyance. They went to great pains to point out that he was 'from Reading and Weston-super-Mare' and that the two businesses were not in any way connected. In 1891 the Wood Street business was repositioned as 'bicycle manufacturers' to take advantage of the sudden public interest in cycling, following improvements in the previous few years to the safety cycle and the introduction of the pneumatic tyre. The premises of Edward King comprised a building with a front entrance on to Wood Street, a side entrance from Albert Street, and the premises adjacent

in Albert Street. Quickly renamed the King Brothers' Napoleon Cycle Works, it was here that they built the machines (specialising in 'Quadrant', 'Viking' and 'Peregrine' branded cycles) and also took in repairs. Of the several bicycle makers that established in Swindon during the cycling boom, it is the King brothers who are best remembered.

King Class Locomotive Mural
Swindon's largest mural to date showed a King Class steam locomotive travelling past the GWR Works, and was painted in 1976 by Ken White and a number of youngsters on a job creation scheme, and was sponsored by Arkell's Brewery. The site was a wall that bordered a car park to the east of the railway village, between Fleet Street and Station Road. Neither wall nor car park still exists.

King of Prussia Inn, High Street
When Eastcott Smith's butcher's shop at No. 4 High Street was demolished, Swindon lost a building that was formerly the most significant hostelry in the town. The shop had been Smith's family business premises for a century and its demise is still regarded as a huge act of vandalism, which took place despite protests and a petition of 1,000 signatures to the local authority. Here was a two-storey, 16th-century building that became The King's Head and, later, The King of Prussia inn. An inventory taken in 1821 describes two attic bedrooms, one containing four beds for soldiers and another with two beds for servants; three bedrooms for guests, a smoking room; a bar; a parlour; a kitchen; a cellar; and a brew-house. Outside, at the rear, were pigsties and stables.

By the 1850s, this inn was 'the most prominent' in Swindon. Pitched markets were held along its frontage, against its walls, and mail coaches picked up their passengers here. It was used by the younger gentry of the old town, including those of the manor's first family, one of whom had a penchant for scattering money outside and beating the street girls with a riding whip as they scrabbled around in the gutter to pick up the coins. The building was at the centre of trade on market days and fair days, and prostitutes did business above the assembly room at the rear. They kept an eye out for both the constable and prospective patrons through a small window on the stairs. It had a number of 'character' and influential innkeepers and owners, including William 'Fat Billy' Webb, who took over from Mary Ellison in 1832; Thomas Washbourne, Edwin R. Fifield and the landowner John Harding Sheppard (1778-1868). In 1863, the Swindon Central Market Company unsuccessfully tried to buy the place from Sheppard (who lived almost next door) in order to convert it into a corn exchange. It closed in 1880, became a butcher's shop the following year and was thereafter held by three generations of the same family, ceasing to trade in 1977 when Eastcott Smith retired. The original building was demolished in 1981.

Most of what was then pulled down – including the stone-built front elevation, the front rooms and the front cellar – had been built between the 1600s and the Georgian era; lost too, was internal beam work of the 1700s. Two cellars at the rear had been built in the later 18th century. Even more importantly, attached to the inn was a Georgian assembly room and ballroom, perhaps the town's earliest custom-built space for musical entertainment. This had early 18th-century egg and dart moulding, carved merman brackets beneath the plaster ceiling and, over the two doors, crests that

depicted a hand with a heart in its centre and a ribbon at the base, surrounded by olive branches. In 1977, the building was bought by the Midland Bank before being acquired by Hannick Homes and Development. In 1980, the then Thamesdown Council gave permission to pull down the rear of the building, on condition that the façade was kept; this was waived the following year and complete demolition was agreed. Having completely flattened the site, the developer then rebuilt the façade in an approximation of its former likeness and created a modern office development within. It is called Eastcott House.

King's Arms, Wood Street About 1840, John Godwin, baker of Wood Street, established an alehouse on his premises; the King's Arms is first mentioned by name in 1842, with Godwin as innkeeper. In 1864, his son, also John Godwin, leased adjacent land to the rear from the lord of the manor, apparently the site of a former windmill, and began to rebuild and extend the baker's shop/ alehouse. (In '*Jefferies Land*', 1867, Richard Jefferies alludes to this: 'Some enterprising persons actually erected a windmill here, but the speculation was unsuccessful; it was taken down and three cottages built with the materials, which three cottages stood where now the King's Arms Inn offers shelter and good cheer to travellers'. John Godwin junior was also the nephew of the owner of the Belmont Brewery. He added a coat of arms to his literature, and called his hostelry an 'agricultural and commercial inn'. The neo-Gothic, three-storey, five-bay façade as it presents today was put up in brick with stone window dressings, flat strings, and quoins, c.1870. It is a compact arrangement with pairs of shoulder-headed lights separated by shafts and capitals. Four gables have roundels, and the symmetry of the two upper storeys is tied together by the chimney stack, corbelled out above the recessed central doorway and emblazoned with the coat of arms at the upper level. Next to the porch is a fussy bay window, clearly intended to give prominence to the entrance, but out of keeping with the rest of the façade. The King's Arms was bought into the Arkell's estate in 1885, and refurbished by them in 1993.

Kingshill House, Bath Road An Italianate-style villa with a central tower was built at the western end of The Sands in the mid-1840s. It was owned by John Henry Harding Sheppard (1777-1868), landowner, brewer, and mill and public house owner, on portions of whose land parts of New Swindon were built in the early 1870s. (John Street, Henry Street, Harding Street and Sheppard Street were named after him; it is said that this was a requirement under which he agreed to sell the land.) During the 1870s, Kingshill House was occupied by brewer, and wine and spirit merchant Richard Bowly, whose business premises were at 10-12 High Street. The property was sold for £950 in 1871. It was later a doctor's residence; it was bought by Swindon Corporation in 1931 and became the maternity hospital. The Seymour Clinic mental health unit used it for a time, and it was then leased to the National Health Service Trust housing mental health services until 2009, and used as a clinic until the lease expired in 2011. It was sold privately at auction in 2012. The main entrance is beneath the three-stage tower with moulded string courses, which was originally finished by a pierced parapet with acorn knop finials. The symmetrical front is of two storeys and five

bays; the entrance has a rusticated surround, a bracketed cornice and depressed pediment with narrow side lights flanking the arched doorway that leads into a vaulted porch and thence the stair hall. Above the ground floor, the tower has a tripartite first-floor window, and paired arched lights to the upper storey. There are paired modillion brackets to the eaves of the flanking elevations, and a run of moulded and plain brackets to that of the tower.

Knapp, Edwin (1826-1885) The son of Edward Knapp, a local builder, by the time Edwin was fifteen he was living with grocer William Brush (and Brush's mother), whose business was established in Wood Street in the 1830s. Edwin soon took this over, adding 'wine merchant' to his portfolio. In 1847, he married Jemima Pearce Prettejohn (b.1823), who came from Stockenham, Devon. The couple had two sons, both of whom went into their father's grocery business. Son William advertised the grocery business separately, alongside his father's advertisements that clearly showed how the latter preferred to increase the wines and spirits side of the business. By 1861, Edwin was employing two men and four grocer's apprentices or assistants, and had one servant at home. He was, in 1864, a member of the first group to make up the Old Swindon Local Board and he became a director of the Swindon Central Market Company in 1866. Jemima died in 1872, and in 1874, Edwin married Ann Edwards (b.1843) of Tetbury, the daughter of farmer Edward Edwards. She was then living at 17 Red Lion Street, London, and the couple were married at St Andrew's church, High Holborn. Soon afterwards, Edwin retired, and the couple went to live at Fairfield Lodge, Bath Road. When he died,

he left just under £903. Ann moved back to Tetbury and thereafter lived 'on own means' at The Green.

Kode House, Bath Road One of the earliest villas to be built when successful tradesmen began to develop the area between Old Town and The Sands, this two-storey, three-bay residence was put up c.1845. Built of limestone rubble (mainly on the two-storey rear extension of the same time) and dressed ashlar, the two storeys are separated, on the front elevation, by a wide, flat string course, with flat pilasters below it and quoins above at each extremity. The pilasters have a hint of a capital, thereby faintly mirroring the flat Doric pillars around the doorway, which has a plainly moulded entablature. The windows are all square-headed, their sills on paired brackets. There are paired modillions at the eaves, very much a feature of this kind of residence in Swindon in the mid-19th century. Originally called 'Fairview', it was leased in 1855 to John Toomer, the coal, coke, salt and hay merchant, who later purchased the property. It was occupied by Swindon Town Club after 1884. (See also Swindon Town Club; Toomer, John.)

Ladd's Mill As early as 1339, a mill stood at the south side of the point at which the River Ray crossed what is now the Wootton Bassett Road near West Swindon. It can be traced through members of the Stichell family between 1618 and 1631, and it was in the occupancy of Thomas People when it was sold, together with the surrounding land, to Revd Timothy Dewell of Lydiard Tregoze. By 1691, it was called 'Arthur's Mill' and was part of the estate leased by John Cullum, a woollen draper of London, to Stephen Lawrence of Broome, Swindon. It remained

in the Lawrence family; was occupied by Robert Boxwell (1724-27); passed to Thomas Ladd (1727-43); and was leased by Richard Wayte from Thomas Vilett in 1744, when it was briefly called Westcot Mill. It became known as Wayte's Mill, situated on the dividing line between Goddard land and Vilett land. By 1773, it was called 'Hall's Mill', after the occupier, Roger Hall, and in 1791, it was bought by Ambrose Goddard.

In 1807, the Wilts & Berks Canal Company rented this mill from Ambrose Goddard, then bought it, and eventually sold it c.1840 to Swindon landowner John Harding Sheppard, and it was still his property thirty years later. Henry Brooks was the miller in 1851. By the 1870s, the mill had fallen into disrepair; it remained gradually decaying, adjacent to six occupied dwellings, until they were all demolished c.1897.

Lady Chatterley in Swindon

Lady Chatterley's Lover, written by D.H. Lawrence and published in 1928, was legally unavailable in England until the ban was lifted following a historic court case involving Penguin Books in 1960. As soon as UK publication became legal, Swindon's bookshops were inundated with requests for the title. Most of the orders were placed by telephone, as the callers did not want to present themselves to the personal scrutiny of bookshop staff. The town's main bookshop Wyman's took thirty-six orders on the first day and had stockpiled 300 requests in just over a week. One man ordered thirty-six copies. W.H. Smith stopped taking orders at 350 copies because the company's head office advised they had received so many requests nationally that it would not be possible to service them all before the end of the year – virtually two months away. Swindon's public library service ordered a dozen copies and started a reservations list, hoping that the book could be read and returned in two or three days. Gray's bakery famously celebrated the event by making a cake in the shape of a book, with the title on the cover.

In 1968, Swindon libraries withdrew from display *The Natural Method of Dog Training* because the RSPCA wanted it to be banned, objecting to certain 'cruel' passages in the chapter entitled 'Breaking Bad Habits'.

Lakes, Goddard Estate

The two lakes that form part of the public parkland on The Lawn estate were created when the landscape was redeveloped at the time of the 18th-century remodelling of the late medieval manor house. They may have devolved on a much older pond thereabouts. It is possible that this stretch of water may have been in some way connected with the underground tunnels of Old Swindon (see Moonraking Legend), or were some kind of outlet for waste water from the settlement on the hill.

Lamarr, Mark (b.1967)

Born Mark Jones, his career as a comedian and television presenter began at the London Comedy Store in 1985. Before that, he attended Park South Infants school and junior school, and Oakfield School, Marlowe Avenue. At the age of seventeen, he left for London and the stand-up comedy circuit. Famous as a strong critic of Swindon, he once described it as 'a very, very narrow-minded and bitter little town' and 'there is an extreme amount of violence in Swindon...when I come back to see my mates, GBH is the phrase they use more than any other; fighting has become an accepted part of night life'. As a reporter on the early morning television programme *The Big Breakfast*, 1992-93, he occupied

the 'Down Your Doorstep' slot. His other appearances include *The Word*, *Planet Showbiz*, *Shooting Stars*, and *Never Mind the Buzzcocks*.

Lardy Cake, Gray's Famous In his ninety-fourth year, Cyril Gray handwrote his own recipe for the lardy cake, and gave it to the author of this book. Here it is.

Ingredients for the cake
275ml/½ pt milk and water mixed
20g/¾ oz fresh yeast
50g/2 oz sugar, plus one teaspoon
450g/1 pound plain flour
1 teaspoon salt
50g/2 oz lard or margarine

Ingredients for the topping
100g/4 oz granulated sugar
75g/3 oz currants
50g/2 oz white fat (at room temperature)
50g/2 oz lard (at room temperature)

For the base of the tin
10g/½ oz white fat
50g/2 oz currants
50g/2 oz granulated sugar

Method
Warm the milk and water in a saucepan over gentle heat.

Mix the yeast, the teaspoon of sugar, and a little warm water in a small bowl and leave for ten minutes.

Sift the flour, salt and sugar into a large bowl, then rub in the lard.

Add the warm milk and water, and the yeast mixture to the dry ingredients and mix to form a soft dough. Knead for three minutes until the dough is smooth. Place in a clean bowl, cover with lightly oiled clingfilm and leave in a warm place for thirty minutes.

Turn out the dough on to a pastry board and knead lightly. Roll out evenly to an area twelve inches square.

Layer the topping mix on to the dough by spreading the lard and white fat over the dough, then sprinkle the currants and sugar evenly over the top.

Fold the dough in half, left edge to right, then fold the bottom edge up to the top to make a square.

Leave in a warm place for thirty minutes.

Roll out again to a little more than twelve inches square, and fold again in the same fashion as above.

Lay baking parchment in the bottom of a ten-inch-square tin, and spread the white fat, sugar and currants over the parchment.

Press in the dough to fill the tin, and leave until it has risen to double its size.

Bake in the oven at 400 F/200 C/gas mark 6 for 30 to 35 minutes until golden brown.

Place wire rack over tin and invert the cake on to rack.

Lardy cake is best eaten on the day it is made.

Lawn, The The Lawn was the manor house of c.1770 on the Goddard estate in Old Town. Until 1850, it was called Swindon House. The Goddard family had lived in Swindon at least from 1400, and Thomas Goddard acquired the manor in 1562. It is likely that a house was then first built on this spot, a hill looking towards the distant Vale of the White Horse, and it remained there until the late 18th-century rebuild. The Georgian property was a brick-built, double-cube construction, with stone dressings and a baluster parapet with pineapple and urn finials. To the east of this was a block with five bedrooms and a large dining room. The main house comprised an outer hall and an inner hall on the ground floor; a lobby; a drawing room;

a dining room with an adjoining study; a billiard room; a library; and a gun room. One staircase led to the bedrooms, of which the master bedroom had a dressing room adjoining. Another staircase led to a nursery, and the servants' quarters. The view from the drawing room windows took in an orangery and a sunken Italian garden, bounded by an open balustrade wall with, at intervals, decorative urns on pedestals.

The estate was laid out c.1800 at the end of a driveway leading from High Street, at which entrance were constructed classical-style, four-bay, single-storey lodges. The drive curved towards the garden, then ran alongside the front of the house, and ended in a series of steps. In the grounds were an arboretum with formal walks, sweeping lawns, and artificial lakes. Beyond the south section of the balustrade wall, where the ground dropped steeply away, were further ornamental gardens not visible from the house. The stables associated with the house became auctioneers' premises in The Planks. The estate also includes two lakes that were probably created in the Georgian period around a single, smaller lake that then existed.

Fitzroy Pleydell Goddard, the last lord of the manor of Swindon, died at The Lawn in 1927, and his widow Eugenia left soon afterwards. The house remained unoccupied from 1931 until it was taken over by the military during the Second World War to accommodate American troops, who treated it badly. They also had several huts in the grounds that were taken over, following the war, as an extension of the technical college. In 1947, the year Eugenia died, Swindon Corporation bought the decaying manor house and the 53-acre parkland surrounding it, at a cost of £16,000. By 1952, the house

had become dangerous, and was demolished. The grounds were opened as public parkland, and remain so today. (See also Westlecot Manor.)

Lawn Cottages This group overlook the Goddard estate, and were built late in the 18th century, when No.1 must have appeared to be quite grand. It is a large, double-gabled, three-bay house, set in a prominent position, of two storeys with attics and hipped dormer windows, built in courses of rough limestone. No. 2 and No. 3 adjacent are made out of a run of what were once much smaller dwellings occupied by estate workers. They are single-storey dwellings with attics that also have hipped dormer windows, roughly built of ragged limestone pieces. They make a nice group in an attractive position.

Lea, Nehemiah (1810-1862) Nehemiah was the son of Edmund Lea, tailor and draper of Wood Street, and his wife Anna (née Long). In 1839, he married Frances (née Francome, b. Purton, 1809). He became a master tailor, and by 1851 was employing eight journeymen. In 1852, he became a director of the Swindon Market Company. The couple had three sons: in the 1850s, Samuel (b.1840) became an ironmonger's assistant at Witney; by 1861 Edmund (b.1843) was a draper's assistant; and Norman (b.1845) was 'an ironmonger's assistant on trial'. Frances died in 1859, and Nehemiah brought in his sister-in-law Mary Francome, a widow, as his housekeeper. He also had a long-time servant, and a lodger Henry Smith, who worked as a cashier at the County of Gloucestershire Bank.

Library Services The Borough of Swindon adopted the Public Libraries Act in

1942. James Swift was appointed as the first Borough Librarian, tasked with overseeing the introduction of a public library service in the town. This resulted in an adult lending, reference, and children's library, which was opened on 14 August 1943 by Professor R.H. Tawney, in the presence of Dr Arundell James Kennedy Esdaile (1880-1956), the famous scholar librarian and bibliographer, who was then President of the Library Association. The library was opened in a temporarily rented room in McIlroy's department store, Regent Street. Administrative offices were squeezed into a nearby corridor. The Borough Council's Surveyor's Department made the necessary alterations, and Libraco, the library suppliers, furnished the place.

It was a huge success; 5,000 people registered for membership before the opening date, upon which 3,104 books were borrowed. A public reading room that could accommodate fifty people, and a meeting room where the Library & Museums Committee could formulate its policies for cultural activities in the town were set up in the former Corporation Electricity Showrooms in Regent Circus. It was to here the junior library was almost immediately relocated. In 1946 the Junior Library was for a while in the Arts Centre, off Regent Street.

The library's literary publication *The Swindon Review* was founded in 1945. In 1946, Harold Jolliffe succeeded as Borough Librarian, and the children's library, renamed the 'Junior Library', relocated to a converted Sunday school, off Regent Street. In 1947, the first library satellite was opened: Pinehurst branch library was established in a former reading room at The Bungalows. In 1948, a 1,300-square-foot reference library was opened in part of the town hall, and the library's administrative offices were

also opened there. J.T. Lea, a Swindon man, who had worked at the Mechanics' Institute library 1936-39 and had been a prisoner of war in Germany 1940-45, was then appointed the first Reference Librarian. He had returned to the Institute for a year after the war, and had been at the public library since 1947. He was to become Chief Assistant Librarian in 1952.

On 26 March 1949, a new single-storey Central Library was opened in prefabricated huts immediately to the east of the town hall in Regent Circus, with stock relocated from McIlroy's, where the former library area became the men's clothing department. The opening ceremony was performed by the writer Compton Mackenzie. This building was intended as a 'temporary arrangement', a custom-built, prefabricated structure, vaguely in a 'T' shape. The short arm connected with the town hall, wherein was part of the reference collection, and comprised a general office, separate male and female cloakrooms, a staff room, a goods in/out room, and a store room; the corridor that connected these housed the library's 'reserve stock' of obsolete books or those most likely to be stolen. The long arm comprised the adult library, of some 3,000 square feet, with an issue desk and telephone exchange at one end. The entrance hall, some 1,200 square feet in area, provided for an 'overspill' of queues at the issue desk. In 1950, the library began publishing *In Print*, its monthly magazine of new acquisitions, and began providing a service to patients at Victoria Hospital.

In 1953, Moredon branch library was opened in Moredon Methodist Church, which had been Rodbourne Parish Council's library and reading room at the end of the 1800s, before the upper room was leased by

the trustees of the local Primitive Methodist Church, Second Circuit for religious services on Sundays and Thursdays. It was into this room that the library was shoehorned, screened from view when services were held. Penhill branch library was opened in a former farmhouse in 1954. Both were in temporary accommodation. In 1956, the junior library relocated into the Central Library building, which had been extended to accommodate it and a cataloguing department.

A custom-built library was opened at Penhill in 1957, another was opened at Walcot in 1958 and, in the same year, sub-branches were opened in Princes Farm at Park, and at Lawn. Pinehurst branch library transferred from the reading rooms to the former Anglican Mission Church on The Circle, retaining the altar steps and altar rail. These were removed when sufficient funds became available for a full conversion, which took place in 1962. When the Mechanics' Institute library closed in 1961, its stock of 25,000 titles was sold off; members of the British Railways Staff Association had first choice; the Swindon Public Library Service bought all of the local collection, all of the railway books, and its choice of the music titles; the remainder of the books were sold to the public. Mrs W.D. Wright, who had been the Institute's librarian for the previous seventeen years, said 'the public library killed us'.

Park branch library went into a permanent building in Cavendish Square, designed by architect Frederick Gibberd, in 1964, the same year that a sub-branch was established to serve Even Swindon, and another to serve Old Town.

Plans fell through in 1969 to establish a new central library on what became the Wyvern Theatre car park. The following year Highworth branch library was opened, in 'temporary buildings' with a predicted lifespan of twenty-five years. In 1973, Even Swindon library was installed in portable cabins in Hughes Street. In 1974, the Swindon library service was transferred to Wiltshire County Council, under the absurd reorganisation of local government that brought Swindon into the equally silly, newly created Borough of Thamesdown. The same year, Wroughton branch library was opened. Swindon lost some of its decent library stock to Wiltshire County during this period. Then, the unitary Swindon Borough Council emerged, and the library function came back to the town.

In 1976, the temporary 1949 central library building was substituted by a larger set of single-storey, equally temporary buildings on the same site at the rear of the town hall. Two years later, Wiltshire County Council considered building a new central library, either on its current site or in Islington Street; Thamesdown Borough Council countered with a proposal for Sanford Street, but this came to nothing. Neither did proposals in 1988 for another site close to the Wyvern Theatre. West Swindon branch library was opened at the Link Centre in 1985. North Swindon library was opened by Mayor Stan Pajak at the North Swindon District Centre, next to the Orbital Shopping Park in 2003. In the same year Even Swindon library relocated into the Even Swindon Community Centre in Jennings Street, and the branch library at Highworth removed into the first floor of the new Oxford, Swindon & Gloucester Co-operative Society's supermarket in Brewery Street. In 2004, economic conditions caused the closure of a small, but very long-established library in New Road at Chiseldon, which had come

under the auspices of Swindon Council, in favour of a mobile unit.

The central library remained in its temporary buildings until 2006, when the whole lock, stock and barrel relocated its 61,000 books to the Paramount Buildings in Princes Street. Little feet were painted on the pathways to direct readers in the right direction. This, of course, was yet another temporary venue for the central library; in January 2007, work began on redeveloping the original town hall site. (See also Central Library.)

Limmex, Samuel Joseph (1842-1935) In 1881, Samuel Joseph Limmex took over an ironmonger's business in High Street begun by Laurence Lawrence in the first half of the 19th century from his family's twin-gabled, three-storey house, with cellar, of c.1708. Lawrence was succeeded by Edward Page, c.1845, whose family and resident shop-man lived on the premises, and then by James Wise, who was described in 1861 as an ironmonger and tinplate maker. He was followed by Joseph Walter, the last owner to live on the premises. It was Walter who sold the business to Limmex.

S.J. Limmex was born in the West Indies; in 1869, at Brighton he married Rebecca Bartrop (b. Uxbridge, Middlesex, 1841), who came with a five-year-old daughter, Mary Ellen (b. Aylesbury, Buckinghamshire, 1864). The couple had a son, Frederick William, who was born at Brighton in 1871, and relocated to Swindon within the next year or so, where their daughter Edith Ellen was born in 1873. They lived in Prospect Place, and Samuel expanded the High Street shop into two adjacent cottages in Wood Street. Then, 1884-5, he rebuilt the cottages to the same height as the house, took down

the original gables of the latter, remodelled the whole frontage, added new windows to the second and third storeys, and put in a whole new shop frontage at street level. He tiled the part of the roof that could be seen from High Street and Wood Street, and covered the back in sheets of tin.

At the rear, Limmex had a tin smithy. He made all manner of galvanised tin items in an upstairs room, beating them out as necessary on a tree stump in the back yard. It was said of him that when he was not working as a hands-on craftsman, Samuel Limmex was surveying his shop and his staff from a high stool behind a high desk in his little corner office. Frederick, who lived at Lynwood, Devizes Road, joined his father's business as an ironmongery salesman; in 1898, he married Maud Emily Walters (b.1874), and died in 1943; his widow survived until 1962.

Samuel retired to Fair View, Liddington, and died in 1935. The business eventually passed to his daughter and step-daughter. It continued to be the epitome of an old-fashioned hardware store, and from 1975 until its closure in October 1999, this landmark shop on the corner of High Street and Wood Street was run by Roy Stevens and a small staff dedicated to upholding the best traditions of personal service.

Lindley, Kenneth Arthur (1928-1990) Ken Lindley – author, illustrator and woodblock engraver – was an inspirational graphic design tutor at the School of Art, allied to Swindon College. Before coming to Swindon, where he lived in Pleydell Road, he taught art at Loughborough College. He was a member of the Society of Industrial Artists, and an associate member of the Royal Society of Painters, Etchers and Engravers, and the Society of Wood Engravers. He is represented

in *The Swindon Review* (No.10, 1958) with 'Still Waters', a piece about canals and waterways, for which he provided a drawing and a painting of the junction house on the North Wilts Canal. He once designed a card for L.T.C. Rolt that showed an engine on the Tal-y-Llyn railway. Among his published works were *Town, Time & People*, 1962, which was almost wholly based on Swindon; *Chapels and Meeting Houses*, 1969, which was introduced by John Piper, whom Lindley greatly admired; and *Of Graves and Epitaphs*, 1965. An early work was *How to Explore Churches*, 1953; and *How to Explore Abbeys and Monasteries* followed in 1961. The following year, he illustrated John Baker's *Cottage By the Spring*, for the Country Book Club. He was particularly enamoured by landscapes – *Landscape and Buildings* was published in 1972 – and the coastline. Some of his most evocative work involves seascapes. *Coastline* came out in 1967, *Coastwise* in 1970, and *Seaside Architecture* in 1973. Cornish scenes were a speciality of this most prolific illustrator, and woodblock engraving was in his soul. In 1970, he published *The Woodblock Engraver*. He also designed a fine cover for Dover Wilson's *What Happens in Hamlet*, published by Cambridge University Press, and a frontispiece for the Nonesuch Press edition of *Hopkins's Poems*.

Link magazine In 1979, Roger Ogle came to Swindon, where he was employed as a community development officer for the then fledgling area of West Swindon. Realising that there was an immediate need for some means of communication between the new residents, he started a newsletter for them that was run by volunteers and was published at approximately six-weekly

intervals. The print run increased as housing developments expanded in West Swindon, and there came a point in the 1980s when that type of newsletter was no longer viable. There was a requirement for an upmarket, properly printed newsletter paid for by advertising. The Link magazine became an independent business in 1987, still targeting the West Swindon community, and was thereafter published monthly. North Swindon was added to the stable in 1994, and in 1997 the organisation was one of the first in the town to create a website. In 2013, Roger Ogle was still the magazine's owner, editor, and principal writer and photographer.

Lister, R.A. & Co. In 1942, the Admiralty took over the Petter Engines' premises, just south of Swindon; thereafter, gun mountings were made there for ships, under the name of Marine Mountings. When these were no longer required, R.A. Lister (founded 1867 at Dursley, Gloucestershire by (Sir) Robert Ashton Lister to make agricultural machinery) hired the premises in order to assemble small petrol motors that drive light agricultural machinery and light vehicles, using parts manufactured at Dursley. Petter and Lister were rivals; Hawker-Siddeley acquired Petter in 1957, and Lister in 1965; the two were amalgamated in 1986 to form Lister Petter.

Little London This lane was thought to have been established by migrant Londoners who settled in a field immediately to the north of Wood Street early in the 19th century. Then, their field was reached via a track called Back Lane (the same that gave access to Albert Street), part of which became known as London Lane, then Little London Lane, and was London Street by 1855. The

lane, at one time flanked by tiny cottages into which were shoehorned the labouring poor, debouched into Cricklade Street. It became the centre of low life and depravity, and Old Town's red light district. Henry Jones, shoemaker, had his business in Little London in the 1840s. By the mid-1800s, the southern end of Albert Street, Little London and Back Lane were effectively a single thoroughfare, albeit one that only its inhabitants would want to traverse. From 1879, the area included the terrace of seven cottages, built off at right angles to the east, and named Victory Row. Little London was always a forgotten part of a neglected area of the town, but possessed, until it was demolished c.1966, Swindon's last thatched cottage.

'Little Theatre', Bridge Street The Great Western Players performed in the theatre of the Mechanics' Institute until 1948, and in the following year they changed their name to the Western Players. Also in 1949, the British Rail Staff Association took over a large building on the corner of Bridge Street and the north side of Holbrook Street. This was part of Albion Buildings, a terrace that was put up of a piece in the 1880s, when it occupied the whole of the east side of Bridge Street between Holbrook Street and Station Road, and numbered 1 to 6 Bridge Street. (No. 1, originally a shop, had been hallmarked for a youth hostel just before the war, but had not been used during hostilities. This was at the Station Road end, and in 1942 it was sold to the Communist Party in Swindon, with a twenty-year mortgage. They sub-let parts as offices to the AEU and the National Union of Vehicle Builders, set up a canteen for servicemen and war workers, and latterly let out the cellar as a meeting place for the local folksingers' club.)

Albion Buildings was constructed of brick in two-and-a-half storeys, with gabled dormers with decorative bargeboards. It had an eccentric but homogeneous arrangement of square-headed windows within pointed shapes, picked out by freestone dressings and further enlivened by decorative arches above the windows, created in brick and in-filled with various decorative treatments. There had been a performance venue here, originally called 'The Harmonic Room', wherein had played the actress and music hall artiste Belle Elmore
(real name Corrine 'Cora' Turner), who was better known as Dr Crippen's second wife, whom he murdered in 1910.

Nos. 4, 5, and 6 were operated by the Great Western Staff Association (later British Rail Staff Association) at street level as a working men's club, and an intimate theatre was created upstairs under the direction of James Ellison, with a large meeting room leading off. He was a one-time foreman in the railway gasworks and was the producer of almost all the plays put on by the Players (the organisation had a succession of names) between 1929 and 1958. The audience were seated on wooden chairs with leather seats (it is said that up to 150 people could be squeezed in), facing a proscenium beneath which hung a heavy curtain, red in colour and trimmed with gold braid. The walls were decorated with Shakespearian murals: the work of William Thompson Hemsley. The actors' two dressing areas were on the floor above, reached by a narrow staircase, and so far away from the toilets, which were on the ground floor of the building, that the cast employed chamber pots in their attic dressing rooms.

The theatre was never formally named, but was identified locally as 'the little theatre

in Bridge Street', and the name stuck. In 1959, the British Rail Staff Association merged with the Mechanics Institution. The sub-leasing scheme of the Playhouse theatre and dance hall had long-since failed. The lease on the Staff Association premises was about to run out, so in 1959 the Western Players mounted *Murder Mistaken*, a psychological thriller by Janet Green, as their last production at the little theatre, and then returned to their former home in the Mechanics' Institute building. The premises in Bridge Street thereafter became redundant, and the whole of Albion Buildings was later demolished. (See also Hemsley, W.T.)

Lloyds Bank building, High Street

Built in 1899-1900 and 1906 respectively, and now Grade II listed, these two adjacent properties are on the site of two former Swindon banks whose origins go back to 1807. Both buildings are of ashlar limestone, three- and four- storey; one has six bays and the other has four. The main bank building is rusticated at street level, with inset round-headed windows, a continuous hood moulding with keystones, similar strings beneath the windows, and flat, rusticated pilasters. All of this detailing is divided from the first floor by a moulded cornice on scroll brackets. The stages of the first floor are also divided by rusticated pilasters; and the windows are square-headed, except for a central bow window with slim columns to the angles, and cap with cresting, that covers two bays. It is separated from the second floor by another moulded cornice beneath a run of square-headed windows (those of the end bays have inset corner pedestals). Above the final cornice are vase terminals on rectangular plinths.

The building adjacent was designed by Waller & Son of Gloucester (Frederick William Waller, the son, 1848-1933, following his more illustrious father Frederick Sandham Waller, 1822-1905.) It is effectively of four storeys, the upper level worn like a crown, with a triangular, pedimented dormer and a run of segmentally pedimented dormers behind a balustraded parapet. The building has four bays. The elevation at ground level is rusticated; there is a canopied entrance, and three inset, arched windows with keystones. Above the entrance, on the first floor, is a bow window, and the three adjacent square-headed windows have triangular pediments. The windows at the third level are all square-headed, and there is a run of dentil mouldings at the eaves. (See also Banking in Swindon.)

Local Government in Swindon

Before the town had any formal local government, parish matters in Swindon were sorted out by 'the vestry'. This was a concept of self-government derived from activities that, in medieval times, took place in the vestry of the church, where parishioners met to discuss village affairs and to elect churchwardens, whose duty was to oversee matters relating to the fabric, fixtures and fittings of the building. In the 1850s, for example, Swindon was looked after parochially by two churchwardens, two overseers of the poor, a surveyor of highways, one inspector of police and two constables, and nine gas inspectors. This semi-formal arrangement developed into a committee, at first formed of more influential people in the community, and later of elected persons of means. These were usually successful business people. Swindon continued with this arrangement until 1849, when Old

Swindon petitioned to set up a local board under the Public Health Act, 1848. This was not taken up, and the old town and New Swindon continued with parish status until the early 1860s, when it seemed likely that the town might be included in a sanitary and highway district with nearby Highworth.

The Local Government Act, 1858 was applied separately to both Old Swindon and New Swindon. In 1864, following the possibility that Swindon might be included in a public health (Sanitary and Highway) district with Highworth, both old town and new town adopted the most recent, 1858 Public Health Act, and set up individual local boards. The New Swindon Local Board first met on 27 April 1864 at the Mechanics' Institute, chaired by the GWR's William Frederick Gooch; the Old Swindon Local Board had its first meeting in the Town Hall, Old Town on 10 August 1864, chaired by the grocer Philip Hawe Mason. Occasionally the two boards co-operated with each other, but not frequently; the old established country town worthies on the Old Swindon committee were always sceptical and suspicious of the motives of the New Swindon group's predominantly railway and industrialist make-up. Even so, in the late 1880s, the two boards discussed amalgamation, but nothing came of it. At a meeting of the New Swindon Local Board, held in 1889, James Hinton astounded his fellow members by declaring that within twenty years Swindon would be large enough to be awarded county borough status. Under the Local Government Act, 1888 no such application could be made until the population reached 50,000.

The New Swindon Local Board opened (1891) its splendid, architecturally designed offices (see Town Hall, New Swindon) in a bid to demonstrate its superiority and hasten an amalgamation of the two areas. In 1894, Wiltshire County Council made representation to the Boards, in a failed attempt to bring both parties together. The local Boards operated until 1895, when they were converted to separate Urban District Councils.

In 1896, Old Swindon once again rebuffed representations for amalgamation by the New Swindon Urban District Council. Then, in the face of growing public opinion in favour of a single authority, the two boards were forced to act. A public meeting held on 23 November 1897 effectively set in motion the procedure for petitioning the Privy Council for a Charter of Incorporation whereby the Borough of Swindon would be formed. This was granted; it was received on 22 January 1900 and became effective that year on 9 November. It was the last Charter of Incorporation to receive Queen Victoria's signature. From 1900, the officers of the council comprised twelve aldermen, and six councillors for each of the six wards of the town: North Ward, South Ward, East Ward, West Ward, King's Ward, and Queen's Ward.

The population reached its borough council target in 1911, by 751 souls. In 1913, Swindon Borough Council investigated the possibility of becoming a County Borough, under the Local Government Act, 1888. The Act stipulated a minimum population of 50,000, and Swindon did not quite meet that criterion, or at least wavered on either side of the mark. At the local government reforms of 1974, Swindon and some nearby villages became The Borough of Thamesdown, a district of Wiltshire County. The name was an amalgamation of 'River Thames' and 'Wiltshire Downs', contracted. In 1997, sanity prevailed, and Swindon then became a unitary authority, and the Borough of

Swindon was restored. (See also City Status for Swindon.)

Locarno Ballroom The Locarno was set up in the redundant Corn Exchange in Old Town, just one such use of the building in the 20th century. The large room was floored in Canadian maple and opened as a public dance hall in 1949. The main resident band associated with the place was Ken Kitching, who also had a residency at the Bradford Hall (now the Arts Centre) in Devizes Road. The Locarno was particularly popular in the late 1950s and the 1960s, when gigs were played there by many of the pop groups that later went on to considerable fame. The Locarno ceased to function as a dance hall in the 1960s. (See also Corn Exchange, Old Town)

Lock-up see Blind House

Locomotive Works, GWR Works Brunel's engine house was the first in a series of buildings intended to make Swindon the base for all manufacturing associated with the broad gauge then in use. The first machinery started on 28 November 1842, although the official opening of the Locomotive Works was 2 January 1843. By 1866, the workforce had reached 2,000 men; eventually the complex, which at one time employed over 15,000 people, was arranged over 377 acres. It came to be known as 'The Works', although this term was extended to cover all of the functions carried out on the site, and those employed there were said to work 'inside'. By 1877, there were 5,000 workers on site; it had reached 7,000 by 1885, and had topped 12,000 by 1898. Within each division there was a series of 'shops', most of which were distinguished by an identifying letter. These were as follows (by the mid-

20th century some had changed to a certain degree, and changes are shown in italics in brackets).

A Shop: engine repairing and painting (*erectors, boilermakers, and painters*). B Shop: engine repairing; included engine tables where locomotives and sections could be dismantled and repaired (*erectors, boilermakers, and painters*). C Shop: engine repairing; also included engine tables where locomotives and sections could be dismantled and repaired (*Concentration yard – for storing scrap and dealing with it*). D Shop: turners and fitters of the locomotive carriage and wagon wheels; equipment included lathes and steel planes (*carpenters and masons*). E Shop: (*electrical shop*) F Shop: general smithy. G Shop: boilermaking, then changed to millwrights. H Shop: carpenters, and pattern makers; later added moulders and included the joinery work for the buildings at the Works, plus the patterns and moulds used by the metalworkers (*pattern makers*). J Shop: iron foundry; contained cranes for lifting wagons of molten metal. J2 Shop: *chair foundry*. K Shop: coppersmiths (*and sheet metal workers*), which dealt with all copper connected to locomotives, and that used for other purposes in the locomotive division. L Shop: painting shops with a frontage on Rodbourne Road. L2 Shop: (*tank shop*). M Shop: (*electrical sub-station*). N Shop: turners and fitters of the locomotive carriage and wagon wheels; equipment included lathes and steel planes (*belt shop*). O Shop: (*tool room*), for making angle iron and similar pieces needed in the construction of carriages and wagons. P Shop: boiler-making and tender-making shops, and the hydraulics riveting plant; it opened in 1875 and the equipment also included travelling cranes and traversers. P1 Shop: steaming

and boiler mounting. Q Shop: fittings for carriages and wagons (*angle iron smith*). R Shop: general machinery and miscellaneous fittings used to make locomotives; included equipment for planing, cutting, drilling, turning, milling and assembling the components of engines and carriages, prior to being fitted together. S Shop: wheelsmiths; steam hammers were used here to weld together parts of the wheels (*springsmiths*). SP Shop: *spring shop*. T Shop: brass workers and gas fitters; all gas fittings needed by the Company were made here (*brass finishers*). TH: (*testing house*).

U Shop: turning and fitting of carriage and wagon wheels; later brass foundry for all brass work associated with the rolling stock. V Shop: boiler-making and tender-making shops, and the hydraulics riveting plant, which also including equipment such as travelling cranes and traversers; it opened in 1875. W Shop: (*turners and machinemen*). X Shop: (*permanent way points and crossings fitters*).Y Shop: smithy; included rows of forges, and carriage and wagon springs were also made here. Z: (*transport*). In 1987, the surviving workshops were designated the Railway Works Conservation Area. (See also Carriage and Wagon Works; Rolling Mills.)

Lodge, The A two-storey, double-gabled dwelling stood on the corner of Marlborough Road and Old Mill Lane. It was constructed of rough stone with dressed stone quoins, and had square-headed windows with hood mouldings and stone mullions. It also possessed a two-storey porch with an upper room, and decoratively moulded, tall chimneys. In 1891, it was leased for seven years to John Jefferies, a Swindon auctioneer. It was demolished in 1965 to make way for an extension to an adjacent motor business.

Lodges, Lawn Entrance From c.1770 to 1963, when they were demolished for no reason whatsoever, the entrance to The Lawn (home and estate of the lords of the manor of Swindon) from High Street was flanked by a pair of fine Georgian lodges. These stood adjacent to the gateway pillars and entrance arches that remain today, and were rectangular, single-storey, classical-style buildings of four bays with flat pilasters. The present round-headed side apertures of the gateway were once the front windows of the lodges.

London overspill The Second World War caused housing, social, and employment problems for families that had lived through hostilities in the capital, and for people who returned there following active service in the Forces. These challenges were ameliorated, under the Town Development Act, 1952, by a number of government-approved 'overspill' towns. On 25 June 1952, Swindon was designated one of these. Between then and the 1960s, some 14,000 people relocated to the town from London, many of them being accommodated in the peripheral housing estates of Penhill, Park North, Park South and Walcot, which were built principally in response to this initiative during the 1950s. The Borough Council also took steps to attract new firms to the town, and were successful in encouraging some forty to set up in Swindon, mostly on small industrial estates newly created for the purpose. These organisations provided work not only for the Londoners, but also for people relocating from elsewhere. By the mid-1960s, around 25,000 people had come to work in Swindon since the Second World War, and the town was considering further expansion. (See also Silver Book.)

Looking to the Future sculpture, West Swindon Centre This sculpture of three sunbathers, two men and a woman, at West Swindon Centre was the work of sculptor Jon Buck (b.1951). In 1983, the Borough of Thamesdown inserted an advertisement in the art press for its first artist-in-residence, allied to the Joliffe Studio in the Wyvern Theatre. Jon Buck was successful, and was given some huts at Toothill in which to work, and where he held workshops and evening classes for residents in moulding clay and plaster. Out of this came the commission for a permanent sculpture, initially intended for an open space at Toothill. Buck, who was influenced by the work of Cezanne, was given a figurative brief. The over-life-size figures of young people (hence the name), created in resin and glass fibre, filled with lightweight concrete, and painted in pastel shades during 1984-5 was the first commission piece of his nine-month sojourn. It was carried out on the theme of 'naked not nude' with which he had been experimenting since his college days in the late 1970s. The figures were installed at Toothill, and were immediately vandalised. After restoration, they were relocated to a landscaped area especially created to receive them close to the Link Centre and shopping complex at West Swindon. There, the piece was wrapped in seasonal patterns, before being unveiled in December 1985 by the Mayor Percy Jefferies. They lounge beside the pond, surrounded by trees and bushes.

Lord Raglan, Cricklade Street This is a good example of the kind of overcrowding that characterised the low lodging houses of Swindon in the 19th century. In 1847, a furniture broker, general dealer and carrier (to Cirencester on Mondays) named Elijah Rushen took over an existing beer-house in Cricklade Street. He lived there with his wife Sarah and continued to sell beer. By 1851, he had converted the property into a substantial lodging house, which immediately gained a reputation as a dosshouse for tramps. In order to help publicise his other business, he named the beer-house lodgings The Carrier's Arms. It became the most densely populated of its type in Old Town. At the time of the 1851 census, thirteen tramps were staying there, as were five lodgers who, along with three females, declined to give their professions. A clockmaker was domiciled there with his wife and daughter, as were a gardener, his wife and three daughters. Other beds were taken by a tailor, blacksmith, painter, agricultural labourer, laundress, servant, and a tinman. George Prier was the landlord 1852-60. The Carrier's Arms was leased by John Arkell (the first property in which the brewer had an interest in Swindon) in 1856, and the property became The Lord Raglan early in the 1860s, named after the Crimean War general.

Thomas Jennaway took it over in 1861, living there with his wife Emma and their daughter. The trades represented there on census night included two labourers, one with his wife and two children; a servant, bricklayer, plasterer and wife, cabinet maker and wife, tinman, chimney sweep, smith, and a woman who did not give her profession. Jennaway was succeeded in 1863 by George Trout, and in 1870 came Fred Cratchley, his wife Ann and six daughters. They were all there on census night 1871, together with fifty-eight lodgers. A group of these comprised an eight-man German band; other musicians included a violin player. A singer of comic songs, an acrobat and a costermonger also had beds. Twelve

labourers with three of their children, four needle-workers plus a child, a cap maker and his child, and a lace worker with his wife had also been put up. Six pedlars were squeezed in, as were two bricklayers, two brick makers, two carpenters, a flower maker, slipper maker, wire worker, tailor, engine driver, paper hanger, painter, laundress, and a smith. Arkell's Brewery bought the Lord Raglan in 1889.

By 1901, its landlord was Angelo Vitti. At the time of the 1901 census, the beds there were filled by twelve general labourers, six street hawkers, two bricklayers, two grooms, two domestic servants, one brick maker, one brickyard carter, one cattle drover, one gardener, one plumber, one general dealer, one soldier, and one bread maker. Only the two domestic servants were women. It seems likely that the lodgers' beds were arranged in dormitory fashion. The Lord Raglan was closed down by the magistrates in 1907; the building was later used as a motor body shop, and was demolished in 1981. (See also Vitti, Angelo.)

Lords of the Manor The manorial rights to Swindon were acquired in 1563. Thereafter, the Lords of the Manor were as follows:

Thomas Goddard 1562-1567
Richard Goddard 1568-
Thomas Goddard -1641
Richard Goddard 1644-50
Thomas Goddard 1651-83*
Richard Goddard 1684-1732

The above were all fathers and sons. The manor then passed to Richard's brother:

Pleydell Goddard 1732-1742

then to his cousin

Ambrose Goddard 1745-54

whose two sons

Thomas Goddard 1757-70
Ambrose Goddard 1771-1815

held the manor in succession. It then passed to Ambrose's son

Ambrose Lethbridge Goddard 1852-95

And thence to his son,

Fitzroy Pleydell Goddard 1895-1927.

In 1931, four years after her husband died, Eugenia Kathleen Goddard left Swindon. The Lawn, the family home, accommodated British and American forces during The Second World War. In 1947, it was bought, together with fifty-three acres of surrounding land, by Swindon Corporation for £16,000, and the house was demolished in 1952.

* a minor until 1669.

Lott, James (1845-1921) Lott's ironmongery and general hardware store was a feature of Regent Street from the late 1870s, and throughout its existence retained its Victorian glass frontage, separated only by slender muntins. It was the last of its type in the town. James was the son of John Lott, a Devonshire blacksmith, and his wife Elizabeth. He was born in 1822 in Hartland, Devon, and she, in 1824 in the same county at Bridgerule. The family lived at Pancrasweek, just a few miles from John's birthplace, where he traded as a blacksmith. James, who had two younger siblings, John and Elizabeth, took up the occupation of smith at an early age. By the time he had reached his mid-twenties, he had made the long journey to Swindon, most probably in order to get employment at the railway works.

In Swindon, James Lott took lodgings with Richard Gadd and his wife Ophelia at 16 Union Street, which had been built in 1865 as part of the old town's expansion towards New Swindon. Gadd was born in Croydon and was an accountant at the GWR Works;

Ophelia was born at Derry Hill, near Calne. When James lived with them, the household also included their two teenage sons. James worked as a blacksmith, almost certainly on the railway, but intended to have his own business and to marry his sweetheart from home. By 1873, he was married to Ellen (born 1850 at Holsworthy, Devon, less than three miles from Pancrasweek). By 1881, James was an ironmonger of 91 Regent Street, and the couple had four children: Elizabeth, 8; John, 4; Charles, 2; and Maud, 1. They could afford a servant, eighteen-year-old Alice Bateman from Bristol, the first of a succession of servants of similar age who attended the Lott family. The ironmongery and general hardware store continued to prosper and, by the turn of the century, Elizabeth and John were both working in the shop. Charles had joined the firm as an ironmonger's assistant, and Maud was attempting to better herself as a student at the college. The two boys developed the business at 50-51 Regent Street after their father's death, and J. Lott & Sons latterly also advertised as heating engineers and plumbers. The business closed in 1968 and the property was subsequently redeveloped.

Lower Eastcott Farm Corporation Street was made up from about 1903, and was named in 1906. Prior to that it had been a fairly narrow, nameless trackway leading north from the Whale Bridge over the Wilts & Berks Canal, and continuing until it met the line of the Great Western Railway. The only property along this trackway until the closing years of the 19th century was Lower Eastcott Farm (known as Eastcott Farm from the 1860s, when it was no longer necessary to distinguish it from Upper Eastcott Farm). This was a typical two-storey, five-bay, cottage-style farmhouse, built of rubblestone, with a front garden edged by a neatly coursed drystone wall. Next to this was a large, stone-built barn with a half-hipped, tiled roof. The attractive house faced eastwards across the track, on the other side of which there were large barns belonging to the farm. Behind the farmhouse was the yard with sheds and pens around its perimeter; adjacent, to the south, was an orchard.

During the latter half of the 19th century the tenant farmers were two generations of the Smith family. These were Edward, and then two of his children William Eastcott Smith and John King Smith. William's home (from the 1880s) and butcher's shop in High Street, Swindon was in the former King of Prussia Inn building. By the mid-1880s, there were already plans to lay out residential streets on the opposite side of the trackway, beside Lower Eastcott Farm (the present-day Manchester Road area), but the land there was still fields, part of the former Vilett estate then owned by the bankrupt Colonel. Within fifteen years, eleven streets were built between Lower Eastcott Farm and County Road. However, the farm's days were really numbered as New Swindon encroached from the west, virtually turning the property on the west side of the track into a smallholding of about 132 yards by 66 yards (dimensions that would easily fit into the area of a football pitch today). It stayed like this until 1903, when what remained of the farmstead was bought by Swindon Corporation to build its electricity works on the site. These premises later became the Swindon Corporation bus depot, and in 2011 were scheduled by urban regeneration specialists Muse Developments for redevelopment under the Union Square scheme for Swindon. (See also King of Prussia Inn.)

Lower Shaw Farm, Old Shaw Lane

Since the 1970s, when it was organised by a community of several families, Lower Shaw Farm has developed organically into a unique educational, environmental and cultural resource for family-related, social and community activities. The 18th-century farmhouse, Grade II listed since 1989, is in grounds that were once part of a much larger dairy farm. Its owner is Swindon Borough Council, which obtained the complex by compulsory purchase in 1973 and then let it on short-term leases to groups wishing to pursue alternative ideas and ways of living. Lower Shaw Farm was initially in the care of organic grower, author, publisher and educationalist Dick (Richard) Kitto (1917-99), and the Foundation for Alternatives in Urban Development, an educational charity under whose auspices he was installed as the farm's first warden. In his time, it became one of the first places to host the World Wide Opportunities on Organic Farms scheme, founded in 1971.

Since 1980, the tenant of Lower Shaw Farm has been Matt (Matthias) Holland (b.1947) who, with his wife Andrea, née Hirsch (b.1958), has created a crucible of small-scale farming, arts and literature, and community living and education, thereby turning it into a valuable local resource with a national and international reputation. In 2006, Swindon Borough Council's Property Department decided that Lower Shaw Farm should be sold for housing development, estimating that they could sell the land for an attractive sum of money. They were reluctant to give the Trustees a new lease. Faced with large-scale public outrage, news press dissent, and a wish, by the Trustees, to negotiate in reasonable fashion, the Council reconsidered matters. In November 2011,

after five years of negotiations, it awarded the Trustees a twenty-five-year lease, which finally ended speculation about Lower Shaw Farm's future.

Since 1994, the farm has been the organising base for the Swindon Festival of Literature, run there and in other venues around the town by Matt Holland. In 2009, Lower Shaw Farm won *The Observer* Ethical Garden Award for Best Community Garden.

The farmstead is 3.2 acres and comprises organic vegetable gardens, partly worked with the help of volunteers; ponds, and areas of trees. It includes the farmhouse, with two late 18th-century wings, and attached 19th-century cheese room. The house is built of red and blue bricks in Flemish bond (alternate (blue) headers and (red) stretchers in each course), of two storeys and three bays, beneath a half-hipped roof. Some of the outbuildings were converted to sleeping quarters in the 1970s and are now guest bedrooms, as well as meeting rooms and workshops. The corrugated barn is now a children's play area.

Documents extant from the early 1700s relating to the farm show that it was connected with branches of the Strange family who later had banking interests in Swindon, and the property-owning Tuckeys. In the 1860s and '70s it was farmed by the Ody family, branches of which also had other farms in the area. Thereafter, a succession of tenant farmers ran Lower Shaw Farm with varying degrees of success, and by the mid-20th century it had fallen into disrepair. (See also Holland, Leslie; Swindon Festival of Literature.)

Lydiard Park The Lydiard Park estate, on the western outskirts of Swindon, was developed out of the Anglo-Saxon Braydon

Forest, and comprises some 260 acres. These are now parkland and farmland. Sometime in the 1600s, the adjacent village disappeared, leaving the manor house huddled together in isolation with the village church, which is almost attached to it. Thereafter, the St John and Bolingbroke family in the house regarded the church as their private chapel. The house was then an internally remodelled medieval-style, cross-winged hall house, at one time owned by the 1st Viscount St John, created 1712, who, as the Tory statesman Henry St John, was Secretary of State to Queen Anne. The house was remodelled c.1738-42 by the 2nd Viscount St John, using the dowry he obtained by marrying Anne Furnese. He tacked on the eleven-bay front and the seven-bay side elevation, creating a dual aspect façade that gives a false impression of four-square solidity. In 1768, Diana Spencer, daughter of the Duke of Marlborough, caused a scandal by divorcing Frederick, 2nd Viscount Bolingbroke, and consolidated this delicious reputation by subsequently marrying Topham Beauclerk, the great-grandson of the liaison of Charles II and Nell Gwynne. In 1868, Henry Mildmay, 6th Viscount Bolingbroke, was in contention with the Great Western Railway Company. He claimed that the early morning hooter, used for summoning the men to the Works in Swindon, disturbed his sleep and was a danger to his weak heart. His attempt to silence it was unsuccessful.

Until 1911, when a dam burst, the extensive grounds featured a superb lake, which then drained away and much of the area was overtaken by nature. Throughout the first half of the 20th century, the family sold much of the furniture from the state rooms, as well as their china, silver, glassware, and personal artefacts. During the Second World War, the grounds supported a military camp for American servicemen, a military hospital, a prisoner of war hospital, and temporary housing accommodation. In 1943, the estate of 147 acres and the house was bought by Swindon Corporation; the house was restored and refurbished, and part of it was opened to the public in 1955. In 1962, the 6th Viscount Bolingbroke loaned his picture collection. This was subsequently bought by Swindon Corporation, who also spent decades trying to find and return as much as possible to the house of what the family had sold. For decades after the establishment of Swindon's library service, part of its large reserve stock of books was kept upstairs in Lydiard Park House.

Lydiard Park House is Swindon's only historic country house, and a Grade I listed building. It is the show house of the town, a snapshot of a stately home in seven rooms of exceptional quality, and is open to the public. Here are displayed saloons and state rooms with finely moulded and plaster-decorated cornices and ceilings, all furnished in accordance with the best periods of the rooms. The hall, library, dining room, morning room, drawing room, state bedroom and dressing room are open to visitors, and all are on the ground floor. In the grounds are 18th-century stables and a gatehouse, and a Georgian walled garden. At the beginning of the 21st century, a seven-year programme restored and remodelled the grounds, reinstated the lake, which revealed a plunge pool beside it, made a feature of the walled garden, and crossed and encircled the estate with numerous walkways. A baluster sundial made around the second quarter of the 18th century and inscribed 'J(onathan) Sissons, London was restored and relocated to the walled garden, and in the grounds is

a rebuilt 18th-century ice house of brick. Many public events take place in the grounds throughout the year.

McCluskey, Marie (b.1948) The woman who made contemporary dance accessible to and in the Swindon community, and brought choreography to previously unwitnessed levels in the town, was born in Shepherd's Bush, London of underprivileged Irish Catholic parents. Her grandmother – who taught music hall songs and folk songs to the young Marie – was an appreciable singer in Ireland, and her great-aunt used her creative and artistic skills as a dancer in vaudeville. Marie was convent-educated and, although she performed in school productions, did not dance until she discovered tap at the age of eleven. Despite being encouraged by the nuns to take Latin 'A' levels, she left school at sixteen and obtained a full grant to take up vocational dance training at Arts Educational in London. This meant she could combine full-time dance with 'A'-level education. With a view, which was never realised, to becoming a professional classical ballet dancer, she joined classes run by the Martha Graham Dance Company of New York, and won a scholarship to work with them in London at what became the London School of Contemporary Dance. She began to teach in London, and undertook necessary cabaret and pantomime work, but was never comfortable with commercial activity.

When she arrived in Swindon (where her husband had obtained a job and a house), she turned heads; the town had not previously seen such vibrant and eccentric hairstyles and clothes as those worn by Marie McCluskey. In 1972, she set up her own dance classes at Holy Family Catholic Primary School, Park North, and for a while taught at Swindon's Judith

Hockaday School of Dance and the Tanwood Dance School. Her own classes moved around venues, and were at one time in the Reuben George Hall at Cavendish Square. In 1976, she responded to an advertisement placed by the local authority for artists to work, unpaid, in a new arts centre being established at the former town hall in Regent Circus. (Since the local government reorganisation of 1974, this site had been home to the Thamesdown Arts Studio.) Marie was appointed to her first community dance post and, for the first time, was able to 'take on board strategic community arts thinking, and make that leap from performing arts to community engagement'. In 1979, she was appointed Dance Director of Swindon Dance, a position that at last carried a salary. In 1984, Marie was awarded the Winston Churchill Scholarship, which enabled her to visit New York for ten weeks to study the training and development of young black dancers at the Alvin Ailey Dance Theater and the Dance Theater of Harlem. In 1991, Swindon Dance achieved National Dance Agency status, and in 1993 Marie McCluskey was awarded the MBE for services to dance. In 1986, she was the founding chairman of the Foundation for Community Dance and, in 1994, the Association of Dance of the African Diaspora. In 2005, Swindon Dance became an independent trust. The organisation is also a commissioning and producing enterprise, and associated companies are Swindon Youth Dance Company, and the professional Swerve Dance Theatre Company, which was formed in 2007.

McIlroy's Department Store, Regent Street Swindon's best- known, most enduring, and much lamented department store was custom-designed by John Norman and built in Regent Street in

1875 for William McIlroy. He was a one-time draper, born in Ireland, who had settled in Reading, where he opened his first general store. The Swindon store's strapline was 'The House for Everything', and the building was a landmark in the town. It was extended in 1902, again in 1925, and a programme of modernisation and interior remodelling was carried out between 1957 and 1960, adding a further 5,400 square feet of shop-floor space. The façade of the building was remodelled in the late 1960s, and it continued to trade until unexpectedly closing in 1998, due apparently to competition from newer and larger chain department stores in the town.

The original store featured walls of glass at street- and first-floor levels, each curving right around the elevations to Regent Street and Havelock Street. Its third storey was of square-headed windows, arranged singly and in pairs, with a scroll pediment and ornamental infill above those on the corner diagonal. Above this was a flight of dormers with stone dressings. The most obvious feature was the clock tower, an amalgamation of Brightwen Binyon's clock tower on the town hall and a Wren-style church steeple. It was built in 1904 and featured a fluted, domed roof topped by an open, minaret-style cupola, above a flat, moulded parapet with corner pinnacles. The clock elevations, set on the diagonal, had inset columns to the corners with a double string moulding, and base and plinth around the feature. The whole sat above a flat, moulded cornice and a base of decorative roundels and corner brackets. The clock tower was raised above the corner of the building, flanked on either side by a short parapet of open balusters, and little pediments with plain ball finials. It was demolished in 1960 because, according to

a statement by the company 'it had become unsafe'. It was a sad day when the store shut down after 123 years of trading.

Magee, Wesley Leonard Johnson (b.1939) By 2013, Wes Magee had published 166 books for children and 8 books for adults. An award-winning children's author, he also has a large international reputation as a poet, and is a performance poet who gives acclaimed poetry lecture tours. Born in Greenock, Scotland, he came to Swindon in 1967, straight out of University of London (where he had started to write poetry), to take up a job as a teacher at Penhill Primary School. In 1968, he married Janet (née Parkhouse) at Plymouth, and also that year won Swindon's annual Ibberson Jones Poetry Trophy for his poem *The Windmill Hill People*. The catalyst for his published poetry was a pupil at Penhill who bemoaned the fact that there were no poems about dinosaurs: Wes wrote 'Stegosaurus'. While at Swindon, Wes Magee wrote the book *Urban Gorilla*, published 1972, which won the Leeds University New Poets Award, and material for *No Man's Land*, and *Headland Graffiti*, both published in 1978.

At first, the couple lived in a flat in Bath Road, later moved to a house at Wootton Bassett, and latterly relocated to Cricklade. Janet taught at Covingham Primary School until their first child was born. Wes eventually became deputy head at Park North Primary School. After the Wyvern Theatre opened in 1971, he was much involved in productions that took place in the upstairs Jolliffe Studio, one of which was an evening devoted to Alfred Williams and his work. Wes Magee left Swindon in 1977 to take up a headship at Welwyn Garden City, and left the profession in 1989 to become a full-time writer.

Magic Roundabout One-way traffic was introduced around Regent Circus from 5 December 1932, and circled the island at the bottom of Victoria Road for the first time on 26 March 1934. The roundabout at the confluence of County Road and Swindon Road came into operation on 15 August 1938. This was later redeveloped into Swindon's infamous 'Magic Roundabout', designed by the then borough engineer Norman Pritchard (1918-2010), who had held the position since 1965. It opened to traffic in 1972, and was so named (colloquially at first) after the popular children's television programme of the same name, which was broadcast between 1965 and 1977. The piece of traffic management features five clockwise roundabouts, and an internal anti-clockwise flow. Despite being feared by visiting drivers to the town, and learner drivers, it is actually very easy to negotiate. In December 2008, a Swindon Borough Council-sponsored Christmas tree was installed, with some difficulty, on the central island, where it was intended to illuminate the festive season. The Council had expected a forty-foot tree, and were not prepared for the delivered tree, which was ten feet taller. It took two attempts to erect it, and it was then dressed with lights. Overnight, vandals put its illuminations out of action. In 2011, a private individual Paul Smith applied to English Heritage for the Magic Roundabout to be given listed status as being historically the first of its kind.

Majestic Ballroom The main swimming bath at the Milton Road baths, when boarded over during the winter months, partly served as a public dance hall known as the Majestic Ballroom. It could accommodate up to 2,000 people and featured visiting bands of the day. The resident band at the Majestic was the multi-award-winning Johnnie Stiles Band, which played there for ten years from 1948, when the place was first used in this way, until the eponymous leader retired ten years later to take over the White Hart public house at Stratton St. Margaret. Gordon Talbot, Stiles's former pianist and arranger, took over the band, which continued to play for public dances until the last one was held there in 1960.

Manchester House, High Street One of the very few surviving 18th-century buildings when it was demolished and replaced by buildings pretending to be old, Manchester House had been for much of that time in trade in High Street. It had been built, possibly in the early 1700s, for a merchant, and was said to have been named after that person's association with the cotton industry in Manchester. Its front elevation was of three storeys and six bays, and it had a cellar. It had been latterly distinguished by a shell canopy over the front door, and a large shop window that replaced two bow windows that were built c.1840. By the time it came down, it was a warren of passages, old doorways that led off at odd angles (and were in some instances bricked up), and little flights of stairs. Its loss was almost as disastrous for Swindon's architectural heritage as was the demise of the King of Prussian inn, a little further along High Street, a few years later.

For much of its time, Manchester House had been associated with drapers and tailors, particularly, in its early days, with the Heath family, who were in the trade in Swindon in the 1600s, and probably lived in a much older building on the same site. Probably in the late 1840s, it passed to a branch of the Strange family, best known as early Swindon bankers, of which Thomas Strange was the

draper. His business at Manchester House expanded into what we would now call an outfitters, and it continued as such through a succession of Victorian proprietors and lessees until the end of the 19th century. Burge & Norris, saddlers, operated from the premises between 1897 and 1915, when the antique dealer Fred Cleverly moved in. Mrs Cleverley, who carried on the business until 1958, maintained that the steps into the cellar were made from tombstones that were once associated with the first independent chapel in Newport Street. After she ceased trading, the place began to decay internally, and was demolished in 1964.

Manor House, The Allegedly a medieval building that internally retained part of its early structure, this building stood on the corner of Albert Street and Wood Street. The site appears to have been a public house at various times throughout the first half of the 18th century, when it was called The Harrow. The façade was rebuilt during the Georgian period, perhaps when it ceased to trade, turning it into a low, two-storey, four-bay house, with square-headed windows with labels and stops. At roof level, there was a plain parapet above a moulded cornice. The house had a substantial square porch, with moulded cornice and decorated frieze, raised above Doric columns. This was taken down in the early 1900s. Latterly, the eastern front contained a shop, the Manor Tobacconist. The Manor House was demolished in 1962, and a development of shops and offices was put on the site.

Market Hall, Cromwell Street The New Swindon replacement for the octagonal market that stood next to the Mechanics' Institute in Emlyn Square between 1854

and 1891 was an open-air market designed by Henry Joseph Hamp, surveyor to the New Town Local Board, and then of 10 Queen Anne's Buildings, Faringdon Street, Swindon. It was built on a triangular site between Cromwell Street, Commercial Road, and Market Street. This had been bought for the purpose in 1889 by the New Swindon Local Board, to whom market rights were transferred in 1890, and by using a £2,300 loan obtained from the Local Government Board to build the market and the approach road, repayable over 35 years. The site was opened to traders on 2 November 1891; on 8 December, it was illuminated by gas lamps. Despite this, traders were not forthcoming, and just before Christmas 1891 the New Swindon Local Board invited tenders for 'building market shops, lock-up shops with verandas, piers, boundary walls, etc'. The work took longer than expected; when the market opened on 15 October 1892, it had also, at £4,500, gone over budget.

For eleven years the space was bounded by a low brick wall wherein were seventeen 'shops', and a number of traders sold from tent-like stalls. This area of about 2,134 square yards was covered in 1903 when a multi-ridged roof was erected, supported by iron pillars and cross-braced beams. Externally, it presented a great flight of gables above blind windows, built of red brick with stone dressings and rusticated pilasters. The roof of the main hall comprised five bays of louvered lights, and a quantity of match boarding. The interior walls were of white, glazed bricks to a height of five feet. Early on, the market hall consisted of thirteen shops arranged on its north and south sides, smaller lock-ups on the west side, and a double row of stalls placed back to back down the centre, and separated by a partition. By 1933, there

were sixty stallholders and sixteen shops in the complex.

The main entrance was on the corner with Market Street. It had a round-headed doorway with a moulded label and deep keystone flanked by flat, fluted pilasters and bases with foliated capitals in which was a pair of very intricate, wrought-iron gates; a triangular pediment above the cornice in a cut-out parapet; and a raised ornamental, segmental pediment. This area became a fish market, with eight marble-topped stalls built with white, glazed bricks, with separate washing facilities and a water supply to each stall. This was a fire engine depot between 1941 and 1959. The main entrance was later blocked off to provide accommodation for Harry's Cut-Price Stores (Harry Conn also had a shop at the west end, outside the market, and a stall in the market hall selling fancy goods, toys and jewellery.) There was a secondary entrance at the south-west corner of the building, next to the market manager's office and the popular but draughty market café. The 1903 covered market was demolished in 1977, and the area it had occupied was thereafter used as a car park.

When this market closed down, many of the stallholders relocated into a purpose-designed market hall in the nearby Brunel shopping centre, which opened in 1976. This was not a successful move, and some eventually went into Swindon's 'five-peak' tented market house, conceived by Eric Reynolds on the basis that what historically went with a market was a pleasure fair, so he designed the 'tipsy' tent arrangement of the market house to evoke the ideas of a helter-skelter and traditional carousel horses. The peaks, in a series of cones, are made of the same fabric as the Millennium Dome in London, built on a steel frame that is bolted together and to the ground. It was erected in just six months in 1995 on the site of the 1892 market in Cromwell Street. The tented market closed in October 2007, and there were plans to re-erect it at the Olympic Village in time for London's 2012 Olympic Games. This did not happen, nor did a scheme to put a restaurant, cafés and shops on the site. The tented market remained, and was re-opened in 2009.

Market Square, Old Swindon

The market place, centred on what would become the Market Square, was probably planned in the 13th century, close to the older settlement on the hill. A covered market cross of unknown age, but probably made of wood and most likely more of a shelter, existed in the centre of the square until it was taken down in 1793. By the 1800s, the space was mostly bounded by cheese lofts and warehouses above a row of old stables, there were a few old cottages, and some open land owned by the lord of the manor. At the beginning of the 19th century, large crowds assembled in the square to hear Wesleyan Methodist preacher George Pocock of Bristol; he continued to preach regularly until 1812. By the 1840s, the markets in the square were very much hit and miss affairs. Corn was sold here, the place was infested with rats, and there were pig and sheep folds in the square. All of this contributed significantly to the insanitary state of Old Town. The town hall was built on the south side, 1852-53; and in 1886, the corn exchange was erected adjacent. A cattle market continued in the square – conducted from a temporary rostrum – until 1887, when Ambrose Lethbridge Goddard removed it to his own land adjoining the cattle sale market in Marlborough Road. The market square was also where the Vale of the White Horse

Hunt famously gathered, to the delight of crowds in the 19th century, opposite Thomas Hooper Deacon's VWH Horse & Carriage Repository in High Street. The market square (where there was a watering trough for horses) was the starting and finishing point for the horse-drawn brakes that conveyed people to and from the pleasure grounds at Coate Water. From 1904, it was the site of the Old Town tram terminus for trams travelling between there, Rodbourne and Gorse Hill, taking in New Swindon. Most of the current buildings on the north and east side of Market Square are modern houses, apartments, or commercial premises. (See also Corn Exchange; Square House; Town Hall, Old Town.)

Markets, New Swindon As the railway village was built, and the early public houses associated with it also went up, a number of the established Old Town firms began to hold sales of cattle, pigs and horses in stable yards. About 1860, William Dore began to sell livestock from a private yard near the Queen's Hotel, opposite the GWR station. The railway company contemplated opening a sale yard in competition in 1866 on nearby land that they owned, but were persuaded that Dore's monopoly was too strong. By the 1880s, Bishop & Day, and John A.Y. Matthews were holding sales of livestock and agricultural implements on alternate Mondays in the square next to the Mechanics' Institute. Much of the history of the New Swindon markets in the 20th century devolves on other entries in this book. (See also New Swindon Improvement Company, and Market Hall, Cromwell Street.)

Markets, Old Swindon The oldest record of a market in Swindon dates it to 1259.

In 1274, it was said to exist to the detriment of the market at Marlborough, but it clearly persisted; in 1289, the town was called 'Chepyng Swindon', and 'Market Swindon' in 1336. It is referred to in a document of 1559, and a fair and market was mentioned at Swindon when Thomas Goddard acquired the manor in 1563. Charles I granted a weekly market to Thomas Goddard in 1626. A fair and market is mentioned in East Swindon in 1640, when it was said to be 'a petty, inconsiderable one', and again in 1667 when the tolls of the market and fairs in Swindon become part of a lease on the marriage of Thomas Goddard to Mary Pleydell. By the time John Aubrey wrote of it in 1672, it had revived into a 'gallant market for cattle', because a cattle plague that began in 1650 at nearby Highworth and continued until well into the next decade had caused its dealers to change their allegiance to Swindon. It was one of thirty similar markets held in Wiltshire in 1718, and the town had a market cross that continued to be mentioned until 1757, mostly at the court leet in connection with requests to the lord of the manor to repair it.

In c.1700, Thomas Goddard acquired a former church house, inhabited by some of the parish poor receiving alms; he ejected them and converted their home into a lock-up market building. Richard Jefferies recorded that this was supported by oak pillars, and was demolished in 1793. William Morris described 'a small circular market or penthouse in the centre of the market place, under which people used to assemble to do their marketing ... not unlike a huge umbrella'. It was low, octagonal, and became dangerously rickety and dilapidated. The market also declined; in 1800, only Mr Tidd of Dammas Lane turned up there once a week and sold meat from his mobile stall. Yet

when, in 1811, Thomas Davis reported to the Board of Agriculture on the agricultural state of Wiltshire, he found Swindon to have 'a pretty good market for cattle'. A small wool market was also held in old Swindon, c.1819 to c.1840. Until the mid-1840s, cattle were sold regularly at Charles Anthony Wheeler's auction yard in High Street.

In 1848, the idea of building a permanent market house was first mooted. The Swindon Market Company was formed in 1852 to do just that, and to demolish the stables and warehouses in the market square, and establish a market for cheese. About the same time, the company of Dore & Fidel were holding livestock sales at the Goddard Arms. By 1852, the various traditional Old Town sales of animals, although taking place at more reasonable hours, had become too much of a nuisance for the inhabitants to bear. It declined from about 1866. In addition, the annual hiring fair for servants, on the second Monday after 11 September, was simply an occasion to display the poorest wretches of the community who could not find other employment. By 1880, it became an excuse for public drunkenness and brawling.

About 1865, William Dore built a sale yard just below Christ Church, and held monthly sales there until 1871. In 1870, he leased some land owned by Richard Tarrant (who owned the house in which Dore's father had lived) in Lower Town, and thereafter held sales there of cattle, sheep and pigs, with increasing regularity. Together, Dore and Tarrant also held horse and commodity sales, and in 1871, Dore bought adjacent land from John Harding Sheppard in Marlborough Road. This became the Marlborough Road Cattle Market; it was laid out to accommodate over 2,000 head of cattle, sheep and pigs, and opened on

27 October 1873. Within two years, sales there had almost eclipsed those still being undertaken in High Street. In 1875, Deacon & Liddiard tried once again with wool; it was an immediate success and continued until the First World War. Intending to retire, William Dore took Henry Smith (hitherto a Newport Street butcher) into partnership in 1876, but Dore died soon after. Smith engaged another partner almost immediately, and the sale yard went from strength to strength. During 1877, fortnightly sales of cattle began at Deacon & Liddiard's yard and, in 1878, monthly sales of cheese. The firm of Dore, Smith & Radway sold about 10,200 head of cattle, sheep and pigs in 1979. The firm later became Dore, Radway & Titmas. In 1889, James Radway held the first of his annual carthorse sales and shows at the Repository.

Ambrose Lethbridge Goddard relocated the High Street cattle market on to his own land in 1887, next to the Marlborough Road cattle market, where he employed William Read to design the site. Read put in a collector's office at the Marlborough Road entrance, and separate entrances for pigs, sheep, horses and cattle. The wrought-iron and cast-iron work for the pens and the standards was supplied by William Affleck of the Prospect Works. The Swindon Water Company laid mains under the yards, and hydrants and taps above it. There was direct access to the adjacent Midland & South West Junction Railway, of which Goddard was a director. This new cattle market opened on 25 July 1887. In the same year, a butter market opened in the market square, but it was not a success. The Swindon Central Market Company leased Goddard's Marlborough Road cattle market from him in 1890, and immediately set about sub-letting. John A.Y. Matthews was the first sub-lessee, in 1890.

With T. Lavington, he held weekly sales of cattle, sheep and horses.

By 1903, the main sellers were the firms of Dore, Fielder & Matthews, and Ferris & Maskelyne, and in 1905, John Maskelyne rented the former butter market at the corn exchange as a provender stores. Thomas Hooper Deacon, who had been holding sales of English and foreign horses in his sale yard (Vale of the White Horse, or Deacon & Liddiard's Horse and Carriage Repository) opposite the market square since 1871 (the premises were greatly expanded in 1874), was granted a licence to sell in the cattle yard. Between them, the firms of Dore and Deacon were selling more livestock in two weeks in Swindon than all the old markets had managed in a typical year. In 1911, John Maskelyne was granted licences to sell sheep, horses and cattle on land at the rear of the Goddard Arms Hotel. Over the next couple of decades, a number of businesses were licensed to sell variously on the Marlborough Road site. In 1930, the Swindon Central Market Company purchased from the Goddard estate that part of the cattle market that it had leased since 1889. During the late 1930s, talks took place between Swindon Corporation and the Swindon Central Market Company about removing the fairs to a site near Ladder Lane, but hostilities intervened, and these were not renewed. In 1949, the company bought William Dore's sale yard and amalgamated it with the rest of the market.

In 1965, Swindon Corporation bought the freehold interest in the Old Town market square and to the various accompanying rights. That year, with the agreement of Swindon Central Market Company, the markets for cattle, horses, sheep and pigs were transferred from The Square to the Marlborough Road cattle market, and on 30 November 1965 the former officially ceased to be a market place. Thereafter, no-one could sell goods there. Two ancient fairs were affected by this move; they were not those of the original charter, which had by now become defunct, but two 12th-century fairs. (The Swindon Central Market Company also retained the rights of the Pie Powder Court to decide disputes arising during the fairs or markets.) Two stallholders affected by this were offered accommodation at the cattle market.

By 1966, Swindon Corporation was taking steps to remove the remaining fair from High Street, where it was causing congestion, and relocate it into the car park of the County Ground. This was carried out that year, after negotiations with Robert Edwards, whose family had been operating the fair since the 1930s. The last market on the Marlborough Road site took place on 18 April 1988. (See also Candle and Lantern; Dore, William; Gin and Water; Market Square; Town Hall, Old Swindon)

Marks & Spencer In 1911, Marks & Spencer bought 90 Regent Street from the London Penny Bazaar Company, and there set up its own Marks & Spencer Penny Bazaar. The shop relocated to a former furniture and upholstery store at 85/6 Regent Street in 1931, and extended these premises in 1964-65 when it took over the adjacent corner site with Cromwell Street, formerly that of the Fox Tavern, which shut down in 1963 after about a century in business.

Marlborough Road cottages Just south of the junction with Newport Street, and almost isolated in their own history, stand a pair of cottages that were built

early in the 1800s. Both of the Marlborough Road cottages have two storeys, one has a single bay and the other has two; both have attics and hipped dormer windows, and were constructed in courses of rough-faced limestone with heavy, flat stone lintels. The larger of the pair has a central entrance, with a room on either side. These cottages, when built, stood at the entrance to the town, where the turnpiked road from Marlborough, arriving at Swindon via Coate, climbed the hill. This part of Swindon was then known as Lower Town, and was a mixture of small thatched cottages with some larger 18th- and early 19th-century dwellings. Almost everything else of these times has gone from Marlborough Road, leaving just these two heroic survivors.

Mason, Philip Hawe Born in London in 1828. By the time he was in his early twenties, Mason had established himself as a grocer in High Street, Swindon, which business eventually took up three adjacent premises. One of these had previously been a grocer's shop and, before that, was The Bull public house. By 1851, P.H. Mason already had a housekeeper, Mary Rushen from Wanborough; he married Martha from Chiswick, Westminster in 1853. The High Street business was a great success and, by 1861, he was employing ten men and three boys. The family lived in Devizes Road. He was the first chairman of the Old Swindon Local Board, which was established in 1864, and the chairman of the Swindon Water Company from 1865. He was also a member of the Nuisance Removal Committee, and a director of the Swindon Market Company. A Methodist, he contributed financially to the fund by which the Bath Road Methodist church was built in 1879. He later emigrated

to New Zealand for the sake of his wife's health.

Mason's Arms Inn, High Street
When it was demolished in 1971, this was the third-oldest hostelry in Swindon. It was built of rough stone in the 1600s, and latterly presented as two storeys and six bays; one bay was occupied by two bow windows. Prior to 1800, it was called the Coach & Horses, and the name was probably changed during the occupancy of Richard Tarrant. There was a stable yard and stables at the rear of the building. Tarrant kept the inn until it passed to William and Caroline Killard in 1841; John Washbourne of Wroughton took over in 1863, and was succeeded by Matthew Washbourne in 1870. Thomas Wheeler came to it in 1870, and the Mason's Arms was bought by Arkell's Brewery in 1886. They retained it for the next eighty-three years. The inn was connected by its own brick-lined underground passages to others in the vicinity. All of this historical interest notwithstanding, the property was demolished for 'urban regeneration' after it was acquired in 1969 by Swindon Borough Council to facilitate road widening and a public car park.

Matheson, Rosa With an MA in Women's History and Research, and a Ph.D. in Women's and Railway History, it is not surprising that Rosa Matheson's great contribution to the history of Swindon has been through her books about female labour and the town's railway works. She was born in London of Romany heritage, and came to Swindon in the early 1980s. Educationalist, historian and teacher, she also founded two charities: Friends of Angel's Orphanage, following a visit to Nepal as part of Health

Partnership Nepal, when she met Amrit Bikram Shahi ('Angel' since his conversion to Christianity) and his wife Aishworya in the private orphanage they had set up in their home in Kathmandu. Her other charity is the Book Project, 'helping women to help themselves', and an allied book called *A Day in the Life of 100 Women in Britain*, which was inspired by the archive of Britain's Mass Observation Unit, the social research organisation that began in 1937. Rosa's books of Swindon interest are:

TRIP - the Annual Holiday of GWR's Swindon Works (History Press, 2006)

The Fair Sex - Women and the Great Western Railway (History Press, 2007)

Railway Voices 'Inside' Swindon Works (History Press, 2008)

The GWR Story (History Press, 2010)

Doing Time Inside - Apprenticeship and Training in GWR's Swindon Works (History Press, 2011)

Mattick, Richard Mallory (b.1949)

The man who has chronicled the history of Swindon Town Football Club, through a number of published works, began to support the team in 1958, and was a director of it, 1985-92. Dick Mattick was born in Swindon, and was educated at Lethbridge Road School and Park Grammar School before taking a B.Sc. degree in Economics at London University. He spent his entire teaching career at Churchfields School, where he was head of the history department. In the 1980s, he joined Swindon magistrates, and latterly became chairman of the Youth Panel. After he retired, he became local secretary of the National Association of Schoolmasters Union of Women Teachers, and an active member of the Old Town Rotary Club. His books about Swindon Town Football Club

are *The Robins* (Barracuda Books, 1989); *The Robins Return 1993-96* (Capricorn Books, 1996); *Swindon Town Football Club* (Tempus, 2000); *Swindon Town 100 Greats* (Tempus, 2002); and *Swindon Town 50 Classic matches* (Tempus, 2004).

Mayors of Swindon

The Mayors of Swindon since the creation of the Borough in 1900:

1900-01 George Jackson Churchward
1901-02 Levi Lapper Morse
1902-03 Frederick George Wright
1903-04 James Hinton
1904-05 William Reynolds
1905-06 William Henry Williams
1906-07 Francis Stook Coleman
1907-08 William Henry Stanier
1908-09 Thomas Hooper Deacon
1909-10 William Henry Lawson
1910-11 Tom Butler
1911-12 George Brooks
1912-13 John James Shawyer
1913-14 Charles Hill
1914-15 William Ewart Morse
1915-16 William Ewart Morse
1916-17 Albert John Gilbert
1917-18 Alfred William Haynes
1918-19 Charles Anthony Plaister
1919-20 Samuel Edward Walters
1920-21 Edwin Jones
1921-22 Reuben George
1922-23 Albert Edward Harding
1923-24 Thomas Charles Newman
1924-25 Richard Evans
1925-26 William Gerald Adams
1926-27 Sampson John Haskins
1927-28 William Webb
1928-29 George Henry Stevens
1929-30 George Henry Hunt
1930-31 John Belcher
1931-32 John Lindow Calderwood

1932-33 William Robert Robins
1933-34 William Henry Bickham
1934-35 Frederick Thomas Hobbs
1935-36 May George
1936-37 Lewis James Newman
1937-38 Harry Edwin Newton Niblett
1938-39 Raymond George Cripps
1939-40 Henry Russell Hustings
1940-41 Francis Edward Allen
1941-42 Leonard Dodson
1942-43 Arthur John Barnes Selwood
1943-44 Frederick Arthur Drinkwater
1944-45 Charles Stuart Macpherson
1945-46 Charles Roundell Palmer
1946-47 George Henry Selman
1947-49 William John Davis
1949-50 Francis Elliott Akers
1950-51 James Bond
1951-52 Arthur Leonard
1952-53 Albert Edward Long
1953-54 Harold Whiteside Gardner
1954-55 Arthur Madge Bennett
1955-56 Harold Thorpe
1956-57 Norman Victor Toze
1957-58 Harold Diment
1958-59 Frederick John King
1959-60 Frank Jewson Jefford
1960-61 Elsie Christina Mary Millin
1961-62 Thomas George Gay
1962-63 Arthur Edward Cockram
1963-64 Charles William James Streetly
1964-65 Mervyn Webb
1965-66 Archibald William John Dymond
1966-67 Lilian Rose Lock
1967-68 Harold George Lewis
1968-69 Alfred James Bown
1969-70 Reginald Alexander Jones
1970-71 John Wilmot Pass
1971-72 Arthur Norman Palmer
1972-73 Peter James Furkins
1973-74 Gladys Lavina Knapp
1973-74 William Thomas Winton

1974-75 Raymond James Smith
1975-76 John Raymond Stevens
1976-77 Leslie Gowing
1977-78 William Henry Collins Turpin
1978-79 Ashley Roberts
1979-80 Gordon Thomas Law
1980-81 Reginald Douglas Clarke
1981-82 Arthur Samuel Miles
1982-83 Michael Bertram John Bawden
1983-84 Arthur James Masters
1984-85 Henry Ernest Garrett
1985-86 Percival Laurence Jefferies
1986-87 Sidney James Daniels
1987-88 Peter Owen
1988-89 James Robert Cordon
1989-90 Robert Kenneth Benson Savage
1990 John Raymond Stevens
1990-91 Derique Joseph Montaut
1991-92 Eric Charles Smith
1992-93 Mildred Violet Haines
1993-94 Gloria Doreen Dart
1994-95 David Ernest Glaholm
1995-96 Bertram Smith
1996-97 Maureen Kathleen Caton
1997-98 Maurice Hugh John Matthew Fanning
1998-99 Brian Ford
1999-2000 Joy Brunt
2000-01 Arthur Archer
2001-02 David Cox
2002-03 Stan Pajak
2003-04 Derek Benfield
2004-05 Peter Stoddart
2005-06 Ray Fisher
2006-07 Mike Bawden
2007-08 Michael Barnes
2008-09 Steve Wakefield
2009-10 David Wren
2010-11 Rex Barnett
2011-12 Ray Ballman
2012-13 Michael Bray
2013-14 Nick Martin

Mazonowicz, Douglas Howcroft (1920-2001) The fifth child of Albert Andrew James Mazonowicz and Lilian Maud (née Howcroft), Douglas was the great-grandson of a Polish immigrant who was forced to flee his own country where he was a person of some status. This man, Alexander Casimir Mazonowicz, and his own father, also Alexander, worked as navvies building the line that brought the railway to Swindon. Douglas, like his siblings, was born in Swindon, and went to Gilbert's Hill school, then Clarence Street school, where he won first prize in a national poster competition. He lived at 37 Rolleston Street, and later at no. 36, where he had a studio in the attic, and attended art and design evening classes at the Technical College. After leaving school, he worked as a fitter and turner in the GWR Works until 1940, when he joined the Royal Engineers and later REME. Discharged from the war, he went to live in Plymouth, to where his mother had previously relocated.

He was to become world renowned for seeking out prehistoric art in situ, principally in France, North Africa – typically Algeria and the Sahara Desert – Australia, North America and Spain, accurately recording it, and reproducing it as silkscreen prints. He also wrote several books and many papers on prehistoric cave art, and some of his work can be seen on display in The Douglas Mazonowicz Collection at the University of Bradford.

In 1968, he was appointed a Research Associate of the Carnegie Natural History Museum in Pittsburgh, Pennsylvania. In 1975, he founded the Gallery of Prehistoric Painters, in Manhattan, and in 1979 was made a Fellow of the Rochester Museum and Science Centre, New York. The Smithsonian Institution of Washington gave him four touring exhibitions, and in 1987 he was made a Fellow of The Explorers Club of New York. Douglas married three times, each marriage ending in divorce. He was under age when he first married, so his mother's permission had to be obtained, and his third marriage was to a wealthy American, Susan Warms Dryfoos (b.1946), the great-granddaughter of Adolph S. Ochs (1858-1935), the one-time newspaper proprietor and former owner of the *New York Times*.

MECA The former Regent Cinema building in Regent Circus was sold by Mecca to Swindon Borough Council in 2008, and remained unused for over two years. In 2010, it was refurbished – retaining its original pink, green and gold ceiling – by GVS Entertainment Limited and renamed MECA (Music Entertainment Cultural Arena). The floor was strengthened to take a capacity standing audience of 2,000 people, and the venue opened in December of that year, with a three-course dinner and an evening of amateur boxing organised by Eddie Neilson, the Birmingham-born (1950) former heavyweight boxer, who has associations with Swindon.

Mechanics' Institution Often confused with the Mechanics' Institution building – the Mechanics' Institute – this was originally the name given to the concept of ideals rather than any bricks and mortar that later supported them. The Institution originated in 1844 as a concept for the betterment of railway employees, and Daniel Gooch began to attract some of the less dissolute of the workforce to the idea of improving themselves through lectures and evening classes which, with the establishment of a small library, formed the

nucleus of the institution's early activities. A part of 'O' Shop in the locomotive department of the Works was set aside for dancing and theatricals in 1844. Over the next eleven years, before it had its own purpose-built premises in 1855, the institution developed programmes of education and self-improvement alongside social activities, operating out of various places inside the Works and undertaking outside or extra-mural activities. During this period, the original paint shop was cleared and adapted for dancing and other amusements, and 'O' Shop was used for theatricals alone.

Mechanics' Institution building, Emlyn Square This building is in the Railway Village Conservation area, and is designated on the statutory list of buildings of special architectural or historic interest. It is Grade II* listed, upgraded from Grade II in 1999 following a report to English Heritage by the New Mechanics' Institute Trust. It is also included on the English Heritage Register of Buildings at Risk and, in 2012, was placed on the Victorian Society's ten most endangered buildings in England & Wales.

Situated in Emlyn Square, the Mechanics' Institution building, more widely called the Mechanics' Institute, has become, since the mid-1980s, the embodiment of the kind of obfuscation, nimbyism, bureaucracy, small-mindedness, and muddled thinking that generally have previously stopped Swindon from elevating and successfully regenerating itself. It was instigated by the Mechanics' Institute Committee of the New Swindon Improvement Company, which was formed in 1853 to provide venues for social, entertainment, and educational activities in the new town. Its Mechanics'

Institute was designed by Edward Roberts of London in Gothic Revival style, built 1853-55, and enlarged in 1905. There were plans, in 1879, to create a new institute building adjacent, designed by Brightwen Binyon, which included a spacious lecture hall, and a theatre. The premises were extended in 1892.

It is built on a double-cross plan with raised central section, in two storeys of limestone rubble, with quoins, string courses and dressings of ashlar. It has, in many ways, an ecclesiastical feel, in no small way suggested by the two octagonal flanking lantern towers to the south elevation, and the plethora of gable ends throughout. There is a seven-bay northern front, and the building has much Tudor-style embellishment, particularly in the treatment of the windows. The weathervane was placed above the north-west turret in 1902. It is a likeness of the Iron Duke Class locomotive Lord of the Isles, which was in service 1851-84. The piece is 46½ inches long, and was made by C.A. Matthews.

The Institute served as a place of relaxation and education for the railway workers and their families. (An original plan can be seen in *The Builder* magazine, 1 July 1854.) It became best known for its reading room, library, and a theatre. The building also had cold water baths, a coffee room, a dining room, lecture rooms, and public meeting rooms. British Railways Staff Association, Western Region carried out extensive alterations to the building, which was reopened by R.F. Hanks, chairman of the western area board, on 20 November 1959. The following year, the Institute merged with British Rail Staff Association, effectively transferring the building to British Rail Engineering Limited. The library closed in 1961, by which time almost every aspect of

its existence was being carried out to a better degree elsewhere in the town. The theatre closed in 1976.

In the late 1970s, Thamesdown Borough Council was given the chance to buy the building, but declined. In 1985, British Rail Engineering offered to sell the building to the council, who wanted to develop it for the arts, for £1. This was also refused, at the eleventh hour, because local authority funding cuts would have meant a severe reduction in funding for existing arts ventures in the town if the council, having bought the Mechanics' Institute, had then to pay for its proposed redevelopment. The building was sold to a private developer the following year when Swindon's railway works closed, and then sold for the second time in 1986. Plans in 1987 to turn it into two nightclubs were vigorously opposed by the local community, who formed the Mechanics' Institute Action Group, and it was sold on. Similar opposition took place when plans were submitted in 1988 to turn the building into a hotel, and this persuaded the council to reject the proposals. This decision was repealed following a public enquiry in 1990, but the work did not take place, and the permission for a hotel expired in 1995. The building continued to deteriorate. Also in 1995, the New Mechanics' Preservation Trust was formed in an attempt to stop the deterioration, maintain a watching brief, and try to find a means by which the building might once again serve the community.

A feasibility study by Swindon Council and English Heritage in 2002 resulted in an urgent works order. In 2003, Mountmead Limited, the then owners, sold the building through Alder King Property Consultants of Old Swindon. The new owner Matthew Singh, of Forefront Estates, was given permission to create apartments, offices, and a café on the site. These were not realised, and in 2004, Mr Singh's company tendered a planning application to turn the building into a hotel, but this was withdrawn in the face of opposition from the New Mechanics' Institute Trust and just before a Government enquiry was due to begin. The Victorian Society declared in 2007 that Swindon's former Mechanics' Institute was one of the country's ten most endangered buildings. Two years later, architects Feilden Clegg Bradley assessed what was required to be done at once, on behalf of the Borough Council who issued an urgent works notice on Forefront Estates. In 2010, Swindon Borough Council was granted the legal right to temporarily take over the building and carry out urgent works with a grant of £250,000 from English Heritage. (See also Playhouse Theatre.)

Mechanics' Institution Library In September 1843, a handful of mechanics and toolmakers set up a small lending library within the Swindon GWR Works, with books that had been donated by friends. The Company enabled them to buy a few more, using funds that had accumulated by way of fines. The library came under the auspices of the Mechanics' Institution when it was formed in 1844, by which time it had around 130 books, and just fifteen members. By the end of the first year, membership had increased to 129, and the stock of books stood at 522 volumes. The first annual report of the Council of the Institution, published in 1845, said that the book selection aim had been to purchase 'only standard works, and such as would be both instructive and amusing'. It went on to say that some eighty volumes were being issued each week, and that 'these books are, in many cases, read by persons

who were previously known to spend a great part of every evening in a tavern'. From the outset, the Company had provided a room in the Works for the library, and by the time it was also taking newspapers and had therefore become a reading room, it was attracting capacity occupancy of some twenty users. The library remained inside the Works until space was allocated for it in the Swindon Improvement Society's Mechanics' Institute building of 1854. By the middle of the 1860s, the Institution had 500 members and some 3,500 volumes on the shelves. Swindon residents could take out books on Monday, Wednesday and Friday evenings, whilst Tuesday and Thursday evenings were reserved for non-residents. The Council continued to select fiction and non-fiction, 'continually replenishing the library with valuable standard books', at such a rate that some 6,600 were on the shelves by 1875. There were 12,000 in stock by 1885, and 20,000 by 1895; when the library reached the 60th anniversary of its founding, it had more than 24,000 books. This figure had risen to around 40,000 by 1942, when Swindon adopted the Public Libraries Act, and established its local authority-run public library service. This effectively created a service with which the Mechanics' Institute library could not compete. It was closed down in 1961, and its stock of books was sold off to members, and then the general public. Some of its best books were bought by the Swindon Public Library Service. (See also Library Services.)

Medieval Swindon See Domesday, Medieval and Later Manors

Mela The first cultural 'gathering' (the meaning of 'mela' in Sanskrit) celebrating regional Asian arts and crafts, clothing and accessories, dance, food, music, and related aspects of lifestyle and leisure activities was held in the Town Gardens in 2003. This free festival, supported by the Borough Council and local businesses and organisations, has since been an annual event in the town, and has continued to take place on the same site.

Members of Parliament for Swindon The earliest known parliamentary representatives for Swindon were John Ildhelfe and Richard Pernaunt, who held office in 1295. Thereafter, few names are recorded. Richard Neel represented the town in 1304, Thomas Crekkelade and Robert Crekkelade in 1422, and Nevil Maskelyne in 1660.

From 1885 until the Swindon Division was created at the General Election of 1918, Swindon was part of the Cricklade Division. Two candidates were returned before multiple-member constituencies were abolished in 1884 by Act of Parliament. Since the 1997 General Election, the town has been split into Swindon North and Swindon South. This is a list of the people who have represented Swindon in Parliament (following general elections in the years shown) since 1868.

1868 Hon. F. Cadogan (Liberal)
Sir Daniel Gooch (Conservative)
1874 Ambrose Goddard (Conservative)
Sir Daniel Gooch (Conservative)
1880 Sir Daniel Gooch (Conservative)
Mervyn H.N. Story Maskelyne (Liberal)
1885 Mervyn H.N. Story Maskelyne (Liberal)
1886 Mervyn H.N. Story Maskelyne (Unionist)
1892 John Husband (Liberal)
1895 Alfred Hopkinson (Unionist)
1898* Lord E. Fitzmaurice (Liberal)

1900 Lord E. Fitzmaurice (Liberal)
1906 John Massie (Liberal)
1910 Col. T.C.P. Calley (Conservative)
1910 R.C. Lambert (Liberal)
1918 Sir Frederick W. Young (Conservative)
1922 Sir Reginald Mitchell Banks (Conservative)
1923 Sir Reginald Mitchell Banks (Conservative)
1924 Sir Reginald Mitchell Banks (Conservative)
1927 Rt. Hon. C. Addison (Labour)
1931 Sir Reginald Mitchell Banks (Conservative)
1934* Rt. Hon. C. Addison (Labour)
1935 W.W. Wakefield (Conservative)
1945 T. Reid (Labour)
1950 T. Reid (Labour)
1951 T. Reid (Labour)
1955 Francis E. Noel-Baker (Labour)
1959 Francis E. Noel-Baker (Labour)
1964 Francis E. Noel-Baker (Labour)
1966 Francis E. Noel-Baker (Labour)
1969* C.J.F. Ward (Conservative)
1970 David L. Stoddart (Labour)
1974 David L. Stoddart (Labour)
1979 David L. Stoddart (Labour)
1983 Simon C. Coombs (Conservative)
1987 Simon C. Coombs (Conservative)
1992 Simon C. Coombs (Conservative)
1997 (SS) Julia K. Drown (Labour)
    (SN) Michael D. Wills (Labour)
2000 (SS) Julia K. Drown (Labour)
    (SN) Michael D. Wills (Labour)
2005 (SS) Anne Snelgrove (Labour)
    (SN) Michael D. Wills (Labour)
2010 (SS) Robert Buckland (Conservative)
    (SN) Justin Tomlinson (Conservative)
* By-election

Messenger, Melinda Jane (b.1971)
Melinda Messenger was born in Swindon and educated at Liden and Dorcan schools. She was then employed locally, except for a short period with Britannia Airlines. She later became a photographic model with the town's Jason Paul Agency, at whose suggestion her breasts were enhanced, when she was twenty-three years old, to 34DD. In 1997, much of these appeared on a poster advertisement for Glevum Windows, their owner wearing only bra and knickers. By the time it was banned by the Advertising Standards Authority for its suggestive content, the picture had appeared on bus shelters in Swindon – sometimes only fleetingly, for several copies were swiftly liberated by admirers – and Melinda was much in demand by competing elements of the national tabloid press. In 1997, when her photograph was published in *The Star* and *The Sun* newspapers, a considerably greater number of people saw even more of Melinda, and her mother famously disapproved of her topless modelling. This launched her national modelling career and provided her with a high profile that provided a springboard for her subsequent career in the broadcasting media. By the time she left Swindon, going firstly to live at Aldbourne, she had completed a number of films and had launched a television career. In 1998, she married Wayne Roberts, with whom she has three children. Melinda was remarkably forthcoming about her experience of suffering pre-eclampsia and severe post-natal depression, and gained much public support. Afterwards, she successfully managed to advance her television career.

Methodist Central Hall Built in 1907-8 as the Central Mission, under the auspices of the Revd Ralph Pritchard, the establishment became best known for its men's mission

called The Swindon Brotherhood. It was built fronting Clarence Street, with its rear adjacent to Regent Circus. The Young Men's Club followed the Brotherhood proper, out of which was formed the Swindon Brotherhood Football Club, which continued to play locally until it was disbanded when its players were required for the First World War. Following hostilities, the Brotherhood Cup for football was instituted and played for in the Borough League. The hall was expanded in the 1960s, when it was used as the venue for public concerts, in particular those held in Swindon by the Bournemouth Symphony Orchestra. It closed in 1971, was soon afterwards badly damaged by fire, and demolished in 1985. Offices were built on the site.

Methodist Church, Bath Road

This Old Town Methodist church was paid for by public subscription (notably by important trades people who lived in the vicinity and who had recently embraced Methodism), was designed by Bromilow & Cheers of Liverpool, built by Thomas Barrett of Swindon, and opened in 1879. It is constructed of rock-faced limestone with Bath stone dressings, and features an east-west apsidal arrangement, the apses having stepped, transomed, blunt-headed lancets and a glazed arcade beneath the eaves. The south front has an arched entrance, flanked by exaggerated trefoil lights with, above, two single-light, blunt-pointed windows flanking one of three lights, each having 14th-century-style cusped tracery in the heads, and the central window featuring a roundel. The south front is flanked by turrets with spirelights connected by an open parapet. Architecturally, it is a hybrid; some neo-Romanesque, a feeling of Early English,

and a measure of Victorian Gothic revival. The church proper is well above the level of the road because the architect designed the integral Sunday schools to be beneath ground level at the front, a device that made the church itself even more elevated and imposing than it might otherwise had been.

Midland and South Western Junction Railway

On 18 June 1872, the town clerk of Marlborough, Robert W. Merriman, circulated a notice to the effect that there would be a meeting of the Marlborough Committee in Marlborough Town Hall at twelve noon on 22 June 'for considering the subject of railway communication between Swindon and Andover', its main purpose being 'to discuss the draft of a preliminary statement proposed to be issued'.

On 28 July 1875, after three years of debate, Lord Ernest Bruce, MP for Marlborough, performed the ceremony aimed at starting work on a railway line between Marlborough and Swindon. Invitations to the event, sent out by company secretary Charles L. Brooke, spoke of the 'Ceremony of Turning the First Sod', at two o'clock p.m., and a 'Luncheon at the Riding School, Marlborough, after the Ceremony'. Luncheon was scheduled for 3 p.m. Tickets were in the hands of solicitors Merrimans & Gwillim of Marlborough.

The Swindon, Marlborough & Andover Railway Company intended to link Andover with the GWR line at Swindon, and possibly continue from Andover to Southampton. They planned a tunnel some 830 yards long beneath Old Swindon (which ultimately proved to be too expensive), and estimated that it would take two and a half years to complete the line. In the event, work did not begin until 1877, and the section opened

between Marlborough and Swindon on 29 July 1881. On 1 May 1882, the line was opened between Marlborough and Andover. The line joined the Banbury & Cheltenham Railway's line at Andoversford Junction.

Ambrose Lethbridge Goddard was deputy chairman of the concern; James Copleston Townsend was its solicitor. Instead of being tunnelled beneath Swindon hill, the line, after leaving (Old) Town Station south of Newport Street, curved westwards towards Rushey Platt, and thence initially into the GWR line at Mannington Bridge, west of (New) Swindon station. The line of the Midland & South West Junction Railway (as it was called following amalgamation with the Swindon & Cheltenham Extension Line in 1884) ran through Cricklade and on to Cirencester. (In the same year, the GWR opened a branch line between Swindon and Highworth, with an interim station near Kingsdown.) A passenger service ran between the stations at Old Town and New Town between 1882 and 1885, when it was discontinued. Rushey Platt station was opened in 1883, and closed in 1905. In 1913, a station was opened on the line at Moredon, and public services ended there c.1935; the station officially closed in 1951 but continued to provide for supplies to the Moredon power station for the rest of that decade.

The M&SWJ line was never very successful, and was taken over by the GWR in 1923. In 1894, Old Town station, built in 1881 and famed for its attractive gardens, was given a licence for its refreshment rooms. These continued, known locally as the 'ghost train' until 1965, four years after passenger services finished in 1961. An enthusiasts' train, the last to run the line, covered the route between the site of the Newport Street station and Rushey Platt in 1972. The station

was demolished, and the bed of this railway line is now a designated linear footpath and cycle route.

Milk Bank, Station Road This name was given to an elongated, grassy mound, east of the Swindon station entrance, and almost opposite the Great Western Hotel. It was separated from the line by a wall alongside what was known as the 'milk platform'. Farmers drove their wagons loaded with full churns of milk on to the incline beside the milk bank, where the churns were taken over by railway porters who proficiently rolled two at a time along the platform and loaded them on to waiting milk trains. The area eventually became a car park.

Mills At the time of the Domesday survey in 1086, there were two mills in Swindon. One was on the estate of Odin the Chamberlain, and the other was on lands belonging to Odo, Bishop of Bayeux. A mill was owned by William de Swyndon in 1303, and two mills are mentioned in a document of 1313, the properties of Robert Avenall and his wife Christine. The exact whereabouts of these mills is not known. (See Church Mill; Deacon's Mill; Ladd's Mill; New Mill; Okus Farm mill; Wood Street windmill.)

'Miss Whiplash' Real name Marion June Akin (b.1952), also known as Lindi St Claire, but more widely and for longer as 'Miss Whiplash', was a former brothel keeper, celebrity prostitute, and dominatrix. She came to Swindon at a very early age during the period when the town was offering council houses to accommodate the so-called 'London overspill' after the Second World War. Marion lived in Kingswood Avenue,

and went to Walcot Junior School, Jennings Street School, and Park Senior School, and attended the Brownies and the Girl Guides in Whitbourne Avenue. When in Swindon, she began the career in sexual services that would ultimately make her the most famous London prostitute of her time, for a while working the town's famous red-light district around Manchester Road. She acquired the name 'Miss Whiplash' at the height of her career, a moniker that stayed with her into her later reincarnations in the escort industry, and as a farmer with ducks, geese, rabbits, etc. In 2009, she made the national news when she was involved in a traffic accident that left her trapped upside down in a stream for nearly twenty-four hours. She has been prospective parliamentary candidate for the Corrective Party, and her autobiography, *It's Only A Game*, was published in 1992.

Mitchell, Enid In 1979, Enid Mitchell completed a study of the Victorian and Edwardian decorative ceramic wall tiles extant in Swindon, thereby adding an important and hitherto unexplored strand of original research to the history of the town. As a notable sculptor, she also contributed, in 1988, a bronze bust of Diana Dors for permanent public display in the Wyvern Theatre. The cement cast for this piece was given to Michael Deacon (1935-98), of the firm of jewellers in Wood Street, whom Diana took to school.

Enid Mitchell was born at Hampton Hill, Middlesex, at the time a rural setting but within the sound of Bow Bells. The family moved to Ealing when she was fifteen, where she attended the Ealing School of Art before spending five years selling furniture for Heal's department store and designing rooms for clients, and was the proprietor of a London

taxi for nineteen years. In the 1970s, after a brief sojourn in Swindon following the death of her husband, she studied for a diploma in art and design at the Hammersmith School of Art, Lime Grove (which became part of the Chelsea School of Art), of which the thesis on Swindon's tiles was part of the ceramics element, and taught evening classes there. At that time, the opportunity arose for her to buy a house in Swindon that was originally built in 1896 by E.W. Beard, and which still had its original fireplace and ceramic kerb. She had the opportunity to study at first hand Swindon's Art Nouveau tiles that were then (1978) 'being destroyed at the rate of about half a dozen examples a week'. (She has identified some of the Swindon tiles extant as being the work of Craven Dunnill of Bridgnorth, Shropshire, and Bermantofts of Leeds, Yorkshire.) Her thesis was called *Art Nouveau Porch Tiles in Swindon, Wiltshire*, and was donated to Swindon Libraries' Local Study Archive in 2011.

Moonraking Legend Wiltshire-born men are known as 'Moonrakers' because of the way in which a group of them fooled excise men into believing that they were raking a pond for the 'big cheese' (a reflection of the moon) instead of the contraband liquor they had hidden there. Throughout the 16th and 17th centuries, the Bell Hotel in High Street was run by Dutch and Flemish wool merchants. It is thought that a smuggling organisation was established to import barrels of gin and brandy, and tobacco for their purposes, and those of their agents on the wool-producing Marlborough Downs and in the Cotswolds, so that the high cost of import duty could be avoided. This was stored around Old Swindon and it is certain that illegal gin was also made and hidden in

the town. (See also Underground Tunnels of Old Swindon.) Swindon has as great a claim to being the source of the Moonraking legend as have any of the other places in the county that claim it; even more so if you consider that elsewhere the contraband was just passing through, whereas Swindon was most probably its ultimate destination. Some circumstantial evidence may be suggested by the collapse of a cellar floor beneath the market house in Old Town, when a tunnel was discovered beneath with a number of grilles in it, thought to have been the cellars of properties that pre-dated the market house. Coloured water was forced down the grilles, which came out in the pond on the Goddard estate.

Moore, Edward Acland (1817-1881) One-time manager of the County of Gloucestershire bank in High Street, and a director of the Swindon Market Company when it was set up in 1852, Moore was born in Plymouth. His life is remarkable for its sudden rise from bank employee to landed gentry. In 1843, he married Charlotte (née Newall, b. Chorlton, Lancs., 1819) in Manchester, and the following year the family moved to The Sands, Swindon, where they employed a cook, a nursemaid, and a housemaid. In the 1840s, Moore was working as an agent for Medical & Clerical Life Assurance with an office in High Street. By 1852, he was manager of the bank, and was still there in 1859. The 1861 census finds him and his family living at Lonlas Cottage, Coedfrank, Cadoxton-juxta-Neath in Glamorgan, where he is described as a colliery proprietor. Twenty years later, the cottage has become Lonlas House, and Moore is a 'land proprietor'. One of his sons, James Herbert (b. Swindon, 1852) became a

captain in the Glamorgan Artillery. Moore died in Plymouth, and Charlotte died in Chorlton, Lancashire in 1887.

Moredon Tree Collection, Cheney Manor Road The collection is maintained under the auspices of the Great Western Community Forest initiative, and lies east of Cheney Manor Road, north of Akers Way and the little River Ray (here called Hreod Burna Brook), which marks its southern boundary. The site was formerly a local authority plant nursery, specialising in growing young trees that were later used in planting schemes around the town. From the 1980s, specific trees were grown there, partly at the request of local residents, and latterly in response to corporate tree-funding sponsorships. There are now examples of many European species, as well as some native to the Americas, Asia and the Far East. Associated with this area is Plaum's Pit, a little to the north, a small lake beloved of fishermen who know of it. (See also Great Western Community Forest.)

Morgan, Henry Frederick Stanley (1881-1959) In 1900, Morgan began work as a draughtsman in the GWR's Swindon drawing office, under the tutelage of William Dean, Chief Engineer at the Railway Works. Three years later, he bought his first motor car. He left the Works in 1906 to open a garage and motor workshop in Malvern Links, Worcestershire, from where he also ran an omnibus service to Wells. In 1910, he began production of his first Morgan car, and the hand-built vehicles are still being made there.

Morris, Desmond John (b.1928) An only child, Morris was born at Hillside House, Purton. His great-grandfather was

the founder of the *Swindon Advertiser*; his mother was Marjorie (née Hunt); and his father Harry Morris was an engineer, trained in the drawing office of the Great Western Railway in Swindon. Harry was a prolific, but commercially unsuccessful, writer of dramatic fiction for children. Desmond's first 'toy' was a typewriter, which he mastered before he could handwrite properly. In 1933, the family moved to 58 Victoria Road, Swindon, where Harry opened a general store specialising in confectionery, specifically to service regular passing trade between old Swindon and the new town. The family lived above the shop; there was a pond stocked with fish at the rear of the premises; and Desmond kept tame foxes, a dog, lizards, snakes, rabbits, mice, voles, chicken, and a stock of guinea pigs from which he supplied Oxford Zoo. The area that is now Queen's Park, the site of the former brickworks, then belonged to his grandmother. It comprised a series of ponds that his father combined, creating one large pond with islands, and stocked the waters with fish. The area was very overgrown, and became the budding zoologist's private domain. Only his then girlfriend, the eventual actress Diana Dors, was allowed in. In the austere aftermath of the Second World War, Desmond established a jazz studio in Swindon, where he painted, developed an interest in the rhythms of Indian music, and installed a drum kit. Harold Joliffe, then Swindon's Borough Librarian, encouraged Desmond to paint and, in 1948, allowed him to hold the first two exhibitions of his surrealist paintings at Swindon's arts centre. By the end of the 1940s, he was associated with the poet Paul Weir, and Ramona Baulch, whom Desmond married in 1952, and the trio made intense and surreal films. Conscripted into the army,

he became lecturer in fine arts at Chiseldon Army College, which meant he could live at home in Victoria Road, and paint in the glass conservatory studio there, whilst simultaneously improving his interests in the natural world and social anthropology. He left Swindon in 1949 to begin his long career in zoology, writing and television presenting.

Morris, William (1826-1891) The founder of Swindon's first newspaper, the *Swindon Advertiser*, relocated to the town from Wotton-under-Edge in 1830. His father James had a bookseller's and stationer's shop in Swindon's Wood Street. William was a Liberal supporter, and an outspoken and influential moralist who did not shrink from exposing anything or anyone acting contrary to his own views. This approach sometimes landed him in court, occasionally meant that his newspaper was banned by the organisers from reporting on certain events with which he had dealt harshly in the past, and made him a number of political enemies. Much of his writing about Swindon during his own lifetime appeared first in the *Advertiser*, which, from 1857, was published from custom-built offices in Victoria Road, (at the time, called Victoria Street) and was afterwards gathered together and published in 1885, with much additional hearsay, as *Swindon: Notes & Relics of Ye Old Wiltshire Towne*. This secured him a reputation as the town's first historian, and it was reprinted in 1970. He died in his sleep, whilst on holiday, at the Wilberforce Temperance Hotel, Bournemouth. (See also Football Pink; Swindon Advertiser; and Swindon Echo.)

Morris, William, Sale of Effects In 1892, the year after the death of William Morris, *Swindon Advertiser*'s originator, the

Swindon firm of auctioneers Dore, Fielder & Maskelyne was instructed by his son, W.E. Morris, to sell his father's library of some 4,000 books, and his collection of furniture, silverware, rare antiques and ephemera, scientific instruments, and works of art. The sale lasted for two days, and took place at the Goddard Arms Hotel. The catalogue showed William to have been a collector on a large scale, whose walls must have heaved with paintings, engravings and prints, who had an overwhelming passion for old Japanese and Chinese furniture and display cabinets, and whose premises were probably stuffed with articles of vertu, curios and bric-a-brac. These included numerous pieces from the Far East and the Orient, and Chippendale and other antique British furniture. Among the rarer items was an antique war trophy 'taken by the British army at the capture of Chin-Kiang-Foo, July 21st, 1842'; three ancient Indian tom-toms; a model of Stonehenge under glass; a handsome four o'clock Sevres tea service dated 1763; a large, handsome French pedestal bronze clock presented by Louis XVI to his physician (which sold for 14 guineas); and 'a pair of paintings on glass by John Gee, an artist who, being born without arms, painted and designed with his feet, holding his brushes and pencils with his toes'. William Morris's collection of books showed that he had the archetypal Victorian antiquary's interests: old volumes on history, antiquities, topography, art, religion, and poetry made up the bulk of the collection, all in fine and rare editions.

Morse, Levi Lapper (1853-1913)

Charles Morse of Purton became a draper and grocer at Stratton St Margaret, where he embraced Primitive Methodism and held their meetings on his business premises at the bottom of Eastcott Hill, Swindon. He gradually established a small business empire in Swindon and elsewhere. His son, Levi Lapper Morse, was to become a business and political giant in the area, and is still remembered as the owner of Morse's department store, second only of its kind in Swindon after McIlroy's, which was situated in Regent Street. Both Levi and his son, William Ewart Morse (1878-1952), were ardent Primitive Methodists. Levi was mayor of Swindon, 1901-2; William held office twice — 1914-15, and 1915-16. The family lived at The Croft, Old Town, and during their ownership the grounds were often given over to Methodist events and, in particular, to Conventions at the beginning of the 20th century. Levi Lapper Morse was Liberal MP for Wilton, 1906-1910, and William Ewart Morse represented Bridgwater for the same party 1923-24. Both father and son were Wiltshire County Councillors, Justices of the Peace, and Swindon Town councillors; both were highly active in Swindon's business and commercial circles. (See also Croft, The.)

Most Terrible Calamity

Pleydell Goddard, brother of Thomas Goddard who was to become lord of the manor of Swindon in 1757, was in Lisbon, Portugal when the extremely violent earthquake that was to kill an estimated 60,000 people struck on 1 November 1755. Six days after the event, Pleydell wrote home:

Dear Brother. Thank God for us. We can never be sufficiently thankful for our almost miraculous escape from a most terrible calamity that ever befell a city. Lisbon is no more — shook to pieces by a most terrible earthquake, and to complete the destruction, the ruins consumed by fire. I have been under the greatest apprehension for what you must

suffer on our behalf, as the news of this misfortune will reach you before you have this assurance of our safety. You will undoubtedly conclude that we have shared in the fall of this unhappy city – I had hoped to spend an agreeable winter here and the climate had begun to have a most desirable effect on my health, but I have nothing now to do but to fly from a country which is one continued scene of desolation. Poor Brosius who received me in the most friendly manner is now so far from being able to accommodate me that he must think himself lucky if he can find a place to shelter himself against the inclemency of the weather. I find his loss uncommonly severe. I need not mention to you how much it is our duty to share it with him. The gentleman who favours me with conveying this calls on me to conclude. How thankful should I be that I can still say you have an affectionate brother, P. Goddard.

Murals in Swindon See Arkell's; Cambria Bridge; Castle Combe; Children's Story Wall; Fairy Castle; Famous Swindonians; Golden Lion Bridge; Gorse Hill; Hinder's; Iffley Road; King Class Locomotive; Queen's Park; St George and the Dragon; Station Site; White, Ken.

Murray John Tower Otherwise known as the David Murray John building (after Swindon's town clerk, whose last major project this was), and The Brunel Tower (for 21st-century marketing purposes), this block was designed to rise in twenty-two storeys of concrete, steel and glass to some two hundred and seventy feet above the town centre Brunel shopping development. It was built for Swindon Corporation, 1975-76. The structural engineers for this were F.J. Samuely & Partners, and opened by the mayor, John Stevens, in 1976. The planned accommodation was sixty-four flats and eight duplex properties. The tower was marketed, possibly to the chagrin of the hotel owners in the town, by a campaign that pointed out 'Finding a hotel room in Swindon is a real problem. The answer could be a company apartment in the David Murray John building'. It now has four floors of office space from ground level, with seventy-two flats arranged on the floors above.

Museums The family of Charles Herbert Henry Gore (1866-1951) came to Swindon in 1869. He was educated at the Great Western Railway school in Bristol Street, and then at King William Street school. In 1876, he discovered the fossilised bones of a prehistoric creature on the site of the Queen Street gasometer, and the find inspired a growing interest in geology and natural history. The following year, he was accepted as an apprentice coach builder in the carriage department at the railway works, and remained there until ill-health forced his retirement in 1900, and he thereafter established a clothier's business in Granville Street. Throughout the whole of this time, his interests gradually developed into a passion, and he amassed a considerable collection of artefacts. In 1919, Gore offered the entire collection to the Swindon Town Council on the condition that it provided a suitable building in which to house his finds. The Council came up with a hall on the east side of Regent Circus; known as the Victoria Hall, it had been built as a Unitarian Chapel, and had been in the occupancy of the Roman Catholics before they moved to their new church of Holy Rood in Groundwell Road in 1905. Gore was appointed curator of his own collection, and he personally classified and

arranged each exhibit that was displayed. This was Swindon's very first museum, opened on 27 October 1920.

In 1930, Gore packed it all up, and relocated to Apsley House, Bath Road. He continued to be curator there until his death, when the town's borough librarian, Harold Jolliffe, was designated Borough Librarian & Curator, on behalf of the Swindon Borough Council's Libraries, Museums & Arts Committee.

In 1961, the museum was put in the charge of twenty-three-year-old Morna MacGregor, who lived in Quarry Road. On her initial inventory of the museum, she discovered six hand grenades of whose existence no-one knew. This discovery involved the Swindon constabulary, Army Southern Command at Salisbury and, in particular, the expertise of Staff Quartermaster Sergeant D.C.H. Maidment of the Royal Army Ordnance Corps' Ammunitions Inspectorate. McGregor left in 1962. Neil (later Sir Neil) Cossons succeeded her, and he was followed in 1964 by the archaeologist John Woodward. Additions abutting the east of Apsley House, built on over the years, were demolished in 1964 when shops were put up with an art gallery above. (See also Railway Museum, Railway Village Museum, and STEAM.)

National Monuments Record In February 1994, the Royal Commission for Historical Monuments began to set up on the former GWR Works site, occupying Brunel's original general offices of 1842-3, which housed the Works' drawing office, and also the original stores and pump house. The property was enlarged and extended in the 1860s, and further built upon in 1904 when a third storey was added. It was completely refurbished and extended 1992-94, and the organisation built a high-tech archive store on previously vacant land, adjacent. The monuments record was officially opened on 30 June 1994 by the Royal Commission's then chairman Baroness Daphne Park of Monmouth. Tarmac, the owners of the site, brought in an industrial compressor to enable the historic Works hooter to mark the occasion. In 1999, the Royal Commission merged with English Heritage, since when the National Monuments Record has been the latter's public archive of photographs and documents at Swindon. The site includes some ten million historic photographs, a public search room, and a library.

National School, Newport Street
In 1764, a 'free school' was opened, funded by voluntary contributions and under the auspices of a board of trustees, in an existing complex of cottage and outhouses on Goddard family land in Newport Street. The first master was Thomas Barrett, who taught reading, writing, arithmetic and religion. Twenty boys and five girls were there accommodated. In 1811, the National School Society was formed; the free school became a National School, and the premises were rebuilt as such in 1836. This was a two-storey, stone-built property, distinguished by its large and finely chiselled name and date stone. It was erected over an existing well, only separated from the schoolroom by floorboards. Just outside the school building was a water pump and a urinal. Just three years before it closed, it had 116 pupils; the water in the pump was said to be 'in such a filthy, stinking state that it is kept locked to prevent the children using it', and the urinal was 'covered in night soil, the seat and floor of the privy in a like state, the whole being most filthy and offensive'. Two

adjacent cottages belonged to the school. The National School's best-known schoolmaster was Swindon-born John Turvey (1755-1850). It closed to pupils in 1871, and in 1909 the premises became the Parish Church Men's Club. The National School building was demolished in 1962.

National Trust, Kemble Drive In 2005, the National Trust brought together 470 members of its staff that had hitherto worked in offices at Cirencester, London, Melksham and Westbury, and amalgamated them at the organisation's new headquarters in Swindon. The Trust chose to establish its complex on a four-acre section of the former railway works, specifically where a rolling mill had stood before it was demolished in 1964. The new building was commissioned in 2002, with a brief to meet the National Trust's sustainability principles in every way. It was designed by Feilden Clegg Bradley of Bath and London, and was developed by Kier Property of Sandy, Bedfordshire. The builder was Moss Construction of Cheltenham, a member of the Kier Group, who beat eighty-six other contenders to win the contract. Work started in January 2004, with underlying criteria to achieve the highest standards of design and sustainability, and deliver replicable strategies that set new standards for green, commercial offices. It cost £10.5 million.

The building was named 'Heelis' to commemorate Mrs William Heelis, better known as Beatrix Potter, who gave land in the Lake District to the National Trust. The Heelis building in Swindon was designed as a two-storey, open-plan environment giving 76,500 square feet of office space, meeting rooms and workshops and, on the ground floor, a shop and café restaurant.

It is a gabled building, constructed on a trapezoidal plan around a series of atria and interior courtyard spaces, with a colonnade to the south. The external walls are clad in a variety of blue bricks in polychromatic style and feature cantilevered brickwork and aluminium panels and forms. Internally, the environment is reminiscent of the nearby former engineering sheds, with a steel frame with pre-cast concrete infill to the first floor. A variety of timbers from the National Trust's forests was used to line the atrium wall and the accommodation stair, and carpet tiles throughout were made from the wool of the Trust's Herdwick sheep. The Trust included billboard-sized reproductions of pictures from its own photo library all around the building, but noticeably in the public areas, and the north facing wall of the central atrium featured five colourful panels, each of five square metres, designed and hand-woven with acoustic quilt by artist Eleanor Pritchard in her Greenwich, London studio. The themes of these – coastlines, woodland, gardens, farmland, buildings – reflect the breadth of the National Trust's assets.

Between 2005 and 2008, Heelis became a multi-award-winning building for sustainability, innovation, and building. These awards included the Brick Development Association Award for Best Commercial Building, and the Best Medium/Large Office Building Award at the International FX Interior Design Awards, both in 2005. The British Council for Offices gave it an innovation award in 2006, and the same year saw it scoop a building award from the British Construction Industry, the British Institute of Facilities Management Award, the Dedalo Minosse International Prize for Commissioning a Building, a RIBA award, and the RIBA Sustainability

Award. It received two Civic Trust awards in 2007, one for sustainability; and was the Sustainable Building of the Year in 2007. In 2008, it acquired building performance awards, and the Fasso Bortola International Sustainability Prize.

New, Edith Bessie (1877-1951)

Edith was born in North Street, the daughter of Frederick New, a railway clerk, and his wife Isabella (née Frampton). The Framptons – William (b.1814), who was a Swindon lad, his wife Jane, who came from Cricklade, and their five children, of whom Isabella was the youngest – lived in Wood Street. William would become a builder in the town, and one of his sons a joiner, but Isabella went into teaching, which undoubtedly influenced Edith's choice of career.

Soon after Edith's birth, Isabella was widowed when her husband was killed at the GWR. She and her three children (the others were Ellen, born 1874, and Frederick, born 1877) relocated to 17 Prospect, where she taught music. The family also lived in St Margaret's Road and, later, at 29 Lethbridge Road. By the age of fourteen, Edith was a pupil teacher at Queenstown Infants School, and the family were then living at the Lethbridge Road house, where her mother also let rooms to make ends meet. Edith continued as a pupil teacher in various Swindon schools 1893-99; she then trained in London at Stockwell Training College for Mistresses, and returned briefly to Swindon in her early twenties as a Board School teacher to teach infants at Queenstown school.

In 1901, Edith moved to London where, after attending a public meeting in Trafalgar Square in 1906, she became active in the suffragette movement. Her work in the Women's Social and Political Union brought her into conflict with the authorities, and she was sent to gaol on several occasions – notably for chaining herself to the railings of No.10 Downing Street, and forcibly trying to gain entry into the House of Commons – and was once fined £25 and bound over to keep the peace. The most famous incident took place in 1908 when she and fellow suffragette Mary Leigh progressed, with a group of militants, from a rally in Parliament Square to Downing Street. Failing to gain entry to Prime Minister Asquith's residence by hammering on the doors, they attacked his windows with stones taken from a bag that Edith was carrying. Two windows were broken; both women were arrested and taken to Bow Street police station, where Edith was bound over in the sum of £2 to appear in court. At her trial, the pair threatened to 'use bombs next time', and were warned by the judge that this would be a hanging offence. For her part in this, Edith was sentenced to two months' hard labour in Holloway prison, where she was interned from 30 June to 22 August. Letters were smuggled in to her, and she wrote to her mother that all was well and she was in good spirits. Her release was greeted with great celebrations by her fellow suffragettes.

For her part in this incident, Edith was awarded, in 1909, the Women's Social & Political Union's Gallantry Medal 'in recognition of a gallant action whereby through endurance to the last extremity of hunger and hardship, a great principle of political justice was vindicated'. She retired to a cottage in Cornwall, where she died at Polperro.

New Mill A mill, on the River Ray between West Leaze and Westcott, is mentioned on a document of 1648. This is likely to have

been the property described as 'White Mill' on Andrew's and Dury's map of Wiltshire in 1773. A map produced by the Wilts & Berks Canal Company in c.1820 calls it 'New Mill', and it is certainly the mill that gave its name to Mill Lane, then only a track, leading from West Leaze Road to West Leaze farm. It stood, long disused, until c.1920, and the adjacent mill house was demolished c.1930.

New Swindon Improvement Company This organisation was formed in 1853, when four-fifths of its shares were held by the council of the Mechanics' Institute. Its objectives were to provide accommodation for the inhabitants of the railway town, establish shops where the artisans connected with the railway works could obtain provisions, put up public buildings, and develop a market place and retail shops. The organisation had its offices in Church Place. Its main project was the octagonal market, built next to the Mechanics' Institute. This had failed by 1888, when the New Swindon Local Board discussed the possibility of providing its own market. In 1889, solicitors Maxwell & Tuke, acting for the Rolleston estate (the greater part of which in Swindon had already been sold), recommended that Major Rolleston sell his land in Cromwell Street for £550, subject to it being used for a market only. This was agreed, and contracts were signed on 8 April 1890. At about the same time, Ambrose Lethbridge Goddard agreed to transfer all of the market rights held by the New Swindon Improvement Company to the New Swindon Local Board. (See also Market Hall, Cromwell Street; Octagonal Market, High Street; and Mechanics' Institute.)

Newport Street A document of 1346 concerning the gift of a tenement by Constance Dolyn of High Swindon to her sons mentions 'Nyweport (meaning 'new market') Street, and is the oldest known recorded name of a thoroughfare in the town. The market referred to is probably that by which the town was known as 'Market Swindon' in 1336, which may have been a recent revival (hence 'new') in the tradition of one that was established adjacent by c.1259, and which had given the name 'Chepyng' (meaning 'market') Swindon to the place by 1289. Market Place, at the northern end of Newport Street, had probably been planned as such in the 13th century, but the street itself would have been a lane that joined the track coming in from Wroughton at its southern end with that arriving at its northern end from Marlborough; the market was established where Newport Street and the Marlborough road met the thoroughfare from Cricklade (now Cricklade Street and High Street). It was alongside this track that people acquired portions of land and put up low, thatched cottages in a piecemeal fashion. The original line of Newport Street remains intact, and although by 1900 some of the old cottages had been re-modelled or rebuilt with brick façades, they still stood above cellars that were several centuries old; many of the ancient rubblestone and thatched cottages, now lime-washed, remained until the 1930s. These included the larger properties close to the junction with Devizes Road: some double-fronted and gabled, although thatched, and others semi-detached of two storeys with dormer windows.

Swindon may have begun hereabouts, but Newport Street was not well kept up, and its footpaths were allowed to deteriorate. In the 19th century, it was called Bull Street after the name of the public house that stood on its west side, and which was originally

called the White Hart but acquired the name after the demise of The Bull in High Street. Newport Street was badly affected by the results of poor sanitation, open sewers and seeping cesspits. That said, it became, in the 1800s, a thoroughfare of small businessmen who mostly carried on craft-based cottage industries from their residential premises. There were other public houses here in the 1700s and 1800s; the Royal Oak, long ago demolished; The George, which in 1808 became the residence of the Nonconformist minister at the adjacent chapel; and The Wheatsheaf. It was here, too, that Swindon's first school was established, succeeded by the custom-built National School in 1835. The face of Newport Street was largely changed, undeniably for the worse, during the latter half of the 20th century, when the cottages and small houses at either end of Newport Street, and those on the north side, were demolished to facilitate road widening and retail redevelopment. (See also Newport Street, the oldest house; Old House At Home.)

Newport Street, the oldest house in Swindon

Nos. 17 and 18 is 'the oldest house in Swindon'. Grade II listed, this is effectively two properties remodelled into one, and is now of three bays and three storeys, with a remodelled Georgian second storey and a 19th-century carriageway through the central bay. This facilitated access to a one-time blacksmith and stables at the rear. The rear elevation has a rare 18th-century barrel window. The bays of the remodelled house are separated by flat bands, and the arch is depressed with a keystone. The windows have louvered shutters. The cellars beneath the property have been dated to the fourteenth century, and there is a later

entrance in one of these (now bricked up) to a tunnel that might have been part of the network known to have existed beneath Old Swindon. This one may have run beneath the roadway towards the Bull alehouse that existed by 1771, later named the White Hart.

The 'oldest house' had been a boarding house when Harold Stanley Lorraine Easthope (1915-2003), art restorer and dealer, and his wife Marjorie Gwendoline (née Fripp) (1920-1990), an art teacher, bought half of the property in 1955 and there proceeded to give painting classes to aspiring local artists. The couple were members of the Society for the Preservation of Ancient Buildings, and Harold also undertook architectural surveys of local buildings (particularly some in Swindon) for Government departments. They bought the remainder of the property in 1962, and in 1970 established the property as an art gallery called Easthope & Fripp, and bearing the legend 'Fine Art Gallery'.

Newspaper Offices, Victoria Road

The façades of the offices at nos. 99 and 100 Victoria Road are two of the finest elevations in Old Town. They were custom-built as offices and printing works for the *Swindon Advertiser*, and are each of three bays; no. 99 is of three storeys, and no. 100 (built as the printing works) is of two. Both have moulded eaves, bracketed out, and first-floor Venetian windows in the prevailing fashion of the time: centrally on the second storey of no. 100, and occupying all three second-storey bays of the building next door. The rusticated façade with quoins at ground-floor level, and square-headed doorway with recessed columns, were put up c.1930.

Newspapers

See Morris, William; Piper, Joshua Henry; and Wyatt, Woodrow Lyle

Nexus sculpture, Freshbrook In 1986, the internationally renowned artist and sculptor Hideo Furuta was commissioned by Thamesdown Borough Council, with the assistance of Southern Arts, to create what became the Nexus sculpture beside the shopping precinct at the centre of Freshbrook. The sculptor was born in Hiroshima, Japan in 1949, and came to Britain in 1985 after a spell in Chile. He took six months to complete the piece at Freshbrook, carrying out the commission in situ, in public. The sculpture comprises three connected (hence the name) slabs of blur pennant stone from South Wales, rough-hewn, building to a pyramid, and set on blocks of wood. Three years after he completed the Swindon commission, Hideo Furuta settled in Scotland, where he died in 2007.

Nicholson's Raincoat Factory In 1919, Nicholson's of St Albans (head office) and Manchester opened its raincoat assembly business in a then derelict, one-time sweet factory in Manchester Road, Swindon, which had also been occupied by Compton's. There, the company made its garments from supplied, pre-cut and pre-sorted material, but it closed in 1922 during a raincoat recession in the UK, and reopened in 1924. Thereafter, it supplied markets for raincoats in many countries throughout the world. Latterly in County Road, it closed in 1972.

Nig Nog Club A brief teaser mentioning the forthcoming *Swindon Evening Advertiser* Nig Nog Club appeared in the paper on 8 April 1932; another mention was made the following day, and full details were given on the 11th. In those days, the words 'nig nog' had no racial connotations whatsoever, but

was only slightly deprecating in meaning 'all silly fellows together having a great time'. The club superseded the paper's Tinkerbell Club (Wendy Hut) and was to be run by 'Aunt Joy', the pseudonym of the newspaper employee Vi Robins, who worked in the sales department. She referred to the members as her 'dear nephews and nieces'. (Mrs Robins was well known, and possibly avoided, for her habit of wrapping her head in vinegar-soaked brown paper when she had a headache.) The whole Nig Nog concept was after the model established by the Northern Echo of Darlington's Nignog Children's Ring in 1929, and was thereafter taken up by a good many provincial newspapers. The badges differed a little from club to club; the Swindon Nig Nog's circular badge was made of tin and plastic (some newspapers produced them in die-stamped brass). It had a dark blue background with a white edge and a white circle in the middle that bore the image of a Nig Nog – a circular, smiling white face with a quiff of hair, all in silhouette. It bore the legend 'Evening Advertiser Nig Nog Club'. It was offered with either a stud fixing for buttonholes ('usually preferred by boys', wrote Aunt Joy) or a brooch for pinning on to a coat or frock.

Membership was open to 'boys and girls of all ages whose parents read the *Evening Advertiser*'. The club intended to run 'novel entertainments and competitions' and the first *Evening Advertiser* Nig Nog outing (2/6d for 'members'; 5/- for grown ups), which took place soon after it was founded, was to the Cadbury chocolate factory at Bourneville. Membership of the *Evening Advertiser* Nig Nog club cost 3d in stamps. In return, a card of rules required members to be 'a friend to lonely and friendless children; not to forget their friends when they are ill,

and always be kind to dumb animals'. In addition, they were enjoined to 'wear a smile and perform a good deed whenever possible, and, above all, must do every little thing they can to help hospitals, charities and other good works'. Aunt Joy encouraged members to write to her with news of themselves, their pets, their families, etc. The nephews and nieces were sent birthday cards on the appropriate dates, on which their names also appeared in the newspaper. They also learnt the Nig Nog's salute, which, according to Aunt Joy, involved inserting the thumbs in the ears and waggling the fingers. The list of the club's first 106 members was published in the paper on 13 April 1932 and, six days later, it was able to report that membership had topped five hundred. For the next twenty-eight years, the *Evening Advertiser* Nig Nog club continued as a daily feature, running its thoroughly wholesome entertainments, competitions, outings, collections and good works. The feature was latterly called the 'Nig Nog Evening Advertiser' and was much reduced in size by the mid-1950s, sometimes comprising no more than a short list of those members whose birthdays fell on that day. It last appeared in July 1958.

North Wilts Brewery, off High Street Richard Bowly always said that his brewing business began in 1865. In 1870, he built his premises, separated from the Godwins' Belmont Brewery only by Britannia Place, and evidently very similar in design. The entrance to the complex was off High Street, through a narrow carriageway arch in a two-storey, three-bay elevation of c.1850. The brewery closed in 1918, and its date of demolition is unknown, but the High Street premises retain the frontage of round-headed arch and flanking windows, with keyed archivolts and bracketed sills to the windows. The upper windows are square-headed with moulded architraves and sills, and the eaves have pairs of modillions. The brewers Courage took over the business, and used these premises as offices; latterly, they have been occupied by a bank. Associated with this property, until they were demolished, c.1980, was a little run of dwellings known as 'Brewery Cottages', built c.1870, which ran off at right angles to High Street on either side of the carriageway that gave access to Bowly's North Wilts Brewery.

North Wilts Canal In 1794, the two canal companies first discussed constructing a watercourse between the Thames & Severn Canal and the Wilts & Berks Canal. Nothing came of it because the T&S Canal Company preferred to navigate a way to London through the upper Thames, which would have required the Thames Commissioners to improve that part of the river. Nothing came of this either. Finally, in 1812, the companies controlling the T&S and the W&B canals reached an agreement, and in 1813, Parliament passed the necessary Act that allowed the North Wilts Canal to be constructed. This waterway opened in 1819, a nine-mile stretch that included twelve locks, covering a total fall to the north of 58½ feet. The North Wilts joined the Thames & Severn at Latton, and met with the Wilts & Berks near the hamlet of Eastcott at Swindon. Its route, although then through open countryside, meant that it would later pass through the Swindon railway works. A six-inch step lock at John Street controlled the amount of water passing from the Wilts & Berks into the North Wilts, and facilitated load measurement for the purpose of levying

tolls on the carriers.

The GWR were to build (and later demolish) at least five un-named communication or access bridges, or footbridges across the North Wilts Canal within their Works, and there were also others within the town. Notably, these were: 1814 John Street (an arched road bridge, built of stone near to the junction of the two canals and close to New Wharf; it was demolished c.1920).

1814 Iffley Road Bridge (demolished c.1920). 1814 Telford Road Bridge (also known as Rodbourne Road Bridge; it was demolished c.1920). North of this was an un-named farm access bridge of the same dates; it was followed by another, also built in 1814 but not demolished until the 1940s; and a third, again to the north, that was demolished in the 1950s.

1816 Moredon Road Bridge (also known as the Purton Road Bridge; it was demolished in the 1930s).

1841 GWR Mainline Bridge, erected north of Sheppard Street to carry the line between London and Bristol over the canal.

1851 Bullen's Bridge (also known as Sheppard's Bridge or Union Bridge). This was said to have been exhibited at the Great Exhibition of 1851, and to have been named after a landlord of the Union Railway Inn, which was situated where the railway line crossed the canal. It was demolished in 1923. 1878 Fleet Street Bridge (also called New Bridge and built by the New Swindon Local Board; it was demolished in 1916).

1881 Midland & South Western Junction Railway bridge (demolished c.1920).

Financial paybacks proving too onerous for the T&S Company, the North Wilts Canal was taken over by the Wilts & Berks in 1822, a Consolidating Act that established the Wilts & Berks Canal Navigation Company. It thrived for the next twenty years or so, bringing salt, coal and iron into Swindon, variously from South Wales, Somerset and the Forest of Dean, and taking out stone from the quarries, and wheat from the surrounding farms. Once the railway lines arrived, essentially following the courses of both canals, the North Wilts in particular went into rapid decline. Ironically, it had helped to carry materials that built the railways. It was particularly affected by the opening of the Cheltenham & Great Union Railway to Kemble in 1841 and to Gloucester in 1845. By 1857, when 'New Wharf' was being built close to the junction of the two canals, imports along it into Swindon were more than sixty per cent lower than they had been in the early 1840s, and almost nothing at all was borne along it out of the town. In 1888, the Great Western Railway Company was granted the right to pipe water from it for its use in the Works. The North Wilts Canal was not used after 1911; the canal company was wound up in 1914, and the canal was completely abandoned by 1927. (See also Wilts & Berks Canal.)

Oasis Leisure Centre, North Star The Oasis complex cost £3 million and was built on the site of former Great Western Railway Company railway wheel and stamping shops, and was opened by the then mayor, John Stevens, on 1 January 1976. Its main attraction from the outset was its lagoon-style pool, which featured a wave-making machine, beneath a glazed dome, and a series of external, enclosed water slides that deposited swimmers into the water. These plastic tubes were known as the 'Domebusters'. There was also a cycle speedway circuit behind the Oasis. The

complex catered for a wide range of indoor sports, and later had the capacity to double as a performance venue (or exhibition area), which could accommodate 3,000 people standing or 1,600 seated. This attracted a number of entertainments that would not have otherwise been considered – the smaller performance venues in the town were not large enough to accommodate financially viable events. By 2012, the complex had become run-down and tired, but Swindon Borough Council, the owners, could not afford to carry out the refurbishment. A property developer, Moirai Capital Investments, planned a £65 million investment that would turn the Oasis into a regional tourist attraction with an on-site hotel, indoor ski slope, and many additional facilities, and formed Oasis Operations Limited for the purpose.

O'Callaghan, Sian Emma (1988-2011) Swindon was united in shock at the murder of young Sian, who disappeared on 19 March 2011 after a night out with friends at Suju nightclub, High Street. CCTV footage from the nightclub showed her leaving the premises alone at 2.52 a.m. When her concerned boyfriend sent a text message to her mobile phone at 3.24 a.m., the signal suggested that the phone was in the area of Savernake Forest, Marlborough, or Pewsey. This was reported to the police, who immediately mounted a vigorous and thorough investigation. Within forty-eight hours of Sian's disappearance, they were trailing a suspect for her abduction. A description of her had been circulated, and Swindon was full of posters, designed by the *Swindon Advertiser* and provided by 4Max Graphic Services. These included one of hoarding size in Old Town, and another in the window of Suju nightclub. Tesco at Ocotal Way printed police posters at its photo centre, and the store provided food and drink (as did staff from Jury's Inn, Fleming Way) for some four hundred people who, from 22 March, joined in the search of Savernake Forest.

On 24 March, outside the Asda Walmart superstore, police arrested Christopher Halliwell, a forty-seven-year-old, self-employed taxi driver, whom they had been watching. They impounded his vehicle, which was displaying the 'missing person' posters of Sian. A vigil was held at St Barnabas Church, Gorse Hill, where some three hundred candles were lit, and the *Swindon Advertiser* published a prayer written by one of Sian's friends. As a result of the arrest, Sian's body was found close to the road in a rural location at Uffington, Oxfordshire.

Suju nightclub closed temporarily (it re-opened on 26 March), and became the focus of a shrine where thousands of floral tributes, artefacts, and written messages were left by the people of Swindon. A beautiful piece of graffiti, including Sian's name and the image of a burning candle, was executed on a wall in the centre of the town. Swindon Town football team wore black armbands at their away game with Brighton on 26 March (as did Swindon Town Ladies Under 21s at their away game with Trowbridge Wanderers, where a two-minute silence was also observed). That evening, thousands of people went to the Polo Ground, off Marlborough Road, and released balloons and lanterns in Sian's memory. A similar event took place in Queen's Park. On 1 April, some three hundred people took part in a memorial walk around Old Town, many with tee-shirts bearing images of Sian; Fr. Mark Paris read prayers, and a two-minute silence

followed. The football club also observed a one-minute silence before their home game with Hartlepool on 2 April, when a statement from Sian's family was read over the public address system. Two days later, dog owners held a memorial walk in Lydiard Park.

Sian O'Callaghan's funeral took place at Kingsdown Crematorium on 18 April, following a drive by the cortège through Old Town, when thousands of people lined the streets. Halliwell was charged with the murder of Sian O'Callaghan on 28 March 2011; he eventually pleaded guilty, and in 2012 was sentenced to a minimum of twenty-five years in prison. (See also Hunter, Frances; and Swinford, Esther.)

Octagonal Market, High Street (Emlyn Square) The New Swindon Improvement Company's earliest venture was a market, designed by Edward Roberts, and built by Edward Streeter of Bath, adjacent to the southern elevation of the Mechanics' Institute. The market was octagonal and surrounded by a low wall made of rough stone from the Swindon quarry, with Bath stone dressings. Each of the sides was forty feet long. Wooden corner posts supported the shallow roof, with the help of additional braces; there was a raised central section, on the top of which was an openwork, cupola-like wooden frame capped by a round, pointed turret. Immediately inside was a walkway that encompassed the entire perimeter, and another walkway ran between the east and west sides, where the entrances to the market were located; an octagonal space in the centre had an octagonal fountain to which water was pumped from the nearby GWR Works. The original intention was to glaze the three sides that did not contain doorways, to be built on top of the perimeter

wall, but this was abandoned and the market remained open. Internally, Roberts allowed for thirty-two lock-up units and thirty open stalls, arranged in an outer circle and an inner circle; those on the outside being open to the perimeter walkway, and the inner ring accessible only from the central passage and fountain area. The stalls were covered by sheets of canvas, and the woodwork throughout was of stained and varnished deal.

On opening day in 1854, eleven lock-ups had been leased in the octagonal market, some by Old Town traders who took the opportunity to open a New Swindon branch of their businesses. There was John Blackford, butcher of Wood Street; Joseph Blackford, butcher of Westcott Place; George Broadhurst, butcher of New Swindon; James Copeland, butcher of High Street; Thomas Chapman, butcher of Fleet Street; B. Holmes, who sold tobacco and snuff; J. Read, fishmonger, whose discarded off-cuts were sufficiently offensive to be deemed a public nuisance; William Stone, boot and shoe maker of Westcott Place; a Mr Williams sold fruit and vegetables; and H. Wilson was the market's general provisions merchant. The Ready-made Clothing Depot had a large, prime corner site next to the east entrance. Almost at once, a beerhouse called the Engineer's Arms was attached to the market building, and seems ultimately to have comprised a ramshackle accumulation of wooden buildings, from which off-sales were sold through a hatch. This gave rise to its alternative name as 'The Hole in the Wall'. It was closed down in 1872.

In 1866, it was discovered that the tolls from market traders were the legal right of Ambrose Lethbridge Goddard, lord of the manor, who had held the licence for the

market since 1855, and not the New Swindon Improvement Company, which had been taking them. An agreement had to be reached with Goddard, arrears paid, and an annual sum set for the future. In the 1860s, the New Swindon Industrial Co-operative Society rented the first of its three retail stalls in the market. A mortgage was raised on the market between 1871 and 1890, by which time it had gone out of favour with the buying public, was neglected by its owners, and had fallen into disrepair. By 1880, it had been described as a public nuisance; all trade stopped; children played there during the day; tramps slept there at night; the woodwork rotted, and the masonry crumbled. The market rights were sold to the New Swindon Local Board in 1890. In 1892, the octagonal market was demolished and its place taken by an extension to the Mechanics' Institute. (See also New Swindon Improvement Company.)

Okus The name 'Okus' is obscure, but ancient. It was written in various covenants and transfers of property from the mid-17th century to the mid-18th century as 'Okesse'; 'Okeys Farm' was being thus described by 1718. It was sold to Richard Goddard in 1724, and mortgaged by Ambrose Goddard to Thomas Villet (Swindon's first family dealing with Swindon's second family) in 1746/7. Andrews' and Dury's *Map of Wiltshire* 1773 records 'Hocus' as some dwellings west of Kings Hill, and 'Oakus grounds' was part of the settlement of marriage between Ambrose Goddard and Sarah Williams in 1776. By 1818, an 'Oak House' had appeared there, and in 1822 'Okus Farm' was leased to Charles Cripps. Much of the old settlement at Okus seems always to have been taken up by Okus Farm, reached either by trackways around Swindon quarries or via tracks

leading off the road between Old Town and Wootton Bassett. The general area of Okus was situated to the south-west of the point where the western part of Bath Road, for so long known as 'The Sands' – because much of it ran through surface sand, gravel and scrubland – split into two tracks (one of which would become Kingshill Road). Children played there, but it was not until the 1930s that Okus began to be built upon, and it would be the 1940s before much was done with the quarry site.

By the end of the 19th century, when the Victoria Hospital had recently been built at the entry to Okus, there were still hardly any buildings to the south or west. The road ended roughly where it was joined by a track that led to Okus Farm, and a fine 17th-century thatched barn that was demolished in 1975. There were quarries and gravel pits to the west of this, a terrace of four cottages for quarry workers; allotments, and a track that ran to another group of dwellings called Okus Cottages. A track that linked all of this skirted the reservoir of the Swindon Water Board before arriving at the hamlet of Okus.

Mill Lane bisected the Okus area, but was not itself built up until the late 1920s. It was so named since the start of the 18th century after a mill that stood thereabouts on the River Ray, and which became better known as Hall's Mill after Roger Hall, who ran it in the late 1700s. The Wilts & Berks Canal Company bought it in 1809. The Mall went into this area in 1906. Belmont Crescent, the 'beautiful hill', which was really a misnomer for the intended 'beautiful view' that inspired it, was built off Mill Lane in 1908. Portland Avenue was laid out adjacent to the quarry at Okus Cottages, close to Sandy Lane, which is a reminder still of the old terrain to be encountered hereabouts. In the 1950s, Tithe

Barn Crescent continued the development of Okus, running around the reservoir site towards the barn itself, which was then still standing.

Okus Farm mill In 1848, Isaac Holdway built a corn windmill at Okus Farm, which he rented from Ambrose Goddard, with £250 he borrowed from Mary Horton of Highworth. Nothing more is known of it, except that it burned down in 1854.

Old Firm, The By the middle of the 19th century, John Hawkins, styled grocer and publican, was the proprietor of a family home and brewhouse on Prior's Hill, Wroughton that was to become known as the Last Chance, at one end of which was also the grocer's shop. The children of John and his wife Sophia included four sons: Thomas; William, who took over the Last Chance in 1901; Charles, who became landlord of the Rising Sun public house in Sun Lane; and Edward ('Ted') J. Hawkins (1870-1937), who was the founder of The Old Firm, the first public passenger carrying service between Swindon and Wroughton. The two public houses ceased trading in 1909, although the Last Chance building remained the property of the Hawkins family until it was demolished in 1987. By 1898, Ted had married Fanny Melinda (née Pearce) and had become a licensed carrier. In 1902, he rented Spencer's Farm in Wroughton's High Street (famed for its large 17th-century thatched barn that stood hard by the road) and was running twice-daily passenger carrying trips between the two settlements, using a four-wheeled wagon pulled by two horses. His business became known as 'The Old Firm', and, embracing motor transport, Ted bought a succession of buses from either Praeter's

garage or Skurray's garage in Swindon. The livery of the company was cream around the top half of the vehicles, with green below. The Swindon terminus for the journey was Temple Street. After Ted's death, the road service licence was taken up by his widow. Although the family's motor buses latterly parked up in Rolleston Street, beside the offices of the Bristol Tramways & Carriage Company (from 1957 the Bristol Omnibus Company), the latter was prevented from picking up passengers in Wroughton. The Old Firm continued for a century, at all times in the hands of the same family, until 1955 when its route was sold to the Bristol Tramways & Carriage Company. The final run of The Old Firm was made between Wroughton and Swindon on 2 July 1955. (See also Tramways; Bristol Omnibus Company.)

Old House At Home, The Until well into the 20th century, many of the properties in Newport Street were low, two-storey, thatched cottages, built of rough coursed stone, and lime-washed. This was particularly true of the western end of the north side of the street, where the downstairs front room of one of the smallest properties was The Old House At Home, a provisions merchant as displayed on a sign above its door. It stood in a small terrace of cottages, immediately to the west of the National School building. In 1910, during a particularly hot spell of dry weather, the thatch on the roof of The Old House At Home caught fire, and hundreds of people turned out to watch the fire brigade deal with it. The premises were eventually rebuilt in Tudor style, three bays and gabled, of bricks at first-floor level, plaster and timber to the upper storey, and with a tiled roof. The rebuild gave the retailer a double shop window with recessed entrance, and the business continued

to trade as The Old House At Home. Both this property and the former school were demolished in the 1960s, and their sites have long been occupied by the forecourt of the Newport Street petrol station.

Ormond, William (1827-1908) Born in Wantage; by the age of twenty-four and yet unmarried, Ormond was living in Abingdon, where he was looked after by a housekeeper. Admitted to the Law Society in 1849, he practised as an attorney and solicitor. In the 1850s, he came to Swindon, joining J.C. Townsend's firm of solicitors, which became Townsend & Ormond in 1859, and married. From then on, he lived the rest of his life at The Limes, Croft Road, which was then a southerly extension of Devizes Road known as 'Shorthedge'. He and his wife Georgina Mary had seven children between 1860 and 1872, who were looked after variously by a nurse and a governess, and the family also employed a cook and housemaids. In 1863, Ormond was a member of A.L. Goddard's committee that began proceedings to establish a permanent corn exchange in Swindon, and in 1866, Ormond became a director of the Swindon Water Company. He was also sometime treasurer and secretary of the Society for Promoting Christian Knowledge. In 1876, Townsend and Ormond separated and thereafter each operated their own practice, the latter working from offices in Devizes Road. Ormond retired in 1897, and continued to live at The Limes with his wife, one of their daughters and her female companion, and two servants. Georgina died in 1906, and William Ormond died in 1908, leaving almost £51,000.

O'Sullivan, (Raymond Edward) 'Gilbert' (b.1946) The O'Sullivan family came to Swindon in 1958, when young Raymond Edward – who would one day take the stage name Gilbert – was just thirteen years old. He was born in Waterford, Ireland, where his father worked in a meat factory, and his mother in a sweet shop, and had five siblings. In Swindon, the family lived at Penhill. He went to St Joseph's Comprehensive School, as did his brothers and sisters, and, from 1963, he attended Swindon College of Art with the intention of becoming a graphic artist. Briefly, he worked as a postal clerk, took up amateur boxing, in which he achieved some successes, and was also in several Swindon bands – notably The Doodles and The Prefects. He moved to London in 1967 where he shared a flat with the Swindon artist Ken White, and rock musician Richard (Rick) Davies. In 1969, he adopted the 'Bisto Kid' image that was his trademark, and thereafter he became one of the most successful recording artists, first appearing on BBC television Top of the Pops in 1970 and thereafter accumulating fourteen Top 40 hits in that decade. His first hit chart single was *Nothing Rhymed*, and his most famous songs are arguably *What's In A Kiss?*, *Clair*, and *Alone Again (Naturally)*. Gilbert was unable to release material throughout the 1980s because of business disputes; the album *Frobisher Drive*, titled after his Swindon home, came out in 1987 but was only released in Germany. Since 1990, he has regularly released albums, and Bygum Records, which was set up in 2001 under the management of one of his sisters, exists to make his music widely available.

Palladium Picture House This was built in Jennings Street, Rodbourne in 1928. It had 622 seats arranged in stalls and on the balcony. It closed in 1958, became a venue

for various businesses, and later became a printing works.

Park, The Faringdon Road The area now known as the Faringdon Road Park began as a general playing field, called 'The Plantation', on land acquired in 1844 from Lt. Col. Thomas Vilett, partly in order to establish a cricket ground. It was then known as 'The Cricket Ground', and has also been called 'Victoria Park', and its perimeter was originally marked by hedging and wooden paling. A cricket pavilion was erected, set back in the shrubbery adjacent to Park Lane, and the New Swindon cricket team played there from its formation in 1847. For the next quarter of a century, the area remained an undeveloped field, except for the cricket area. In 1871, a corner of the field was annexed and screened off with foliage, and there a drill hall was built for the use of the 11th (Wilts) New Swindon Rifle Corps. This also had to accommodate female pupils as an overspill schoolroom. In the same year, the field began to be developed as pleasure grounds, when gardens were developed on the eastern side. By 1873, it had a park keeper's lodge and significant glasshouses. Ornamental formal gardens were laid out, and these were particularly concentrated inside the main entrance gateway from Church Place. From there, the vista was one of a large island bed, flanked by larger areas of planting, and formal beds with fountains, decorative bowls on pedestals, and ornamental urns.

A small bandstand was built on a circular lawn within the park, and was used by the Corps' twenty-two-man band under the direction of bandmaster William Hawkins. It had an ogee-shaped roof with a cupola and conical cap, and was surrounded at ground level by very intricate wrought-iron railings that included a dog rail. The park continued to be developed as a general pleasure ground, oval in shape, with a walkway around the perimeter and seats placed at regular intervals beside the path. The original perimeter fencing was replaced by a wall made of red bricks which, in 1897, was given a capping of Staffordshire blue engineering bricks, made by Joseph Hamblet (1819-94) at his Piercey Brickworks, West Bromwich. Metal railings were added, most of which were removed during the Second World War in the Government's drive to reuse metal for the war effort. The park remained under the control of the Park Improvement Committee of the Mechanics' Institution until 1925, when it was taken over by Swindon Corporation in a swop deal whereby the GWR obtained land in Gorse Hill. Most of the park's buildings, features, and ornamental beds have disappeared over the years, and it is today a large open space of mown grass, surrounded by mature trees and shrubs. In 2009, the brick pillars were restored, and the missing railings were replaced by new ones with mild steel bars and cast-iron finials. (See also Juvenile Fete.)

Park and Ride Swindon's first park and ride scheme opened at Groundwell, to the north-east of the town, in 1998. It was suspended in 2009.

Park House, Church Place Church Place was originally called Park Road when it was built to give the best view of the open space that was the GWR's pleasure ground immediately to the west. The largest building in this road, a three-storey, four-bay, gabled house with basement, was built in 1876 of brick with stone dressings, and given a significant porch. It was put up at

the end of a terrace of fourteen cottages, built to the south of Taunton Street in 1853, the most western of which was removed to make way for this large corner building. Park House is a riot of bay windows, square-headed and segmental-headed windows with either mullions or sashes, and tall chimney stacks. From the beginning, it was the home of Dr George Money Swinhoe, who had been appointed medical officer of the GWR Medical Fund Society in 1859 when he lived and practised in London Street. Park House was let free of rent to the GWR surgeon from 1897. Swinhoe held this position until 1908, after which the GWR Medical Fund Society rented Park House as a home for some of its medical staff. It later became the company's medical administration headquarters. It was bought by Swindon Borough Council in 1968. The property was renovated in 1984, and this Grade II listed building is today a business centre, offering virtual and actual office accommodation for rent.

Pattern Store This historic building, erected in 1897, stands between the Designer Outlet Village and the residential development of the Penzance Drive area. Since 1998, when the two lower floors were opened as the Pattern Store Bar, this three-storey, seven-bay and basement property has been a succession of bars and restaurants. Here, the GWR's draughtsmen worked on the patterns; blueprints, and the forms and moulds used in castings and repair work were stored in racks on the two top floors. The workshops were at ground level, and the basement housed the pattern makers' canteen. The brick building, with twenty segmental-headed windows on its main face, was constructed around steel pillars and girders. An exceptionally wide staircase

was constructed between each floor, admitting on to each level through a wide, semi-circular iron door. Each of the ceilings was barrel-vaulted in brick, and the floors were composed of black wooden blocks the size of bricks. An ornate, circular staircase gave access from the upper floor to a metal turret on the roof, where a large tank with a capacity of 230,000 gallons was situated that once supplied water to the GWR village. An arrangement of pulleys enabled heavy objects to be lifted, on the outside of the building, and admitted through doorways on to the appropriate floors. Internally, items were let down by a similar system, through a series of trap doors. Much of this arrangement and other fixtures and fittings from the pattern store's past remain in situ. Beneath the building are a number of now blocked-up tunnels that at one time allowed access to different parts of the GWR Works. Some are forty feet underground. In front of the building is the locomotive turntable, where newly built locomotives were brought to be photographed before being put into service.

Penhill In 1951, Swindon Corporation bought Penhill farmhouse and two hundred and fifty acres of land immediately to the north east of the borough, which was then part of the parish of Stratton St Margaret. That year, it began to build on the east side of this land, laying out a dozen or so roads and naming them after Wiltshire towns and villages (as would be the whole estate). The farm complex was divided by Cricklade Road, immediately to the west of which were farm buildings that were demolished; to the east, the farmhouse was retained, which in the 1960s became the club house for the Swindon branch of NALGO (National Association

of Local Government Officers). The Penhill development became the first focus for incomers to the town under the 'London overspill' arrangement of 1952, although it had not been begun with that in mind. Also in 1952, the borough boundary was changed by shifting it a few hundred yards to the north to include the new area, and between then and 1955 an additional sixty roads were added to complete the housing estate (only a couple more went in during the 1960s and 1970s). The estate was intended to be self-sufficient, with its own schools (Penhill North Infants, 1955, Penhill Primary, 1956); a shopping precinct, a branch library, and St Peter's church (consecrated in 1956). In 1958, the Deer's Leap public house was built on Penhill Drive, where it became, 1960-62, the venue for Swindon's Modern Jazz Club. The Penhill Amenity Area, which was opened in 1966, was a recreational area of the estate, comprising a bowling green, and facilities for putting, tennis, and cricket. There were tea rooms and changing rooms, and walkways with planted beds and borders.

Penny Readings The earliest penny readings in the town, very much part of the social infrastructure of Swindon during the 19th century, took place in the assembly room at the Goddard Arms hotel, High Street. This was the principal venue for wholesome public events and entertainments (as well as the main meeting place for societies, etc.) before the town hall was built in the nearby market square. Penny readings were an innovation of the 1850s, and their prime purpose was to provide an alternative form of leisure activity for adults to that offered by the public houses, and at the same time underline codes of morals, ethics, patriotism and religion. The patron of the

penny readings was the lord of the manor, there was an organising secretary, and some local luminary was usually present, in order to add distinction to the proceedings. Each programme typically included readings of solemn poetry and prose, classical piano pieces, and the occasional song, and was mostly presented by well-known people in the community, such as clergymen, piano teachers, and the like.

Penny readings were transferred from the Goddard Arms to the town hall in Old Swindon in 1853, and in New Town were held at the Mechanics' Institute from the time it opened in 1855. They were typically held on Monday evenings in Old Town, and on alternate Tuesday evenings in the new settlement. From 1861, tickets were available from the offices of the *North Wilts Herald*. These events were 'free to working men and their wives', otherwise admission cost one penny, two pence for the padded seats at the front of the hall, and three pence for a seat reserved in advance. The takings from each session were donated to charitable and other causes that required to be funded by public subscription. Whilst the penny readings held in Old Town were of a more sober character, by the 1870s the readings at the Mechanics' Institute had become more humorous, and comic songs were often sung.

Pest House, Okus In 1753, Ambrose Goddard gave land in a spot on Okus Field, west of the Swindon quarries, for an isolation hospital to be built for those with infectious diseases, under the auspices of the Vestry. This was the pest house, shown on Andrews' and Dury's map of Wiltshire, 1773, as the smallpox house – reached via a trackway from Hocus [sic]. From 1864, it was under the joint control of the Old Swindon Local Board

and the New Swindon Local Board. People who wanted to gain admittance on their own behalf, or that of a friend or relative, had first to apply to the Inspector of Nuisances or the Local Rate Collector. The hospital contained apparatus needed to disinfect clothes and bedding, and was in the charge of 'a qualified nurse'. This building was closed and dismantled in 1888, and was superseded in 1892 by an isolation hospital designed by Henry Joseph Hamp, surveryor to the New Town Local Board, and built in red brick in Gorse Hill. This was extended in 1931. The wards here were dedicated to patients with diphtheria, typhoid, and scarlet fever. It is now the Hawthorn Centre.

Peter Pan Statue, Town Gardens
Allegedly at the time of the First World War, apprentices at the GWR Works made a two-foot-high statue of Peter Pan, which was placed on a base of stones in the rose garden in the Town Gardens in Old Swindon. There it remained until 2004, when it was removed in pieces after vandals had spray-painted it and latterly ripped off its head. In 2010, Richard Beale, parks and green spaces officer for Swindon Borough Council, commissioned a replacement from Pangolin Editions of Chalford, who firstly welded the surviving pieces back together and then used their in-house commercial artists to restore the missing and damaged areas. They then made a mould of silicone rubber, and used this to cast a replacement in lead. This was placed in the Arts Centre in Devizes Road, where it was felt the piece could be better looked after and appreciated. Pangolin also made resin copies at the same time; one of these was placed in the Town Gardens and officially unveiled by actor Richard Vincent, who was playing Peter Pan in the Wyvern

Theatre's 2010 pantomime of the same name, and the other was put into store. In 2011, the statue was again decapitated by vandals.

Phoenix Players One of the earliest of the Swindon Public Library ancillary societies was the Poetry Circle, established in 1946. This group met regularly in the Regent Street arts centre to read and discuss poetry; they also read verse plays, and these proved sufficiently popular amongst members for them to form a drama section in 1954. This was named the Poetry Circle Players, and it gave its first public performance (*The Firstborn* by Christopher Fry) in September of that year. From 1956, the Players put on their performances at the Arts Centre, Devizes Road. The Poetry Circle ceased to exist in 1963, so one of the members of the drama section, Ashley W. Huish, who was at the time Swindon Public Library Service's Central Lending Librarian, suggested that the name of the amateur drama side might be changed to The Phoenix Players as it had 'risen from the ashes of the Poetry Circle'. This was immediately adopted, and the group have since continued to present three shows annually, mounting almost two hundred productions by 2012.

Picture House The Picture House was Swindon's first indoor cinema, although it was not purpose-built. It was set up in Regent Circus c.1910, utilising the premises of an insurance broker and a room at the rear that had previously been used for Sunday schools. The rather eccentric manager, a Mr Hunt – locally known as 'uncle', was distinguished by his thick moustache, and his preferred raiment of breeches, gaiters and a Stetson hat. The Picture House closed down in 1913, and became in turn a motor

repair workshop, bus office and florist's shop.

Pilgrim Centre, Regent Circus

The centre comprises the Central Church for worship, a conference centre with rooms for hire and, on the ground floor, the Roundabout Café. The Central Church was a combined local ecumenical initiative, c.1968, of the Baptist Tabernacle, Church of Christ Broad Street, Congregational Church Sanford Street, Methodist Central Hall, and Trinity United Reform Church. Two-thirds of the Pilgrim Centre building of 1989-90 (it opened on 17 November 1990) is owned by the Baptist Church; the Methodist Church and the United Reform Church each own one-sixth. The building was designed by Peter Reynolds of Oxford, and was built by Moss Construction as part of the redevelopment of Temple Street by Rosehugh Plc. It is of seven bays and three storeys, is on part of the site of the former Baptist Tabernacle, and is of orange brick, with a pedimented central section of steel, glass and concrete. There is a spirelet on the roof.

Pinehurst

This was Swindon's first local authority residential housing development, built at the town's north-eastern boundary with the parish of Stratton St Margaret. The original layout of what became known as 'Swindon's garden city' was by Sir Raymond Unwin (1863-1940), the promoter of residential developments that were peripheral to their host towns. Although the area began to be developed about 1919, the first roads of the estate proper were laid out there in 1924, and some eighteen in all were built over the next twelve years. They were all named after species of British trees, and this theme was continued with another

five roads built in Pinehurst in 1947, and a further handful in later years. It had its own school, a series of single-storey wooden huts, which was put up in 1935. The area devolved on 'The Circle', whose wide greens had temporary prefabricated bungalows on them until the 1960s.

Piper, Billie (b.1982)

Named Leian Paul Piper until her parents changed their minds, Billie Piper grew up at Nine Elms, West Swindon; she went to Brookfield Primary School and then Bradon Forest School, Purton. When she was just fifteen years old, she became the youngest female artist to have a UK number one hit single. The song was 'Because We Want To', and she began her short but successful singing career, for which she was to get her first awards, as just 'Billie'. She had two further first-place singles: the follow-up 'Girlfriend', and then 'Day and Night' in 2000. There were only two albums, 'Honey To The B' and 'Walk of Life'. Billie's struggle with anorexia during this period is well documented. In 2001, she married television presenter and disc jockey Chris Evans, from whom she was divorced in 2006. She gave up singing in 2003 and became a successful television and film actress, achieving great acclaim for her part in an episode of *The Canterbury Tales*, and later for her role as Rose Tyler in the television series *Doctor Who*. She became hugely successful in several television series called *Secret Diary of a Call Girl*, the dramatisation of Dr Brooke Magnanti's life as a high-class prostitute, as detailed in her *Belle de Jour* blog and best-selling books. She has starred in numerous other films and television productions, in which she has become established as a splendid character actress. At twenty-four years of age, she

published her autobiography, *Growing Pains*. In 2007, she married the actor Laurence Fox.

Pitched Market see Gin and Water Sales.

Planks, The This was essentially a walkway and carriageway between the Market Square and The Lawn, a public way from Lower Town, just off High Street. Its purpose was to allow free passage to the estate's stables, coach house and cottages, and to give access for the incumbent and worshippers to the old church of Holy Rood. Its name is derived from the flagstones (plank stones) with which the raised footpath was paved. The original trackway was frequently used by horses and carriages, causing the surface to become very muddy, so the raised pathway and retaining wall were constructed on the north side in order that people walking to church in bad weather did not arrive with wet, dirty shoes and clothes. The low, capped retaining wall is extant. Several buildings bordered the walkway until well into the 20th century, the most notable being the former vicarage; the walkway began beside the entrance to the vicarage garden and almost opposite the Goddard family's stables. The vicarage, a 17th-century building of stone that had been enlarged in the late 1700s, was latterly business premises and demolished in 1973. In the 19th century, Ambrose Lethbridge Goddard, lord of the manor, erected posts across the way and, as a result, a lengthy altercation ensued between himself and William Read, Surveyor to the Old Swindon Local Board. The Planks was the site of a chapel, begun for the Wesleyan Methodists in 1813. From 1866, part of the walkway from Market Place was beside the Corn Exchange.

The estate's former stables and coach house remain, and were used as private auction rooms until they were closed in 2003 and subsequently redeveloped. This property is long and low and built of limestone rubble, a single storey with an external staircase leading to what were the groom's quarters in the attic. It has a semi-hipped, stone tiled mansard roof with five flat dormer windows, above, in part, a range of panelled double doors. The gate pillars have ball finials. At the estate end of The Planks are an early 19th-century house, and two cottages (originally built as three for estate workers to live in) of 1798. They overlook the parkland. The house (No.1), built of coursed limestone rubble, is a large, double-gabled, two-storey and three-bay property with a stone-slated roof and three dormer attic windows. The square-headed windows have splayed stone lintels. The cottages (Nos. 2 and 3) are single storey, also of coursed limestone rubble, and with hipped dormers to the attic.

Playhouse Theatre, Emlyn Square
The Mechanics' Institute had an integral theatre that was known as The Playhouse. The room was essentially a hall (it had formerly been called 'the large hall'), some seventy-eight feet long and thirty-three feet wide with a panelled barrel-vault of a ceiling and panelled cornice, and much decorative attention paid to the heavily curtained stage area. The auditorium, which had a sloping floor, could seat seven hundred people on tip-up seats, one hundred of which were in the circle. A fly tower was built in 1930, the year that a devastating fire destroyed the Institute's reading room. This necessitated a remake of the theatre, which was reopened in 1931, and became a professional theatre two years later. Almost from the start, the

refurbished auditorium doubled as a venue for dances, and most of Swindon's crop of local bands played there from the 1930s. It was a favoured venue for Swindon girls and service personnel during the Second World War. In 1949, the administration of the Playhouse theatre and the dance hall at the Mechanics' Institution was leased to a private individual who for a short time afterwards hired out these venues, and public dances continued to be held there until about 1950.

The ceiling was a striking and ornately decorated barrel vault, mirrored in the low, remodelled proscenium arch of the stage. This was protected by an asbestos curtain that could be dropped in under half a minute. The stage was fifty-five feet wide, and thirty-three feet deep, and the proscenium opening was twenty-eight feet. It was lit from above by a lantern that was designed to open in the case of fire and in such a way that flames and smoke were conducted away from the auditorium. Leading off the stage were a scenery holding area, a property room, six dressing rooms, and toilets. The dance floor was beneath the stage of the Playhouse and built of maple wood with rubber shock insulators above the concrete foundations. The theatre was also used by the town's amateur theatrical and musical organisations, giving public performances. In 1954, the Playhouse theatre was converted, renamed the Regal Ballroom, and re-launched principally for dances, although it was thereafter also occasionally used for theatrical performances. The otherwise cold and rather featureless hall had a small balcony at the rear, which had been intended as a platform for orchestras playing at the dances. (See also Mechanics' Institute.)

Plessey Company Following a succession of wartime bombing raids on London, Plessey, a maker of radio components, decided to relocate from Ilford, Essex. It chose the comparative safety of Swindon, where it opened its electronics factory in Kembrey Street in 1940, in a former First World War powder factory. It began there with just ten employees, but its rapid expansion in electrical and electronic systems and components for the technological advances of the time meant that in a little over a decade it was employing about two thousand people. In 1957, it built a factory at Cheney Manor. This was Swindon's first industrial estate, which had opened two years previously. The railway workshops went into decline from the 1960s and their pole position as a local employer was overtaken by the emerging motor manufacturing industry, Plessey then becoming the second-largest employer in the town.

Plumley, Gladys Fanny (1897-1975) One of the best-known characters in mid-20th-century Swindon, largely due to her encyclopaedic knowledge of consumer law and social issues that she used in her work with the Swindon Council for Social Service in Catherine Street, the Citizens Advice Bureau. Gladys was born in Highworth, the daughter of William and Blanche Plumley, and the family relocated almost at once to Cricklade Road, Swindon. In 1941, she joined the staff of the SCSS; she took over as secretary in 1954, and resigned in 1970 due to failing eyesight. She lived at 499 Ferndale Road. Her friends called her 'Plum'; to the thousands of Swindon people who sought her advice in her thirty-year career she was 'Miss Plumley', possessed of

a strict disposition, a steely bespectacled eye, and an incisive recall. She was also an ardent user of Swindon reference library, whose holdings of law books, statutes, and British patents supplemented the material held in her own office.

Police Swindon acquired its first official constabulary in 1839, a branch of the Wiltshire County force that was established in that year. The town's first police station (the police house with a cellar that served as a cell) was Canford House, Devizes Road, and another was later added in Newport Street. By the 1860s, the force comprised a superintendent, and inspector and two constables in the Old Town, and, in the New Town, just one sergeant. A police station was built on Eastcott Hill in 1873; it had eight cells, a courtroom and residential accommodation. This was an attractive, vaguely Italianate building famed for its moulded and arched central section with a Venetian window. It was demolished in 1973.

Swindon police squad cars were first fitted with radios in October 1949. The town's policemen on the beat were first issued with two-way radios on 17 February 1966, and Swindon was the first force in Wiltshire to have them. In 1969, Swindon's multi-storey Fleming Way police station was built, and this was eventually demolished in 2006. It had been replaced in 2005 by a new police headquarters at Gablecross, near Stratton St Margaret.

Population figures for Swindon Swindon was a sizeable village for the 15th century; it has been suggested that some 600 people then lived in the settlement on the hill, and that figure remained fairly constant until the mid-1600s. A figure of 580 is estimated for the population in 1676; by 1697, there were 791; and the number had advanced to 800 by the year 1700. Over the next century, it developed into a small town, and for the first half of the 19th century remained relatively under-populated. New Swindon was established adjacent to the railway works, and by 1843, some 417 workers, including 100 engine drivers and firemen, and six foremen, were accommodated there. The population of new town exceeded that of old town some time in the 1850s. The 1901 official Census figure, the first after the old town and the new town become administratively one, was the first for thirty years to return a single figure covering both areas. In 1968, the Borough Council predicted that the population of the town would reach 296,000 by the year 2000:

1801 1,198
1811 1,341
1821 1,580
1831 1,742
1841 2,495
1851 4,876 (combined old town and new town)
1861 6,856 (combined old town and new town)
1864 7,287 (of which 3,120 old town)
1871 11,720 (of which 3,892 old town)
1881 19,904 (of which 4,818 old town)
1891 32,838 (of which 5,543 old town)
1899 43,000*
1901 45,006
1903 46,525
1904 48,200 (local authority estimate)
1909 50,000*
1911 50,771
1912 53,334
1915 51,647 (Registrar General's estimate)
1921 54,920
1925 56,880*

1931 62,401
1935 60,400*
1940 64,840*
1945 65,520 (Registrar General's estimate)
1946 66,150*
1947 66,560*
1949 70,000*
1950 68,000*
1951 68,953
1961 91,775
1962 94,566
1963 96,450
1964 97,460
1965 98,440
1966 98,410
1967 97,920
1968 97,840
1969 98,300
1970 98,100
1971 91,033
1973 61,990*
1974 94,900*
1981 102,561
2001 155,432
2005 184,000*
(*unofficial estimates made at the time)

Post Office, early services In the late 1820s, Charles Rose, innkeeper of The Bell, High Street, opened Swindon's first post office; it occupied part of the hostelry's public bar, and the mail was handled by any of the inn's employees who happened to be free of other duties at the time. Rose was styled 'post master', and his directory entry stated: 'Letters from London arrive (by mail cart) from Marlborough every morning at seven, and are despatched every evening at seven. Letters from Birmingham, Gloucester, Worcester and the North arrive (by cross post) from Highworth every evening at seven, and are despatched every morning at

seven. Letters from Wootton Bassett arrive (by cross post) every evening at half-past six, and are despatched every morning at seven'. In winter, an additional quarter of an hour was allowed for the arrival of the latter.

Charles was succeeded by Thomas Rose in 1839, formerly a farmer, on the same premises; Thomas was soon to style himself 'post office, architect, surveyor and builder'. There was an immediate change in advertised arrival and collection times. 'Letters from London and parts East arrive every afternoon at twenty-five minutes past one and every night at five minutes before twelve, and are despatched thereto every morning at half-past one and half-past nine. Letters from Gloucester, Cheltenham and the West arrive every morning at ten minutes before three and a quarter before eleven, and are despatched thereto every day at a quarter past twelve and every night at half-past ten. Letters from Marlborough arrive (by mail cart) every night at twenty minutes before ten, and are despatched thereto every morning at four. Letters from Newbury and Hungerford arrive (by mail cart) every night at ten minutes before eleven, and are despatched thereto every morning at three. Letters from Highworth and Cricklade arrive (by mail cart) every night at half-past nine, and are despatched thereto every morning at four. Letters from Wootton Bassett arrive (by horse post) every night at twenty minutes before ten, and are despatched thereto every morning at four.'

In the early 1840s, the post office was taken out of the Bell Hotel, and removed to Wood Street, two doors to the east of the King's Arms, in a room off a narrow passage where business was transacted through a small window. This was kept shut, and was only opened upon application. 'Letters to be

registered must be given in at the window at least half an hour before the closing of the box. Money orders issued and paid from 10am until ½ past 11am, & from ¼ past 12pm until 6pm except Sundays, when the office is closed during the hours of divine service.' By 1848, the postal service in Old Town was making money out of latecomers: 'Late letters will, however, be received, to go forward by the mail which is in course of preparation for despatch, on payment of a fee of 1d per letter for the first ½ hour after the box is closed, & 2d per letter afterwards, until the bags are made up, which fee belongs to the revenue & cannot, therefore, at any time, be dispensed with'.

At about this time, a sub-post office was set up in New Swindon, where John Holmes Sewell, chemist and druggist, was also designated 'postmaster and receiver of mail'. 'Letters received through the Swindon post office arrive at 5am for morning delivery, & at 3pm for the afternoon delivery. The letter box is closed at 20m past 8pm.' In 1848, the New Swindon office regretted that: 'There is at present no morning mail for London, which was the case formerly, and which was discontinued on account of the letter-carrier being unable, from the extent of delivery and increase of letters, to deliver at the Swindon office in time for the departure of mail.' The matter was resolved by 1850 when, 'letters from London and all parts arrive (from the Old Town office) every morning (Sunday excepted) at nine and afternoon at three, and are despatched thereto at half-past ten in the morning and half-past eight in the evening'.

About 1850, the Old Town post office was relocated, with Thomas Rose, to Bath Buildings, Bath Road, where Thomas Newbold Bott was officially appointed to the full-time position of postmaster in 1856.

The post office was again relocated; this time, to the opposite side of Wood Street. Sunday opening was reduced to between 7 a.m. and 10 a.m. In New Swindon, Sewell took his chemist's business to High Street, Old Swindon, c.1856, and the post office in New Town was transferred to 1 High Street (Emlyn Square) in the charge of Robert Arthur Taylor ('receiver of mail, postmaster, grocer, chemist and druggist').

By 1900, Swindon's main post office was in Bath Road, and there were sub-post offices in Regent Street, Westcott Place, Clifton Street, Rodbourne Lane, Gorse Hill and Ashford Road. Swindon's first custom-built head post office was opened in Regent Circus in 1901, and Henry Durden transferred there from Bath Road as head postmaster. The main building was square, of three storeys and three bays, with dormers to both roadside elevations, plus a two-storey, five-bay annexe along Princes Street. It had its front doorway on the eastern diagonal. By this time, the town's sorting office was sited on the 'Milk Bank', immediately to the east of the New Swindon Railway station, but was relocated to Regent Circus in 1935. A new sorting office was built beside the site of the Wilts & Berks Canal, 1963-64, and soon afterwards a head post office was relocated close by. After demolition of the Regent Circus premises in 1972, its place was taken by commercial buildings on the east side of Theatre Square.

Post-war Planning In 1942, Swindon Town Council formed a post-war planning sub-committee, which commissioned William Robert Davidge (1879-1961) to prepare a survey and report on post-war planning in Swindon. Davidge was a very experienced town planning consultant with

impeccable credentials; he was a Fellow of the Royal Institute of British Architects and, 1926-27, President of the Town Planning Institute. He presented his first draft in 1943, and the following year completed his post-war planning report. At about the same time, the Town and Country Planning Act, 1944 was passed, which conferred sufficient powers on local authorities that, in Swindon's case, would have enabled most of the main recommendations to be carried out. The post-war planning sub-committee prepared a report which was approved by the council and published as *Planning for Swindon 1945*. The public were able to view an exhibition, based on the report, and held that year in the Town Hall, Regent Circus. The aim of the programme of post-war redevelopment was to create 'a town worthy, perhaps beautiful, in appearance, and the provision of such varied services and amenities as will make it a vastly more enjoyable place to live in'.

Powder Factory Early in the First World War, a factory was built on a sixty-acre site, close to the railway line between Swindon and Highworth, for the purpose of making ammonium nitrate, used in munitions as an oxidizing agent in explosives. It was known locally as the 'powder factory', 'nitrate works', or 'munitions works'. The whole area was covered in what looked like a succession of low aircraft hangars, and was distinguished by two tall chimneys that stood close together beside the railway line. The factory closed in 1919, after which a succession of industries used the buildings. These included a dairy and Plessey, the electronics company. The chimneys were pulled down at the outbreak of the Second World War, in case they proved to be markers for enemy bombers approaching the town,

and the site was taken over by the Ministry of War as a supply depot. The area is now immediately to the north and west of part of Bridge End Road; sections of the trading estates at the east of Kembrey Street and Elgin drive, and the BMW Works are on the former powder factory site.

Powell, (James E.) 'Raggy' (1849-1930) Swindon's best-known rag and bone man was born into relative poverty and received little education, yet he understood there was money to be made in people's cast-offs. After he came to Swindon, c.1890, he led his horse and cart around the town, giving pennies to women and children in exchange for these commodities. He also bought rabbit skins, and kept a slaughter house in Regent Place. Reuben George taught him to read and write, and he developed an interest in bric-a-brac, collectables, and antiques after attending lectures at the Mechanics' Institute. Thereafter he also bought pictures and prints, furniture – which he paid carpenters to repair and refurbish – and books, storing and exhibiting for sale much of his stock on premises in Regent Circus. A number of the pictures and prints he acquired were put into new mounts by him and presented either to various public institutions in the town, such as the GWR Medical Fund hospital, or the museum, which was initially set up in Regent Circus. He also hand-wrote captions for many of the exhibits that he donated. In 1901, he became a councillor. During the First World War, he organised free shows at the Empire Theatre for families of servicemen, and in 1920 he was made a freeman of the Borough of Swindon. Always conscious that he had received very little formal learning, many of his benefactions were for the education of the

young; one such, made in 1918, was the gift of a piece of land in Savernake Street. He also gave the site of what was to become Gorse Hill recreation ground. The fine sculpture of the seated Charlotte Corday on display in the town hall was donated by Raggie Powell. He died at his home, 63 Eastcott Hill.

Presbyterian Lecture Hall, Dixon Street Architect Orlando Baker, who had offices in Regent Street, designed this hall, built in Early English ecclesiastical style in 1885. It had a 1,560-square-foot lecture room that featured an open collar beam roof, an entrance porch and lobbies. The floors were 'covered with Lowe's patent wood block flooring'. It was used by the Trinity Presbyterian Church, and was the meeting place for their Band of Hope.

Pressed Steel Company Ltd Pressed Steel was formed at Cowley, Oxford, in 1926 to make car panels. When it was unable to extend this site, it bought part of the site of the former Parsonage Farm, off Bridge End Road at Stratton St Margaret, in 1954 and built (1954-57) an additional car body plant, which actually began production in 1955. The business was particularly successful in immediately attracting men from London who had come to Swindon with their families; this followed the Government's approval in 1952 to designate Swindon as an 'overspill' town to alleviate the capital's work, social, and housing problems resulting from the Second World War. The Pressed Steel premises at Swindon were doubled in size in 1958, and extended further in 1962. Its better rates of pay also encouraged railway works' employees to defect, as ironically, it began to lay the foundations for an alternative industry to that of the railway in the town.

Within a decade or so, it would become a larger employer in Swindon than the railway.

The Swindon site continued to make car panels, through several changes of ownership, but never complete vehicles. In 1965, Pressed Steel was acquired by the British Motor Corporation. This organisation had acquired, in 1953, the long-established body panel makers Fisher & Ludlow, then of Castle Bromwich near Birmingham (who supplied panels for Morris cars, the organisation that had set up Pressed Steel). BMC immediately amalgamated the two, and Pressed Steel at Swindon became Pressed Steel Fisher. In 1966, BMC was renamed British Motor Holdings; two years later, this merged with British Leyland Motor Corporation, formed in 1968, and the Swindon site was renamed British Leyland. In 1975, BL was nationalised and became British Leyland Limited. BL became the Rover Group in 1986, and in 1990 this organisation went into partnership with Japan's Honda. It was this association which kept the old Pressed Steel site at Swindon viable. In the 1980s, Honda had collaborated with British Leyland, and in 1985 it built a huge factory for car production on part of the former Vickers Armstrong site at nearby South Marston. This became Honda of the UK Manufacturing, and was only a short distance from the Rover Group site at Bridge End Road. When MG Rover was bought by BMW in 1994, the latter acquired the Swindon pressings plant. In 2000, BMW sold MG Rover (which went into administration in 2005), but kept the Stratton site as a wholly owned subsidiary, and reinvented the business there as Swindon Pressings Limited. The site was considerably reduced in size by demolition in 2006 and officially named the BMW Plant Swindon.

The facility is designated 'The home of MINI Panel Production'.

Primitive Methodism Writing in *Swindon Fifty Years Ago* (published in 1885), William Morris described how Primitive Methodist meetings were held irregularly in the 1820s in several cottages occupied by working-class families in Eastcott, some associated with Upper Eastcott Farm, an isolated farmstead that then stood, amidst trackways, roughly where Regent Circus is today. The movement progressed in the town from c.1828, consequent upon the newly formed Brinkworth circuit. In 1849, Thomas and James Edwards enabled the town's first Primitive Methodist chapel to be built in a field they owned alongside a farm track that ran north-west from approximately what is now Regent Circus. This chapel was enlarged in 1863 to include a schoolroom, and was rebuilt on the same site in 1876. By then, the track had become Regent Street.

Throughout the previous decade, Primitive Methodist meetings had also taken place in Old Swindon, firstly in a room near Albert Street, and then a chapel in Prospect Place (built 1870-71) and one in Gorse Hill built at about the same time. Following the formation of the Swindon Circuit in 1877, based on the Regent Street church, Primitive Methodist chapels were built at Clifton Street (1882) and Rodbourne Road (1883). Levi Lapper Morse gave land in Rodbourne Cheney, where a Primitive Methodist chapel was built in 1894. The Circuit was split into two in 1900, the No. 1 Circuit devolving on Prospect Place, and Regent Street being the base for the No. 2 Circuit. The Manchester Road chapel was set up in 1902, and in 1903 another was built in Butterworth Street. The Rodbourne Cheney chapel was superseded by a new one in 1906, when the 1894 building became a school, and this remained in use until 1961 when the Methodists relocated to a chapel in Moredon Road and the 1906 building was acquired by the Baptists. The two Circuits continued until the Methodist Union of 1933.

Primitive Methodist Church, Regent Street The Primitive Methodist Church in Regent Street was designed by Orlando Baker in vaguely Italianate style and built by George Wiltshire in red brick with Bath stone dressings. The building was almost fifty-nine feet long, and thirty-six feet wide. The Regent Street façade was of three storeys and seven bays, with a central doorway, two flanking doors, and flights of steps at right angles to Regent Street. Internally, the arrangement was similar to that of the Baptist Tabernacle, built a little closer to Regent Circus, in that the main room was galleried, which was supported on iron columns and had decorative ironwork fronts, and could be gained from a lobby at the west end. Some six hundred people could be accommodated on seats made of red deal. A schoolroom, measuring thirty-eight feet, by thirty-two feet, by nine feet, was put in beneath the chapel, and classrooms were added to the rear. Later road widening swept away the classrooms, caused an amount of remodelling to the Regent Street frontage, and necessitated some additional building at the south-east of the original structure. What had been a beautiful, symmetrical building now became an ugly façade, quite out of shape, and the whole building assumed a disproportionate aspect, menacing the end of Regent Street. The stone dressings picked out the extraordinary mismatch of round-headed windows that adorned the visually

illogical add-ons of the years. This ghastly building was topped by an open cupola and spirelet. The flight of steps, described as 'an eyesore and a source of great inconvenience' was removed in 1889. A new Methodist Sunday School building was opened behind the chapel in 1895 and these were seconded to the War Office during the Second World War. In 1946, they were leased to Swindon Corporation, and became an arts centre. The church was demolished in 1957. (See also Primitive Methodism.)

Princess Margaret Hospital, Okus

Plans to build the hospital began in 1950, in the wake of a report which estimated that within twenty years the Swindon hospital would have to serve a population of 190,000. The foundation stone was laid on the Okus site in May 1957 by HRH The Princess Margaret. Sir George Schuster, then chairman of the Oxford Regional Hospital Board, officially opened the first phase of the hospital – out-patients and accident departments – in October 1959. The architects were Powell & Moya, the consulting architect was R. Llewellyn Davies, and the main contractor J. Gerrard & Sons. Eventually, the hospital comprised a main ward block, opened by Princess Margaret at a ceremony held on 22 April 1966. There was also an accident and emergency department, opened 1974, a nursing floor with its own theatres and treatments suite, a hospital for psychiatric and geriatric patients, a maternity unit, doctors' flats, midwives' hostel, theatre blocks, offices for administration and services, and car parks. In 1999, work began on its replacement at Commonhead. The Princess Margaret hospital officially closed on 3 December 2002, was demolished in 2004, and the site

was subsequently developed as a residential estate. (See also Great Western Hospital.)

Prospect Foundation, The

In 1980, the Prospect Foundation was established as a homecare nursing service for people approaching the end of their lives. The organisation became known as 'the Swindon charity'. Support for it grew in the community, and in 1985 it was given four beds in the former Victoria Hospital in Bath Road. Prospect's reputation for patient care grew, as did local appreciation for its services, and it was increasingly called upon as Swindon expanded over the next decade. The Foundation's president, David Margesson, led a community fund-raising campaign that brought in some £3 million and, in the mid-1990s, this was used to build a dedicated hospice in Moormead Road, North Wroughton, which opened with just ten beds. In 2008, the Foundation launched an additional service, Prospect At Home, giving end-of-life care in the place where most people would choose to be, and which is more acceptable to many families.

Quarries, The

There is evidence that deposits of white Purbeck stone, lying just below the surface of the ground between the summit of Swindon hill and its descent towards the west, were worked by the Romans who settled in the vicinity. Immediately to the north of the limestone, lie sandy deposits, after which Bath Road was originally known as 'The Sands'; to the south, a roadway that was later built up, and named Westlecot Road in 1886. The deposits of stone seem to have been little used after the Roman era, until, according to antiquarian John Aubrey, they were 'discovered' about 1640 on land then held by the lord of the

manor, Richard Goddard. This led to the area being worked from c.1642, as sections of it were leased to businessmen by succeeding members of the Goddard family. The plots were worked by families of stonecutters – eventually, in some cases, by a succession of several generations – and had lime kilns built on them.

A number of these workings were collectively known as 'The Quarries', which continued in profitable operation until around 1730. A network of trackways provided access across the area, and the individual lessees were expected to erect fences around their individual plots. Those who failed to do so, were brought before the Court Leet, where they were charged with keeping their quarry in a dangerous condition.

Most of the stone dug there was used locally, and on paving or rough walling projects, as hayrick supports, or as gravestones. Some of it was transported overland and then floated by Thames barge to London. By the mid-1700s, the lessees were quitting the business, and stone cutting on Swindon hill declined until 1790 when a new seam was opened at Kingshill, which provided stone for the bridges over the Wilts & Berks Canal, and canal-side buildings. The canal gave a renewed impetus to Swindon stone cutters and masons who, with a pool of labourers, once more worked the quarries and used the canal to export Swindon stone. Work in the quarries quietened by the late 1820s, but revived after 1840 when stone was needed in building Swindon New Town, once the railway had arrived. Between then and the end of the 19th century, a wide range of Swindon tradesmen, businessmen and architects leased sections of the quarries for their own use and, between 1860 and 1880, three short terraces of quarry workmen's

cottages were built on what became Quarry Road.

Most of the Swindon quarries were exhausted by 1885, although people still occasionally leased plots. One of these was local builder Joseph Williams, who did so in 1899. Another was Edwin H. Bradley, who bought a section and thereupon established his company's headquarters. Quarrying finally ceased in the 1950s.

Quaving-gogs The colloquial name by which the people of Swindon knew the area of damp and reputedly dangerous land to the north of the hill, across which the Swindon section of the Wilts & Berks Canal was built c.1804, and where the Great Western Railway Company's line and Works were built from the 1840s. There were variations of the name; 'quavy quogs' for example, suggested a fearsome place, and although described as being full of rabbits that might be a source of food, it was avoided by the local inhabitants. The area was a quagmire, where water hung in foetid lakes on heavy, slow-draining clay, where there were marshlands to inconvenience the unwary, and where vegetation was sparse and unlovely. Almost certainly, most of the roadways that were subsequently built between the line of the Wilts & Berks Canal and present-day Cheney Manor went down in an area that would have included, at least in part, this unsavoury area.

Queen's Park In 2001, Queen's Park was placed on the English Heritage *Register of parks and gardens of special historic interest in England*. The park was created out of a one-time brick and tile works, amidst clay pits and a lake. It includes a lake with islands, surrounded by walks and open

spaces, and the relics of buildings that were once there. There are a number of sculptures and examples of modern art.

The land was under private ownership, but derelict and much overgrown, when it was earmarked for compulsory purchase under the local authority's report *Planning for Swindon 1942-44*. Its subsequent layout and composition, which took place in two phases between 1949 and 1953, was a co-operative effort between the then borough architect, J. Loring-Morgan, and Maurice J. Williams, who was the town's general superintendent of parks and allotments.

The oldest entrance, from Groundwell Road, bears a plaque, and was completed in 1950. It led into an integral rose garden and garden of remembrance for those killed in the Second World War, and was opened that year on 15 November by Princess Elizabeth. On 30 May 1953, the High Sheriff of Wiltshire, Sir Noel Arkell, commemorated the coronation of HM Queen Elizabeth II by opening the parks western section, at which point it was named after the monarch. The entrance between Durham Street and Lincoln Street was built in that year. In celebration of Swindon Borough's diamond jubilee, further land was bought.

The Drove Road entrance was added, and the mayor, Cllr. Miss E.C.M. Millin, opened it in 1960. The park continued to be developed internally until 1964, notably with the addition, 1960-63, of Loring-Morgan's glasshouse. Most of this, which contained a cactus house and a tropical garden, was demolished in the 1980s and early 1990s. During the later '90s, a landslip occurred, and part of the park was shut off.

Queen's Park Mural In 2007, a local arts initiative, Artsmad (a joint venture between the Arts Council of England and Swindon Borough Council) oversaw the creation of a pictorial wall on a shelter beside the lake in Queen's Park. The wall had previously been the canvas for ad hoc 'tagging', when the opportunity was taken to turn it into a quality piece of community art. Photographer and community artist Lynette Thomas came up with the idea, after realising the detrimental effect of the tagging. It fitted well with Artsmad's aims of improving the lives of children and young people; art students from Commonweal School provided the original suggestions, then an 'open day' was held on site during which youngsters were encouraged to suggest or draw ideas for the wall – ideas that would capture the spirit of the park. Some of these young people were also actively involved in painting the work. Once the suggestions had been approved by the Queen's Park Community Council and Swindon Borough Council, muralist Tim Carroll, then a member of another Swindon art group, ArtSite, translated the ideas into reality. The project, officially called the Queen's Park Project, was backed by Swindon Borough Council and co-ordinated by Claire Smith.

Queen's Royal Hotel, Swindon Station The hotel occupied the two upper floors of each of the three-storey, Georgian-style station blocks, identical in shape and external elevation, built on each side of the main line at Swindon station, linked by a covered walkway. The floor below, on each side, was taken up by two refreshment rooms, separated by rows of columns. This complex, which became known as The Queen's Royal Hotel & Refreshment Rooms, was built by Joseph D. & Charles Rigby and leased to them in 1847. They immediately

sub-let the refreshment rooms to Samuel Young Griffiths, owner of the Queen's Hotel, Cheltenham. Between 1842 and 1895, all trains stopped at Swindon station for ten minutes, so that travellers could refresh themselves, but from the very beginning there were innumerable complaints about the food and drink. The situation did not improve under a succession of managers. John Rouse Phillips purchased the lease in 1848, and the Great Western Railway Company bought it back in 1895, by which time the hotel was hardly a going concern.

An interesting note appeared about it in the Swindon Directory of 1876: 'The "Queen's Royal" may be accessible, but few of the travelling public know it, or would venture to intrude within its splendid precincts for purposes of shelter. Especially does this apply to the poorer classes, who often have to wait for several hours to meet a train. The Queen's Royal Hotel and Refreshment Rooms have also been redecorated and otherwise embellished, and are generally admired by the thousands of passengers who daily alight at the platforms. Proprietor, Mr George Moss, whose urbanity and excellent arrangements are much appreciated'. In 1888, it was also announced that 'a considerable staff of young ladies and other assistants are necessarily engaged'. The hotel hardly survived in business into the 19th century, but the refreshment rooms remained until the old station was rebuilt in 1972.

Queen's Tap, Station Road This heroic survivor of a public house is now dominated by adjacent multi-storey office buildings. It was built on the corner with Wellington Street by Joseph D. & Charles Rigby in 1840, and first licensed the following year. This was part of the contra deal under which they were also contracted to build three hundred railway village cottages at their own expense. It is a little two-storey, three-bay gem, built of coursed rubble limestone with ashlar dressings beneath a hipped bay roof with dentil mouldings. The square-headed windows have splayed lintels with keystones, and the freestone quoins are used decoratively. The Tuscan portico to Station Road, and the half-height Tuscan pilasters, cornice and engaging corner windows, give it a pleasing eccentricity. Between 1841 and 1850, the original square building was extended by single-storey additions on either side, and considerable stabling was put up at the rear for the use of the Queen's Royal Hotel. In the 19th century, sales of cattle and horses were held in the stable yard at the rear of the premises. What remained of the stables in 1991 was then demolished.

Radnor Street Cemetery The cemetery is today a designated local nature reserve, close to the town centre and approached from Radnor Street, Clifton Street, Dixon Street, and Kent Road. Within it are five paths radiating between the centre of the grounds and the perimeter walkway. It was laid out on an eleven-acre site in 1880 on grounds made available by businessman James Hinton (mayor of Swindon 1903-4), paid for by a co-operative funding agreement between the Old Swindon Local Board and the New Swindon Local Board (which each provided an equal number of members to the eight-member Burial Committee). As the cemetery was created and laid out, a good many boulders were revealed. Some of these were used in making the access roads and pathways, and others may still be seen intact today. Swindon architect William Henry Read's design for the Radnor Street

grounds incorporated an apsidal-ended chapel with a Gothic-style campanile and a vestry, built in Early English style, a separate cruciform-on-plan coffin lodge and mortuary chapel, and a lodge for the caretaker, all at a cost of £10,000. The work was carried out by Phillips & Powell, and George Wiltshire, builder, monumental mason and sculptor, of Bath Road, Swindon. The iron railings on the surrounding stone wall, and the entrance gates, were supplied by William Affleck of the Prospect Works, off Eastcott Hill, and Edwards & Co. of the Castle Works, off Wood Street. Close by the main chapel is a sandstone cross, on an octagonal plinth and base, which is a war memorial. The first burial was on 6 August 1881, and by the last day of that year interments had numbered ninety-four. By the time it had been open for five years, 1,290 people had been interred there. This was the resting place for a number of prominent Swindonians, as well as many paupers, before the grounds were closed to further burials in 1970. By that time, more than 33,000 people had been laid to rest in the cemetery. The area was designated a nature reserve in 2005.

Railway Mission, Wellington Street This little wooden building, with its corrugated roof, was built in 1903, in support of the Railwaymen's Christian Association that had been active in the town for about twenty years. The band of decorative woodwork in the timber-framed, square panels on the east elevation, fronting the roadway, gave it a conservatively 'magpie' appearance, and there was a drop pendant to the apex between plain bargeboards. On the roof were two skylights, and a small cupola, and the entrance was beneath a corrugated porch. The mission was run almost exclusively by women, until Revd D.J. Laurie was appointed superintendent in 1938. The building was destroyed by fire in 1979.

Railway Museums in Swindon The forerunner to a permanent display of railway artefacts and memorabilia took place in 1953, when a railways exhibition was held at the central library in Swindon. One of the exhibits was a panorama of the town, dated 1849, showing the GWR Works as they were then. A scale model of the locomotive 'Lord of the Isles' was a very popular exhibit and there were a good many books and photographs in the collection.

The Great Western Railway Museum opened in Swindon on 22 June 1962 with an inaugural luncheon for railway dignitaries and civic luminaries at the Mechanics' Institute. The museum was in the former lodging house, known as 'The Barracks', which had been built in the 1840s to accommodate the intake of railway workers from Wales and the South Midlands. The hostel was bought by the Wesleyan Methodists in 1866, converted, and opened for worship in 1869; it closed in 1959. During 1961, the entrances were enlarged sufficiently to admit locomotives, a main hall and a smaller exhibition hall were created, and a caretaker's flat was installed. The first locomotives to go in included the Hawksworth Tank Engine.

In pride of place among the exhibits was the fifty-one-ton *City of Truro* locomotive, designed by G. J. Churchward and built in the town's Works in 1903, and which distinguished itself by reaching 102 mph in the following year. It was withdrawn from service in 1931. *The Lode Star*, also designed by Churchward and built 1907, was there,

too; it weighed over seventy tons, and was withdrawn from service in 1951. There was also a reconstruction of Stephenson's *North Star* – the original of which pulled the first GWR passenger train in 1838, and which was broken up in 1906 because a museum could not be found in which to house it.

The Swindon railway museum was opened by R.F. Hanks, chairman of the Western Area Board of the British Transport Commission, the organisation that was a joint partner in the venture with the Swindon Council. Some seven hundred people visited on opening day. John Betjeman was an early visitor, and the first to make a television film there; his 1962 *Men of Steam* featured the exhibits.

The first caretaker at the GWR Museum was Ernest Neighbour, a former post office sorter in the Torbay area. He ascribed his success in landing the job as being partly due to his interest in museums, but in particular to his interest in trains, since they were used to transport the royal mail. Ernest had very recently relocated to Swindon, where his abilities as an amateur actor and operatic singer were soon in demand. This enabled him to thereafter tread the boards under the sobriquet of E. Hilton Neighbour.

By 1968, footfalls at the railway museum were in serious decline, and its future was in doubt. Funds needed to be raised in order to 'save' it. Matters worsened, and it seemed possible that the collection might have to be broken up, some of it being relocated to Bristol. This did not happen, but plans were formulated in 1972 – by which time British Rail was no longer in partnership with the Corporation over the running of the museum – 'to move Swindon's railway museum to a new site (possible where there were nearby BR tracks), as part of a plan to liven it up'.

Railway Station Joseph D. & Charles Rigby built the GWR Company's railway station at New Swindon in 1842. This comprised a Georgian-style building on each side of the main lines, linked by a covered walkway. The two blocks were identical externally and in their first-floor plan, and also in having cellars, kitchens and station workers' accommodation in the basement. The ground floor was mostly taken up by first class and second class refreshment rooms, and the two upper floors comprised the station hotel, with bedrooms on the north side, and lounge areas to the south. The station facility became known as the 'Queen's Royal Hotel and Refreshment Rooms', and the profits from both were intended to recompense Rigbys for their original capital expenditure.

From the moment the station opened, until 1895, every passenger train travelling past Swindon stopped there for ten minutes. This enabled engines to be changed, and the passengers were able to take advantage of the luxuriously appointed refreshment rooms. The food and drink, however, did not come up to standard, and there were complaints. John Rouse Phillips purchased the lease in 1848, and the Great Western Railway Company bought the rights in 1895. In 1968, the arrangement of platforms was changed, and amalgamated into three. The old station was ornate and full of character, but by the time most of it was demolished in 1972-3 the platform approach had become leaky, smelly, and very discoloured. Just one of the original Brunel station buildings remains. (See also Queen's Royal Hotel.)

Railway Village A planned model village of three hundred cottages, intended to house railway employees at Swindon,

was planned in 1841. The design – to a grid plan on either side of an open square or promenade – is often ascribed to Matthew Digby Wyatt, the architect of Paddington station, although there is no documentary evidence that it was other than Brunel's own. Work began on two fields north of the Wilts & Berks Canal, purchased from brewer John Harding Sheppard. The building firm of Joseph D. Rigby & Charles Rigby themselves defrayed the cost (Swindon stone was used, and Bath stone, probably including some from the making of Box tunnel) on a contra deal under which they then leased the cottages back to the GWR Company. Bristol Street and Bath Street were built first, in 1842-3, followed by Exeter Street and the north side of Taunton Street by the end of that year. The south side of Taunton Street, London Street, Oxford Street and Reading Street were all added 1845-6. Faringdon Street was built piecemeal 1846-51. In about 1860, the blocks of buildings were put up facing each other across the open space that was to become High Street (later Emlyn Square).

The village was built following a symmetrical layout and a strict hierarchical structure. The rows of small back-to-back cottages were finished by larger houses, some gabled, to be occupied by company foremen and their families. They were approached from the rear through little stone arches set in the end terraces. The properties had brick-walled back yards with wash houses and privies. The best properties faced the railway line, and the houses of the Works' managers were built a little apart from those of the workers. Properties assigned to professionals in the railway service were built facing away from the rows of workers' cottages; the largest ones being erected 1850-55, and built to overlook the park. Some of the cottages were one-up-one-down, with adjoining front doors paired in a v-shaped porch, to lend a pleasing aesthetic detail.

The streets of the railway village ran at right angles to a square; four were constructed on each side, and each was given the name of a town with a GWR station. Those to the west of Emlyn Square were named after stations to the west of Swindon; stations to the east of Swindon provide the names for roads to the east of Emlyn Square. The final row of cottages was built in 1866, by which time several building firms had been involved, and although a small number of buildings have since been demolished (including the last six), it today includes 356 residential properties.

In 1948, the railway village passed into the ownership of British Rail. Swindon Borough Council bought back most of the properties in 1966, and restored the village 1969-82. The railway village was designated as a conservation area in 1975, and in 1987 it became part of a larger conservation area that included the former GWR Works.

Railway Village Museum, Faringdon Road Next to the former Wesleyan Methodist Chapel (previously 'The Barracks') at 34 Faringdon Road (renumbered from 1 Faringdon Street in 1929), is one of the GWR Works' so-called 'foreman's houses' of the early 1860s. It is the end building in a terrace of sixteen, and is built in two storeys and two bays of courses of squared rubble stone from the Swindon quarries, with squared, ashlar door and window surrounds, and a roof of Welsh slates. The original sash windows and front door are present. It has a front garden, and a back yard with an outside lavatory, and a

later (c.1890) kitchen lean-to and wash house. The property was refurbished, and furnished as it would have been c.1900, as part of the Swindon Borough Council's (continued by its successor, Thamesdown Borough Council) programme of modernisation and preservation of the railway village, after its purchase by the local authority in 1966. The house was opened to the public in 1980 as the Railway Village Museum.

Rea, Minard Christian (1822-1857) It is doubtful whether Swindon's iconic Mechanics' Institute would have been built without the involvement of Minard Rea. Rea, born at Christendom in southern Ireland, was a protégé, a pupil, and thereafter a lifelong friend of Daniel Gooch. In 1848, he was appointed locomotive superintendent of the Bristol & Exeter Railway, whose locomotives were at the time being repaired and generally looked after at the Swindon locomotive works. In 1850, he was appointed the GWR Works superintendent at Swindon, in succession to Archibald Sturrock, who had effectively held the equivalent position of Works manager since 1842 when he was engaged to employ workers even before the enterprise was operational. Minard Rea was a prime mover in improving the social conditions for the railway workers. He suggested that the Mechanics' Institution, then being held in a room in the locomotive works, should be placed on a firm footing; and he opined that a company should be set up to build a market house for railway village occupants (who mostly had to shop in the Old Town at the time) and a Mechanics' Institute building. This resulted in the formation of the New Swindon Improvement Company, of which he was the first chairman. It was Minard

Rea who used his influence with the GWR Board of Directors, through Daniel Gooch, obtaining their agreement to lease their open space in Emlyn Square at a negligible rent to the New Swindon Improvement Company for the purposes of erecting a market house and an institute. Minard Rea was president of the Medical Fund, and vice-president and treasurer of the Mechanics' Institute. In 1851, he became Worshipful Master of the Royal Sussex Lodge of Emulation at Swindon, and thereafter championed the cause of freemasonry in Wiltshire. Towards the end of his life, he spent time abroad for the sake of his health, and resigned his position shortly before he died, thereafter being much missed by the railway rank and file.

Rea, Stuart Keith (c.1820-1848) The elder brother of Minard Christian Rea, Stuart Keith Rea was the Swindon railway works' first doctor, in the sense that Daniel Gooch persuaded him to come to Swindon in 1843, live in the railway village, and set up a general practice whereby the employees might benefit. Rea's marriage to Ann Pavy of Wroughton in 1846 was the first to be held at the then newly built St Mark's church; just over a year later, their only child was baptised there. Rea seems to have lived firstly in Exeter Street, and then Bristol Street, which was large enough to accommodate his domestic arrangements, consulting room/ surgery and dispensary. All the accounts of Rea attest to his unflinching hard work in the medical care of a community that was much afflicted by tuberculosis, small-pox, and typhoid fever. Stuart Rea succumbed to tuberculosis, his demise being hastened by his insistence on attending a fatal train accident at Shrivenham in 1848 whilst he was seriously ill. He died less than three

weeks later, and was buried in St Mark's churchyard; his widow died in 1907.

Read, William (1817-80) Born at Stratton St Margaret, Read was to become a general surveyor, appraiser of property, and a land and house agent in Swindon. He took up office as the parish surveyor of highways in the town in 1842, and in 1847 became surveyor to the GWR Medical Fund. He married Louisa Ann (née Hawkins) from Oaksey in 1848. The couple took up residence at Croft House, a large residence built at Croft in the 1840s for the solicitor James Copleston Townsend. Their first child, Ann Louisa, arrived in 1849, and the second, William Henry, was born at Croft House in 1850. In 1852, William Read was one of the directors of the Swindon Market Company upon its establishment. During the 1850s, the family downsized from Croft House and moved into smaller premises at 31 Wood Street. This is a very conservatively executed, late 18th-century building in red brick, of three bays and two storeys with an attic with three dormer windows. The centrally placed entrance is beneath a fluted Tuscan portico; the square-headed windows have splayed lintels, and sills. It is now Grade II listed.

In 1855, William Read was famously involved in litigation with Ambrose Lethbridge Goddard, lord of the manor, when the latter built a wall beside his estate that encroached on the public highway. He was also in dispute with Goddard in 1859 when the lord of the manor complained to a vestry meeting that Read was making repairs to the market place in The Square, Old Town when, as owner of the market, it was Goddard's sole right to do so. Read had provided new posts and stalls. It was pointed out that the Goddard family had failed for so long to carry out their responsibilities to the market place, that the parish had long since (some said for as long as 200 years) had to unofficially shoulder the responsibility of upkeep. Despite angry protests from Goddard, Read's posts and stalls stayed.

Read also went on to fulfil the role of surveyor for the Old Swindon Local Board, the New Swindon Local Board, and to be a director of the Swindon Central Market Company. He was the first secretary of the Swindon Water Company at their formation in 1865, and he helped to arrange the grand ball at the opening of the Corn Exchange in 1866. Wherever he lived, he always kept keys to the building in Newport Street that housed the Old Swindon fire engine (another set was kept at the police station, Canford House, Devizes Road). When William Read died, the tailor and draper John Chandler bought 31 Wood Street.

Read, William Henry (1850- 1901) The second child of William Read, surveyor, and his wife Louisa Ann, William Henry Read was born at Croft House. He was sent to be educated at Henry C. Lavander's New Park Street Grammar School, Devizes, afterwards returning to 31 Wood Street, where the family had taken up residence. He became self-styled as 'civil engineer', although he would later make his mark on Swindon as an architect. In 1876, William Henry married Susannah Elizabeth (née Chandler, b.1851), daughter of the tailor John Chandler, who lived just two doors away at No. 35 Wood Street. The newly married Reads took up residence at Moravia House, 10 Bath Road, which the young architect had designed himself. After the death of his father in 1880, his mother came to live at Moravia House.

William Henry Read and Susannah had four children before she died, and he remarried in 1893.

Although Read's father had often been in dispute with Ambrose Lethbridge Goddard, lord of the manor, it was to William Henry that the latter turned to design his new sale yard for livestock, which opened in 1887 adjacent to the cattle sale yard of Dore, Smith & Radway, off Marlborough Road. William Read was also the architect of several fine buildings in the town: notably, Anderson's almshouses in Cricklade Street, beside the churchyard at Christ Church; the Baptist Tabernacle in Regent Circus, New Swindon; Clifton Street Schools; and the Victoria Hospital at Okus.

Red Brick Publishing There has only ever been one publishing house in Swindon. In 1979, Peter Sheldon (b. 1946), a former pupil of Sanford Street School, who had then been a teacher at Ferndale School for five years, published *Swindon In Camera, 1850-1979*. It was a book of Victorian and Edwardian photographs of the town, annotated with descriptive text, and set in comparison with contemporary photographs (now themselves historic photographs) taken from the same perspective as the originals. This was followed, also in 1979, by *Roadways*, a history of Swindon's street names, which he co-wrote with Richard Tomkins. Both books were published by Picton Publishing of Chippenham. In 1980, the Borough of Thamesdown Museums Service published Sheldon's *A History of Swindon and District Mineral Water Manufacturers*. At this point, Sheldon and Tomkins formed Redbrick Publishing, primarily to publish the results of their own research into Swindon's history. His first title under this imprint, featuring annotated historic pictures of Swindon, was the forerunner of the series of similar books – *Swindon In Old Photographs* – that first appeared in 1988 under the Sutton Publishing imprint and were to become so successful for The Swindon Society. Here is a complete list of the Swindon titles published under the Redbrick imprint, and its brief offshoot, Golden Lion Publications.

A Swindon Album (Peter Sheldon, 1980)

A M&SWJ Railway Album (Peter Sheldon, Barrett, Bridgeman and Bird 1984)

Golden Lions and Silver Screens (Peter Sheldon, 1982)

Stronger Through The Years (Richard Tomkins, 1982)

Stratton In Camera (Revd Dr. F.W.T. Fuller, 1984)

Swindon's Pride (Peter Sheldon, 1984)

Fishing For The Moon (Peter Sheldon, 1984)

A Swindon Retrospect (Frederick Large, 1984. A reprint of the 1932 3rd edition.)

Swindon's Other Railway (Barrett, Bridgeman and Bird, 1985)

The Day Alma Cogan Came To Town (Peter Sheldon, 1986)

Lost For Words (John Rich & Peter Sheldon, 1986)

Stratton Revisited (Gerald T. Dancer, 1987)*

Further Up The Crossing (Ken Ausden, 1987)*

St Luke's Church, Broad Street (Revd Dr. F.W.T. Fuller, 1987)

The Railway Works and Church in New Swindon (Revd Dr. F.W.T. Fuller, 1987)

Swindon Through The Years (Peter Sheldon & Richard Tomkins, 1988)

The Changing Face of Swindon (Peter Sheldon & Richard Tomkins, 1989)

Swindon and the GWR (Peter Sheldon & Richard Tomkins, 1990, in association with Alan Sutton Publishing)

* In 1987, these were the only two titles to be published by Golden Lion Publishing. Redbrick also marketed two other titles, written by Joe Silto (q.v.). Following the publication of the 1990 title under the Alan Sutton banner, Redbrick Publishing ceased activity. Richard Tomkins left Swindon to live and work in California, and Peter Sheldon retired from teaching to become a dealer in second-hand and antiquarian books – trading as Go-Between Books – specialising in topography, architecture, history, and historical biography.

Red Cow, Princes Street By the mid-1700s, a cottage beer house had been established in Cow Lane. This appears to have been a rough establishment, associated with a number of unpleasant innkeepers, and it closed in 1879. Its name, the Red Cow, was transferred the same year to a small public house, then newly built on a nearby corner with Princes Street. This was a neat building, of brick with stone dressings and quoins, narrow, arched windows with large keystones on the ground floor, and presenting seven bays and a corner splay to Princes Street. The tiny entrance was at right angles to the road. Swindon Borough Council purchased the premises in 1962, and demolished it in 1968.

Redlands see Redville House.

Redville House, Charlotte Mews When it was built by Swindon chemist and general retailer Charles Anthony Wheeler in the 1840s, this red brick residence, beside the drive to The Lawn in Old Town, was known as Redville House. The property was later named 'Redlands'. It is now apartments, having previously

served as a Toc H hostel from 1923, when it was acquired from solicitor John Lindow Calderwood (1888-1960), who was a partner in the Townsend practice from 1919. (From 1922, Calderwood lived nearby at The Hermitage, which was also built by C.A. Wheeler.) Toc H sold Redville House in 1977, when it became a care home for people with mental disorders; the premises were converted to eight residential flats in 2010.

Redville House had a long association with Swindon solicitors. By the mid-1850s it was the home of solicitor John William Browne, whose offices were in Wood Street. Browne seems to have taken in the young solicitor Henry Kinneir (1832-1915) when he arrived in Swindon in the 1850s, having been admitted in 1854. This was the year of his marriage to Harriett Elizabeth (née Tombs, 1828-99), born in Bridgwater, Somerset, the daughter of William Tombs, a banker and magistrate. By 1858, Kinneir had leased Redville House from J.W. Browne, and the two solicitors went briefly into partnership as Kinneir and Browne. This was dissolved by mutual consent on 6 February 1860, at which point Henry Kinneir began in practice on his own, and he continued to live at Redville House. Following the death of his first wife, Kinneir was married in Kensington, London, on 22 November 1900 to Susan Sarah Durnford, (née Tombs, 1846-1923), a widow. Susan's father was Samuel Tombs, solicitor; her brother, Henry Coggan Tombs (1832-96), born at Bridgwater, went into partnership in Swindon with his brother-in-law as Kinneir & Tombs. The Kinneir family continued to live at Redlands, and were still there at the time of Henry Kinneir's death. Redlands is of three storeys and four bays, with double two-storey, two-bay extensions. It is Grade II listed.

Regal Ballroom see Playhouse Theatre

Regent Cinema In 1929, the 1,322-seat Regent Cinema opened, with integral Compton Wonder Organ, in Regent Circus, next to the site of the former Picture House. Its first manager, A.G. Harman, had spent the previous three years at the Electra Palace, but stayed at the Regent until he retired in 1948. In 1950, J. Arthur Rank, the organisation that owned Gaumont-British Cinemas, requested that its name be changed to Gaumont. Because of the Swindon cinema's location, this was not done immediately. From 1962, it was called the Odeon. It closed in 1974 and became a full-time bingo hall, having previously trialled it on Sundays, and was later converted to the Top Rank Club. This closed in 2008. (See also MECA.)

Regent Circus The first residential properties, eventually a terrace of sixteen buildings, went up facing south on the site of the northern side of present-day Regent Circus in the 1850s. This terrace was called York Place. Its immediate neighbour was Upper Eastcott Farm, which stood adjacent, with its outbuildings and half a dozen associated cottages, amidst a number of trackways. In the mid-19th century, this was in an isolated spot; south of the track (later to become Regent Street), between Upper Eastcott Farm and the line of Fleet Street, was open countryside, as was the case east of Eastcott Hill. Much of this land was part of the Rolleston estate, which did not become available for redevelopment until after 1885.

In the 1850s, the owner of Upper Eastcott Farm built a number of small properties adjacent to the farm cottages, which he rented as residential and retail, allegedly calling the development York Place. The idea of creating a square devolving on York Place was formulated in the early 1880s. When, by the mid-1880s, the New Swindon Local Board decided to build their offices in York Place, this gave impetus to the finishing of Victoria Road, which would connect it with Old Town, and to new residential and retail developments in the immediate vicinity. The square was laid out 1886-88, firstly by doubling the width of the footpath running along the front of York Place, then building a footpath right around the perimeter of the square, and finally by increasing to fifty feet the width of the roadway alongside York Place. This roadway curved out of the square to the east, past the six cottages that comprised Buscott Terrace (between the junctions with Rolleston Street and Byron Street), eventually becoming, when Victoria Road was 'officially' ready c.1888, the point from which the people of New Swindon began to climb the hill to the old town.

First the east side of present-day Regent Circus, and then the west side, began to be built up. Fine residences were established, such as Eastcott House, and Concrete House with its portico, well-defined quoins, moulded cornice and pediment, and finials. Their middle- class occupiers were sufficiently distanced from the emerging trade at the west end of Regent Street, but close enough to take advantage of it. Regent Place and Eastcott Terrace Place (now demolished but formerly on the site of present-day Wyvern Theatre and Theatre Square) ran roughly parallel to each other, immediately behind York Place, and at right angles to it. During 1888 and 1889, a large number of houses and shops were built at the northern ends of New Road (Victoria Road), Rolleston Street, and Eastcott Hill, close to York Place. Shop fronts went into the York Place terrace from about

1890. The first suggested name for the new square was Trafalgar Square but, this being considered rather too grand, York Square became the briefly used alternative. The name Regent Circus was used from about 1900. Soon afterwards, a fine Edwardian villa was built of red brick on the corner of Regent Circus and Commercial Road. Double-fronted to Regent Circus, of three bays with two tiers of bow windows, No. 34 featured tall, ornate chimney stacks, which were also built of bricks. The Commercial Road elevation had a third- storey oriel window, a large bow window, and an eight-bay, two-storey extension. Typically for Swindon, it was demolished in 1964.

Commercial Road was built in 1890 to converge with Regent Street, on what was then called York Square. This really became the focus of New Swindon when the town hall was erected in 1891, at a time when Regent Street had reached York Place. The Head Post Office was built on the corner with Princes Street in 1900, and horse troughs were put up on each side of the square. Some fine Edwardian villas were built on the west side of the square at the turn of the 20th century, and Regent Circus was supposed to have been the site of the town's first (open-air) cinema. A clockwise, one-way system was adopted for traffic around Regent Circus in 1932. (See also Art Deco; Cinemas in Swindon; Free Christian Church; and Museums)

Regent Street Beginning as the eastwards extension of Bridge Street, across the line of the Wilts & Berks Canal at the Golden Lion public house, Regent Street began as a trackway towards Upper Eastcott Farm (close by present-day Regent Circus). Until the 1850s, it ran through fields, land whereupon bricks were made and dried, and waste land, and was only occasionally punctuated by isolated cottages or small terraces of low dwellings. Beyond, on either side, was open countryside, with the occasional distant cottage marking a point alongside some other track. Then, Regent Street began to develop as an extension of Bridge Street, although neither was at first named. The former acquired little runs of cottages and modest individual houses, and grew almost entirely residential. This soon changed as the cottage occupants realised the need for trades to support the new town that was continuing to grow out of the railway works. At this point, around the mid-1860s, it was ironically named after the great trading thoroughfare in London.

By the 1870s, Regent Street contained a few small terraces of one-up-one-down cottages, some modest detached properties, and a handful of front-room traders. There were then about the same number of businesses in Regent Street as there were private houses in the eighty-eight recorded properties between the Golden Lion Inn and the Rifleman's Arms, at the entrance to York Place (where is the present-day Regent Circus). No gentrification of Regent Street occurred; it would always remain socially inferior to High Street and Wood Street, its equivalent in Old Town.

Within twenty years, the whole street had been transformed into the retail and commercial hub of New Swindon, places of worship also went in early, and the elements of social infrastructure quickly followed. A large number of the terraced properties were converted to retail at street level, custom-built shop fronts went in, and dedicated shop premises were put up. Where there had been considerable roadside gaps twenty years

before, large business premises now rose up to three storeys in height, and both sides of the street were packed with properties whose large glass frontages were packed with the products of their trades. By 1900, it was vastly superior to Old Town in a retail sense, and has since remained so. The street once had two-way traffic, and latterly one-way traffic running west to east. It finally closed to all traffic in 1971, was pedestrianised, and opened as such in 1976.

Renault Building see Spectrum

Rhinoceros, The Of all Swindon's historic 'red light' area lodging houses, The Rhinoceros in Albert Street was the one that packed most undesirable excesses into the shortest period of time. It existed for only about twenty-four years, yet has a sustained place in the folklore of Swindon. Disorderly conduct, murder and mayhem were all associated with this establishment, which was opened c.1845 by one-time dressmaker Lucy Rogers (b.1801), an unmarried woman. Prostitutes lived and worked there, and violent acts took place on and off the premises. Rogers's daughter Lucy Jane was married to Joseph Patchett, (which he variously spelled as Paget, Pagett or Padghett), a former plate layer, who was associated in the enterprise from its beginning. He was a bombastic individual, who had no regard for the law, which he appears to have often broken, and which acts frequently landed the business in court.

The premises had a shooting gallery that was run under the auspices of Patchett, and a room at the rear was used for all kinds of illegal entertainments. Downstairs, half a dozen drinking rooms and club rooms were clustered off the large bar area; beneath was a cellar, and there were five bedrooms above, which all helped its reputation as 'the most notorious house in town'. Patchett was described as a 'waiter' there in 1851, when the beds were otherwise taken by two females with unspecified occupations, five general labourers, three hawkers, an ostler, a bell-hanger, a fishmonger, a cordwainer, a carpenter, and a bricklayer.

In 1857, an argument at the Rhinoceros resulted in Lucy Rogers fleeing the premises, dressed in her nightdress and in the company of her daughter, pursued by Patchett. He knocked down his mother-in-law and she struck her head, later dying of this injury; he was charged with manslaughter, but was acquitted. The public house was sold on as a business but, its reputation and activities failing to improve or impress the magistrates, it was closed down in 1869 on the grounds of being a home to prostitutes. The premises became a private residence, and were demolished in 1963. (See also Little London; Vitti, Angelo.)

Richard Jefferies Museum see Coate Farmhouse

Richardson, Billie In the 1930s, a short, tubby chap who lived in Lincoln Street, and was employed as a clerk at the GWR Works in Swindon, made a wider name for himself by recording a series of comic songs on the Regal Zonophone label. He was a member of the Swindon GWR Male Voice Choir, an amateur thespian, and a regular broadcaster on 2LO radio who also made it on to the national BBC radio network. He made several appearances in local pantomimes, and famously played KoKo in The Mikado at the Empire Theatre, Swindon, where he also appeared in

Florodora. At other times, he assumed the persona of a country yokel. In this guise, he made his recordings, notably *Out Come Mother And Me*; *Oi Baint Be As Soft As Oi Looks*; *Wot's The Price O' Swedes*; *There Baint No Flies On Me*; *Her Showed Oi The Way*; and *Gooseberry Tart*. Bert Fluck, Diana Dors's father, was a pianist, and his work is to be heard (although not credited) on some of these records as the accompanist to Richardson's voice. On other Richardson recordings, the accompanist is Arthur Ford, a long-time organist and choir master at Swindon's Baptist Tabernacle in Regent Street. The little man had deep connections with the Victoria Hospital, and was the prime mover in establishing the hospital's Carnival Week.

Rifleman's Arms Hotel, Regent Street When it was built as a small, two-storey hostelry, c.1854, the Rifleman's Arms stood in some isolation at the Upper Eastcott Farm end of the trackway that led across the Wilts & Berks Canal. Within the next thirty years or so, this area would be built up as the new town's shopping centre, Regent Street. At that time, there were only about three shops, a beer house, a couple of small terraces, and a handful of detached properties spread out between the Rifleman's Arms and Fleetway (the present Fleet Street). The public house was licensed in the late 1850s. At that time, it occupied part of a substantial wedge-shaped plot of land, with a walled stable courtyard through which the stables were reached directly off the main road. In 1888, the Rifleman's Arms was rebuilt to three storeys, with its characteristic shoulder gable and pinnacles. The rebuilding took in a cottage immediately to the east, and provided a large first-floor assembly room.

The result is essentially as the public house presents today, although the low wings were added later. In 1891, the pub hosted the first meeting of the Swindon & District Trades Council.

Rimes Coaches The forerunner of Rimes Coaches, which worked out of the Central Garage, just about where Princes Street met Regent Circus, was the Swindon (later Motor) Charabanc Company. When the town's first telephone exchange opened in 1893, they were given the number 'Swindon 1', and this number was retained by its successor. Albert Rimes was the company's proprietor. Following the formation of the Borough of Swindon in 1900, their charabancs were allowed to display the Swindon coat of arms. In the 1930s, Rimes was really just a taxi company, and it added coaches in the 1940s. Albert's successor, Maurice Rimes, still had only three coaches when the business was taken over in 1958 by George Keen, of Heddington, Calne, and his son Des Keen, who were already operating their own bus services. They kept the name Rimes at the Central Garage, Swindon, although the premises were thereafter used only as an office and workshop, and initially retained the premises next door that had been used as the company's booking office. Keen's manager was Len Collins, a director of Swindon Town FC in the 1960s and '70s. The company's expanding fleet of coaches was kept at Hills (the builders) yard in Swindon, until the coach firm eventually built a garage and workshop at Bramble Close, and the Central Garage continued to be an office until the admin side of the business was relocated to 102 Commercial Road, c.1970. The company had forty-five vehicles when Rimes ceased business in 1988.

Rink Cinema This cinema opened in 1914 in the old Corn Exchange in Old Town; it was named after the skating rink that preceded it. It closed at the end of 1949.

Riot Act in Swindon Just once has the civil Riot Act been read in Swindon, and that was from the Town Hall, Old Swindon on 2 April 1880 by Superintendent George North. This followed voting for the Cricklade constituency, which then included Swindon (won locally by Mervyn H. Nevil Story Maskelyne for the Liberal Party), in that year's general election. A mob went on the rampage through the new town and Old Swindon, smashing the windows of public houses whose landlords they felt were turncoats in their support of the Conservative candidate (Daniel Gooch, who was also elected) over that of the favoured Liberal. When they arrived in Old Swindon, the town's chief of police stepped forward and shouted: 'Our Sovereign Lady the Queen, chargeth and commandeth all persons being assembled, immediately to disperse themselves, and peaceably to depart to their habitations, or to their lawful business, upon the pains contained in the act made in the first year of King George the First for preventing tumults and riotous assemblies. God Save the Queen'. That, and the sudden presence of a large force of police officers, did the trick.

Rodbourne This is an area immediately to the north-west of central Swindon, north of the railway line. It is built on either side of the modern-day Rodbourne Road. This thoroughfare, and its continuation south of the railway line (the present-day Park Lane), was once a track that ran between Fleetway (the ancient 'le flet', now called Fleet Street/ Faringdon Road) and the ancient village of Rodbourne Cheney. Before the Conquest, the settlement at Rodbourne Cheney was named Hreod Burna after the 'reedy stream' that ran nearby. By Domesday, it had become 'Redbourne', and the le Chanu family that held the manor in the 13th century added the suffix that became 'Cheney'. The track that joined Fleetway with Rodbourne Cheney passed through Even Swindon (at one time in the parish of Rodbourne Cheney, and in which was the present-day Park Lane).

Even Swindon was developed in the early 1870s as a working-class suburb, and the track became a road; this was the Rodbourne Road (i.e. the road to Rodbourne Cheney, known locally as 'The Lane' or 'Rodbourne Lane'). Residential Rodbourne began to be built up from the 1870s. Row upon row of two- and three-bedroom, two-storey terraced properties were laid out primarily on farmland in Even Swindon and Rodbourne Cheney and built of brick with occasional stone decorations such as plaques. These streets, mostly put up by speculative builders with the ever-increasing GWR workforce in mind, were mostly built to the west of Rodbourne Road, although the few earliest roads went in to the east of it, north of the GWR brickworks. These, and the associated kilns, were immediately to the east of Rodbourne Road, on land on which the company would soon build some of its extensive workshops.

By 1886, most of Rodbourne had been planned and was under construction, although much of it had still not been built. Guppy Street, Henry Street (later renamed Hawkins Street), Linslade Street, and William Street (later renamed Manton Street) were partially built in the 1870s, but it was during the next two decades that Rodbourne

was properly developed. The earliest public building along the Rodbourne Road was the Dolphin Inn. This was built 1872-3, opposite the brickworks, but was ultimately able to take advantage of trade issuing from the GWR Works once the company had established an entrance on to the Rodbourne Road.

Indeed, Rodbourne Road grew commercially with the dual purpose of serving its own community as well as capturing trade from the railway works. Small shops went into its residential terraces, clustered around the GWR exits and, after 1904, the tram terminus close to Bruce Street bridge. Percy Street was partly built in the 1870s (completed by 1890), and a Methodist Chapel was constructed on its north side in 1879 to serve the area. In 1880, Even Swindon school was built at the junction of Hughes Street with Rodbourne Road, and extended in 1895. The first working men's club in the area, Even Swindon Working Men's Club, opened in Morris Street in 1883, the same year as the first Primitive Methodist Church was built in Rodbourne Road. Even Swindon Working Men's Club built new premises in Percy Street in 1888, when its former venue became Morris Street Working Men's Club.

The following year, land was provided for a recreation ground near the western end of Morris Street, on part of which there had stood a small brickworks. This became known as the Mannington Rec, and is still so called. Also, a new Rodbourne Road Primitive Methodist Church was built, 1889-1900. In 1901, the Cellular Clothing Company established a factory on the corner of Morris Street and Rose Street in order to attract female labour, in which it would become very successful. Reading rooms were built on the corner of Rodbourne Road

and Morris Street in 1902, as an extension of the Mechanics' Institution. Jennings Street school was built in 1904. The Rodbourne Arms was built in 1905 at the northern extremity of the area, on the corner with Whitworth Road (it was demolished in 2011 and a supermarket was built in its place). St Augustine's church was opened in Summers Street 1908. Also that year, the ecclesiastical parish of Rodbourne was formed from parts of the parishes of Rodbourne Cheney and St Mark's, Swindon. Between 1928 and 1958 the area had its own cinema, The Palladium in Jennings Street.

Rogers, Don (b. 1945) Even before he retired from professional football, Don Rogers had emulated Swindon's other great footballer, Harold Fleming, by opening a sports shop. Rogers's premises were in Faringdon Road. That was in 1968, the year before he scored the second and third goals in Swindon Town's 3-1 win over Arsenal in the 1969 League Cup Final. Born at Paulton in Somerset, he signed for Swindon Town straight from school in 1961, and stayed – playing in the outside left position – until he moved to Crystal Palace, eleven years later. Following a spell with Queen's Park Rangers, he returned to Swindon for the 1976-77 season, where he played for the Town each side of a loan period with Yeovil. He retired at the end of that season after injuring his hip, and subsequent hip replacement surgery put paid to his playing career. Later, he managed Lambourn in the Hellenic League. The south stand at Swindon FC's County Ground was named the Don Rogers Stand for the start of the 2008-9 season.

Rolleston Estate Areas of land lying in particular to the south, south-west, east and

south-east of the railway village were key to the residential development of Swindon, and in physically linking the new town with the old town. These lands devolved on the estates of the Vilett family (known as Swindon's 'second family', the Goddards being the first), who were lords of the manor of Eastcott. They became the property of Col. William Vilett Rolleston, who lived on The Square, Old Town, and who inherited them from his uncle, William Vilett. Their wholesale release to speculative builders was desired by all parties, but this was made impossible when Col. Rolleston was declared bankrupt in 1874 and his estates became the object of a suit in Chancery. (The bankruptcy was annulled in 1880.) The trustees of the estate were thereafter able to release only small plots of land, and much more slowly than was required. More land was released in 1885, which enabled Commercial Road to be built in 1890, together with a bridge carrying it over the canal in 1890, and a number of streets leading off on either side. In 1897, the trustees were able to sell off some fifty acres to the east and north-east of the emerging new town, thereby enabling speculative builders to develop an area roughly between the railway line and where Broad Street is today.

Rolling Mills, GWR Works Arguably, these are more readily remembered by the general public than other parts of the Swindon GWR Works, perhaps due to the public house of the same name in Bridge Street. The Works established its rolling mills in 1861 for the purpose of augmenting and reforming previously used iron into new rails for the track. Iron workers were brought in from Wales to do the job, and they established, from 1864, the Cambria Place

estate community. One of them was William Ellis, the rail mills manager from the outset, who lived at 7 Fleetway Terrace. The rolling mills were said to be the noisiest, hottest part of the Works. By 1866, they were considered to be autonomous within the GWR undertaking at Swindon, separate from the locomotive works with which they shared the same site. In 1872, they were described as: 'furnaces of seething iron incessantly belching forth huge lumps of white metal'. Here, day and night, white-hot lumps of metal were pulled from the furnaces and smashed beneath the great steam hammers; they were then removed to the rollers which extruded the metal into rails of the required shapes and lengths for cutting by a rotary saw. The result was then trimmed and cooled, and became lengths of track.

In the face of improved manufacturing technology and alternative raw material, the rail mills became unprofitable and obsolete by the 1880s, and were closed down. The rolling mills machinery, however, went on to process much of the scrap metal produced as the result of other manufacturing processes around the Works, and by the 1890s was rolling scrap wrought iron and bar iron. (See also Carriage and Wagon Works; Locomotive Works.)

Rolling Mills public house The Rolling Mills public house was built and so named in 1861 on the site of a beer house of c.1855 called Sir Charles Napier and an adjacent commercial school (run by the beer house keeper), on the corner of Bridge Street and King Street. The owner was Henry Trimble (b.1805), a one-time soldier who gave up the military sometime in the 1840s and became employed as a schoolmaster in Tintagel, Cornwall. By the time his former establishment in Swindon was named The

Rolling Mills, Trimble and his family had relocated to Cheltenham, where he was still occupied as a schoolmaster. The Rolling Mills was a two-storey property with four bays to Bridge Street and two to King Street, with a corner doorway and unprepossessing shop windows at street level. Clinch & Co. bought it in 1904; it was renamed Porters café bar in 1988, and the Rat & Carrot in 1994, but did not survive as a hostelry.

Roman Swindon The first Roman town in the area of Swindon hill was established in the vale immediately to the south-east, close to present-day Stratton St Margaret and the Roman Ermine Street. This town was predominantly a military settlement, and archaeological evidence has shown that it was one of considerable proportions and a very important part of Roman Britain. In 1989, earthworks were uncovered revealing artefacts of what might have been a very early Roman site. The 2nd-century Roman community site at Groundwell Ridge, a little to the north of the hill, was discovered in 1997 and has been described as being 'a real jewel in the crown of southern England'. Foundations of Roman buildings have been excavated to the north and east of the hill, and considerable amounts of pottery and coins have been recovered from the period of Roman occupation. Swindon hill was known to the Romans. A Roman burial was found there; archaeology also revealed remains of Roman buildings in the Old Town Market Square, and there is indisputable evidence that the Swindon quarries were used at that time. Perhaps the town's earliest roads were then built to convey the stone into the vale, and particularly to the settlement at Durocornovium. Most of the Roman artefacts discovered on the quarry site –

pottery, coins, etc. – may simply have been dropped or discarded by those who had business there. The notable exception was the site of a Roman villa, discovered at Okus in 1897, and possibly associated with some overseer at the quarries.

Royal Oak, Newport Street It is likely that by the 1840s there was a well-established brewhouse in one of the cottages on this site, and wool spinning was carried out as a cottage industry in the outhouse of adjacent premises. All of these properties were bought up in the mid-1840s, and remodelled as a hostelry to serve trade entering the town from the Wroughton road. The present two-storey façade, of two bays to Newport Street and three to Devizes Road, is a little later and is distinguished by its use of green ceramic tiles as plinth, pilasters, window aprons, and fascia, the last mentioned having a particularly attractive styling of the public house's name. The central entrance has a triangular pediment, and there are notable old lamps on either side of the building. The windows are square-headed with sills and sashes, except for two bow windows to Devizes Road.

Running Horse, Wootton Bassett Road The present building was erected by Arkell's brewers in 1891, on the site of the Royal Oak, which began in 1825 as a brewhouse belonging to John Garlick. (This surname was associated with other inns in the area: a little further along the Wootton Bassett Road was The Wheatsheaf, run by Sarah Garlick (1815-85) after her marriage to Thomas Purse. The Wiltshire pronunciation of 'purse' as 'puss' led to this inn being misnamed 'The Sally Pussey' after this one-time landlady.)

The Running Horse and its car park are on, and adjacent to, the site of an ancient and long-standing mill and some associated cottages. The earliest reference to this mill is dated 1339, when Robert de Calcot, who then owned High Swindon, granted it to William and Margery Godhye. It was owned by William Stichell at the time of his death in 1618; in 1659, when the tenant miller was Thomas People, John Stichell sold it to Timothy Jewell, the vicar of Lydiard Tregoze. By 1691, it was known as Arthur's Mill, and was then owned by a London woollen draper named John Cullum, who leased it to Stephen Lawrence of Broome, whose family had part-owned it in William Stichell's time. The Lawrence family ran it until 1724; Robert Boxwell followed until 1727; and at that date it passed to Thomas Ladd, who occupied it until 1743. Even today, the Running Horse is said to be on the site of Ladd's Mill.

That notwithstanding, Richard Wayte became the occupier in 1744. The property was then owned by the land-owning Vilett family, and although they liked it to be called Westcott Mill, a map of 1756 calls it Wayte's Mill, standing right on the boundary line between Vilett's land and that of Thomas Goddard, lord of the manor of Swindon. In 1778, the miller was Roger Hall. In 1791, Ambrose Goddard bought the mill from the Viletts for £30, but his ownership was short-lived. A section of the Wilts & Berks Canal Act, 1795 enabled the Wilts & Berks Canal Company to 'purchase or rent mills and land which might suffer from the diversion or use of their streams for the canal, which the Company could work or use from time to time'. The Company exercised its option in 1805, and put in a succession of millers until the late 1830s, when it sold Ladd's Mill, the public house, its outbuildings and adjacent cottages to John Harding Sheppard. Henry Brooks was the miller in 1851. The mill was included in a sale of Sheppard's property in 1870, but thereafter it fell into disuse and ruin before being pulled down c.1897. The public house was purchased by Arkell's in 1883, and remains in their estate. Six occupied cottages, 'Ladd's Mill Cottages', remained on the site, but were pulled down to make way for the Running Horse car park.

Sage, Sampson (b. 1799) Born at Doulting, Somerset, Sampson Sage married Eliza (née Crabb, b. Oxford, 1805) at Trowbridge, Wiltshire in 1823 and the couple settled for a while at Dunston, Lincolnshire, where he was employed as a surveyor of works. Thereafter, they moved around: in 1829, they were at Weston House, Warwickshire; they were living at Shipston-on-Stour by 1834; 1837 found the family at Honiton, Devon; by 1841, they were at Norton, Lincolnshire. By 1844, they were in Swindon, living at Prospect Place, and Sage was styled surveyor and architect. In 1848, he restored St Mary's church at Rodbourne Cheney; he was the man who designed the market house that was built in the Old Town square in 1852-3; and in 1858, Sage was the architect of the National School at Broad Town. By 1861, one of their sons, William Sampson (b.1841) had joined his father as architect's assistant, and the family had moved on to Llanstadwell, Pembrokeshire.

St Aldhelm's Chapel, Edgeware Road This little building stands on part of the site of the demolished St Paul's church. It was built by the firm of E.W. Beard, and opened in 1966 as a chapel of ease, with a hall and a courtyard. Alterations over the years have made the chapel smaller, whilst

covering the courtyard with buildings — principally the Rainbow Bookshop, built in 1979, and St Aldhelm's Resource Centre. The site is open daily to the public; low mass is celebrated here, and there are regular services for the Russian Orthodox Church. The Resource Centre has a stock of religious books, videos and other study material, and the Country Market (formerly Women's Institute market) is held in the chapel hall on Friday mornings.

St Augustine's Church, Summers Street This vaguely Romanesque, basilica-style hall church was built of red brick in 1907-8 to the design of W.A.H. Masters. It was the successor to the Rodbourne Lane Mission. The bricks were paid for by the public, but the church was never completed to its original plan, and remains a six-bay nave with an eastern, aisled, polygonal apse; a porch, vestry, and a single bell cote. The exterior features triple, blunt-headed lancets inset into the brick wall, beneath shallow arches at clerestory level, with a brick corbel table above, and single blunt-headed lancets separated by shallow, single-storey pilasters at ground level. The interior features a double-purlin roof on queen posts, and a Romanesque-style font. The vicarage was built in 1913 in Morris Street.

St Barnabas Church, Gorse Hill Built in 1885, of Swindon stone with ashlar and freestone dressings, in Early English style from designs by J.P. Seddon of Westminster, St Barnabas cost £3,200. Originally, it comprised just a clerestoried nave of six bays and a central turret with a single bell, until the south aisle and vestries were added in 1894. Most of the windows are single lancets. The south porch, originally intended to be a tower,

was built in 1912. The large font was made of Pennant and Mansfield 'marbless',[sic] and the sedilia, piscina and credence featured blue Pennant stone. The adjacent Sunday school building and concert hall, of Swindon stone with Bath stone dressings, was designed by Swindon architect John J. Smith, and built of Swindon stone, brick, and Bath stone dressings. The vicarage was built in 1892, and demolished in 1977.

St George and the Dragon Mural Thamesdown Community Arts' first attempt at mural painting, carried out in 1975, was a frightening and brightly coloured depiction of dragon slaying on the Knight Tyres building in Manton Street, Rodbourne. The picture, painted by Ken White, was based on part of Paolo Uccello's composite picture of the same name of c.1470 in the National Gallery. Its background in Manton Street suggested the chalk downland of Dragon's Hill, close to White Horse Hill and Uffington Castle, and each of the protagonists occupied one-half of the composition. St George charged in from the right, plunging his lance into the head of the great, green-winged serpent, which was poised to attack from the left, all fangs and dripping blood, claws and anger. The work was co-ordinated by group leaders, but carried out very much on an ad-hoc basis by children of secondary school age. Despite its X-certificate nature, the painting was restored in the 1980s, but was lost in 1989 when the building on which it was painted was demolished to make way for a new configuration of roundabouts and bridges at Bruce Street.

St John the Evangelist Church, Aylesbury Street Designed by F.B. Wade of London, St John's was built of stone

in Early English style in 1883. It comprised chancel, nave, vestry and organ chamber, and was established as a 'daughter church' of St Mark's. The windows of the nave were arranged as groups of three stepped lancets, separated by two-stage buttresses with steep set-offs; those of the chancel were two-light cusped lancets, and there were three tall, stepped, two-light lancets at the west end. Also at the west was a stone-built, lean-to porch with pointed doorway and a run of little pointed windows; and on the roof was an open bell turret containing a single bell beneath a slender spirelet. The church closed between 1921 and 1926, and was demolished c.1958.

St Luke's Church, Broad Street

Designed by W.A.H. Masters, St Luke's was built 1911-12 (next to a former church of 1903 that is now the church hall) in 14th-century style. The building has a crocketed bell cote at the western end, and a castellated façade with square-headed, 14th-century-style windows.

St Mark's Church, Church Place

This church was designed in Decorated style (although its cluster columns have earlier influence and give it a disarming hybrid feel) by the firm of George Gilbert Scott and W.B. Moffatt (who also designed St Mark's vicarage and the GWR's Bristol Street school), and was built 1845-6 by William Sissons of Hull. The church has a nave of five bays with clerestory and a large, five-light, curvilinear west window; chancel with south chapel; south aisle with chapel; north aisle; north vestry; and porch. The clerestory has pairs of two pointed segmental windows, with fleuron decoration in the heads, between flat, gabled buttresses, and there are similar windows to the aisles. Until 1846, the parish of St Mark's was under the jurisdiction of Old Swindon. The cost was defrayed by a £500 bequest, specifically to help build a church and school, made by George Henry Gibbs, a GWR director who died in 1852, plus further funds obtained by generous public subscription. Lt. Col. Thomas Vilett gave sufficient land for the purpose, and the church cost £6,000 to build. Its first incumbent was Revd Joseph Mansfield. The building is distinguished by its three-stage tower and 140-foot-high, ribbed and crocketted broach spire to the north-west. The chancel screen was designed by Temple Moore. The church sold its original organ to the Mechanics' Institute in 1855, where it thereafter accompanied musical entertainments, and bought a new one. The building was enlarged in 1897. In the transept is a fine window by Martin Travers. In a radio broadcast in 1948, John Betjeman famously said: 'If ever I feel England is pagan, if ever I feel the poor old C. of E. is tottering to its grave, I revisit St Mark's Swindon. This corrects the impression at once'.

St Mary's Church, Lydiard Tregoze, West Swindon

Of the chancel and chapel of St Mary's, the 17th-century antiquary John Aubrey wrote: 'in this it exceeds all Churches in this countie'. The nave has a wagon roof; that of the chancel is a blue sky covered in stars, and of c.1700. Beneath, is a church packed with interesting pews and other wooden furnishings, some of it Jacobean. This is a 15th-century church, having still some of the painted glass and medieval wall paintings that were there before the St Johns took it over in the 17th century and made it their family church. Much of it was done by Sir John St John, who died in 1648. In

went the great east window, the painted and gilded chancel screen, the Stuart coat of arms above, the Jacobean pulpit and pew, and the wrought-iron altar rails. St John's tribute to his parents is the large painted triptych against the north wall; to himself, it is the tomb he designed with his own life-size effigy next to his wives and the thirteen children he had by his first wife. Also on the north wall is the life-size, fully armoured 'Golden Cavalier', the Royalist Edward St John, who was killed in 1645 during the English Civil War. He stands beneath a marble-curtained canopy, attended by pageboys. Against the south wall are the kneeling likenesses of Nicholas and Elizabeth St John, erected in 1592. Above the south-east doorway is a pedimented conversation piece depicting Sir Giles Mompesson and his wife Katherine (née St John). The church makes a fine group with Lydiard Park House.

St Mary's Church, Rodbourne Cheney

This is the medieval church of what was once a separate village, built on a slight rise and still in a commanding position despite the residential developments of the 20th century around it. Until its restoration in 1848 by Sampson Sage, the Swindon architect who lived in Prospect Place, it had a tower at its crossing. The restoration cost £3,000. St Mary's now has a 19th-century tower, which incorporates some Perpendicular masonry at its west end, with part of an Anglo-Saxon wheel cross built into its north side. The church otherwise comprises chancel, nave, north aisle, and a south porch with an early 13th-century entrance. Indeed, it is Early English at heart, supported by Perpendicular work. A piece of Anglo-Saxon cross shaft with interlacing is set into the west wall of the north aisle.

The windows at the east end are three stepped lancets of the same period; the other windows are Perpendicular-style, depressed arch and square-headed type, each with two or three lights. There are monuments from the 17th, 18th, and 19th centuries within, and some chest tombs in the churchyard. The persistent legend surrounding this church is that a golden altar was buried somewhere close by, and then forgotten.

St Paul's Church, Edgware Road

Designed by Sir Arthur Blomfield, and built of brick in 1880-81 in Early English style by D. and C. Jones & Company of Gloucester, this church was created to serve a town centre parish that originated by amalgamating part of that formerly belonging to St Mark's with some of Christ Church. The materials used in its construction came from Thomas Turner's Swindon Tile & Pottery Works in Drove Road. St Paul's consisted of chancel, nave of four bays with clerestory, porches to the north, south and west, and a bell cote projecting from the western gable end, with a single bell. The building featured pairs of blunt-headed lancet windows with continuous strings around the heads, and circular windows in the clerestory and in the gable at the west end. It cost almost £6,000. Internally, it had a four-bay arcade of pointed arches on circular stone pillars with flat moulded capitals. The church had a fine, painted, three-bay wooden chancel screen with, on each side of the opening, a bay of three lights, divided by turned muntins, and having quatrefoil and trefoil headings. The head of the pointed opening was a cinquefoil, and the whole was topped by a cornice of quatrefoils and a decorated cresting. A vicarage, designed by John Bevan of Bristol, was built adjoining the church in 1884. The

church was demolished in 1963, and the site was acquired by F.W. Woolworth; St Aldhelm's chapel of ease, built on part of the site, is in use today for services and as a resource and study centre, and includes a book shop.

St Saviour's Church, Ashford Road Built in 1889-90 of wood on a brick base by volunteer labour supplied by GWR employees who intended it to be mainly for their own use, St Saviour's consisted of chancel, nave, vestry, western porch, and a trefoil-gabled turret bracketed out on the gable end, with a single bell. The interior was overwhelmingly of wood. The building was enlarged in 1904-5, also by volunteer labour, and ended up looking like a series of wooden sheds with deep, plain barge boards, bolted together. It was encased in stone in 1961.

Salmon, Nicholas John Cook (1824-1857) Born at Faringdon, he was, at seventeen, a solicitor's clerk living at High Street, Ramsbury; latterly, he advertised himself as an accountant. He took a similar position in Swindon, where he lived in Prospect Place, and by 1848 was secretary of the Swindon Gas & Coke Company, established in 1841. He was also the Inspector for Watching and Lighting and, in 1852, he became a director of the Swindon Market Company. He was the inaugural secretary of the Swindon Water Company in 1857, but did not live to see its first meeting, for he died on 8 October that year.

SALOS Swindon Amateur Light Operatic Society was born in January 1951 out of the demise, through lack of support, of the Swindon Operatic and Musical Society. (The forerunner had been the Swindon

Amateur Musical & Dramatic Society, formed in 1922.) The promoters of SALOS were Edgar Young, then editor of the North Wilts Herald; a retired professional opera singer Arthur Carron; Swindon Press manager Eric Blanchard; Grahame Hill, who would become its first and long-term president; and W.S. Bobby, then manager of the Empire Theatre. In 1951, its committee raised sufficient subscriptions to underwrite any financial shortfall in its first production (as it did for several subsequent shows), and it gave the first of its annual public performances. This was *The Arcadians*, which played for a week at the Empire Theatre in 1952. Three productions were put on at this venue before it closed in 1955, whereupon SALOS transferred to the Playhouse in the Mechanics' Institute, Emlyn Square, where it remained until relocating to the Wyvern Theatre when that opened in 1971. It has been there ever since.

Salvation Army The Salvation Army was probably in Swindon in the early 1880s, setting up in the former Methodist chapel behind the Corn Exchange in Old Town. Known first as 'The People's Hall', this soon became the Salvation Army Barracks and was, by 1887, under the direction of Captain John Poole. At that time, it set up in the Gospel Hall, Bridge Street, New Swindon under Captain Read, who lived at 3 Andover Street. The Salvation Army moved out of the old chapel in Old Town in 1901, relocating into premises in North Street. Outdoor services were held in both the old and new towns during the week, and the Bridge Street section also held services at the Mechanics' Institute. They built a citadel in Fleet Street in 1891, and acquired premises in Chapel Street, Gorse Hill in 1907.

Sanitary Conditions, Board of Health Enquiry Into On 23 August 1849, one hundred and sixty two residents of Old Swindon petitioned the General Board of Health, under the Public Health Act, 1848, requesting an enquiry into the sanitary state of the town. The Board sent Inspector George T. Clark in 1850, who looked 'into the sewerage, drainage, and supply of water, and the sanitary conditions of the inhabitants' of Old Swindon, and published his report in 1851. Clark found that no map or plan of the town then existed. He was also frustrated by the townspeople's dichotomy: on the one hand, they felt that Swindon needed to have an overhaul of its sewage and water provision arrangements, but on the other, many held the mistaken belief that adoption of the Act meant that the General Board of Health could compel the town to undertake works at its own expense. George Clark found that typhus was rife in parts of the town; there were no sewers in Old Swindon; that open gutters discharged all manner of effluent into the streets; individual dwellings had no house drains; house refuse was contained in cesspools or thrown into the streets, and wells for drinking water were frequently contaminated by seepage from nearby cesspools. He found that the water supply was of inferior quality, and that street gutters ran with everything, including the washings from slaughterhouses. Cesspits were a great cause for concern, described thus: 'This is a pit or well ten to twelve feet deep, in some few cases lined with brick, but in most cases merely sunk into the earth. Upon this is placed the privy, and it is the common receptacle for various kinds of filth. In houses of the better class, this cesspool is deep and large, and covered up, and is emptied from time to time. In the cottages it is more frequently open, that is to say covered only by the privy house, and in one case, its contents were, at the time of my visit, overflowing into the yard.' The contents of cesspools seeped into neighbouring cellars and ground floors. George Clark inspected numerous premises for himself, and took the evidence – oral and written – from many inhabitants. He announced that a sewerage system should be constructed in Swindon, and an effective supply of water be obtained. He recommended that the Public Health Act be applied to Swindon, and that a local Board of Health should be set up there. Although the situation was dire, the Act was not adopted, and Swindon continued to operate in this ancient, insanitary way for several years more.

Sapphires, The This was a short-lived (1961-64), but very promising Swindon amateur rhythm band, which started up just as the traditional jazz revival was on the wane. Members of the band were Tom 'Trigger' Bradley (guitar and vocals), Geoff Exton (keyboards), Alan Minns (bass), Alan Warren (lead guitar), Dave Davies (drums 1962/63), Clive Bridgeman (drums 1964) and, variously, Keith Lewis or Neil 'Ned' Pike (rhythm guitar). The band rehearsed at 155 Clifton Street and played at the Locarno, and McIlroy's ballroom, where they supported several well-known national bands of the day, and at other halls around the town. These included The Moonrakers on Sunday lunchtime gigs. Had they chosen to take it, the potential for big breaks and a professional career was promised by performances that The Sapphires gave in Birmingham in 1963 and Liverpool in 1964. (See also Bradley, Thomas Frederick.)

Savoy Cinema The 1,775-seat Art Deco-style Savoy cinema opened on the site of some shops that had been demolished in Regent Street in 1937. The cinema was designed by the Scottish architect William Riddell Glen (1884-1950), who, in 1929, became the 'in-house' architect for Associated British Cinemas. Thereafter, he either designed new cinemas for them or adapted former theatres for showing films. He was occasionally called upon to remodel wonderful buildings designed only a few decades earlier by the great theatre designer Frank Matcham. The Savoy became the ABC (owned by Associated British Cinemas) in 1960 and was converted in 1974 to a three-screen venue. The ABC was acquired by Cannon in 1986, was so named from 1987, and closed in 1991 to become a theme bar. From this point in time, Swindon had no town centre cinema.

Saxon Swindon Archaeology in the Old Town market square, and a little to the east of it, has shown that in the 5th century, the Saxons took over the Romano-British hilltop site. Evidence has been found of a small residential development of wood-framed and plaster huts, and pottery has been recovered from the 6th and 7th centuries. The Anglo-Saxons also created land charters for apportioning their holdings around the settlement on the hill.

Schools in Swindon In 1764, a 'free school' was opened in Newport Street; it became a National School in 1811. Consequent upon the success of the free school, a number of questionable dame schools, charity schools, and doubtful fee-paying schools were opened in Swindon in the later 1700s. Some operated a parallel learning and earning system. By 1830, Ann Batt was running a school in Wood Street, probably from the same premises where her sister Louisa was a 'professor and teacher of music'. In 1833, the Government first grant-aided schools, and a Nonconformist school was opened for girls in 1835. William Morris records an early 18th-century school in a thatched cottage elsewhere in Newport Street, and this was taken over by Martha Large in 1830, when it was exclusively for girls. At the same time, there was another school adjoining the Bell & Shoulder of Mutton public house, and George Nourse's Classical and Commercial School for Young Gentlemen, advertised as a 'gent's boarding and day school', was in Prospect Place.

Ann Batt's school in Wood Street would later be run by Louisa Haines. Martha Jefferies had the Ladies' School in High Street; Catherine Nourse, wife of the young gentlemen's George, had added a ladies' school in Prospect Place. The premises beside the Bell & Shoulder of Mutton were, by the 1850s, in the hands of James Steger, who looked after the boys, and his wife Emma, who taught the girls. She was eventually to relocate to the Nourse's establishment in Prospect Place. There was a Ladies' Boarding School, run by Martha Tanner, in Victoria Street, whilst Ann and Jane Smith ran another for girls who attended daily. A day school was also attached, in the 1850s, to the Independent chapel in Newport Street.

In 1844, the first school was built in New Swindon. It was financed by the GWR, designed by George Gilbert Scott and W.B. Moffatt, and erected next to St Mark's churchyard. Its position served a dual purpose: slightly away from the better houses of the GWR village so that the children would not disturb the occupants, and next to the church for spiritual guidance.

Its first master was Alexander James Braid; his wife Jane Braid was the mistress, and the infants were looked after by Louisa Rette. The charges were 4d per week for juniors, 2d per week for infants; the fourth and subsequent children from the same parents were admitted free of charge. Although intended for the children of GWR employees, parents who had no connection with the railway could pay one shilling per week to have their offspring educated in the GWR school. These buildings were demolished in 1881.

In 1857, a separate GWR infants school was erected adjacent. This building, of rock-face rubble with ashlar quoins, remains in Church Place, although it ceased to be a schoolroom in 1879. Education at the GWR schools came under the management of a local committee in 1858, and was thereafter available for government inspection.

The Swindon Academy was opened by Revd R. Breeze in 1856, and the following year Mr & Mrs Steger opened a mixed school in Market Place. In Devizes Road, in 1858, Miss Cowell established a school for young ladies. Mr S. Snell opened his Swindon High School in 1859 and, in New Swindon in 1861, Miss Sykes began a school in Fleetway Terrace. Revd J.H. Snell's Classical & Commercial School opened in the Congregational church schoolroom in Victoria Street in 1866. A Wesleyan school opened in The Planks in 1867; George Nourse relocated his academy to Victoria Street in the same year, and the Misses Cowell took over the girls in his former Prospect Place premises, whilst Mrs Fentiman took over the boys. The 1870s saw the emergence of still more private schools: the Middle Class Boys' School; the Alexandria House Young Ladies' School; two private preparatory schools for little boys; Grosvenor House School in Victoria Street and, close by, The Middle Class Girls' Collegiate School.

The Elementary Education Act, 1870 made school attendance mandatory for children aged between five and fourteen. This could be done by voluntary means, but should there be any shortfall in available places, a local School Board was required to be established. This Board had the power to levy rates sufficient to build and operate the required number of schools. This is what happened in Swindon; College Street school was built, which, in conjunction with King William Street school, provided enough places to meet the requirements of the Act, for a while.

The King William Street school, built by Revd Henry George Bailey as a church school and which caused the National School in Newport Street to close and its pupils to be transferred, was opened in 1871. When College Street school was built by the GWR in 1873, there was no longer a need for the Company's school adjacent to St Mark's church. The College Street building was an imposing two-storey affair with two gabled wings and a four-bay central section, and was put up for its 'employees' infants of both sexes and older daughters'. It was demolished in 1961, and part of the rear of the faceless Parade shopping centre was put up in its place. A Catholic school was opened in Regent Street in 1875, and rebuilt in Groundwell Road in 1899 as Holy Rood Catholic school.

Swindon formed a School Board in 1877, under the Education Act, 1870. It first met, at 28 High Street, on 10 November 1877, and declared that henceforth 'all schools under the control of the Board shall be opened with the reading of the Bible, singing a hymn,

and prayer'. Sanford Street school went up in 1881, designed by Brightwen Binyon of Ipswich and built by D.C. Jones & Co. of Gloucester. The establishment of the School Board did not stop the private schools from proliferating, but it did encourage them to advertise the various examinations for which their pupils were being prepared, and the successes they had in them. In 1869, Samuel Snell took over the Classical & Commercial School relocated to 1 Lansdown Road, where he made much of his pupils'successes in the Oxford and Cambridge local examinations and the College of Preceptors examinations. Also in the late 1870s and 1880s, W. and F. Jenkins (and 'professors of French, Music, etc.') also prepared pupils at their Middle-Class Boys' School, Sandhill House, 17 Bath Road, for the same examinations as well as Civil Service examinations and Naval Engineering examinations.

At 26 Victoria Street, Mrs Sykes continued to prepare pupils at her Middle-Class Girls Collegiate School for 'competitive examinations'. Mrs and Miss Brown now had Alexandria House in Avenue Road, wherein was their Young Ladies' School until 1880, when they were succeeded by Miss Maculla, who relocated it to 4 Strathearne Villas, Devizes Road. The Misses H. and C. Cowell opened their Educational Establishment for Young Ladies at 3 Lansdown Road. The Misses Roby, together with a 'resident foreign governess and a Master for the Accomplishments' offered their Collegiate Classes for Young Ladies at 3 Gloucester Villas in Bath Road. At 16 Victoria Street, the Misses Doughty conducted their Grosvenor House School for Young Ladies, instructing them in 'music, French, Latin, drawing and other accomplishments pertaining to a finished

education'. They also had a Preparatory School for Little Boys on the same premises.

In 1900, the Old Swindon District Council and the New Swindon District Council amalgamated to form the Borough of Swindon and, under the Education Act, 1902, the new borough became the education authority. Swindon Education Committee was formed in 1903 and began at once to organise university lectures in the town. A branch of the Workers Educational Association was established in Swindon in 1908. Swindon schools were reorganised into primary and secondary schools in 1946, and several of their then existing infant departments were transferred to other wholly infant schools.

Swindon and district schools were opened as follows:
1836 National School, Newport Street (demolished 1962)
1845 GWR School, Bristol Street – boys, girls and infants
1857 GWR Infant School, Bristol Street
1871 King William Street School – boys, girls and infants (enlarged 1890)
1871 Holy Rood Catholic School
1873 College Street (enlarged 1896; demolished 1962)
1875 Stratton Education Centre
1875 Regent Street Catholic School – boys and girls (built 1860)
1878 Gorse Hill School – boys, girls and infants
1879 Gorse Hill – infants
1880 Even Swindon
1880 Queenstown – infants
1880 Gilbert's Hill – girls and infants
1881 Westcott – infants
1881 Sanford Street – boys
1885 Clifton Street – boys, girls and infants
1885 Queenstown – girls

1885 Wroughton Infant School

1890 Gilbert's Hill – girls

1891 Lethbridge Road – girls and boys

1891 Even Swindon – boys, girls and infants (enlarged 1894)

1892 St Mark's – girls and infants

1892 Westcott Place – boys and girls (enlarged 1896)

1892 Rodbourne Cheney School

1892 Beechcroft Infants School

1894 Grange Infants School (now Community School)

1894 Grange Junior School (now Community School)

1896 College Street – girls and infants

1897 Clarence Street – boys and girls

1899 Holy Rood Catholic School – infants and juniors

1900 Bishopstone CE Primary School

1900 Southfield Junior School

1903 Euclid Street (became a secondary school 1918)

1904 Higher Elementary School, Euclid Street

1904 Clarence Street – infants

1904 Jennings Street

1907 Ferndale Road – junior and senior

1913 Rodbourne Cheney Primary School

1926 Ferndale Road – infants

1927 Commonweal School, The Mall

1935 Pinehurst

1935 Kingsdown School

1938 Drove Road Infants School

1946 Drove Road – girls

1950 Headlands Grammar School

1955 St Luke's School

1956 Highworth Warneford School

1960 St Andrew's CE Primary School

1960 St Mary's Catholic Primary School

1960 South Marston CE Primary School

1962 Goddard Park Primary School

1962 Ruskin (formerly Upper Stratton) Junior School

1963 Holy Family Catholic Infant and Junior School

1964 Churchfields School

1964 Lawn Secondary School

1964 Park South Junior School

1964 Penhill South Junior School

1964 Westbourne Secondary (amalgamation of Westcott and Jennings Street schools)

1965 Lainesmead Primary School

1965 Moredon Senior High School

1965 Nythe Primary School

1965 Westrop Primary School

1967 The Ridgeway School, Wroughton

1969 Dorcan Technology College

1969 St Catherine's Catholic Primary School

1970 Wroughton Junior School

1972 Crowdy's Hill School

1972 Seven Fields Primary School

1975 Colebrook Infant School

1975 Colebrook Junior School

1975 Haydon Wick Primary School

1975 The Chalet School

1975 Westlea Primary School

1981 Oliver Tomkins CE Junior School

1982 Northview Primary School

1983 Hreod Parkway (amalgamation of Hreod Burna and Moredon S.H)

1983 Oakfield School (formerly Park Senior High)

1984 Oliver Tomkins CE Infant School

1984 New College (on site of Walcot and Richard Jefferies Schools)

1985 Brookfield Primary School

1985 Robert Le Kyng Primary School

1986 Greendown Community School

1991 Wanborough Primary School

1994 Tregoze Primary School, Hay Lane

1995 Haydonleigh Primary School

1998 Drove Primary School

1999 Abbey Meads Community Primary School

1999 Liden Primary School
1999 Mountford Manor Primary School
1999 Peatmoor Community Primary School
2000 Catherine Wayte Primary School
2000 Eldene Primary School
2000 Lethbridge Primary School
2000 Oaktree Nursery and Primary School
2003 Bridlewood Primary School
2004 St Francis School
2005 Lawn Primary School
2005 St Joseph's Catholic College (formerly school)
2006 Brimble Hill Primary School
2006 Even Swindon Primary School
2006 Moredon Primary and Nursery School
2006 Nova Hreod School
2006 Orchid Vale Primary School
2006 Red Oaks Primary School
2006 Uplands Secondary School
2007 Isambard Community School
2007 Millbrook Primary School
2007 Covingham Park Primary School
2008 Ferndown Community Primary School
2008 Toothill Primary School
2009 Oakhurst Community Primary School
2009 Shaw Ridge Primary School
2009 Swindon Academy (formerly Headlands GS)
2010 East Wichel Primary School
(See also National School.)

Seven Fields Nature Reserve Now bounded by the residential developments of Haydon Wick, Abbey Meads, Penhill and Pinehurst, this public area of unimproved grassland is owned by Swindon Borough Council. The local authority bought it during the development of the Penhill estate in the 1950s, but it then continued to be worked for its hay for more than thirty years. The area was declared an open space in 1984, was adopted for conservation by the local community four years later, and became a designated local nature reserve in 1995. Penhill Copse, to the north, covers three and a half acres and is the largest wooded area, although there are other smaller standings of trees and runs of hedges throughout the site, which is partly bisected by a small feeder stream. The seven fields are Spring Field, Long Meadow, Lark Meadow, Cemetery Field, Old Events Field, Half Moon Ground, and Furrow Field. Each area is rich in fauna and flora, and the overall management is in the hands of council rangers, with the assistance of the Seven Fields' Conservation Group.

Shakespeare Unit In 1945, the Swindon & District Theatre Guild was formed, and by 1947 it had twenty-six local amateur musical and dramatic societies under its umbrella. In that year, a group of amateur actors in Swindon performed a week's run of *A Midsummer Night's Dream*, with incidental music by Félix Mendelssohn-Bartholdy, at the Arts Centre in Regent Street. The scenery, designed by John Comben, was painted by students at the Swindon School of Art; costumes and wigs came from C.H. Fox of London; and pipe music was played by members of the High School recorder band. This was the first production by the Shakespeare Unit, an ancillary society allied to The Swindon & District Theatre Guild, performing under the aegis of the Borough of Swindon Libraries, Museum, Arts & Music Committee. Its secretary was Arthur W.J. Peck. The Unit's first seven annual productions raised money for the Mayor of Swindon's Community Fund.

The performances usually included music, some of which was especially written; the 1956 production of *King Lear*

included music by Louis Thresher (who composed for several of the productions), with lyrics by Swindon poet Paul Casimir; for *The Merchant of Venice* in 1963, Swindon tenor and reference librarian Keith Hardy wrote and sang, 'Tell me, where is fancy bred'; Justin Hayward accompanied 'Lady Mortimer's Song' in *Henry IV Part 1* in 1964; and for *Antony & Cleopatra* in 1966, H.S. Fairclough orchestrated the National Anthem from the earliest known source of the melody, and it was played by members of the Swindon Musical Society. Between 1956 and 1969, costumes for each play were provided by the Shakespeare Memorial Theatre/ Royal Shakespeare Theatre, Stratford-upon-Avon, augmented by the Swindon & District Theatre Guild's own wardrobe, and the Bristol Old Vic supplied the costumes between 1970 and 1974. The Shakespeare Unit mounted twenty-eight productions, known as the Annual Shakespearean Festival, finishing in 1974 with *Hamlet*. The Swindon & District Theatre Guild still runs the Harold Joliffe One-Act Play Festival, named after Swindon's great borough librarian, which takes place annually at the Arts Centre.

Shaw Ridge Cinema An out-of-town cinema, the seven-screen Metro-Goldwyn-Mayer multiplex, opened at Shaw Ridge, West Swindon in 1991. Just afterwards, seven years after the death of Diana Dors, film producer David Puttnam unveiled a statue of the actress, designed and created by sculptor John Clinch, adjacent to the MGM. This cinema was bought by the Virgin Cinema Group in 1995, and by UGC (founded in 1971 in France as Union General Cinematographique) in 1999. The Blackstone Group, an American private equity firm,

bought the cinema in 2004, joining Cine-UK, which had been formed by three venture capitalist organisations in 1996, to trade as Cineworld. This was its title from 2005.

Sheep sculpture, Marlborough Road The Old Town livestock market opened in 1887, a dual venture between Ambrose Lethbridge Goddard, the lord of the manor, who held the market rights, and the firm of auctioneers Dore, Smith & Radway. The last sale was held there in 1988, and the area is now partly residential, a roadway leading off through what was once the entrance into the sale yards. The point of entry is marked by a bronze of the old Wiltshire horned sheep, sculpted by Jon Buck, one-time artist-in-residence for the Borough of Thamesdown. (See also Looking to the Future sculpture.)

Ship Inn, Westcott Place During the 1840s and 1850s, Elizabeth Cave carried on the occupation of beer retailer from a house in Westcott Place, immediately to the north-west of which was a small terrace of cottages. The premises and the business were taken over briefly, c.1857, by James William Bannister, and acquired by George Smith in 1858, from when it was named 'The Ship'. He was followed between the mid-1870s and mid-1880s by John, and then George, Looms and, in 1875, by the wonderfully named John Churchward Porter Stancombe. The Ship as it currently presents is the result of a rebuild in the 1890s, when the public house was owned by the Cirencester Brewery and the landlord was Alfred Webb. Elizabeth Cave's original premises are extant; they are the next door property in Westcott Place. The rebuild was on the site of the cottages (demolished for the purpose) and some land adjacent to

the east (formerly gardens) then acquired from the Rolleston estate. The fact that its shape is determined by the triangular corner plot between Westcott Place and Birch Street means that the work must have been done no earlier than 1892, the date of the latter.

The hostelry is a narrow building of red brick with stone dressings, in two storeys with canted bow windows towards Faringdon Road Park. The initials of Cirencester Brewery Limited can still be seen in an octagonal brick plaque high in the gable on the south front. Webb relocated to The George, Eastcott Hill in 1898, and Walter John Groves took over for a short time following his departure. The building featured a winged dragon on its roof ridge, a fine and rare example of ornamental work by Bermantofts of Leeds, who made tiles and architectural ceramics. In the later years of the 20th century and the early years of the 21st, The Ship became known as an Irish pub, and latterly suffered from a poor reputation. It closed in 2006, acquired new owners Enterprise Inns, was completely refurbished, and reopened as The 12 Bar, dedicated to music and comedy. It closed in 2012. The premises are supposed to be haunted by several ghosts. (See also Swinford, Esther.)

Silto, Joseph (1911-2007) Joe Silto was the author of *The Railway Town* (1980) and *A Swindon History 1841-1901* (1981), which were privately published by him at 157 Faringdon Road. He researched and wrote them following his retirement in 1972 from the GWR Works in Swindon, where he had been employed as a marshalling inspector dealing with carriages and wagons and, latterly, a foreman in the factory transport department. Joe was the son of William Alfred ('Billy') Silto (1883-1959),

a one-time Barnsley footballer who joined Swindon Town in 1909 and played for them until he retired from the game in 1920, and went to work shovelling in the coal stage on the railway. William later became landlord of the Goddard Arms at Clyffe Pypard and, from 1937, of The Ship Inn, Faringdon Road, Swindon. In 1936, Joe was captain of the England table tennis team, and thereafter was much in demand for exhibition matches against some of the world's legendary table tennis players. He was also a cricketer of note, and a player with Swindon Cricket Club.

Joe married his wife Nella (née Crew) in 1940, and the family lived in rooms above The Ship. During the Second World War, Joe served in North Africa, Italy and Normandy. His wife died in 1953, the year the family left The Ship, and Joe never remarried. His son, William Silto (born 1948), has written *Of Stone and Steam: The Story of Swindon Railway Village* (Barracuda, 1989).

Silver Book, The In October 1968, the Swindon Expansion Project Joint Steering Committee published *Swindon A Study for Further Expansion*, called 'The Silver Book' because of the colour of its cover. The responsible committee was drawn from the Swindon Borough Council, Wiltshire County Council, and the Greater London Council, and their deliberations had come about following a proposal made in 1966 by the Minister of Housing & Local Government that they should consult on the further planned expansion of Swindon. This was to be done under the Town Development Act, 1952, and had at its core the proposition that Swindon might accommodate some 75,000 people from London by 1981. All of this came about following the Ministry of

Housing & Local Government's *South East Study*, published in 1964, which suggested a major population expansion in the Swindon area, and a further study carried out in 1965. This was commissioned of Llewelyn-Davies Weeks & Partners jointly by the Ministry, Swindon Borough Council, Wiltshire County Council, and Berkshire County Council (the Newbury area also having been earmarked for further expansion in the *South East Study*. The 1965 report was called *A New City*, which suggested that Swindon might take an additional 125,000 people by 1981, and would have a population of more than 400,000 by the end of the 20th century. The Minister of Housing & Local Government scaled this projection back to 75,000, and estimated a town of 250,000 people by the year 2000. (In the event, the figure was about 180,000.)

Skurray, Ernest Clement (1865-1940) From the 1850s, Francis Skurray was a corn factor in the town. In 1893, he built the five-storey Town Flour Mills beside the Wilts & Berks Canal, adjacent to the Whale Bridge in Princes Street. The business was then styled 'F. Skurray & Son'; the latter was Ernest Clement, by then also a corn dealer, who would later take over the mills, offices and outbuildings on the south side of the canal. The mills had their own wharf, where the corn was off-loaded from canal barges, and from where flour was taken away. They operated until 1924, when the buildings were substantially demolished, although traces of them remained until the mid-1960s.

Ernest thought that electricity had a bright future. In 1895, the town adopted the Swindon New Town Electric Lighting Order. He was chairman of the Electricity Committee, 1901-03, the first person to hold office, and was there when the generating station was built, in 1902, for Swindon's first electricity undertaking.

He also saw a bright future for motor transport. In 1899, Ernest bought his first motor car, thereafter combining the businesses of motor engineer and miller on the Whale Bridge site, and contracting for the purchase and supply of motor cars. He transferred the motor sales and repairs business to Thomas Deacon & Thomas Edmund Liddiard's Vale of the White Horse Repository site in Old Town in 1924 (which they first leased in 1875), accessed beside Manchester House in High Street. (The Princes Street premises remained a motor dealership, although in other hands, until 2005.)

This three-storey Georgian property, with double bow windows to the first two floors, had once been the residence of John Henry Harding Sheppard, brewer and extensive land and property owner in and about the town. Ernest Skurray converted the domestic rooms into offices, and made vehicle workshops out of the outbuildings at the rear. The street front was rebuilt in double-gabled, mock-Tudor in 1927. The street-level interior became the showroom for new cars, the gleaming vehicles displayed incongruously in a panelled and beamed drawing room setting. The firm was acquired in 1960 by Rank Hovis McDougall, the conglomerate of millers. The company remained here after Ernest's death, although the mock-Tudor frontage was taken down in 1967. Its replacement, a ghastly glass and concrete box typical of the time, was opened in 1971 by Joseph Rank, chairman of the owners. Three years later, Skurray's was added to the portfolio of motor franchises owned by Grose Holdings Limited. In 1984,

the business relocated to Drove Road, and in 1998 also set up at Hillmead, West Swindon. Skurray's left the Drove Road site in 2008, and the following year was acquired by motor trade professionals Nick Plevey and Nigel Harvey.

Smith family, butchers see King of Prussia Inn; Lower Eastcott Farm.

Spear, Walter J. (1885-1925) In 1913, Walter J. Spear set up The Picture House at 121 High Street, Wootton Bassett. At the time, he was a dairyman, living and working in Swindon. His father was a 'steam engine maker/fitter' in the GWR Works, and, prior to his own marriage, Walter had been living as a boarder at 40 Curtis Street, Swindon in the household of Francis Elms, a gas fitter and plumber for the GWR. Walter married Francis's daughter, Edith Frances Mary Elms, in April 1911. The couple afterwards lived at 37 Commercial Road, Swindon, which was where he established and maintained a dairy. Walter Spear was no longer the owner of The Picture House by 1920, and it had by then been renamed The Mascot Cinema. The dairyman died at his Commercial Road, Swindon address on 15 December 1925.

Spectrum Building, West Swindon Known locally as 'The Renault Building' because it was designed for car manufacturer Renault to use as its UK parts distribution centre, Sir Norman Foster's iconic steel (painted bright yellow) and glass building was erected 1980-82 at a cost of £8,266,400 and was opened in 1983. The main features are the twenty-seven tubular steel masts, each 16 metres high, carrying perforated steel beams that each support an area of corrugated steel roof decking. The structure is 288 metres long, 96 metres wide, and includes three hundred and sixty Macalloy tendons, the tie-rods that support the beams, and fork connections at either end. The building was designed as a huge single-storey warehouse, comprising twenty-four bays each 24 metres square, with a two- storey entrance, and office suite, training centre, restaurant and other service accommodation at one end; at its highest, it is 10 metres, and 7.5 metres at its lowest. Ove Arup & Partners were the constructional engineers, and it won several architectural awards. These include the *Financial Times* Architecture at Work Award, a Structural Steel Award, and a Civic Trust Award, all in 1984, and the Constructa Prize for Industrial Architecture in Europe, 1986. Renault suspended four car frames in the lobby area and used the building as a backdrop to some of its publicity; in 1984, Roger Moore as 007 filmed scenes there from the James Bond movie 'A View To A Kill'. In 2001, Renault relocated, selling the building to the Burford Group in 2003. Since then, it has been variously occupied, and has sometimes been remodelled internally to suit the needs of each occupant, as Foster's original flexible design was intended to facilitate.

Square House, Old Town The distinguished building in Flemish bond that stands on the north side of the former market square in Old Swindon was built of local bricks in the mid-18th century. It is locally known as the 'King's Press', after a business that once occupied it, and which name was written along the flat string course on the southern elevation. Formerly it was called 'Square House'. The building is of two storeys with attic and dormers, and has three

bays, of which the central section is forward of those that flank it. The whole façade is consolidated by a cornice of dentil moulding. The building is owned by a London investment company; it was remodelled internally in 1984, since when it has lost any original features or evidence of previous use, and is leased to Lloyds TSB, which formerly used it as office accommodation.

Stanier, William Arthur (1876-1965) W.A. Stanier was the grandson of Thomas Stanier, a japanner in Wolverhampton where his son, William Henry Stanier (1849-1924), was born. The latter came to Swindon with his family in the early 1870s, settled in 4 Church Place, and William Henry was employed as Stores Superintendent at the Great Western Railway Works. He became the town's mayor in 1907, and Stanier Street was named after him. Latterly, he lived at 97 Bath Road.

His first son, William Arthur, was born in the railway village. He joined the Company c.1897, by which time the family were living at Oakfield, Bath Road, had a spell in the drawing office, and in 1901 was described as 'engine mechanical inspector'. At that time, the family had moved to Marlow House (one of a pair – with nearby Station House – of Jacobean-style, gabled villas built north of the line by the railway company to house senior management; both were later demolished about 1914 to facilitate an extension to the wagon works). W.A. Stanier spent some time in London from 1904, and returned to Swindon as Assistant Works Manager in 1912; in 1920, he was promoted to Works Manager. He was particularly popular for the ways in which he supported the social life in the town throughout difficult times in the 1920s. In

1931, he became Chief Mechanical Engineer for the London Midland & Scottish Railway, and was responsible for several locomotive designs. He was knighted in 1943.

Station Site Mural, Old Town In 1986, artist Les Holland (1908-2005), then living at Purton, painted a mural commemorating the former Midland & South West Junction Railway on the site of the company's Swindon Town Station, off Newport Street. The mural was put up alongside what is now a cycleway, beside the small industrial estate that now occupies the position of the station in Old Town and the track.

Steam Railway Museum The GWR Railway Museum in Faringdon Road closed in 2000, and its contents were transferred to the newly created Steam Museum of the GWR, in historic buildings on part of the former railway Works site. This museum actually opened on 13 June 2000, but was officially opened on 27 June by Prince Charles. The bulk of Steam was created out of the former 'R' shop in the locomotive works. 'R' shop was opened in 1846 in an area that had been covered to house fitters, turners, and machine men and which was extended in 1864. It was situated between Brunel's original engine house of 1843 (which, by 1847, was completing one engine per week), a wall of which remains, and the machine and fitting shop (part of four sections that comprised 'A' shop) that was erected in 1846, and incorporated a blacksmiths' shop of the same date. 'R' shop was gradually extended in the 1870s and, when complete, covered 3,694 square yards. The original cast-iron columns are still in place. The conversion was carried out with the participation of English Heritage and the Royal Commission for Historic Monuments.

Stevens, Frederick Charles (1934-2010) Fred Stevens, the originator and owner of the locally famous, black- and orange-liveried Collectors Corner at 227 Kingshill, was a major supplier of local history books, documents, ephemera, and artefacts to the historians of Swindon. He also supplied material to the local history archives at the central library, and to the Swindon museum. During the 1990s, he wrote a weekly column on aspects of the town's history for the Swindon *Evening Advertiser*, illustrating it with postcards, photographs, and items from the collections in his shop. He also had a monthly Saturday morning slot on BBC Wiltshire Radio, talking about Swindon's history, and answering questions from listeners. It was during this period that he used his radio programme in the ultimately successful cause to save Swindon's museum from closure; he organised a petition on air, and auctioned the signatures of Swindon Town football players who supported it.

Fred Stevens was born in London Road, Whitechapel. In 1959, he was working for the Parks Department of Camberwell Borough Council and living in south London with a pregnant wife, in an upstairs flat that had no running water. Hoping for something better, he wrote to ten different new town councils asking for a job in their parks department, with accommodation; Swindon offered him one as a tractor driver, and gave him a council house in Park North. He later bought his own house in Lansdown Road. One day, he parked his tractor outside the offices of the Bristol Omnibus Company in Regent Circus, and went in covered in mud and wearing his Wellington boots, to see whether the Company had any vacancies. He was interviewed on the spot, and offered a job on the buses. He spent two years taking fares, then two years as a driver (the minimum necessary to ensure that the Company, which taught its employees how to drive buses, did not claim the cost back from drivers who then left their service). In 1966, he joined Rimes Coaches in Princes Street, and was the first of their drivers to take a party abroad. He should have dropped off his charges at Gatwick airport and waited for their return; but in those less stringent times, he 'chatted up one of the air hostesses, and she let me on to the plane with the rest of the party!'.

Collectors Corner developed out of his own love of collecting, mostly stamps and coins, then postcards and cigarette cards. Time off in other towns enabled him to go around their antique shops, and this led him to organise the first antiques fair to be held in Swindon's town hall, and to build up a spare-time ephemera and bric-a-brac business. At one time, he had a stock of some 15,000 postcards, and for twenty years he had a stall at antiques fairs all over the country. Eventually, he sold his home in Lansdown Road, and bought outright the − by then derelict − former car parts shop on Kingshill. Whilst he still worked for the Bristol Omnibus Company, he opened Collectors Corner daily between 2 p.m. and 6 p.m., and all day on Sundays. He left the buses rather than work under their planned, scheduled rostering system, which would have played havoc with his opening times. He placed a small advertisement in the *Evening Advertiser*, and opened Collectors Corner on 1 April 1985, when 200 people turned up. Fred Steven's corner shop, always an extension of his own life-long interests, was a cornucopia of badges, books, buttons, coins, cigarette cards, ephemera, postcards, recorded music and toys.

Strange, Thomas (1795-1883) In 1807, the draper James Strange, and the grocer Richard Strange took on two partners and established the bank Strange, Garrett, Strange & Cook. In 1822, James's son Thomas married Mary Slark (b. Chelvey, Bucks, 1794). When James died in 1826, Thomas took over his drapery business in High Street, immediately to the north of the Goddard family's driveway, and also became a partner in the bank, thereafter called Thomas & Richard Strange & Co. He and Mary had four children: Edward, b.1826; Louisa, b.1829; Sarah, b.1830; and William, b.1837. Thomas and Richard's interest in the bank continued until 1842, when their bank was taken over by the County of Gloucestershire Banking Company, and Thomas, who had hitherto described himself as a 'banker and draper' (also undertaker, and proprietor of the ready-made clothes warehouse) became 'draper and fund-holder'. By 1861, the family and their two servants were living at Springhill Villa, Bath Road.

Stredder, (Henry) Robert (b.1941) Between 1976 and 1991, Robert Stredder was a member of the Groundwell Farm community in Swindon. He also established the annual London to Brighton cycle race, and was at one time Robbo the clown of Zippo's Circus. Sir Joseph Paxton, famed landscape architect and designer of the Crystal Palace, was his great-great-uncle.

Robert Stredder was born at Shipston-on-Stour, Warwickshire, the son of a chartered accountant. His grandfather had a farm, and young Robert 'had a Laurie Lee-style upbringing'. He worked on local farms and became a member of Ilminster Young Farmers, near Chipping Campden. Educated at Malvern College, he later studied Law at Birmingham University (but did not want to become a lawyer), trained as a teacher, and became involved in drama and the theatre. During the 1960s, he taught English and drama in the East End of London, and began busking and performing street theatre in Covent Garden, and acting in other performance venues.

In the mid-1970s, he was involved with Action Space in London, a group that made inflatable play structures and facilitated adventure play and drama with children. He relocated to Wales, where he wrote poetry, before joining the Action Space community that had recently been set up at Groundwell, and which used the property as a base for their activities locally and in inner cities around the country. During this period, he specialised in creative events that featured family-oriented improvised theatre. As 'advance publicity clown' for Zippo's Circus in the 1990s, Robert toured primary schools. As a long-distance cyclist, he twice completed rides between Land's End and John O' Groats, and cycled between London and Venice. Forty people turned up for the first London to Brighton bike ride, which he organised from Groundwell Farm in 1976 (currently some 30,000 cyclists take part).

Street Cleaning, Early Before it was taken over by the local authority, the task of keeping the streets of Swindon clean fell to individuals. The right to deal in 'scrapings and parings', as the potentially profitable excreta was called, was bid for annually by lot during sales that were held on 1 June, usually at the Goddard Arms hotel. In 1846, for example, cleaning the streets of Old Swindon, and the area between the town on the hill and Wootton Bassett, was contested

under the following lots:

1. From Swindon to the top of Kingshill.
2. From thence to the (Wilts & Berks) Canal.
3. From thence to the handpost at Mannington.
4. From thence to the brow of the Hill at Whitehill.
5. From thence to the Lodge Gate.
6. From thence to the west corner of Agbourn Coppice.
7. From thence to the fourth Mile-stone.
8. From thence to the Gate, in the occupation of Ann Rudler.
9. From thence to the stream of water crossing the road by William Watts's.
10. From thence to the Turnpike Gate.
11. From thence to the borough of Wootton Bassett.

SWINDON PARISH ROAD

12. From Mr Blackford's Corner to the Wharf Bridge.
13. The scraping and sweeping of all the streets in the Town of Swindon.

The purchaser of Lot 13 will be required to remove the sweepings of every Thursday and Saturday, and at any other time the Surveyor may direct.

Sturrock, Archibald (1816-1909)
Born in Dundee, where his father John was a banker, Archibald Sturrock became sufficiently friendly with Daniel Gooch to be invited to join him, at the age of twenty-four, in the London offices of the Great Western Railway Company. In the early 1840s, Sturrock was re-deployed to Swindon, taking charge of the railway workshops there and eventually living in a large custom-built house between High Street (later named Emlyn Square) and London Street. This building was eventually demolished to make way for the carriage and wagon works. From 1843, Sturrock was the superintendent (or manager) of the Swindon locomotive Works, and he was living in the town when, on 30 January 1845 in St Marylebone, London, he married Caroline Sophia Fullerton, who was born (in 1820) in Madras, where her father Charles was employed by the East India Company. It was during Sturrock's incumbency as the first manager of the Swindon Works that a series of recessions in the latter half of the 1840s made it necessary for him to reduce the workforce, in particular that of 1847 when two-thirds of the men had to be dismissed. The couple's first two children, Caroline and Gordon, were born in 1848 and 1850 respectively in the town. In 1850, the family left Swindon in order for Sturrock to take up a position with the Great Northern Railway. They set up home in Peterborough with Caroline's widowed mother Sophia and three servants, before removing to Doncaster where, in 1852, Caroline's death was associated with the birth of their second daughter, Georgina. Archibald Sturrock died in Chelsea, London, at the age of ninety-two.

Swindon Advertiser When it was launched by William Morris on 6 February 1854, the four-page, large format *Swindon Advertiser and Monthly Record* – printed on a hand press – was the country's first penny paper. To begin with, it was published monthly to avoid the stamp duty then payable on newspapers that were issued more frequently than every twenty-eight days. When these restrictions were relaxed in 1855, Morris brought out a weekly edition of his paper, then renamed the *Swindon Advertiser & North Wilts Chronicle*. Following its founder's death in 1891, the *Swindon Advertiser* passed into the hands of Morris's sons, Frank, Samuel and William

Edwin, who had each worked in the business for some time. In 1906, it became the *Swindon Evening Advertiser*, and remained in the family until 1920 when the business was acquired by Sir Charles Starmer, for which purpose he established Swindon Press. Until 1925, when news stories took their place, the front page of the paper was devoted to advertisements. In 1995, the *Advertiser* changed from broadsheet to tabloid format, and in 2005 the name changed from *Evening Advertiser* to *Swindon Advertiser*. (See also Morris, William.)

Swindon & Cricklade Railway This standard-gauge heritage steam railway runs over part of the single track bed of the former Midland & South West Junction Railway; the 2½-mile (in 2011) section it currently occupies north of Swindon was opened in 1883 and closed to passenger traffic in 1961. The S&CR Society was formed in 1978, and has since restored the line between the former Blunsdon Station, which is now its main visitor centre, and Hayes Knoll Station to the north, where it has its locomotive sheds. In 2011, the Society opened the line running south of Blunsdon Station as far as a new station at the Mouldon Hill Country Park, part of the Great Western Community Forest area, and also a section of half a mile north of Hayes Knoll station towards Cricklade. The future intention is to progress the line to Cricklade in one direction, and to create a link, via a proposed station at Sparcells, with the mainline at Swindon. All work is carried out by volunteers, including restoration of the steam and diesel locomotives, and the collection of historic carriages and wagons. Much of the railway's income is derived from its visitors and the programme of locomotive-driving tuition and special events.

Swindon & District Monthly Review The first issue of this short-lived monthly publication came out in November 1960, with an introduction by the then mayor, Elsie Millin. This explained that the magazine was the idea of 'a group of Swindon men', and its objective was to provide a publication that would appeal to all sections of the community. The publication's offices were at 41 Havelock Street, where, from 1962, the same editor and his secretary also ran its sister publication, the Wiltshire Courier. In its inaugural editorial, those 'Swindon men' said of the Swindon & District Monthly Review that 'while much has been written about the old folk, we plan to make them our special interest'. Hedging its bets, it would 'also have its educational value for the younger generation'. In fact, there was little of either; it was topical in its news, comment and letters; it had, for its first few years, an excellent monthly article on jazz and jazz bands written by Tony Bowd, the secretary of the Swindon Chinese Jazz Club; and it leant heavily towards the visual and performing arts. Some of the general pieces, and a number of biographical articles, were contributed by Mark Child, then a librarian at Swindon Central Library. R.J. Blackmore wrote on aspects of the town's history. The last issue was dated December 1965.

Swindon & Highworth Railway Five miles of track were laid between 1879 and 1881 to connect Swindon station with Highworth. The developers were the Swindon & Highworth Light Railway Company, founded in 1872 for the purpose, although the line was taken over by the Great Western Railway in 1882. It was known locally as 'the bunky line'. There were stations at Stratton St Margaret, South Marston, Stanton

Fitzwarren and Hannington. The line was opened to passengers in 1883 but declined during the 1920s. Goods went out along it from Swindon, but little came back, and it was probably at its most useful supplying commodities for some of the engineering works along its length, particularly Vickers-Armstrong at South Marston in the 1940s. The line was officially closed in 1953, although it continued to operate early morning and late afternoon workmen's trains until 1962. Freight stopped in 1965. At Stratton, the station was built immediately to the west of, and below, a particularly steep hump-backed bridge, of which nothing now remains, that carried the main road over the line. GWR employees who lived out of town could order their allocation of company-supplied coal and wood from the ticket office at Stratton station.

Swindon Business News The first issue, an initiative by Lorne Barling, who edited SBN until his retirement in 2010, was published in October 1982. Barling had previously worked for the *Financial Times*. The offices are in Wood Street, and the editorship was taken over, in 2010, by Robert Buckland, whose experience in journalism had been with the *Swindon Advertiser* and the *Western Daily Press*.

Swindon Chinese Jazz Club Between the 1920s and the 1950s, jazz was rarely heard in Swindon. It was confined to brief improvised sections inserted into the sweeter music played by the numerous amateur and semi-professional dance bands that operated in public halls around the town. The 'Trad Jazz' boom of the 1950s changed all that. This scene was opened up in Swindon when John Cole and the Ray River Jazz Band

held weekly sessions on Sunday evenings at the Swindon Corporation Transport Social Club, held in the loft above Rimes' Garage in Princes Street. The jazz club secretary in the late 1950s was Anthony John ('Tony') Bowd, an analytical chemist at AERE Harwell. His paternal grandfather had been station master at the Old Town station on the Midland and South Western Junction Railway at the beginning of the 20th century. Tony was a keen trad jazz fan, and this association enabled him to meet many of the named jazz bands of the day when his club also presented them at The Majestic Ballroom (the covered-up swimming baths) and the Locarno in Old Town. Jazz in Swindon was about to become less ad hoc.

In September 1960, the inexplicably named Swindon Chinese Jazz Club opened in McIlroy's ballroom, Regent Street, with Mickey Ashman's Ragtime Jazz Band on the stage. The club was owned by the very eccentric Buonaventura Manzi, self-styled 'Uncle Bonny', who lived in Surrey and drove around in an ancient London taxicab. He also ran the Oriental Jazz Club in Newbury, and the San Pan Jazz Club in Chertsey. Part of Uncle Bonny's dress consisted of a straw boater and a bow tie. He justified the oriental title by annotating the club's publicity literature, and prefacing his interval notices of forthcoming events in Swindon, with the words, 'Chop Chop, Velly Good'. Tony Bowd, then twenty-eight-years-old, got the job of club manager on the recommendation of his friend Dave Backhouse, who knew Manzi through the Cana Variety Agency. Tony's sisters Patricia and Eileen were the cashiers for the Swindon enterprise.

The venue inside McIlroy's was situated next to the famous store's bedding department, and operated each Thursday

evening, 8 p.m. to 11 p.m. McIlroy's always had two members of staff on duty during the club evenings. These were the night security man, and the catering manager, whose glass-fronted office was in the kitchen next to the staff rest room, which doubled as the band room. The emergency fire exit was through the kitchen to an outside staircase.

The club brought many of the named semi-professional and professional traditional jazz bands of the day to Swindon, most of them booked through the Lyn Dutton Agency. When The Temperance Seven came in 1961, it was the week after their first single *You're Driving Me Crazy* was released, and had shot to number one in the pop charts. The attendance was the largest in the history of the club. By the end of 1962, the club had ceased to be profitable. In the spring of 1963, Manzi gave it up and it was taken on by John Smith, who had been running a jazz club in Oxford. It finally closed, with a concert by Kenny Ball's Jazzmen, in July 1963.

'Swindon Disease' Because so many former Swindon railway workers presented with epithelioid mesothelioma, an asbestos-related cancer, during the first decade of the 21st century (although the problem had been acknowledged since the 1980s), the condition was colloquially named the 'Swindon disease'. Asbestos was widely used in the Works, and many of those who handled the substance or were exposed to it did not use face masks. Victims have alleged that sacks of blue asbestos lay around where the substance was used, that it was used as a spray for insulating purposes, and that workers might sometimes 'play' with balls of the 'putty-like' substance. They cite times in the 1950s and 1960s before the potentially devastating effects of asbestos were known.

Occasionally, specks of ingested asbestos lodged in the lungs of some workers who then went on to developed the disease over a long period of time: typically twenty to fifty years. It allegedly also affected wives of railway workers, apparently as a result of handling their husbands' contaminated clothing. Mesothelioma was preceded by pleural plaques, an early indication of adverse exposure to asbestos, although this was not necessarily a sure sign that the disease would develop. The disease came to public notice in Swindon from about 2005, followed by a series of successful law suits instigated by families of some of the victims. These claimed that even when the danger of exposure to asbestos was known, this was denied or ignored, and victims claimed they were not given protective clothing, masks, or information on safe handling. In 2003, a mesothelioma memorial garden was established in Queen's Park, in memory of Swindon victims of the disease. It was centred around an inscribed sarsen stone, and was opened by the mayor, Stan Pajak.

Swindon Echo Politician, journalist and newspaper proprietor, Woodrow Wyatt (1918-97) owned a newspaper group (Woodrow Wyatt Newspapers) that mounted the only serious competition to the *Evening Advertiser* and the *Wiltshire Gazette & Herald*. This was the short-lived, weekly *Swindon Echo*, published in tabloid format. Its great appeal was the colour process by which it was printed at Banbury (soon after Wyatt had taken over the *Banbury Guardian* and introduced the colour process there), and it was published from 1962 to 1966.

Swindon Heritage The first issue of the colour quarterly history magazine *Swindon*

Heritage was published in January 2013. Its headings were set in Gill Sans, and it had eighty pages, of which sixteen were advertising. The idea for *Swindon Heritage* came from Mark Sutton (the author of the 2006 book *Tell Them of Us: Swindon War Dead*) who was its executive editor, and Frances Bevan, (historian, journalist, and the compiler of the website *Swindon in the Past Lane*). The magazine's editor, also responsible for design and layout, was Graham Carter (researcher, journalist, and the compiler of *Chronicle of Swindon*, the *Swindon Advertiser's* history of the town, published in 2006). Funding for the magazine's production costs was facilitated by the Mechanics' Institution Trust. (See also Chronicle of Swindon.)

Swindon Festival of Literature

The first Swindon Festival of Literature was founded and organised by Matt Holland of Lower Shaw Farm, West Swindon, and was held 6-14 May 1994. Events took place at the town's Link Centre, Town Hall, Arts Centre, and at Lower Shaw Farm. Afterwards, Matt continued to organise the Festival as an annual event.

The catalyst for what rapidly became an important and successful programme in the town's literary calendar was a decision taken by Swindon Chamber of Commerce in 1993 to mark its centenary in some way. The Chamber's then executive director, Peter Stratford, employed a London-based firm of consultants, Gunner Brothers, to determine how this might be done, and at the same time asked its members for ideas. The consultancy recommended a series of six disparate events, each with a 'celebratory feel', and these were held, one per month, in halls and hotels around the town. One of the Chamber's members, Dominic Winter of Dominic Winter Book Auctions, suggested 'something bookish'. The idea was accepted in principle by the Chamber, but was not developed by them. They may have been persuaded by the widely quoted but apocryphal notion that 'Swindon is a cultural desert', although no-one had ever determined whether this, if true, was through lack of desire or lack of opportunity.

A mutual friend put Winter in touch with Matt Holland of Lower Shaw Farm, who had run reading groups at Swindon College, organised poetry groups, and held writing workshops at Lower Shaw Farm. He presented the Swindon Chamber with a proposal for a five-day celebration of books and writing. Stratford declared himself to be 'gobsmacked' by the proposed line-up, and was sufficiently impressed by the concept to finance the first venture. The dramatis personae included Michael Foot, one-time leader of the Labour Party who had recently retired from politics, and who spoke about political satirists. Clive Ponting – the former senior civil servant who less than a decade before had been involved in a landmark case that had called into question the validity of aspects of the Official Secrets Act – had just published *Churchill*, a reappraisal of the wartime leader. Fiona Pitt-Kethley had much to say on the subject of sex in prose and poetry allied to her new book, *The Literary Companion to Sex*. There was also Professor Stanley Wells, the greatest contemporary authority on Shakespeare and his works. The response to all of this was a vindication of Matt Holland's belief in the project; the people of Swindon 'came out of the woodwork' in support of the venture. The first Swindon Festival of Literature was a success, and there were immediate calls from

newly converted Festival followers for the event to be repeated.

Despite all the interest in the first festival, Swindon Chamber of Commerce declined to give financial support to the venture in 1995, saying that it 'had not quite fitted our client profile'. Swindon Borough Council's Arts Services were approached, but were reluctant to support the Festival, saying that 'literature was too long a word for Swindon'. However, the project found favour with David Allen, then Head of Swindon Borough Library Services, who felt that the library should be involved, although it would not be able to provide any funding. This led to co-operation in kind by the Borough Council, which provided venues free of the usual hire charge. Dominic Winter Book Auctions, Holland Handling scrap metal dealers, and Lower Shaw Farm financed the 1995 Festival, and all three have stayed loyal to the present day, continuing to offer support in cash and in kind. When, by the turn of the century, it was clear that the Festival had become a much-enjoyed fixture and increasingly successful year-on-year, Swindon Borough Council gave a grant to part-fund the annual event, and continued to offer the Festival's main venue, the Arts Centre, on favourable terms. Grants received from Arts Council England, and from other sources, also help to fund the event. (See also Chamber of Commerce; Lower Shaw Farm.)

Swindon Music Festival An annual event, the Festival began in 1909 when six choirs competed in front of one adjudicator in the Mechanics' Institution building. The event resulted from a suggestion by Reginald George Cripps. Over the years, many classes were introduced, typically dance, choral, instrumental, piano, opera, verse and elocution. At its height, there were more than 1,500 entries, requiring up to ten adjudicators. Until the Playhouse theatre at the Mechanics' Institute closed in 1976, it was the major venue for the events, although several others were also used around the town. Today, the festival is a registered charity and devolves on the Arts Centre in Devizes Road.

Swindon Musical Society The Swindon Musical Society originated in the 1920s as the Swindon Choral Society, comprising an orchestra and chorus. It changed its name in 1947 when, as the Swindon Musical Society, it performed *Mlada* by Rimsky-Korsakov at the Empire Theatre. Between *Mlada* and the time the society ceased to operate in 1955, it staged nine more productions at the Empire: *Hugh the Drover* by Vaughan Williams in 1948; *Sadko* by Rimsky-Korsakov in 1949; Bizet's *Carmen*, and *The Mikado* by Gilbert & Sullivan in 1950; Stanford's *The Travelling Companion* in 1951; *Goyescas* by Granados, and Weill's *Down in the Valley* in 1952; *The Snow Maiden* by Rimsky-Korskov in 1953; and Massanet's *Cinderella* in 1954.

During this period, the Swindon Musical Society's chorus rehearsed in the Drove Road school's hall, and its gymnasium was taken over by the dancers. The soloists, chorus, dancers and orchestra came together for the first time in each case just two days before the show was scheduled to open at the Empire. Alterations to the routines were commonly made at the very last moment, when everyone got together. The audience on the opening night (Monday) was always made up of children from various schools, accompanied by their teachers, and this was regarded as the final dress rehearsal.

Thereafter, the Society played the week to packed houses, and usually to the highest praise, even by critics from London.

Swindon Opera In 1960, Swindon reference librarian Keith Hardy, a talented tenor, was the major force in establishing Swindon Opera. His fellow founders were Ivor Jones, a professional bass singer; the one-time professional opera singer Arthur Carron (real name Arthur Cox, an accountant by profession); one of Carron's pupils, Colin Ockwell; and the singer and singing teacher Vera Bennett. The company's opening performance was *The Beggar's Opera*, followed up in 1961 by *Die Fledermaus* (which the company was to produce four times over the years). Swindon Opera performed at the Arts Centre, staged three productions at The Playhouse in the Mechanics' Institute, Emlyn Square, and then relocated to the Wyvern Theatre. Despite the high quality of its productions, the Wyvern Theatre became too expensive as a venue; the company was caught in the trap of having to charge seat prices that Swindon opera-goers found unattractive, and thereby failing to obtain sufficiently large audiences to be profitable. Following the failure of *The Merry Widow* in 1996, Swindon Opera thereafter mounted its productions at the Ellendune Hall, Wroughton, also putting on a very successful 'Opera by Candlelight' and dinner event. The last of the annual productions was *Orpheus in the Underworld*, staged in 2002; this was followed by *The Magic Flute* in 2006. Two years later, as the group approached its fiftieth year, its members mounted a fund-raising campaign that enabled it to stage *Carmen* for two nights, and to full houses, at the Wyvern Theatre. It was to be the last production by

Swindon Opera, which was dissolved at an extraordinary general meeting in July 2010, and the relatively small credit balance was donated to the Prospect Foundation, Swindon's local charity.

Swindon Review, The In 1945, the Libraries, Museums, Arts & Music Committee of the Swindon Town Council launched a slim periodical, *The Swindon Review*, under the general editorship of the Borough Librarian. Being a local authority enterprise, it had to have stated, lofty objectives. These were: 'To offer to the occasional poet, essayist or story writer the chance to submit his work to local readers. Not so much to make a factual record of the art movements in the town, as to capture some of the spirit that inspires them. To preserve for our keen satisfaction tokens of friendship with writers with much more than local reputation; writers whose names are nationwide in fame but who, in the belief of the work being pursued in Swindon, is deserving of encouragement, have given us the articles that add so much distinction to these pages.' It carried advertising from the beginning. Two issues were published in the first year, thereafter more or less annually; the page size was reduced from issue 6; and the final issue, number 10, came out in 1958. Several of its regular contributors of poetry and literary prose were Swindon library staff. James Swift was the borough librarian, 1942-46; Hilda J. ('Noddy') Nockolds was the children's librarian, who also wrote poetry; and Paul Casimir was the reference librarian – a successful published poet and champion of Richard Jefferies, who wrote '*Richard Jefferies and Other Writers*' in 1956. Other local poets contributed; Norman G. Liddiard's work was to appear regularly,

as was that of Marguerite Johansen Dean, who became a winner of the W. Ibberson Jones Trophy for Poetry. There was illustrative material from Hubert Cook and Harold Dearden, and examples of the work of sculptor Carleton Attwood.

Swindon Society, The Formed in 1972, The Swindon Society was set up to 'further the interests of Swindon, its surroundings, and its history' and to make slide copies of historic photographs about the town. In 2013, it had 153 members. Over the years, it amassed a considerable number of historic photographs, currently holding over 15,000 images. Some of these have been published in its fine *Swindon In Old Photographs* series of books, which include extended picture captions. All were published by Alan Sutton Limited, the first in collaboration with Wiltshire County Council Libraries and Museums Service. The first selection came out in 1988; thereafter, the second selection in 1989; third selection, 1991; fourth selection, 1993; fifth selection, 1995; and sixth selection, 1998. *The Swindon Album* is an extension of this series, and some of the pictures were also reprinted in *Swindon* in Sutton's Britain in Old Photographs series. In 2000, the Society published *A Century of Swindon*. The Society has also published videos on the history of the town. Members use the Society's slides to give talks, and the organisation does an amount of charity fundraising.

Swindon Tile & Pottery Works see Turner, Thomas.

Swindon Town Club In 1884, a private social club was formed in Swindon for businessmen and other professional gentlemen. The Swindon Town Club was established with offices at Fairview, Bath Road (then still known as 'The Sands'), which it leased from the Toomer family, who lived across the road in Apsley House. The Club's founder-president was Captain Cornwallis Wykeham-Martin. It was incorporated under the Companies' Acts with five hundred available shares, the nine inaugural shareholders being almost entirely the main, and most prosperous, businessmen of Old Town at the time. This was an attempt by them to maintain exclusivity, and preserve the kind of dignity that they felt to be lacking in the railway town that had been built immediately to the north. Bath Road was a highly desirable address in which to locate the venture. Soon, the original shareholders were joined by a flurry of like-minded others, of similar social or business status, again almost entirely from Old Town. The social and drinking club was developed at 59 Bath Road, in premises that had been designed by W.H. Read, and built in 1893. All subscribers paid an entrance fee of one guinea. Officials of the club who lived on site included a steward and stewardess, and a ball-marker. Members could meet, eat, read, smoke, and play cards or billiards, and some great dinners were held in the dining room. Mostly, the club continued to operate in a low-key fashion, largely financially dependent on the amount of alcohol bought over the bar. Some years were financially successful, and others were not. In the early 1930s, the club closed, only to reappear in 1933 with a sprinkling of the old order on its committee, and an infusion of new blood. The club's longest-serving steward, and coincidentally the only female one in its history, was Ellie Choulles, who served 1972-87. The Swindon Town Club was more or less at an end by 1992. Then,

the premises were bought by a restaurateur from Scotland who refurbished the place with a view to continuing as a social club. It lingered on, unprofitably, for the next four years. In 1996, 59 Bath Road was bought by Peter Southerden, who opened it as a veterinary surgery the following year.

Swindon Town Football Club In 1881, the Old Swindon Cricket Club played a game of football against a team put up by St Mark's Young Men's Friendly Society. Immediately afterwards, Revd William Pitt suggested that the two sides should amalgamate and become an amateur football club. This they did very successfully, and were regular holders of the Wilts Cup. To begin with, the club's colours were black and white, then black and red. They played at various unsuitable fields around the town, before establishing themselves at The Croft in 1884, where they played in green shirts, and changed at the Fountain public house in Devizes Road. As soon as they went to The Croft, they began to engage professional players. They were founder members of the Southern League Division One in 1894, when their headquarters were at the Eagle Tavern, Regent Street, run by H.W. Thomas, who claimed that the football results were received there 'by the telegraphic machine'. The club relocated to the County Ground in 1896. In 1901, their shirt colour was changed to maroon; from the following season, the lighter red was introduced, which has since continued. Between 1908 and the start of the First World War, the team was successful in the league, twice winning the Southern League Championship, and had good runs in cup competitions. In 1920, the club was one of the founder members of the Football League Division Three (South). The team played in

that Division until it gained promotion to Division Two for the first time at the end of the 1962-3 season. The following season, it gained a record for a newly promoted club, in being undefeated in its first nine games; but the league success was not to last. Swindon Town Football Club won the Football League Cup Final at Wembley in 1969, and the Anglo-Italian Cup in 1970. In 1990, the team won promotion to League Division One, but the club admitted thirty-six breaches of League rules and were instead demoted two divisions by the Football League. At the end of the 1992-3 season, the team gained a place in the FA Premiership. During its sojourn there in the 1993-4 season, it won five matches, drew fifteen, lost twenty-two, had 100 goals scored against, ended the season with just thirty points, and was relegated.

Swinford (Esther) 'Hettie' (1884-1903) In 1903, Swindon reacted in horror following the cold-blooded murder of nineteen-year-old popular barmaid Esther 'Hettie' Swinford at her place of employment, the Ship Inn on Westcott Place. She was born in Fairford, where her father, Edwin, was a farm labourer. At the time of her murder she had worked at the Ship Inn, on and off, for three or four years. During 1902, Hettie became betrothed to Edward Richard Palmer, a twenty-five-year-old one-time labourer at the GWR Works, and banns were read for their proposed wedding in St Mary's church, Rodbourne Cheney. The marriage did not take place; he had apparently spent their savings, which were intended to buy furniture for their house, so Hettie broke off the engagement. Palmer left the town, stating that he had heard something about Hettie that meant he would not marry her. He was away for about a year, being employed as a

gardener in Reading and Marlow. Palmer wrote to Hettie, who, in the meantime, was seeing another young man, claiming falsely to have been in Canada, and stating that he again wanted employment at the railway works. On the day of the murder, he left his lodgings at 62 Bridge Street and spent some time with friends at the Mechanics' Institute before going to The Ship, where he drank a bottle of Bass beer before confronting Hettie. Although the two did not quarrel, she rejected his advances. He shot his former fiancée in the chest, in the otherwise empty bar parlour of the hotel. The landlord's wife, Isabella Ann Matthews, heard the shot, which went through Hettie's heart as well as other vital organs, and was first on the scene. Her husband, Walter Ernest Matthews secured the murderer in the bagatelle room. When he was taken up by the police, Palmer was found to have a picture of Hettie about him, on which he had written 'the curse of my life'. This suggested a degree of premeditation to the court when Palmer was tried. Nor did it go well for him that the police were aware that he previously had carried a revolver for about nine years, and they had tried to apprehend him in possession of it. At one point, his brother had deprived him of it, but it had lately been restored to him. Palmer was found guilty of murder and sentenced to death, and was hanged at Devizes gaol on 17 November 1903. The funeral was arranged by Henry Smith, a GWR coach builder who made coffins and conducted funerals on the side. The cost of Hettie's coffin and all the funeral expenses were paid for by Mr and Mrs Matthews. The decorative memorial cross on her grave in Radnor Street cemetery was paid for by public subscription, such was the degree of local feeling. Over the years, the memorial and the rest of the grave

fell into disrepair; in 2009, it was all restored and re-erected free of charge by Highworth Memorials. (See also Hunter, Frances; and O'Callaghan, Sian.)

Tanner, Mollie Hilda (b. 1927) 'Miss Mollie' – the dancing teacher to literally thousands of children in and around Swindon – the daughter of a railway worker, was the first baby to be born in Osborne Street. She was born Mollie Woodcock. In the course of a musical career spanning six decades, she and her girls worked with some of the legendary stars of theatre and television, particularly in pantomimes, and there is hardly a theatre in England they have not played. They also appeared eight times on the television programme *Opportunity Knocks*. An early pupil was Diana Dors, and the list of now well-known professional actresses and dancers that owe their musical beginnings to 'Miss Molly' is quite staggering. They include the Hollywood actress Catherine Zeta Jones. Many of her former pupils now run their own schools of dance in distant corners of the world. Her charity work is legendary – in particular, in relation to the Prospect hospice locally, and further afield with Great Ormond Street Hospital – but she refused to accept the OBE.

During the Second World War, Mollie was a performer with ENSA – Entertainments National Service Association – in Swindon. She was working in the offices of the Great Western Railway in Swindon – where her boss was the piano-playing Bert Fluck, Diana Dors' father – when she met John Tanner, who would become her husband. He was also a GWR office worker, a part-time pianist, and they met in the back of a lorry going to an ENSA gig. Thereafter, he became her permanent pianist, later using the sheet

music he inherited from Bert Fluck. In 1943, Molly began to give dancing lessons to half a dozen girls in her father's shed, preparing them for a show at her younger sister's school. When it was over, they did not want to stop, and that was the beginning of the Tanwood School of Dance. Within six years, she had personally achieved four fellowship degrees. Her dancers' first concert, a charity affair, was in 1946. Her dancing school became associated with the pantomimes at the Empire Theatre, in conjunction with Harry Lester and his Hayseeds orchestra. In 1951, they gave a charity performance there for *HMS Affray*, the Royal Navy submarine lost at sea with 75 lives. Mollie Tanner was the last person to leave the stage of the Empire Theatre when it closed in 1955. She established the Tanwood Kindergarten in 1956, and became a dance adjudicator in 1958. Mollie Tanner was a Justice of the Peace for twenty-three years, and was also a tax commissioner.

Technical College Swindon had a School Board from 1877, but adult education remained in the hands of the Mechanics' Institution. Early in the 1890s, its board began to hold talks with the Wiltshire Education Committee with a view to establishing a permanent building for technical instruction in Swindon. A competition for this was held in 1892, but immediately alterations were made in order to reduce costs. These included omitting fireproof doors, and constructing the building of brick instead of the intended stone. The Swindon & North Wiltshire Technical Institution was designed by Silcock & Reay of Milsom Street, Bath, and built by J. Long & Son of Bath. It cost £12,000 and was partially financed by the rates, also receiving a grant of £3,500 from the Wiltshire County Council, and another from the Department of Science and Art in London.

The three-storey building opened on 27 January 1897 in Victoria Road, on a site provided by Major Rolleston. It was built of red brick, with moulded brick cornices and stone ornamental dressings, 'in the English Renaissance style', with Dutch gables and a built-out central section. The School Board was abolished in 1902, when an Education Committee was formed under the auspices of the Swindon Borough Council, adopting the Education Act, 1902. Under this Act, the Mechanics' Institution relinquished its involvement in technical education to the Education Committee. In 1926, the Victoria Road technical institution was refurbished internally, reorganised, and reopened as a College of Further Education; it was renamed 'The College' in 1926.

During the 1950s, a number of residential terraces were demolished immediately to the west of the college – Edmund Street, Horsell Street, and most of Byron Street and Rolleston Street – to make way for a car park and a six-storey college extension. This was designed by Charles Pike & Partners, and F.I. Bowden, the Wiltshire County Architect, built by Gee, Walker and Slater Ltd, and cost £402,000. It gained a Civic Trust Award, and was opened in 1961 by the Duke of Edinburgh. At that time, it had seventy tutors and twelve technicians, and was divided into six departments: arts, building, commercial studies, engineering, household arts, and science and mathematics. The end terraced house immediately to the north of the building in Victoria Road was used as the tutors' staff room. A lower extension was built in 1969-70, adjacent to the west of the 1961 college. In 1971, Swindon Technical

College was opened at North Star, on the site of the former railway works.

The Regent Circus site was all closed down in 2006, and the property was then bought by Ashfield Land, who obtained planning permission to create a retail and leisure development on the site. This scheme was shelved in 2008, in the face of recession, but the owners submitted further plans for a £100 million redevelopment of the site in May 2010, and the college extensions were demolished by Wring Demolition in 2012. The Victorian building was subjected to an arson attack on 17 March 2013.

Tented Market see Market Hall, Cromwell Street.

Theatres see Arts Centres; Empire Theatre; Little Theatre.

Thomas, Edward (1878-1917) The war poet who was killed at Flanders, spent several boyhood holidays at a cottage in Cambria Place. This was the home of his Welsh grandmother, his uncle – a fitter in the nearby GWR works – and his aunt, who was a waitress in the refreshment rooms at Swindon station. Whilst collecting material for his biographical homage *Richard Jefferies* (published 1909), Thomas stayed in Broome Manor Lane.

Thomas, James (1874-1949) Jimmy Thomas, firebrand champion of the workers, orator, union representative, and Member of Parliament, was born into poverty at Newport. He was the son of an unmarried woman whom he believed to be his sister, and who rejected him even when the truth was disclosed, and was raised by his grandmother. In 1886, he left school,

and three years later was employed with the Great Western Railway as an engine cleaner. He became politically active as a very young man, and was vociferous in what he considered to be shortcomings in the way that the railway company behaved towards their workers. Over the next few years, he became an official of a number of political organisations, and a strong union activist. In 1899, he came to Swindon where, despite having to work desperately long hours in the marshalling yards on the railway, he still found time to be elected to that year's Annual Union Conference. His political career began in the town when he was elected a Labour Party councillor. His association with Swindon was, however, relatively short-lived, for he was invited to stand for Parliament in Derby, and was elected its Labour MP in 1910.

Tile and Pottery Works Swindon Tile and Pottery Works were situated a little to the north of the Gas & Coke Company's works on Brockhill, now the southern part of Drove Road. They developed from the tile and pottery works at Stratton St Margaret, which, in the 1850s, comprised only a small brickworks that was taken over by Thomas Turner and developed over the next twenty years into a substantial undertaking. When Swindon's expansion outside the railway village really took off in the 1870s, Turner established his second works between Old Town and New Swindon, taking his clay from clay pits where now is Queen's Park. There were a number of comparatively small kilns scattered about the site, where Turner employed 'steam power and the most approved modern appliances' for producing 'the high-class goods for which Mr Turner's works are celebrated'. His company made

'flower pots, rustic armchairs, elegantly moulded tablets, rustic and ornamental pottery, vases and horticultural pottery, and all kinds of ware adapted for domestic use'. An advertised feature of the site was the cleanliness that attended all of the manufacturing processes, which the company was eager to show off to visitors. (See also Turner, Thomas.)

Toomer, John (1824-1882) John Toomer was born in Hampshire; he came to Swindon in 1849, lodged with Henry Cuss, a Wood Street grocer, and started to deal in coal out of the Swindon railway depot. The following year, he took over A.W. Deacon's corn stores, situated on the north side of the market square in Old Town, and established a hay and corn trade. Mr Deacon had owned the building almost since the two cottages that previously stood on the site were converted by Phillip Pavey, a miller of Elcombe Hall, Wroughton, early in the 19th century, into a corn, manure, and general agricultural dealers. Toomer soon built up a business as a coal, slate, lime, coke, salt and hay merchant, operating firstly out of the Swindon station depot, then from premises on The Sands, and later in Victoria Street — all the while opening similar, smaller depots at the neighbouring railway stations.

By the early 1860s, Toomer was employing twelve men and two boys, and was a member of the Old Swindon Local Board. The family were living at 43 The Sands, Bath Road. In the twenty years from 1857, John's wife Mary Ann (née Reynolds), a Swindon girl whom he married in 1855, gave birth to eleven children; fortunately, the family could afford several servants, and a nurse to look after the children. In 1864, he became a director of the Swindon Central Market Company, formed that year in order to arrest the decline in market activities under its predecessor, the Swindon Market Company, which had been in existence since 1852. He was also instrumental in obtaining the site for the corn exchange, next to the town hall in Old Swindon, where the land and cottages were owned by the then lord of the manor, Ambrose Goddard. When that building was opened in 1866, Toomer part-sponsored the inaugural dinner, organised the accompanying ball, and was responsible for hiring the musicians. In 1870, he bought Apsley House, Bath Road as his family residence. Built c.1830, this was an imposing building that had been owned, since 1862, by coal and coke merchant Richard Tarrant, who was Toomer's rival at the New Swindon station depot. The family moved in, with a cook, a housemaid, and several servants, and for the remainder of his life John Toomer used the yards at the rear of the premises to store a number of the commodities in which he traded. He was a long-time member of the choir at Christ Church.

Town Gardens The town gardens were planned for nine acres adjacent to the old Swindon quarries, on land bought for the purpose by the Old Swindon Local Board from the lord of the manor for £700, and were opened in May 1894. A further £3,000 enabled the main entrance wrought-iron gates to be put up; a park keeper's lodge to be built over one of the former tracks into the quarries; paths, borders and beds to be laid out; ornamental walkways and rustic bridges to be constructed, and the whole area to be fenced off. A maze, bowling green, tennis courts, and a fountain on an island in the middle of an oval pond were also included. The grounds were further developed in 1902,

and again in 1905 when they were extended and a new entrance made from Quarry Road.

The refreshment kiosk was made in 1914 by the Great Western Railway, which conveyed it by rail and set it up at exhibitions throughout the country as a mobile trade stand for their own publicity purposes. It was sold to Swindon Council in 1942. It is timber-framed and octagonal, and built of panels, its roof forming a canopy that ends in a decorative fascia. Above is an octagonal lantern with a similarly swept roof, ending in a ball and spike finial. In 1927, the maze was removed and a rose garden planted in its place. An aviary was built of wood, wire and glass, close to the entry in Westlecot Road, in 1928. The shape of the pond was changed in the mid-1930s.

The open-air concert bowl occupies part of the principal quarry site. Built 1935-36, and designed by J.B.L. Thompson, the borough surveyor, it has a double entrance and iron turnstiles, and an Art Deco-style stage area in a sunken arena. After a period of disuse, the bowl was restored in the 1990s. The ornamental octagonal bandstand was made of cast iron with a roof of lead and aluminium by the James Allan Elmbank Foundry of Glasgow. It too, was opened in 1936, on 6 May, by Alderman Mrs May George. It has a square clock tower topped by a weathervane, later replaced by a clock surmounted by a ball finial. The old aviary was replaced by another, of glass and metal, in 1994. (See also Peter Pan Statue.)

Town Hall, New Swindon By 1887, the New Swindon Local Board had decided to build public offices adjacent to what was then known as York Place, a terrace leading east from the Rifleman's Arms hotel. After much discussion, the design was thrown open to competition, which attracted twenty-seven entries. The winning architect was Brightwen Binyon of Ipswich, selected by a committee from the final four who were: (William) Henman & (James) Timmins of Birmingham, who came a highly commended second; J. Beale of Westminster; and Swindon's William Henry Read. The builder of the Board's new offices was J. Reed of Plymouth. The foundation stone was laid in 1890 by H.J. Birch, chairman of the New Swindon Local Board.

The building, a likeness of neo-17th-century Dutch architecture, was opened by the Marquess of Bath on a very wet day in 1891, at the end of a procession that began in Old Town. It is of two storeys (three beneath the large gables built over each of the two end bays) and nine bays. The return on the north side is of six bays. Built in pink bricks with stone banding and dressings, horizontal and vertical string courses, it presents a riot of windows, pediments, pierced parapets, finials, cupolas and turrets, and has two-storey attics. It predominantly features a ninety-foot-high clock tower above the west front, beneath which the main entrance porch above five steps faces Regent Street and is topped by a balcony. On this, local worthies were presented to the people at election times and on other civic occasions, visiting royalty and other dignitaries were presented to the people, and around it foregathered the populace for various ceremonies. Beyond the main porch is a spacious hall with columns, pilasters and arches, and a sweeping staircase rising to a suite of offices. There are two large doorways on the north side. When the town hall opened, these were occupied by the Board's senior officials and those of the county court; other rooms were available for public meetings. In 1938, the Civic

Offices were built in Euclid Street, and local government relocated there.

In 1893, a public drinking fountain was erected beside the town hall, paid for by the Swindon United Temperance Board. The railings at the front of the town hall were installed in 1997, designed by Avril Wilson, an artist and blacksmith, who based the tops on hand gestures, using metal forged by Richard Quinnell.

Town Hall, Old Town In 1793, Thomas Goddard, then lord of the manor of Swindon, turned out a number of the parish poor from a former church house that he owned in High Street and converted it into a lock-up market house on which he then levied rents. The building was timber-framed and octagonal, and continued in trade until 1843 when, in poor condition, it was demolished. Swindon then had no market building, although farmers in particular agitated for one throughout the first half of the 19th century.

In 1852, the Swindon Market Company was formed. This was a body of professional men and retailers who, in the same year, persuaded Ambrose Lethbridge Goddard to lease a site on his land immediately to the south of the square in Old Town. Goddard wanted somewhere to house offices for the administration of the town; farmers wanted a market house. Several cottages on the site were demolished and their gardens flattened to make way for the new development.

The plan was to incorporate the two requirements of local administration and market house. Sampson Sage, architect of Prospect Place, designed the building, and it was built by George Major of Quarry Cottage, Horsefair Street (Devizes Road). The two-storey, five-bay market house, with a central pediment and Tuscan pilasters,

and part open parapet, had a rusticated ground floor with a range of open arches at street level, and was a striking façade. The main hall measured 1,300 square feet, and could accommodate 600 people. The building opened in 1853. However, it failed in its original purpose because it was not ambitious enough, and there was an almost immediate decrease in the corn trade. Within a few weeks of opening, the cellars and part of the ground floor were leased to William Brown, wine merchant (it became Brown & Nephew in 1862, and Brown & Plummer in 1882), who enclosed the arches. The rest of the ground floor became a sack office and general store. In 1873, the wine merchant took possession of the whole ground floor. He also built a small, square, two-storey building abutting the east side of the town hall, as 'cash wine stores'.

The place became officially the 'town hall' when the town's magistrates relocated there in 1853 from the Goddard Arms Hotel, where the courts had been held, and remained in the new building until 1873. A room upstairs was leased to the Swindon Local Board between 1864 and 1874, and another, also from 1864, to the Swindon Water Company. A new organisation, the Swindon Central Market Company, acquired the interests and premises of the Swindon Market Company, including the market house/town hall, in 1874. By the 1880s, it had ceased to be a town hall, and the upper area was being advertised as public 'assembly rooms'. In 1891, all public affairs were transferred to the then newly erected Town Hall in New Swindon.

Townsend, James Copleston (1825-1885) The man whose name is still associated with the most enduring firm of solicitors in Swindon, and the town's best

domestic building – No. 42 Cricklade Street, although it is no longer occupied by the firm – was born at Awliscombe, Devon. He was admitted as a solicitor in 1847 and, in 1852, became a partner in the Swindon firm of William Morse Crowdy and Alfred Southby Crowdy, the latter being his brother-in-law. The firm was then well over a century old, and had been in the Crowdy family since the late 1700s. Its address was given as High Street, where its principal was described as a 'commissioner for taking acknowledgements of married women'. J.C. Townsend built Croft House, a substantial residence at Croft famously associated with the Morse family of drapers and Methodists who bought it from one of James's sons in 1896. James lived there in some style with his wife Annie Elizabeth (née Fox), a Londoner, their children, and several servants (at the 1881 census, there were three). Amongst his several public offices, he was the first chairman, in 1857, of the Swindon Water Company, and clerk of the Old Swindon Local Board and the New Swindon Local Board, both in 1864. He was also the solicitor for many of the undertakings of the day. J.C. Townsend died on a train, and on its arrival at Swindon station he was carried into the refreshment rooms there, and is buried in the churchyard at Christ Church. (In his fine monograph *Townsend's Swindon & Newbury: From the 18th century to 1996*, published by the firm, Graham Young suggests that the company's move to 42 Cricklade Street 'was probably in the 1850s on the initiative of James Copleston Townsend'.)

Trades in 18th-century Swindon

In 1697, Swindon was a very small town, indeed. An inventory, taken in that year, revealed two bakers, two barbers, four blacksmiths, two butchers, four carpenters, one chandler, one cheese factor, one collar maker, one comb maker, three coopers, one currier, three drapers, one felt maker, one glazier, one glover, one grocer, six innkeepers and ale-house keepers, one ironmonger, two joiners, thirty-nine labourers, fourteen masons, one quiltmaker, one saddler, twenty servants, seven shoe makers, two slaters, six tailors, one tobacco cutter, one translator, four weavers, one wheelwright, and one wool man. There were also three bailiffs, and thirty-one widows were listed for the same year; nine women and one man were receiving alms. By 1702, very little change had taken place in the composition of the occupations, or the number of people carrying out each. An extra bailiff had been appointed; the town had acquired four bakers, two gardeners, a miller, and a surgeon. The number of people in receipt of alms had doubled to twenty.

Tramways

Tramways In 1883, a proposal was put to the Old Swindon Local Board that a public steam tramway system might be laid down to connect the market square in Old Town with the GWR train station in New Swindon. This was followed, almost immediately, by a suggestion that a system of horse-drawn trams might be possible, also under the auspices of the local authority. Then, interested electric lighting companies proposed that the New Swindon Local Board might be interested in adopting their product. Electricity came to Swindon under the Swindon New Town Electric Lighting Order, 1895; this was followed by the dual-purpose Swindon Corporation Tramways & Electricity Bill, 1901. Under this legislation, the Council formed an Electric Light & Tramways Committee, and developed proposals for eight miles of track

for an electric tramway system, linking the then borough boundaries with the already suggested internal route, and others also being proposed. Work began in 1903 on digging up a number of roads in the town to accommodate a more modest, and less expensive, 3½ miles of forty-two-inch track. This connected Old Town market square via Wood Street, Victoria Road, Regent Street, and Bridge Street, with a terminus at the junction of Bridge Street and Fleet Street known as 'Clappen's Corner' or 'The Tram Centre'. Extensions led into Rodbourne, where the terminus was near Bruce Street railway bridge, and Gorse Hill, where the tramway terminated near to the Duke of Edinburgh public house. A tramway spur was put in between Wellington Street, en route to Gorse Hill, and the GWR station.

The Corporation ordered its first seven tramcars from the famous tramcar firm of Dick, Kerr & Co of Strand Road, Preston, Lancashire. They were numbered, painted in cream and crimson lake, and lettered in a style universally employed by the maker, and were brought to Swindon by rail. Each tramcar featured an ingenious latticework catcher at either end of the vehicle, just ahead of the wheels, that was activated if a bar built proud of the headlights struck an object on the track. The catcher dropped, and a bell rang to alert the driver to the problem. The system began in September 1904 following an inauguration ceremony by the mayor James Hinton.

There would be thirteen Swindon Corporation Tramways vehicles over the period of the undertaking, and a shed was built next to the electricity works to accommodate them. Trams were popular in Swindon, but were not particularly profitable. A fatal accident happened on 1 June 1906 when the packed tramcar No. 11 descended Victoria Road, gathered speed, and fell on to its side on a curve at the foot of the hill. Five people were killed, and more than thirty people injured. The tramway manager and the driver of the car were censured because the vehicle had been operated despite a reported problem with the brake mechanism. The residents of Swindon had to pay extra in their rates over the next three years for the Corporation to meet the substantial claims for compensation made against it. Meanwhile, No.11 was repaired and put back into service. Swindon's last public electric tram journey in service was made in 1929, by tramcar No. 1, by which time Leyland Titan motor buses otherwise comprised the Swindon Corporation public transport fleet. The tramlines in Swindon were removed 1929-30.

Trinity Presbyterian Church, Victoria Road Now a nursery school, the church was built of red brick on the corner of Victoria Road and Groundwell Road in 1899. It was built in Decorated style, as exemplified by the large west window with its four pointed lights, a sexfoil and quatrefoils in the spandrels, and dagger motif. From 1978, in conjunction with other churches in the town, it became the United Reform Church. Its congregation transferred to the Pilgrim Centre when this opened in 1990 in a new development on the site of the former Baptist Tabernacle (one of the establishments with whom the Presbyterian Church had formed its association in the late 1970s) in Regent Circus.

Trip Holiday In 1849, some five hundred members of the Mechanics' Institution at Swindon went on an unpaid excursion to

Oxford, on a train provided free of charge by the Great Western Railway Company. They called it 'The Trip'. This led to an annual unpaid trip day, which always took place on the first Friday in July. By the 1860s, there was a choice of venues. These trip days developed into the first 'trip' week's holiday (without pay) for Swindon railway works employees using GWR rail transport, which was arranged in 1913. This was suspended during the 1914-18 war, and resumed in 1919, still without pay. Few Works' employees could really afford to go away, and cartoons drawn at the time show tradesmen queuing up at front doors, waving unpaid bills, whilst the occupants try to hide within. Certainly, in order to afford a day or two away, the breadwinners tried to find temporary part-time jobs during the rest of the week. Eventually, the trip period was extended from the first Friday in July until a week the following Monday. The successor to this was the annual Works holiday in July when the establishment closed down for two weeks. The GWR first gave employees a paid week's holiday in 1938, increasing this to two weeks, ten years later. The Company variously allocated a number of free passes annually to certain employees, depending on their status in the organisation, who also benefitted from cheaper coal, wood, and even railway sleepers (known locally as 'the allocation'), which could be ordered either at an office in the Works, or at Kingsdown station.

Tritton House, Bath Road Built as a gentleman's residence called Grafton Cottage, just as Bath Road was emerging as a fashionable area, c.1835, Tritton House obtained it name in commemoration of Sir G. E. Tritton, who twice unsuccessfully contested the Swindon constituency for the Conservative Party (he was also unsuccessful elsewhere as a Liberal Party candidate). It remains the rather superior property to those in the next door Bath Road Terrace, of which it is really a part. This is a three-bay, two-storey house, built in Flemish bond brick, and stone. It has a pretty wrought-iron canopied porch, an interesting fanlight, and a slate roof with lunette attic windows. The rear extension is 19th century, as are the attractive canted and hipped bay windows with fluted iron columns to the front. The house's best-known owner was the 19th-century auctioneer Henry Smith of the firm Dore, Smith & Radway. In 1973, it was acquired by the Swindon Conservative Association, which worked out of the front rooms and sub-let other rooms as offices to other companies.

Tuckett, Angela (1906-1994) Angela Tuckett played hockey for England in Germany in 1935, on which occasion she angered her Nazi hosts by her open opposition to their propaganda. In the same year, she published a book of poems, *Verses Against War and Fascism*. In her 80s, she was at Greenham Common, still a peace activist, and supporting the women's movement there. She was also frequently to be encountered in the streets of Swindon, accompanying her increasingly thin octogenarian voice on the melodeon, in support of what she saw as the rights of sections of oppressed workers. A collection of seventeen of her songs was published in 1978 as *Sing and Stay Human*, and she was a member of Swindon Folksingers' Club from its inception in 1960, and sang at its meetings to the end of her life. In 1962, she married Ike Gradwell, secretary of the Swindon Communist Party, and after his death she wrote and published

Ike Gradwell, Man of the People — one of several publications of interest to the town's local historians. Others include *Up With All That's Down, A History of Swindon Trades Council, 1891-1975* (Quill Press, 1971), and some manuscript items such as *History of the Swindon Trades Council*, and *History of the 1926 General Strike in Swindon*, which are in the county archives. In 1972, she published a book of poems, *Yesterday, Today and Tomorrow*.

Turner, Thomas (1839-1911) The most obvious, tangible reminder of this businessman, proprietor of the Swindon Tile and Pottery Works, off Drove Road, are the two 'catalogue' houses and the nearby works' manager's house beside the eastern entrance to what is now Queen's Park ornamental gardens, constructed around the site of his works and clay pits. Examples of some of the decorative motifs made at his works appear on Belle Vue Terrace, Hunt Street, of 1895. Turner Street, off Westcott Place, built in 1893, is named after him. These houses were built with his own bricks, as were other streets that linked Old Town with New Swindon. On these, and on his houses in Lansdown Road, Kingshill and Westcott Place, there is a repeated pottery plaque or keystone, the face of a bearded man surrounded by shell motifs and running vines. This was said to be the likeness of Daniel Lynch, who worked at Turner's brick, pottery and tile yard at Stratton St Margaret. The places in Swindon that Turner owned were frequently designed by architect and surveyor John James Smith of Station Road, New Swindon, and they sometimes bear Turner's signature letters 'TT' on a decorative date stone, and have a string course of flat wall tiles with a running vine of ivy leaf.

Turner was born in Cheltenham and, after his marriage, came to live in Stratton St Margaret, where his children were born. In the 1860s, he took over a small brickworks in the village and established there a large tile and pottery works; in the 1870s, he built up the Drove Road works in Swindon, centred on clay pits that had probably existed as such since the 18th century. His bricks and pottery decoration were used to build and embellish St Paul's church, Edgeware Road, Swindon in 1881 and the chancel that was added in 1883; they were the building blocks of the Wilts & Dorset Bank building of 1884 on the corner of Wood Street and Cricklade Street; and were used in the extensions of the museum and chapel at Marlborough College.

In the 1880s, the family moved into Grove House, Drove Road, with their servant, Annie Lewis, who had also been born in Cheltenham. In 1875, Turner was the only Swindon representative on the nine-man board that took over the running of the Wilts & Berks Canal when the original company sold out, facing failure. In order to enhance his business contacts, he became an inaugural shareholder in the Swindon Town Club when it was formed in 1884. He died in Brighton, and is buried in Swindon at Christ Church. The Swindon Tile & Pottery Works was taken over by Thomas Bazzard in 1896. (See also Catalogue Houses.)

Turnpike Tolls All of Swindon's main roads were first turnpiked between 1751 and 1775. For example, charges were imposed on the Faringdon road in 1758, and the Marlborough road — where there was a toll house at Coate — in 1762. Tolls were charged depending on the kind of wagon, the width of its wheels, and the number of horses drawing

it. In the days when roads were not surfaced, the weight of the load and the width of the wheels that were bearing it had a great impact on the condition of the road. Tolls had to be imposed to keep it in reasonable repair. The prices levied for travel between Coate and Marlborough in 1819 were:

Each horse drawing any coach, carriage, etc. 4½d

Each horse drawing any wagon or cart

with strakes over 9 inches wide 2d

with wheels 6 inches but under 9 inches wide 3d

with wheels under 6 inches wide 6d

Millstones in pairs or singly, drawn by five horses 2s 6d

Millstones drawn by more than five horses 2s 6d

plus 1s for each horse beyond five.

On particularly rural roads, there was a need to bring in more money, and to tax the movement of farm animals. At the same time as the above charges were levied at Coate, the road to Knighton demanded:

Each horse drawing any coach, carriage, etc. 6d

Each horse drawing any wagon or cart

with strakes over 9 inches wide 3d

with wheels 6 inches but under 9 inches wide 4½d

Each horse drawing cárts and wagons with broad wheels

that do not roll a flat surface 6d

Each horse without wagon or carriage 2d

Cattle by the score 1s 8d

Pigs by the score 10d

The Turnpike Trusts ceased to operate after Parliament passed the Highway Act, 1862.

Twinning Swindon has been twinned with Salzgitter in Germany since 1975, and since 1990 with Ocotal, a town in mountainous country in northern Nicaragua. In 1991, Swindon formed a town twinning working party, which eight years later became the Swindon Town Twinning Network. The Network's committee, on which there are representatives of each twinned town, meets four times a year, when opportunities for international visits and co-operative projects are discussed, and reports are made on visits by personnel from twinned and non-twinned regions. In 2003, Swindon entered a twinning arrangement with Torun in Poland, primarily in recognition of the wave of Polish immigrants who settled in the north Wiltshire town following the end of the Second World War, but latterly including those who came in the first decade of the 21st century when Poland joined the European Union. Communication between the two is facilitated through the Torun and Swindon Twinning Enterprise. For the whole of 2010, Swindon was also twinned with Walt Disney World in Florida, where a plaque was unveiled in the presence of Mickey Mouse to commemorate the event. This came about when the Walt Disney organisation accepted nominations from British towns for the purpose. The winning entry, a video with a rhyming voice-over, was made in 2009 by 20-year-old Swindon resident Rebecca Warren, an employee at the town's Nationwide call centre. It beat off the competition from twenty-four other towns, to become Walt Disney World's first-ever twinning venture.

Underground Tunnels of Old Swindon At one time, Swindon was a centre for some kind of smuggled commodity; circumstantial evidence suggests that this was probably contraband liquor. Several of the tunnels that were built beneath the old

town, supposedly for the purpose of storage and escape, remain, although mostly bricked up. Some have been dated to the 16th and 17th centuries. All of the known tunnels run between premises that are, or were, on either side of the arterial Cricklade Street, High Street, and Marlborough Road, or the adjacent Newport Street, and they appear to link former inns and significant houses. Those discovered to date are detailed below.

Cricklade Street – now residential, and renamed Betjeman House, this double-fronted, gabled and part timber-decorated, tile-hung property was once two dwellings with a beer house attached. In the mid-19th century, it was the Plume of Feathers public house, later the Oddfellows Arms. An underground tunnel was discovered running alongside the roadway towards High Street.

Cricklade Street – no.42, now contemporary apartments, is built above a brick-vaulted cellar with three twelve-foot-wide tunnels leading off. The two longest extant portions of these tunnels are each over 100 feet long, before being blocked off, and travel towards the Goddard Arms Hotel. During the Second World War, these were one of the twelve designated public air raid shelters in Swindon.

Cricklade Street – a tunnel, discovered in the 1960s, issues from the rear of the Goddard Arms Hotel, running across the back of the place and into what is now the car park of the bank next door. The inn was built about 1820, by extending a small thatched ale house called The Crown, which existed in the 16th century.

High Street – now rebuilt as commercial offices named Eastcott House, this was formerly the King of Prussia inn, with a Georgian assembly room at the rear. Two tunnels were found here during excavations for foundations.

High Street – a tunnel was discovered beneath a 16th-century building on the east side of the street, which had been a long-standing haberdashery business, when it was demolished in the 1970s.

High Street – entrances to tunnels were found running off twenty-five-foot-deep wells beneath former solicitors' offices on the west side of the street.

The Square – in the 1950s, at least two barrel-vaulted tunnels, each about six feet high, were discovered apparently leading down Dammas Lane.

The Square – a tunnel, containing a grille, was discovered leading off one of the cellars beneath the premises of wine merchants Brown & Nephew, later Brown & Plummer, beneath the market house on the corner with Marlborough Road. When a coloured dye was put down the grille, it emerged to the south-east in the pond on the Goddard estate. This gives credence to Swindon's claim to the Wiltshire 'Moonraker' legend.

Newport Street – a mid-18th-century malthouse, later the White Hart public house and, later still, The Bull, stood on the north side of the street, but was demolished in the 1960s. There was a tunnel entrance in one of its cellars.

Newport Street – the 'oldest house in Swindon' has cellars that were built in the 14th century. In one of them is a blocked-up tunnel entrance. This house has medieval foundations, and a remodelled Georgian second storey. In the 20th century, the house was home, art gallery and business premises to Harold Easthope, art dealer and historic buildings inspector, and artist Marjorie Fripp. Mr Easthope was of the opinion that the tunnel entrance in his house connected with that beneath the White Hart, almost opposite.

Newport Street – in 1967, T.E. Gardner said that he discovered a ten-foot-wide shaft whilst working in the late 1940s beneath Gilbert's furnishings shop on the corner with Marlborough Road. The tunnel appeared to run under Marlborough Road.

Marlborough Road – the Mason's Arms public house, opposite Newport Street, was demolished in the early 1970s. Before this happened, the writer of this book was able to inspect a number of brick-lined tunnels beneath it. Three of the larger ones, each about eight feet wide, were dated to the 17th century. They pointed in several directions (before becoming blocked up), notably towards The Lawn (former house of the lords of the manor of Swindon) and towards High Street. In one instance, one tunnel branched off another.

East of Marlborough Road – The Lawn, known as Swindon House until 1850, was built on the site of a medieval dwelling. The Goddard family lived there from 1653 until the 1920s, and the place was demolished in 1952. Several of the tunnels beneath the old town seem to point in its direction.

East of Marlborough Road – an entrance to a tunnel was recorded in a row of cottages near to the site of the one-time church pond.

Vallis, Edward (1823-1911) Born in Devizes, Vallis came to Swindon in 1855 and set up as a stationer and accountant in Wood Street, quickly adding bookselling, collector of rent and debts, and sub-distributor of stamps to his portfolio. His address was 'the stamp office'. He married Mary Hewlett of Stroud in 1853; the couple had two daughters and a son, and his wife's unmarried sister Helen Hewlett lived with them. The family had one servant. Vallis's career was in the ascendant, and he made a name for himself as secretary to the Swindon Gas & Coke Company, secretary to the Swindon Water Company, secretary of the Swindon Central Market Company, clerk to the Nuisance Removal Committee, and the assessor and collector of assessed property and income tax. Then, in 1862, Mary died.

In 1865, he married Harriet Sarah of Great Marlow, Buckinghamshire, who came to live with him in Swindon, where the first of their children was born in 1867. In that year, the family left Swindon (the stamp office passed to Joseph New, stationer) and moved to Lupus Street, Pimlico, London, where they had a fancy goods shop. In 1891, Edward and his wife were living at The Ship public house in Walsworth, Hertfordshire, in the household of their son, Alfred Hardy Vallis, who was the publican.

By 1901, Edward and Harriet had retired to a flat in Ackworth Street, Lambeth, and she died in 1904, leaving her husband just over £6,000. In 1911, the year he died, he was once again living with his son, this time in Fulham.

Vickers-Armstrong In 1938, the Air Ministry identified a 125-acre site at South Marston, to the north-east of Swindon, as being potentially suitable for the manufacture of aircraft. This site was quickly developed by the Ministry of Aircraft Production, which came into being in 1940, with the purpose of taking on the responsibility for procuring aircraft supplies that would otherwise have devolved on the Air Ministry. It instigated research, design and development, and the repair of aircraft, and provided for the storage of armaments and equipment pending the operational requirements of aircraft in the field of battle. Vickers-Armstrong came to the site in 1940, during the Second

World War, after the company's works at Southampton were bombed, and facilitated several of the requirements of the Ministry of Aircraft Production. In the early 1940s, the Ministry of Aircraft Production also built a number of prefabricated bungalows to house key workers at Vickers-Armstrong and their families, notably 'The MAP Bungalows', consisting of West Lane, Westdown Drive, Eastdown Drive, Northdown Drive and The Paddock at Upper Stratton. These were let by the Highworth Rural District Council, and were demolished in the late 1960s. What became known as Supermarine Spitfires were made by Vickers-Armstrong at Swindon. The site was bought by Vickers from the Ministry of Aircraft Production in 1945. Several other jet fighters, notably the Attacker, Scimitar and Swift, were made there.

Vickers later diversified into a number of activities in two areas of the South Marston site, separated by the former airfield. It was turned into a light-medium design and manufacturing centre, turning out hydraulic equipment, electron linear accelerators, mixing and compounding machinery, nuclear engineering, and medical equipment. By the late 1960s, several distinct activities occupied the Vickers site: Design and Procurement Division; Hydraulics Division; Radiation & Nuclear Engineering Division; Mixing & Compounding Machinery Division; Commercial Products Division; and Vickers All Wheel Drive.

As a reminder of its wartime role, a restored Spitfire was for some years displayed at the front of the works. This was Spitfire Mk 21, LA226, whose first flight was made from Vickers' South Marston runway on 9 January 1945. It was later taken on charge by the RAF and delivered to 33 Maintenance Unit at Lyneham, then transferred almost at once to 91 (Nigerian) Squadron at West Malling and had its first operational sortie on 13 April 1945. In 1958, in poor condition, it was delivered to the Central Flying School, Little Rissington. Eventually, the Ministry of Defence donated it to Vickers in recognition of the company's contribution to the fighter role of the RAF in the Second World War, and it was restored by volunteer labour (it took 750 hours) at the South Marston works.

The South Marston site was sold off by Vickers Property Division, and became an industrial park from the 1970s, used mainly for light engineering, warehousing and distribution. Much of the area was acquired by Honda in the 1980s.

Victoria Hospital, Bath Road

Ambrose Lethbridge Goddard gave land 'on Okus Fields at the western extremity of The Sands', and William Henry Read designed the Swindon & North Wilts Hospital to occupy it. Queen Victoria gave her permission for the place to be named after her, in commemoration of her Golden Jubilee, and the hospital was opened on 29 September 1888 by Charlotte Goddard, wife of the benevolent lord of the manor. It had cost £1,960 to build, paid for by voluntary funding, and was furnished with donations from well-wishers. More voluntary funding, and gifts of additional land, enabled it to increase in size over the next couple of decades, mostly through the efforts of the Swindon Hospital Saturday Committee, which was formed in 1885 for the purpose.

Initially, there were three wards: the male ward had six beds; the female ward had four beds and two cots for children; and there were two beds in the accident ward. A mortuary was added soon afterwards. The medical staff comprised 'all the medical gentlemen

of the town'. The committee of management thought that the annual running costs would be between £400 and £500 and with this in mind decided that only six beds should be available to patients for the first year. Before they could be admitted, potential patients were assessed by a committee, and then examined by the resident doctor. Once installed, they could be visited on Tuesdays, Thursdays and Saturdays, between 3 p.m. and 4 p.m. Guided tours of the building were available on Wednesdays, between 2 p.m. and 4 p.m.

Read's original design allowed for an additional wing, which was erected in 1894 at a cost of £700, and provided a sitting room for the matron, an operating room, and an accident ward. In 1905, a lodge was built on the east side of the hospital precinct. The hospital was extended in 1923, and again in 1930 when a foundation stone was laid by the Countess of Radnor; the opening ceremony was performed by the Marchioness of Lansdowne. Later, the Victoria Hospital was recognised as a training school for nurses, under the auspices of the General Nursing Council. It continued as a general hospital but concentrated on specific areas of medicine as the nearby Princess Margaret Hospital gradually took on patients during its early years. In 1993, it became a psychiatric hospital and closed in 2007 to be redeveloped for residential use.

Victoria Road Before the 1840s, a short street extended northwards from Bath Road (then still known as The Sands), to the junction with Prospect Place, hardly more than one hundred yards away. Beyond that, lay the hill, sloping down towards the marshlands through which ran the Wilts & Berks Canal, and which area was crossed by a single bridle way. On these lowlands, New Swindon would be built from the 1840s. The short street had not been named by 1844, but appears on documents as Victoria Street in 1848. The name was probably suggested by that of Albert Street, built c.1841, which ran parallel to it and was named after the Queen's consort. Immediately beyond Victoria Street were allotments, gardens and orchards. All of this was private land, but a trackway was gradually worn across it, over the years, by the footfalls of people trudging between the emerging new town and Old Swindon on the hill. (This was an alternative to the earlier route from New Swindon, forged out across fields and eventually emerging into Prospect Place.)

As early as the 1840s, the southern section of what was to become Victoria Street was effectively an extension of Wood Street in terms of commerce and trade, most of which was on its east side. Here, at that time, were a private ladies' finishing school and a private ladies' boarding school; the residences of the high bailiff of the county court, the town's main auctioneer, and a couple of residents of independent means were there; and the street was also home to tailors and drapers, a carpenter, and a tanner. There was one common lodging house, and one beer retailer; but all in all, early Victoria Street was most respectable.

Thus it remained until 1871, when the Old Swindon Local Board proposed extending it to link Old Town and New Swindon. This was begun in 1873 and largely laid down but not finished by 1875 when it was called New Road. Thereafter, there were numerous complaints to the respective local boards about the state of this section of roadway, the residents of both towns by now considering the initial work

to have been a waste of money. In the 1880s, it was firstly designated Jubilee Road, and then Victoria Street North, and it became the major road between the two towns by about 1888, by which time it had been largely made up. It was lined by trees in 1889. Then, there were plans in place to link the square at York Place (which became Regent Circus) with Faringdon Road, so it was assumed that the whole of this street, which began in Old Town, would, when completed, be named Victoria Road. However, the section between Regent Circus and Faringdon Road was named Commercial Road in 1890 and its continuation across the canal was called Milton Road in 1895. By 1899, the section of the thoroughfare between Bath Road and Regent Circus was entirely built up, and it was this part that was named Victoria Road in 1903.

Vintner, Market Square Built adjacent to the town hall in the 19th century, this little square building was distinguished by the decorative capitals and round, moulded arches to the two-light windows and the doorway of its roadside elevation, and the continuous mouldings around its window jambs. It was at some time owned by John Jefferies, grandfather of the writer Richard Jefferies, and became a wine, grocery and provisions merchant, notably Ackerman and Cosser & Bond, before ending its retail days as an off-licence. The building was demolished in 1971 to facilitate road widening.

Vitti, Angelo (1861-1940) Vitti's lodging house is synonymous with its forerunner, the infamous Rhinoceros public house and lodging house in Albert Street from which it was converted by the exiled Italian.

Vitti was born in the small farming village of Settefrati, in the Province of Frosinone, south-east of Rome. In 1883, he arrived in the West Midlands, possibly to join an established Italian community there, where he met Mary Carter from Wolverhampton. The couple came to Swindon and, in 1885, married in the recently opened (1883) Roman Catholic church in Regent Circus. Why they came to Swindon is unknown, but by 1894 the couple had settled into 26 Albert Street. These premises are significant, because they had formerly been part of a series of adjacent lodging houses run by Sarah White and latterly her husband Daniel during the 1880s and early 1890s. Lodgings were to provide a significant part of the Vitti family's income. Family life was very special to him, and each of his children, (he had ten, of whom two died) even when married, lived very close to his premises.

By 1901, Vitti was the landlord of The Lord Raglan, Cricklade Street, and he and Mary (to whom he always referred as 'Maria') lived there with their first three children. They probably stayed there until 1907, when the Lord Raglan was closed down by the magistrates. This gave Vitti the chance to turn his attentions to the former Rhinoceros public house in Albert Street, which had been closed down in 1869. The family moved into this by 1911, by which time Vitti's grocery and provisions corner shop was doing well at 22 Albert Street, in which short thoroughfare he also owned five more properties. (In the 20th century, the grocery store became A.Vitti Sons & Company.) He also had his own railway coal wagon, and dealt in furniture. The fact that he only ever spoke broken English and wrote in the same fractured way, seems to have been no deterrent to his success. Thousands of people

went through his lodging houses; he gained a reputation for providing cheap bed and board and for helping those who passed through who had fallen on hard times. By the time he died in 1940, Vitti owned properties all over Old Town and New Swindon, notably in Regent Street, Commercial Road and Byron Street. His wife Mary survived him until 1944, and both are buried in Radnor Street cemetery. (See also Albert Street.)

Wantage Sisters Revd William John Butler (1818-94) came to Wantage, Berkshire (now Oxfordshire) in 1846, and two years later founded there the Anglican Community of St Mary the Virgin – the Wantage Sisters. The Sisters came to St Mark's parish in 1891, at the request of Canon Hon. Maurice Ponsonby (vicar of St Mark's 1879-1903, who became Lord de Mauley), to help in parochial work among the families of the railway employees. In 1895, Ponsonby laid the foundation stone, and the community built themselves a narrow, four-storey mission house on Milton Road (now on the corner with Tennyson Street, which was being built at about the same time). The architect of the mission house was a High Church Anglican, A. Mardon Mowbray of 31 St John's Street, Oxford, and the builder was William Frederick Loxley of Cowley, Oxford. Externally, it featured blunt lancet windows, mostly in pairs, and decorative wooden bargeboards to the gables. Internally, it included a soup kitchen, a large mission room, a waiting room, and a visitors' room. In 1899, a new Lady Chapel was built on the first floor above the mission room adjoining St Mark's mission house. It was used by the Sisters, the laity, and parish associations, and by the whole parish at a weekly Communion. By 1903, it had become established as an accepted centre for parish activities. The mission house closed in 1970, and was converted to residential apartments.

In 2011, only one Sister remained alive who formerly lived there. She recalls that between 1960 and 1970 there were five Sisters at the mission house: the Sister Superior; a Sister working within the parish of St Mark's, another allied to the daughter church of St Luke's; one engaged on moral welfare working out of a downstairs office; and another in the kitchens. A girl with learning difficulties helped in the kitchen and in the house, and four needy women who looked after themselves but joined the Sisters for dinner lived on the top floor. There was a bookshop on the first floor that also sold crucifixes, statues and rosaries. The Sisters let out rooms in the evenings, which led to their singing of Compline on Wednesdays being drowned out by that of the Welsh Choir practising in the room below. The Salvation Army came to pray in the chapel at the end of the day, after the Sisters had gone to bed, leaving the front door on the latch to facilitate entry. At one time, Terry Waite was on the staff.

Water Tower, Bristol Street The cast-iron water tower was designed to hold a 50,000-gallon-capacity tank, and was created in the GWR Works and constructed in 1871. It supplied water to all of the Company's workshops. The tower, now a notable landmark, stands close to what remains of the GWR school. It is sixty-four feet high, and built around a timber-faced, square-on-plan shaft, in four storeys or lifts separated by cast-iron girders. These are braced diagonally, and there are decorative interlaced circles to each level. Each lift is of three bays, and on the top of the structure is

a platform that supports the tank. This is a replacement of 1979-80, and is six feet deep.

W.D. & H.O. Wills The company started manufacturing tobacco in Castle Street, Bristol, in 1786. In 1913, the company began building its (No.5) tobacco factory in Colbourne Street, which opened in 1915, and received supplies of tobacco from a bonded warehouse in Bristol. It became an impressive structure in red brick, presenting a two-storey, sixteen-bay façade to the front elevation, with a central porch section surmounted by a shoulder pediment; the whole building was tied together by a blind parapet, a plain moulded cornice, and dentil ornamentation. There were several steps up from street level. In 1917, production of cigarettes stopped in Swindon, and, for the rest of the First World War, shell cases and other ammunition cases were made and stored there, under the auspices of the Ministry of Munitions, together with a variety of military equipment. It was not until mid-1919 that the military vacated the factory and cigarette production was resumed. The Gold Flake, Regal King Size, and the (Wild) Woodbine were the products traditionally associated with Swindon – products that were made by a predominantly female workforce. A small Fowler 0-4-0 shunter locomotive was built in 1933, named 'Woodbine', and used in the factory. Wills' provided a playing field in Shrivenham Road for the use of its workers, established a wide range of medical facilities at Colbourne Street, and maintained a convalescent home for employees. The factory closed in 1987 when production was transferred to Bristol. Tesco bought the building, which was demolished c.1988, in a £17 million deal that also included the sports ground, and a Tesco superstore was later built on the site.

W.H. Smith Then under the chairmanship of Hon. David Smith (great-great-grandson of the founder of the firm and known within the company as 'Mr David'), the national seller of books, newspapers and magazines began work on its new warehouse, distribution centre and administrative headquarters at Greenbridge in 1965. The seven-storey building was designed and built under the auspices of the firm's in-house architect, H.F. Bailey, and consultants Johns, Slater & Haward of Ipswich. The main contractors were Modern Engineering of Bristol (a company that was in business 1947-84) and which held the patents for System Silberkuhl, the concrete and steel roofing construction system of repeated crescents that at the time made this the largest unsupported roof in Europe. This was erected under the eye of their in-house architect, Ivor Hollingsworth. The quantity surveyors for the project were Thurgood, Son & Chidgey of London, and heating and lighting was designed by Barlow, Leslie & Partners of Croydon. The complex opened in 1967. The premises became the headquarters of W.H. Smith in 1985, and have been greatly remodelled and expanded over the years. In 1975, the company opened a newly built office block on the corner of Farnsby Street and Faringdon Road, and named Bridge House after its London offices. This was converted to residential apartments in 2006. (See also Book Club Associates.)

Wainwright, David (b.1929) and Vera (1928-91) During the latter 1950s, and the 1960s, many of the amateur theatrical productions in Swindon bore the names of David Wainwright and his wife Vera Bennett, who was then soon to be a professional singer with a national reputation. Vera was born in

Swindon; David came from Manchester, but was living in Nottingham when the two met in 1946 at St Paul's College, a teacher training establishment in Cheltenham. They married in 1952 and settled in Swindon, where Vera had already established herself as a singer and pianist. The couple joined Swindon Amateur Light Operatic Society, in whose productions they both played leads, and also became performing members of the Adastrians Drama Club. David directed productions for the Adastrians, and also for SALOS, which the couple left in 1959 to join the newly formed Swindon Opera.

By now, Vera was performing with her singing partner Michael Chivers, and David directed them in 'Showboat'. In 1967, the singing duo auditioned for Issy Bonn, the Jewish entertainer who had become a theatrical agent, and they thereafter set out on a professional career together working the club circuits and performing in summer seasons and pantomimes. At the same time, David was appointed headmaster at the new Covingham Park School, Swindon. When their professional singing career became less attractive, Vera returned to Swindon, where she taught singing whilst continuing to give concerts with Michael Chivers.

In 1983, David and Vera formed Stage Struck, in order to give their pupils the chance to perform in public. This they first did in 1983 at the Arts Centre, where, by the time they arrived at the Wyvern Theatre two years later, they had performed five shows. Even though David was still teaching, he directed them in 'Fiddler on the Roof', 'The King and I' and 'Most Happy Fella', and in 1985 they put on 'Anne of Green Gables', 'Love From Judy' and 'Chrysanthemum'. In 1988, Vera Bennett and Michael Chivers played opposite each other in one of their productions. Vera wrote all the musical arrangements for Stage Struck and, at the end of one year, they gave twenty concerts in less than two months.

After his wife's death, David continued with Stage Struck for a while, and in 1999 contacted one of its former star pupils, Jane Marie Osborne, for help with that year's show. After her successful appearance on *Opportunity Knocks* in 1986, when she was nineteen, Jane had spent the next few years working in professional theatre and on television. In 2000, she took over the running of Stage Struck with her husband Geoff Marsh, introducing comedy and variety to the shows. In 2002, the company performed its first pantomime, Aladdin, at the Arts Centre, and has since put on a variety show at the Wyvern Theatre each May, and a pantomime at the Arts Centre each December.

Water in Swindon In 1851, George T. Clark, a superintending inspector of the General Board of Health, published the report of a survey he had made the previous year under the Public Health Act, 1848 into the sanitary conditions of Swindon. His investigation had been carried out in response to a petition signed by 162 residents, including the lord of the manor, several ministers, a bailiff of the county court, four solicitors, and eighty-six of the town's more important shopkeepers and tradesmen. Clark saw the most appalling, insanitary conditions, and a water supply that came from backyard wells that were generally contaminated by effluent leaching from adjacent privies, cesspools, pigsties and dung-pits. Most houses had no water that was suitable for drinking. It was a long report, in which Clark made several recommendations; he determined that what

Swindon needed was a complete programme of clean, piped water, and drains and sewers, and the estimated cost of bringing that to a town of just under 3,200 inhabitants would be about eighteen shillings per year over thirty years. There would be no supply of fresh water to Swindon until fifteen years after his report.

In 1857, the lord of the manor, the vicar, and nine leading tradespeople established the Swindon Water Company, to remedy 'the want of an adequate supply of pure and wholesome water for domestic purposes', and to 'lay mains pipes – capable of yielding eighteen gallons of water daily to each individual – in every public street in Old and New Swindon'. The Company was formally registered and sold shares, commissioned a report into how their intentions (which also included the provision of one hundred street hydrants) might be attained, and at what cost.

Then they basically did nothing until 1864, when some of the directors changed and the Swindon Water Company began again to sell shares. They also successfully prevailed upon the Great Western Railway Company to provide half of the capital required to supply Old Town and New Swindon with water, in an agreement by which the railway company's works could have any surplus. In 1866, the Swindon Water Company contracted Henry Potter of Stepney to build their water works at Wroughton, under the direction of James Fenton, civil engineer of Westminster. Potter also constructed the reservoir at Overtown and the 35,000 feet of associated pipework needed to convey the water into the town via Wroughton Road and Croft Road. Fresh water was first pumped into Old Swindon in 1868. At about the same time, the first dwellings in New Swindon

to receive clean, piped water – the newly built Cambria cottages – were fed from a spring just to the south, close to the Wilts & Berks Canal. The originator of the scheme was Welshman William Ellis, manager of the Great Western Railway Company's rolling mills in Swindon. Meanwhile, the company's model village received its water in a processed, but still very impure, condition from the Wilts & Berks Canal, via storage reservoirs on the Works' site, until its arrangement with the Swindon Water Company. The supply proved insufficient for the needs of the expanding Works, so a borehole was sunk near Kemble station, and water was at first brought by train from there, but was later piped.

The Swindon Water Board was formed in 1895 under the joint auspices of the Old Swindon Urban District Council and the New Swindon Urban District Council, and purchased the entire water undertaking; in 1900, it became the responsibility of the Borough of Swindon, which built a reservoir at Okus in 1902. Ogbourne Water Works came into operation in 1903, pumping water to Wroughton for conveying onwards to Okus. All existing water undertakings continued to be developed and expanded, and in 1934, the Latton pumping station and water scheme was opened by Sir E. Hilton Young, the Minister of Health.

Wearing, William Brewer (1818-1912) Born at Trowbridge, Wiltshire, Wearing married Ruth (née Evenden) in Malling, Kent in 1844, and died at Cirencester, to where he relocated some time after his retirement. He was in Swindon by 1845, where he was manager of the County of Gloucestershire Bank in High Street, having transferred from the bank's branch in

Cheltenham. He was, from 1859, a director of the Swindon Water Company, and a director of the Swindon Central Market Company from 1864. He had two sons: William, who became a bank manager, and John Evenden, who was a civil engineer; and two daughters, Annie and Kate. The family lived in Bath Road (Gloucester Villas and No. 25), always had servants, and occasionally bank clerks as lodgers.

Weigh House, GWR see Archers Brewery

Weir, Paul (1920-2006) Philosopher and painstaking poet who claimed that 'it takes years to formulate ideas'; a man obsessed with ideas and communications through art; someone with whom young and old could easily communicate. Weir was born in Liverpool and called William, a name he found disagreeable and which he changed when he was a teenager. His father, having sought employment in America, was killed in 1927 when a rock fell on him whilst he was working on alterations to Sing Sing prison in Ossining, New York State; some time afterwards, his mother was killed by a tram in Liverpool.

Paul went into aircraft engineering, and arrived at Short Brothers, then on part of the site of the Great Western Railway Works in Swindon, via the Air Ministry in 1941. His was a reserved occupation. He was domiciled in a house in Bath Road that had been commandeered as a hostel for Short's workers, and was not required to do military service until hostilities had ceased. He met his future wife Hilda at a police ball, held in the town hall, Regent Circus, and the couple were married in 1943, and bought a house in North Street.

Weir became a founder member of the Swindon Philosophical Society, and a member of the societies devoted to film, arts and poetry. He once said that he was 'frequently kept up into the small hours of the morning by Freud, Einstein and Darwin. He moved with Short Brothers to the South Marston site that became Vickers-Armstrong, for whom he was an aircraft inspector and captained a company cricket team for a number of years. Always interested in scientology, Afro-Indian primitive art, and animal behaviour, he became, in the late 1940s, part of a group that included the surrealist painter and anthropologist Desmond Morris, sculptor Carleton Attwood, film-maker Colin Simpson, and artists Leslie Cole, George Reason, Wally Poole, John Iles and Michael Hall. His film with Desmond Morris – *Time Flower* – was judged the best amateur movie of 1948. In 1950, he won a high recommendation for directing, scripting, and acting in a film about the life of Vincent Van Gogh.

Paul Weir once said that 'poetry is the most sophisticated way man has of expressing his intelligence'. He was published in *The Swindon Review*: 'Between' and 'Wood' appeared in No. 1, 1945; 'Finis' was published in No. 6, 1953; 'Here Is An Old Man' was in No. 7, 1955; and 'Newton's Third Law' and 'For Love' were both printed in No. 8, 1956.

Welsh Baptists Welsh Baptists arrived in Swindon in 1861 to work at the GWR locomotive works, in particular the rolling mills, and at first held their services in a room behind the Greyhound public house in Cambria Place. They relocated in 1866 when their little limestone chapel was built beside the Wilts & Berks Canal. (See also Cambria Baptist Chapel.)

Wesleyan Methodist Chapel, Faringdon Road By the mid-1860s, the Wesleyan Methodists, who needed larger premises, had negotiated with the GWR to buy some land close to the Mechanics' Institute, for the purpose of building a chapel. Almost at once, the railway company came out of recession and bought back this land, on which to build their carriage works, offering instead to sell them the empty Barracks, nearby. Swindon architect Thomas Smith Lansdown drew up plans for converting the Barracks to the needs of the Wesleyan Methodists. This involved converting the north and south wings of the building (some ninety feet apart) into one large room, and covering it with a single-span roof. The work was carried out by builder Thomas Barrett. A commemorative stone was laid by Sir Francis Lycett in 1868.

The conversion included a remodelling of the Faringdon Street elevation, with three doorways set between two 66-foot-high staircase turrets that led to galleries overlooking the three-aisled main body of the chapel. This had an area of over 6,100 square feet and could seat in excess of 1,100 people (2,000 if they also packed the side galleries). The chapel was lined in Bath stone, the plaster ceiling had forty-seven panels, and was supported on two rows of cast-iron columns, each twenty-nine feet high. All of this was painted in blue and gold. The wall to Reading Street was pierced with two-light, pointed windows cusped with trefoils and cinquefoils in the heads. In all, natural light came through forty-seven windows. Inside the front doors, Lansdown placed a large vestibule, and administration offices, and he included a 2,200 sq. ft. schoolroom above, admitting to the galleries in the chapel. The building was opened for worship in 1869,

and closed in 1959. In 1962, it was internally remodelled as the Swindon Railway Museum, and remained as such for the next thirty-eight years. Since 2000, it has had several incarnations in community service. (See also Barracks, Emlyn Square; Railway Museums in Swindon.)

Wesleyan Methodist Chapel, Newport Street Built in 1813, the Methodist chapel, just off the market square in Old Town, was erected behind a row of little cottages. A schoolroom was added in 1842. In 1862, by then behind the Corn Exchange and adjacent to The Planks, the chapel was rebuilt on a cross plan, with an octagonal core. This later structure comprised a succession of gabled projections, with a steeply pitched roof, topped by a stubby spire. The gable ends had three-light, 14th-century-style, moulded and pointed windows with hood mouldings and little label stops, and there were single clasping buttresses at the corners. The octagonal chapel was in use until 1879, when the congregation relocated to the purpose-built Methodist church in Bath Road, passing on the octagonal chapel to the Salvation Army in 1880. The building was later used as a stable, then a garage, and eventually a general storehouse, before demolition in 1937.

Wesleyan Methodists Wesleyan Methodism arrived in Swindon with George Pocock, a travelling preacher who had allegedly been converted by John Wesley, and who conveyed himself by means of a tent-like structure with sails. William Morris quotes the authority of an eyewitness who recalled an appearance by Pocock in 1812. Meanwhile, William Noad, who lived on the Coate road, obtained a licence for services

to be held on his premises. He was from a long-standing Swindon family, many of whom held parish offices. The Methodist chapel of 1813 in Old Town was followed by custom-built premises in Bridge Street, New Swindon, which were demolished in 1858 and superseded by larger premises in Faringdon Road. By 1869, the Wesleyan Methodists had successfully negotiated for The Barracks, the former lodging house in Faringdon Road, and would remain there for the next hundred years. In 1862, the Old Town chapel was demolished and a new chapel with an octagonal core was built on the same site, by then close to The Planks and behind the Corn Exchange. Between 1870 and 1890, they opened six mission chapels around the town, and left the Planks site in 1880 for a purpose-built church in Bath Road. The chapel was taken over by the Salvation Army and demolished in 1937.

Western Players This theatre group, highly active today, can apparently trace its line back to 1854, when the newly formed Mechanics' Institute Amateur Theatrical Club performed the one-act farce *The Lady of Munster*, written in 1830 by the songwriter and dramatist Thomas Haynes Bayly. This took place inside the Swindon railway workshops, most probably on a stage set up in part of the original Painters' Shop. On the night that the Mechanics' Institution building opened in High Street (Emlyn Square), New Swindon in 1855, the players, having settled on the Mechanics' Institute Dramatic Club as their name, performed the farce *Binks the Bagman* by the Irish playwright Joseph Stirling Coyne, and a melodrama, *The Rent Night*. The venue was the large hall on the first floor of the Institution, where a permanent stage

had been built for theatrical performances. The players tinkered with their name over the next few years: it was the Mechanics' Institute Dramatic Society in 1861, and in 1898 it became the Great Western Railway Amateur Players. Until at least 1870, all of the group's members were men. Female parts in the productions were taken by non-Society members co-opted from elsewhere and, from the very first productions, professional actresses were sometimes engaged for important roles. Another change of name in the early 1900s saw the group emerge with the rather prolix name of The Great Western Railway (Swindon) Mechanics' Institution Amateur Theatrical Society, under which title, in 1904, they staged their first production, *Checkmate* – a farce by Scottish journalist and dramatist Andrew Halliday. Since then, the Society has staged between two and four productions each year. In 1933, it became the GWR (Swindon) Amateur Theatrical Society; it first performed as the Great Western Players in 1936, and took the name Western Players in 1949. The players have had a succession of 'homes', namely the Swindon railway workshops, the Mechanics' Institution, the Little Theatre in Bridge Street, and the Arts Centre in Devizes Road.

Westlecot Manor, Mill Lane The manor house at Westlecot is on the site of a property that predated the present building. This earlier dwelling was probably a farmhouse that belonged to the nuns of Lacock Abbey, and which was built on land that had been gifted to them in Swindon, in the 13th century, by Katherine Lovel. She was a relative by marriage of their founder in 1226, Ela, wife of William Longspée. By 1535, the manor of Wicklescote or Westlecote was let to John Goddard of Upham. It was bought

by him in 1540, following the Dissolution of the Monasteries, and was later merged into the manor of Over and Nether Swindon, or West and East Swindon. Thomas Goddard acquired the manor of Swindon in 1563; he may then have made some improvements to the former Lacock Abbey property at Westlecot.

The present Westlecot Manor is presumed to have originated as recorded on the date stone 'TG 1589', let into the south wall. Thomas Goddard's son Richard, and then Richard's eldest son Thomas, acceded to the manor of Swindon, and it is reasonable to suppose that the branch of the family subsequent to John Goddard continued to occupy the old building at Westlecot. The date stone referred to above suggests that it was either remodelled at that time, or was completely rebuilt by a Thomas Goddard. This could have been a sibling of Richard who held the Swindon manor from 1568 (following the death of the original Thomas), but who lived at Westlecot. A more likely contender for the rebuild might be Richard's own son, another Thomas Goddard, possibly on his marriage. His date to the succession of the Swindon manor is unknown, but he held it until 1641.

Westlecot Manor is Grade II listed. It is built of coursed limestone rubble from the Swindon quarries, and is variously of two storeys with attic rooms, or three storeys in the gabled sections. The cellar was partly walled up in the 1960s, so its full extent is not known.

The original house is what now comprises the front gable wing, which includes the porch and the two-storey, single-bay sections on each side. The adjoining north section of the property is not coeval with these but, certainly at the rear, appears to be not much later. A heavy, two-stage buttress supports the porch wing, which comprises the entrance, a dog-leg staircase, and rooms above on two levels. The two wings at the rear are half-hipped.

The lintel above the main entrance is decorated with triglyphs. The windows throughout are square-headed, of between two and five lights, and all are divided by stone mullions. Those to the ground floor have hood mouldings with plain returns, as do those to the second level on the north gable to the rear. The window above the entrance has a segmental relieving arch in dressed stone. With the exception of the window in the north wall of the porch, which is original, all of the windows are 20th-century renewals.

The roof is tiled and has hipped dormer windows; all of this has the appearance of being done as a piece when major work was carried out in 1926. A date stone 'FPG 1926' attests to this, and shows that the property was then still held by the Goddard family. Fitzroy Pleydell Goddard (d. 1927) was the last lord of the manor of Swindon, and the last of the Goddard male line to live in the town. It has been suggested that the two-bay north section, which can clearly be seen on the front elevation as an addition, was put up at this time. It is also of coursed limestone rubble from the Swindon quarries. However, this may have been a substantial rebuild of that part of the house. Clearly, however, 1926 is the date for all of the windows, and the square-leaded panes they contain.

Inside, there is more evidence of the extent of the refurbishing and remodelling of 1926. The position of doorways, front to rear, suggests that the property was built on a cross passage plan with a kitchen at the rear. The staircase leading off the hall is likely to be late 17th century; it includes heavy

turned balusters, and is associated with wooden panelling with drop pendants that are probably part of the 1926 refurbishments done in Georgian style. The work done at that time also included the wooden panelling around the interior walls, various decorative chimney pieces, doors and door cases, the soffit of a segmentally arched opening on the ground floor, beams, and many of the roof timbers.

Several fireplaces, built in 1589, are extant and in situ on the ground floor; notably, they have depressed arch stone lintels, with or without chamfers. Next to the fireplace in the original kitchen is a deep recess, which is likely to have been originally a spice cupboard or a salt cupboard.

In 1926, the date of the major rebuilding, Westlecot Manor was occupied by T. Hartley. Soon after the death of Fitzroy Pleydell Goddard, it was occupied by Thomas Alexander Sutton, who had offices at 42 Cricklade Street (otherwise the premises of solicitors Townsend, Wood & Calderwood), and who was land steward to Goddard's executors. Thomas Alexander Sutton (1888-1945) was the son of Alexander George Sutton (whose father was Sir Richard Sutton, 4th Bt.) and Eugenia Kathleen (née Merry). Her second husband was Fitzroy Pleydell Goddard, who, by reason of that marriage, became step-father to T.A. Sutton. Sutton lived at Westlecot Manor with his wife Gwendoline (née Forsyth-Forrest), whom he married in 1913 and divorced in 1943.

By 1949, the property had become a nursing home, run by Marjory E. Banham (1900-58), Winifred Mary Banham (1893-1971), and Edith A. Goldsmith (1883-1966). Westlecot Manor became, in 1951, one of the first buildings in England to be listed. By 1961, it seems to have been in the sole charge of Winifred, and Edith was living at the nearby Lodge. In 1967, the resident proprietor of the nursing home was Peter R. Leckie.

In its first thirty years as a nursing home, Westlecot Manor was variously a residence for retired gentry and persons of means, and a home for the mentally handicapped. An in-house surgery was associated with some of these. In the mid-1980s, it became a residential home for the elderly. Throughout this period, the ground floor and first floor were substantially remodelled, mostly by means of partition walling that enabled sixteen bedrooms to be created. Local authority permission was granted to owners Richard and Margaret Brown in 2001 for change of use to a single dwelling. This was carried out in 2004, after the remaining four residents were re-housed and the property was sold. The old rooms were then reinstated to their original dimensions, many of the original features were exposed, and the interior was refurbished as a family home. It was later purchased by a property developer as a private residence.

Whale connections The word 'whale' is *cetus* in Latin. In 1804, a hump-backed bridge was built over the Wilts & Berks Canal at a point where the canal crossed the farm trackway that would eventually become Princes Street (although this part of the roadway was not built up until the late 1880s). The shape of the bridge suggested its name. In about 1840, the Wilts & Berks Canal Company built a terrace of twelve cottages and stables on the north side of the waterway (just east of the Whale Bridge intersection). These were to house canal maintenance workers, bargees and their horses, and steps were built between the properties and the

towing path, to facilitate access. The terrace was named Cetus Buildings, and it became the western part of Medgbury Road after the latter was built in c.1878. It included a beerhouse, which was rebuilt c.1845, close to the Whale Bridge, and known as The Whale. David Backhouse, the author of *Home Brewed*, recorded words allegedly written by its first (and brief) keeper Jonas Head and displayed outside the pub: *This is a true authentic Whale/Look at his head and regard his tail/And come in and taste my ale!/There is no better ale I tell 'ee/Than Jonas draws from out his belly*. The Whale Bridge was also noted for its particularly foul, but strangely charismatic, 19th-century, iron-built, men's urinal. In modern times, the site of the Whale Bridge became a road traffic island and roundabout with pedestrian underpasses; this was all removed in 2011 and the area redeveloped to include a pedestrianised plaza, as part of Swindon's planned Union Square development, renamed Kimmerfields in 2013.

Wharf House, Drove Road Built early in the 19th century, this was a beautiful, two-storey, four-bay Georgian residence, immediately south of the Wilts & Berks Canal and beside Drove Road bridge, at a point close to where the Magic Roundabout is now. It was associated with the adjacent Swindon Wharf, and stood, with a nearby stable block, in its own grounds. William Cobbett, writing in *Rural Rides* of a visit made through Swindon in 1826, remarked of this building: 'Just before we got to Swindon we crossed a canal at a place where there is a wharf and a coal-yard, and close by these a gentleman's house, with coach-house, stables, walled-in-garden, paddock *orné*, and the rest of those things, which, all together,

make up a villa, surpassing the second and approaching towards the first class. Seeing a man in the coal-yard, I asked him to what gentleman the house belonged: "to the head un o' the canal," said he. And when, upon further inquiry of him, I found that it was the villa of the chief manager, I could not help congratulating the proprietors of this aquatic concern; for though I did not ask the name of the canal, I could readily suppose that the profits must be prodigious, when the residence of the manager would imply no disparagement of dignity if occupied by a Secretary of State for the Home, or even for the Foreign, department. I mean an *English* Secretary of State; for as to an *American* one, his salary would be wholly inadequate to a residence in a mansion like this.'

The house was called Canal House until the 1870s, and was lived in by the clerks and superintendents of the canal company, notably the Dunsford family. They established a coal yard beside Wharf House and the Swindon Wharf, which was later used by other local coal dealers. Later, Wharf House was home to auctioneer William Rogers Titmas, and from the 1890s it was the residence of Henry Gilling and his family. They were corn and animal feedstuffs dealers, grocers, dairymen, sellers of milk, and the proprietors of the 'English Butter Factory', which stood on the corner of Station Road and County Road. Under their ownership, Wharf House was renamed Fairholm. At this time, the environs of the wharf had become full of the remains and rotting hulks of wooden barges and other vessels, and a depository for metal canal-side fittings, fixtures and machinery. The house was sold in 1936 and demolished in 1937. A succession of motor car garages and showrooms were built on the site.

White, Kenneth Leslie (b.1943) At fifteen years of age, Ken White was hotting rivets, and from 1958 was sign-writing and stencilling numbers on carriages, at British Rail's Swindon Works – the third generation of his family to go 'inside'. He left the railway workshops in 1962, and enrolled at Swindon Art School, with the intention of becoming a full-time artist. Eventually, he became a mural artist, and one of the greatest exponents of trompe l'œil in the world. In 1982, he produced what has been called one of the most spectacular murals ever painted in London; this was two full-sized, classic 18th-century façades on a 2,500-square-foot wall of the Royal Opera House, overlooking the Jubilee Gardens piazza in Covent Garden. Famous in his own town for a fine series of huge wall paintings depicting aspects of railway history, local history subjects, and local personalities, it was as an international muralist that he achieved most lasting recognition. There are Ken White murals across Europe and North America, and he was the originator and painter, in 1984, of Virgin Atlantic airlines' flame-haired, 1930s-style Scarlet Lady.

Ken White's most lasting mural in Swindon is his recreation of a street scene of c.1908 around the Golden Lion bridge, which stood in Regent Street, on the end wall of a terrace at the junction of Princes Street and Fleming Way. He first painted this in 1976, restored it in the 1980s, and completely renovated it in 2009 at the request of Swindon Borough Council, making some pictorial changes and using brighter colours. A friend of the singer Gilbert O'Sullivan since the 1960s, Ken designed the box for 'Caricature: The Box', some seventy-three tracks covering about thirty-five years, and sold in the USA. The cover features a woodcut portrait of the singer by Ken, who also sings on the 1969 recording of 'Mr Moody's Garden'. In 2009, he donated one of his kidneys to his 29-year-old daughter, Laura, who had for nine years been suffering from an auto-immune disease that caused kidney failure. By 2010, when he received the *Wiltshire Life* magazine Award for Arts and Music, he had painted well over one hundred large murals worldwide, and more than forty around his home town. In the last few years, he has concentrated on paintings of life in the railway Works, and many of these, as well as some of his Swindon pictures, have been turned into lino prints.

White, Walter James, murderer see Hunter, Priscilla Frances

White House, Corporation Street Built in 1841 as a speculative venture in an isolated spot, this public house was called the Queen's Arms until 1910. It was one of Swindon's 'Queen' triple; the others were the Queen's Tap (built 1841), and the Queen's Royal Hotel (built at the town's station in 1847). Auctioneer William Dore held successful sales of livestock at the Queen's Arms during the 1860s, causing the GWR to abandon plans to build their own sale yard on nearby land. The White House was demolished in 2004.

Whitehead, George (1857-1917) Born in Bury St Edmunds, Whitehead married Sabina Maria (née Sturgeon, from Cockfield, Suffolk) in 1877. By the time he was sixteen years old, he was described as a school teacher. His father Benjamin was a 'professor of music', which meant he gave music lessons, and his mother was a laundress, as was his sister Mary Florence.

The family relocated to Swindon during the 1870s, setting up home at 36 Prospect Hill, where George was also styled as a 'professor of music'. Later in that decade, they moved to 9 Bath Road, where both he and his father set up as 'professors of music', and where George and Sabina's daughter May Beatrice was born in 1887. Thereafter, George became a property developer and builder, specialising in the area around Gorse Hill. He built Florence Street in 1894, naming it after his sister, and Beatrice Street in 1899, which he named after his daughter. In 1899, he built the Princess Hotel, Beatrice Street; in 1900, he added a boating lake alongside Beatrice Street and Florence Street, which he created out of old clay pits, and on which he levied an admission charge. The lake was bordered by trees, there was a covered walkway with climbing plants, and an extensive stepped landing stage to facilitate boating. The Princess Hotel received its first licence in 1901, by which time Whitehead was living in Bath Road with just one servant. The hotel in Beatrice Street became his home for the rest of his life, and, following his death, was bought by George's of Bristol by auction in 1917. Whitehead left more than £44,000 to his daughter May Beatrice. Whitehead Street, built 1892, was named after him. The lake that Whitehead had created was filled in during 1974, and the area is now partly a retail park.

Wick Farmhouse, West Swindon

The farm grew up beside Hay Lane, a prehistoric track, and it may be on the site of a Roman settlement. The dwelling was probably that referred to in the 13th century as 'la Wyk' (after the Anglo-Saxon word for an outlying farm), and there have certainly been farm buildings here continuously since the 16th century. The front part of the present farmhouse, which dates from c.1700, may have been built above medieval remains. Today, the main group comprises one detached and two semi-detached properties; one of the latter is the two-storey, three-bay farmhouse proper with large attic rooms, and the other comprises the old dairy with cheese lofts above that have been converted into a dwelling. The stables and one-time brewhouse (later grooms' quarters and harness room) were also converted to residential. The work of conversion and renovation was carried out in 1995 by a private developer, Paul Price of Eastleaze Farm.

The farmhouse is built of dark red bricks, mostly laid in Flemish bond with lime mortar. The roof is hipped to the north, built of stone tiles, and has dormer windows. The St John family (the Lords Bolingbroke, of Lydiard Park House, Lydiard Tregoze) owned Wick Farm from the 15th century until it was sold by auction in 1930. There were successions of tenant farmers, notably the Clark family, who were in residence 1839-87, and the Kinchin family, who were associated with nearby Windmill Leaze Farm and who brought Wick Farm into the 20th century. There was no electricity in the farmhouse until 1955. In 1986, the buildings, and the only remaining four fields belonging to it, were sold to Thamesdown Borough Council, and for the next five years the farmhouse was the base for the Thamesdown Archaeological Unit, which was investigating the archaeology of West Swindon. Plans were formulated between 1985 and 1992 to remodel Wick Farmhouse into a Christian centre for people suffering personal problems or marital disharmony, but the propositions were turned down by the Borough Council, and the property was sold into private hands.

Wild West Show in Swindon In 1903, Col. William Frederick Cody (1846-1917) brought his Wild West show to Swindon for one day only. It was part of a tour of one hundred towns and cities in the UK, which began the previous year with a three-month residency at Olympia, London, and finished four months after the visit to Swindon. Cody, a former pony express rider, marksman, frontier scout in the Sioux Wars, and one-time committed buffalo slayer – from which he earned the sobriquet 'Buffalo Bill' – turned showman in the 1880s and thereafter toured the USA and Europe. A special siding was prepared at Swindon station to accommodate the seventy-five-foot-long, brightly painted boxcars that housed the paraphernalia, the horses, and the personnel that made up his 'Congress of Rough Riders of the World'. Upon arrival, Bill was dressed in fringed buckskins and wearing a white hat (No. 1100 in J.B. Stetson's catalogue of the period). The civic dignitaries who came to welcome the middle-aged American superstar found themselves surrounded by horsemen in wide-brimmed Stetsons, fully costumed cowgirls, and colourfully blanket-wrapped and feathered Red Indians. The show was to have taken place at Beechfield, off Marlborough Road, but, at the last minute, this site was considered to be too small to accommodate the eight hundred performers and their five hundred horses. The venue was changed to Corpe's Field beside Wootton Bassett Road, where a 382,500-square-foot arena and seating area was enclosed in canvas and illuminated by electric light for the two performances. Some 20,000 people witnessed what the show's publicists called 'a veritable kindergarten of history-teaching facts; not on fiction founded'. Cody and company did not remain long in Swindon; even before the second show had finished, some of the associated tents and equipment were already being loaded back on to the train at Swindon station.

Williams, Alfred Owen (1877-1930) Alfred Williams, the 'hammerman poet', was born in Cambria Cottage at South Marston, but is claimed by Swindon because he worked at the Great Western Railway Works between 1878 and 1914. His father was Elias Lloyd Williams, a carpenter, and his mother was Elizabeth (née Hughes). Williams left school at the age of eleven, and went straight 'inside' at the GWR; he worked in the stamping shop of the carriage and wagon works, operating a steam hammer. His brothers were also employed in the Works. Williams's bitter and most evocative book, *Life in a Railway Factory*, published 1914, chronicles the harsh conditions there. He used almost every spare moment, day and night, to teach himself Greek, Latin, Sanskrit and French, simultaneously building his own house – 'Ranikhet', where he lived with his wife Mary – writing articles and poems, giving lectures, and running a market garden to make ends meet. He served with the gunners in India. In 1923, he published *Folk Songs of the Upper Thames*, said to have been collected as he travelled some 13,000 miles on his bicycle, 1916-18. In all, he found about 800 songs, of which one-third went into the book, apparently with any bawdy passages changed or censored by Williams. In the 1960s, his manuscripts were discovered in the archives at Swindon Central Library; by 1970, they were classified, catalogued and indexed by Ivor Clissold and Colin Bathe of the Swindon Folksingers' Club, advised by Frank Purslow. Williams's work brought him little fame and hardly any financial reward

during his life, possibly because the class structure of the day was unwilling to accept a 'scholar' railway labourer, who might have been expected to 'know his place'. A group was formed in 1969 called Friends of Alfred Williams, and the following year they organised at South Marston an exhibition of his work, and work by others whom he inspired. In 1972, the library at Swindon College was named 'The Alfred Williams Library'. (See also Alfred Williams Heritage Society; Hammerman, The)

Williams, Charles (1849-1922)
Charles Williams was the man whose workmen built Swindon's New Queen's Theatre, later renamed the Empire Theatre, in just thirty weeks in 1898. He was the son of Charles Williams, a builder from Gloucester, but was himself born in Swindon, after which the family moved to Watchfield. He began his working life as a carpenter, seeking employment in London, where he met Mary Ann Lilley, and where the couple married in 1869. Their son, also named Charles, was born in 1872 and, sometime after this, the family relocated to Swindon. By 1881, Charles had become licensee of The Dolphin Hotel and public house (opened 1873) in Rodbourne. He gave that up in the 1880s and moved to 1 Bury Terrace in Farnsby Street, where, by 1888, he had set himself up as a small-time builder. He was one of the builders of the streets of Rodbourne, and is particularly associated with part of Redcliffe Street, which was developed in the early 1890s. He is known to have built cottages, small houses and terraces, shops and warehouses variously around New Swindon, mostly between the mid-1880s and 1900.

As business improved, the family moved around the town, always to better addresses.

By 1895, Charles Williams, builder and contractor, had lived at 98 Commercial Road, 39 Commercial Road, 12 Victoria Road, Regent Street, and Princes Street, where his business continued between 1895 and 1915. He owned land next to the County Ground, which he sold to Arkell's brewery in 1896, the year Swindon Town Football Club relocated there. Arkell's clearly saw the potential for trade in this location, and immediately built the County Ground Hotel on this land, which opened the following year. Charles Williams's son, Charles Williams, mirroring his father's early years, had begun his working life as a carpenter and joiner, but was immediately installed as the first 'hotel proprietor' of the County Ground Hotel. In retirement, Charles the former builder lived at the hotel with his wife, his son and daughter-in-law Winifred, and their son, who was also unoriginally named Charles Williams.

Williams (Josephine) 'Josie' (b.1959) Because of the eccentric and exaggerated way in which she delivers her poems at her public performances, her contrived Wiltshire accent, and her interesting costume, Josie Williams has been described as 'Pam Ayres on acid'. She was born at Upper Stratton, went to Kingsdown School, and the Swindon College of Art in Euclid Street, before embarking on a career in photo journalism and becoming a Licentiate of the Master Photographer's Association. In 1994, she published *The Wiltshire Hall of Fame*, a book that featured her images of celebrities who lived in the county at the time. It accompanied a touring exhibition of the same name. *Light Fantastic* was her 1996-97 touring exhibition of colour abstract photographs, taken with long exposures, of

the motorway at night. This was followed, 1997-98, with *Round The Bend*, another touring exhibition that featured unusual aspects of 'archetypal characters in society'. Much of her portraiture was carried out in black and white. She achieved national fame in 1998 with her book of poems, *Erotica Out of the Blue*, partly because of the bawdy nature of the poems but more especially for the parts of Josie Williams that she photographed to accompany the pieces. The book was launched – with the help of glamour model Andrea Mickalski – at the Goddard Arms, Clyffe Pypard. Some of Josie Williams's poems were set to music and recorded. Josie performed her erotic poetry in the Poetry and Words tent at the 1999 Glastonbury Festival, together with Swindon College of Art student Kat Jameison, otherwise known as Nymphonium the wood nymph. The pair developed this into their *Ball & Chain* show in which Josie and Kat toured London venues, dressed respectively in the guise of a reluctant bride-to-be and her bridesmaid. Josie is also community arts development officer at Commonweal School.

Wilts & Berks Canal In 1793, the idea was first discussed of linking the Kennet & Avon Canal near Trowbridge with the River Thames at Abingdon. The intention was to make a navigable waterway that could bypass the upper Thames whilst still giving access to London. Its promoters hoped to bring coal along it from the Somerset Coal Canal, and use it to transport agricultural materials throughout the region. The Wilts & Berks Canal was authorised by Act of Parliament in 1795. It reached Swindon in 1804, and arrived at Newbury in 1810. In all, with a number of short branches, it had fifty-eight miles of waterway.

Bridges were built over the Swindon stretch of the Wilts & Berks Canal as follows:
1803 Rushey Platt Bridge (later called Kingshill Road Bridge, and situated at the foot of Kingshill; it was demolished c.1918).
1803 Black Bridge (a wooden bridge originally allowing farm access, and later linking Tennyson Street and Curtis Street; it was demolished c.1885).
1803 Golden Lion Bridge (this was originally a wooden bridge).
1804 Drove Road Bridge (a stone road bridge that serviced Swindon wharf, and was demolished c.1930).
1804 Whale Bridge (between Princes Street and Oriel Street; it was demolished in 1863).
1806 Wooden bridge, at location later to become known as Golden Lion Bridge.
1806 Marsh Farm Bridge (also known as Ivy Bridge).
1806 Green Bridge (a field access bridge, it was demolished in 1956)
1806 Nythe Bridge (also called Nythe Road Bridge; it was demolished c.1930).
1806 Stratton Wharf Bridge (carried Ermin Street, and was demolished in 1955 to facilitate Nythe housing estate).
1870 Golden Lion Bridge (or Regent Street Bridge, replaced the wooden bridge of 1803 and was built and maintained by the GWR; it was demolished in 1918).
1877 Cambria Bridge (flat-span bridge of steel, built by Swindon Corporation to carry Cambria Bridge Road).
1885 Queenstown Bridge (a girder bridge that joined Wellington Street with College Street and was built at a cost of £900; it was demolished in the 1920s).
1890 Milton Road (or Commercial Road) Bridge (a replacement for Black Bridge, as the Rolleston estate was developed for residential).

1883 Midland & South Western Junction Railway Bridge at Rushey Platt.

1893 Replacement Whale Bridge designed by Henry Joseph Hamp, who was surveyor to the New Swindon Urban District Council, and built at a cost of £1,200, joining Princes Street with Oriel Street; replacement Cambria Bridge, also designed by Hamp and costing £1,500, which included widening both approaches.

1898 Marlborough Street footbridge (built to link with Albion Street; it was demolished c.1918).

1907 York Road Bridge (built by Swindon Corporation; it was demolished in 1963).

There were also some un-named bridges, usually associated with field tracks or to facilitate farm access. One was built east of Nythe Bridge in the mid-1800s, and was demolished c.1930.

The Wilts & Berks Canal, although prospering until the 1840s, never really delivered the anticipated positive influence on Swindon's trade and prosperity. Freight gradually transferred from it on to the railway and, in 1875, the canal company sold out to a group of independent businessmen. By 1875, the Swindon stretch was virtually disused; it became almost completely silted up, and was regarded as a public nuisance. The following year, a new company was set up to administer the canal (its directors included Thomas Turner of the Swindon Tile & Pottery Works), and it ran boats between Swindon, Bristol and Gloucester. The canal again had new management in 1891, ceased to function in 1906, was dredged in 1908, eventually closed down under the Wilts & Berks Canal Abandonment Act, 1914, and partly filled in. Today, its course becomes Canal Walk (its 19th-century name) in the town centre where this leads on through The Parade, Canal Green, and Fleming Way shopping areas. (See also North Wilts Canal, and Coate Water.)

Wilts & Dorset Bank Building, Wood Street

This imposing building was designed by G.M. Silley of Craven Street, London for the Wilts & Dorset Banking Company. It was erected on the corner of Wood Street and Cricklade Street in 1884, and was opened in 1885. The site had been variously occupied throughout the 19th century by John Blackford, the butcher; Henry Tarrant, the boot and shoe maker; and Joseph Gay, the surgeon. It is a three-storey building, bowed on the corner, of brick with heavy stone dressings, rusticated pilasters and heavy string courses. The bricks were supplied by Thomas Turner's Swindon Tile & Pottery Works in Drove Road. There are four bays to the Wood Street elevation and three bays to Cricklade Street. The decorative motifs are concentrated on the rounded corner entrance elevation. They include flat, fluted pilasters and a decorated architrave surrounding the doorway; and there is a moulded, open ogee pediment above, decorated with a garland. The central window has a segmental shell pediment, and the flanking windows have flags and dropped tails. The Wilts & Dorset Bank was taken over by Lloyds Bank in 1914. Barclays bought the bank building (2-4 Wood Street) from Lloyds in December 1919, and put their own signage on the Cricklade Street elevation. In 1932, Barclays also bought 6 Wood Street, and a flat at 1 Cricklade Street wherein they installed the bank manager; in 1974, the bank bought 5 Devizes Road, and the business relocated there as Barclays Swindon Old Town Branch. The Wood Street property was sold by Barclays in 1976, and

went out of the banking business. It has since been a restaurant, and a hairdressing business.

Wiltshire Courier This short-lived monthly county magazine was established by a group of Swindon businessmen, and operated out of an office at Havelock Street with just an 'editor' and his secretary. The company's name was the Swindon & District Review Limited. The first issue of the Wiltshire Courier was dated October 1962, and the final issue was dated May 1966. It occasionally included articles about Swindon.

Wiltshire Gazette & Herald Swindon's other newspaper, the Conservative *North Wilts Herald*, known as 'the weekly' to differentiate between that and the Liberal *Swindon Advertiser*, was first published, from 19 Bath Road, on Saturday 22 June 1861. It came about because certain influential people, notably Ambrose Lethbridge Goddard, the lord of the manor, and Henry Calley, of Burderop Park, were disenchanted with Morris's stance in the *Swindon Advertiser*. They engaged Joshua Henry Piper (1837-1885) in talks about forming a competitor. In the event, the paper was established by a group of Swindon businessmen, headed by the Swindon solicitor James Copleston Townsend, who thought that a publication with a county or farming bias might be a good thing. Piper took on the role of editor.

The newspaper's first proper editorial offices were in Devizes Road. Piper became the proprietor in 1865 and immediately put changes in hand to print on a steam-operated printing press. Its editor also adopted an acquisitive policy, amalgamating

with it some seven other local town and area newspapers within the *Herald's* first decade. Piper came from Bristol, his wife Anne from Exeter, and at first they lived at 13 Bath Terrace, Bath Road. He founded the *Evening North Wilts Herald* in 1881. In 1884, he was a founding member of the Swindon Town Club. He died the following year at his home, then 19 Bath Road, having suffered chest pains and vomiting following a business meeting in London. He was buried at Christ Church. The Piper family kept control of the *North Wilts Herald* until 1922, when it was bought by Swindon Press, the then owners of the *Swindon Evening Advertiser*, who the following year merged the *Evening North Wilts Herald* into the *Swindon Evening Advertiser*. In 1941, the *North Wilts Herald* became the *North Wilts Herald & Advertiser*, then, nine years later, it was re-styled the *Wiltshire Herald & Advertiser*. In 1956, this was amalgamated with the *Wiltshire Gazette*, previously published in Devizes as an independent newspaper with a long history. The resulting publication became the *Wiltshire Gazette & Herald*.

Women's Institute markets A Women's Institute market was established in May 1944 on open ground on the east side of the Town Hall, Regent Circus. It sold fruit, vegetables, poultry, and other produce, and remained there until June 1965 when it was removed some three hundred yards to a small area in Byron Street, adjacent to the Technical College car park. There, it continued to sell farm and country produce, preserves and cakes, from three covered stalls and two open stalls. It changed its market day from Tuesday to Friday in June 1967, but closed down in the same year. A group of Swindon WI members resurrected the market in 1981,

selling a wide range of produce and products each Friday from the foyer of the Wyvern Theatre. There, the markets were patronised by the general public as well as people who were appearing on stage at the theatre. By the mid-1990s, the theatre increasingly needed its foyer for other purposes, and the WI market was often relocated to rooms elsewhere in the theatre complex, where it was less well patronised. In 1995, it relocated to an upstairs room in the Pilgrim Centre, Regent Street, in which position it was hardly more convenient. This was also the year when for legal and other reasons (the Women's Institute being a charity, whilst the market was a co-operative) the two had to separate; the market became the Swindon Country Market. In 2005, it moved out of the Pilgrim Centre and into the church hall of St Aldhelm's chapel, Edgeware Road, where it sells home-baked products, jams and preserves, garden produce and plants, and other crafts every Friday morning.

Wood Street Known to have been named as such by late in the 16th century, the thatched cottages of Wood Street were then very much tenanted by quarry workers and associated trades such as carpenters and blacksmiths. It has been suggested that the name might have derived from a wood store there, or because of a wooded area that stood adjacent, or from the local pronunciation of Wootton – it being the highway to Wootton Bassett. William Morris recalled that it was at some time in the 19th century called Windmill Street, after a windmill that stood in the vicinity of the present-day King's Arms Hotel, and at other times Blacksmith Street, on account of the several forges that were to be found there. Even into the 1800s, agricultural tradespeople were much

in evidence here, although the gradual gentrification of the street began early in the 19th century. Private schools set up here, adding to the developing upmarket 'feel'. It was then one of the 'two principal streets' ascribed to the town, and had begun to be developed in a way that Newport Street – the oldest known of Old Town's thoroughfares – did not. That is to say it became, during the 1800s, a place wherein the better class of tradespeople inserted their businesses and where there were residents of 'easy means' in the larger premises that were being redeveloped out of the older cottages.

In the mid-1800s, Wood Street still had a number of thatched cottages, but during the 1860s and 1870s most of these were swept away. Some of the existing properties were re-fronted – notably the King's Arms Hotel – and new, architect-designed buildings were erected for the purposes of commerce and trade, which reached their peak in Wood Street in the 1870s. Today, some of the best 19th-century buildings in Old Town line the north side of Wood Street. A number of these are described individually. Some notable buildings extant on the south side include a fine 19th-century oak shop front in a two-storey building at No. 9. The varnished woodwork is a riot of decorative motifs: balusters and fluted muntins; carved egg and dart, and leaf decoration; baluster-style glazing bars and similarly decorated pilasters. The central doorway, within a glazed, canted entrance, is similarly treated. This is a beautiful survival in a much older building that also has two windows to the first floor, one a bay, and which features moulded cornices, egg and dart decoration, entwined rings, and a bracketed sill. (See also Banking in Swindon; Bowmaker House; King's Arms Hotel; Wilts & Dorset Bank building.)

Wood Street windmill At the death in 1324 of Aymer de Valance, lord of the manor of Swindon, his estate included one windmill. This is thought to have been on the site of the present-day King's Arms Hotel in Wood Street. The street was once called Windmill Street after one of this mill's successors, which was, in its turn, demolished about 1840 in favour of three new cottages.

Woodhams's book depots, Bath Road The importance of education and religion in the latter half of the 19th century was exemplified by the Woodhams siblings, who arrived from Kent, c.1858. They were four of the children of farmer Abel Woodhams (b.1805) of Edenbridge, and his wife Mary (b.1809, also Edenbridge). Their son George Woodhams (b.1840, Edenbridge), an out-of-work miller, came to Swindon with his Tunbridge Wells born sisters Ellen (b.1835) and Eliza (b.1837), and Maria (b.1848, Edenbridge). Their mother also came to Swindon with them. Immediately, the three sisters established their 'fancy repository' at 5-7 Bath Road, which was also the family's place of residence. Mary set up a ladies' school in nearby Victoria Street. By 1871, the fancy repository had become the Misses Woodhams' Stationers and Booksellers, and was specialising in religious books, and the school text books and other educational material published by the National Society. This organisation's stated objective was 'Promoting the Education of the Poor in the Principles of the Established Church'.

In the mid-1870s, the Woodhams's repository changed its focus in the face of developing social trends and became the Swindon depot for books published by the British & Foreign Bible Society, and the Society for Promoting Christian Knowledge. The latter announced, in 1875, that it had established its depot at the Misses Woodhams's, and asked potential subscribers to apply to the Swindon treasurer and secretary, William Ormond, the Swindon solicitor. The secretary of the British & Foreign Bible Society in Swindon was Richard Strange, the treasurer was Thomas Strange, both of the well-known family of Swindon bankers that, earlier in the century, had helped to establish Nonconformist worship in the town. The secretary was Revd Henry George Baily, the vicar of Christ Church. By 1878, the secretary of the National Society in Swindon was Revd H.R. Hayward of Lydiard Millicent (who by then was also secretary of the SPCK). Woodhams's was latterly run by Maria Woodhams alone; it was re-designated Woodhams & Co in 1892, but was gone by 1895.

Workhouse A document dated 1584 mentions a church house in Newport Street. A document dated 1706/7, recording retrospectively, mentions a former church house wherein were living 'a few poor people in receipt of alms'. It describes how this church house, being required as the site of a market house, was appropriated for such and the inhabitants lost their homes. There is not further evidence of accommodation for the poor in Swindon for the next sixty years.

A quarter of a century after the idea to build a workhouse in Swindon was first proposed by the vestry, one was erected, c.1790, to house the parish poor. The site chosen, on land owned by Ambrose Goddard, lord of the manor, was just west of the road to Wroughton, on a track known as Quarry Lane, immediately to the south of Swindon quarries. Little is known of this building,

except for a 19th-century description, made in retrospect, that it was built of bricks, had a yard outside, and a tunnel-shaped, brick-lined cellar that may have been used for nefarious purposes. Within forty years of opening, the building had fallen into disrepair and, c.1844, was sold. It was converted into tenements, which between them allegedly held up to twenty families. The building was demolished in the late 1850s.

Two houses were built on the site, and both were first occupied in 1861, when they were described as being 'newly built on or near the site of the old workhouse'. Springfield Villa was built for retired draper Thomas Strange, who relocated there with his family from Bath Road. The house was named after the field thereabouts, one of whose several springs debouched into the Wroughton road. The adjoining property was Sanford House, which was leased by Ambrose Lethbridge Goddard, lord of the manor, to Philip Hawe Mason, the grocer of High Street, who hitherto had lived in Devizes Road. Sanford House (sometimes wrongly named on maps as 'Sandford') was named after A.L. Goddard's wife, the former Charlotte Sanford, whom he married at Wellington, Somerset, in 1847. Strange and Mason lived in these properties for the next twenty years. By 1886, Quarry Lane had been built up, the majority of its length becoming Westlecot Road, and the eastern portion taking the name Springfield Road after the same topographical features that inspired the name of the Villa a quarter of a century before.

Workmen's Hall, Cricklade Street In 1877, a group of well-meaning tradespeople and professionals opened the Workmen's Hall in Cricklade Street 'as a free place of resort for men on weekday evenings'. This was rather an odd description, since the hall was open from 5 a.m. until 10 p.m. as 'a great convenience to those whose labours or necessities call them early from their homes, or whose means are limited'. The hall was in the care of Mrs Trinder, wife of Albert Trinder, watchmaker of Victoria Street. Amongst the committee of benefactors were William Brown and Alfred Plummer, wine merchants (although an aim of the establishment was to provide an atmosphere that was 'dissociated from intoxicating drink'); Arthur Stote, the resident boys' master at King William Street school (opened 1871); William Henry Read, architect and surveyor of Morava House, Bath Road; William F. Church, corn dealer of Cricklade Street; and George Barnett, of Belle Vue Road. The premises provided newspapers and periodicals, bagatelle, chess, draughts, smoking and 'other means of recreation'; as well as breakfasts and dinners, tea, coffee, cocoa and 'other refreshments at a reasonable tariff'. The venue was funded by subscriptions and other voluntary contributions. These dwindled and the place was in financial trouble by 1881, and closed shortly afterwards.

Writers of Swindon's History Swindon's first historian was William Morris, founder of the *Swindon Advertiser* (see Swindon Legends). In 1885, his book *Swindon Fifty Years Ago* was published; though extremely flawed in many respects, it was virtually all that was available on the town's history for the next eighty years. Volume IX of *The Victoria History of Wiltshire*, which included Swindon, and which was published in 1970, was to a degree indebted to William Morris's work. In 1931, a native of Swindon, Frederick

Large (1852-1934) privately published *A Swindon Retrospect 1856-1931*, a small but useful volume of personal recollections and reminiscences. He was a tailor's son, born in Victoria Street, but later moving to Prospect, and Fred became a reporter on the *North Wilts Herald* newspaper. In 1950, Swindon Borough Council published *Studies in the History of Swindon*, a five-hander of a book, in six parts, of which five were generally too difficult and arcane for most people to consider buying. David Douglas of Bristol University wrote the introduction; L.V. Grinsell provided the town's story up to Saxon times; H.B. Wells tackled manorial and church history, and Swindon in the 19th and 20th centuries; life before the railway age was described by H.S. Tallamy; and John Betjeman wrote about architecture. The stock of books and piles of dust covers were kept in the boiler room and in the clock tower of the town hall, and copies could be bought from the central library. It is an interesting book, but its commercial failure meant that fifteen years after publication, most of the stock was still lying around, and was eventually destroyed.

In 1960, the Swindon History Class was formed, which met every Tuesday evening in the local history room of the Swindon reference library. They met to undertake individual local history projects under the tutelage of Professor Harry Ross, of the Extra-Mural Department of Bristol University, who lived in Wellhead Lane, Westbury. An example of their work was the compilation and card indexing of Swindon place names; another produced a listing of local history source material held in various archives. Since the mid-twentieth century, others have researched areas and topics of Swindon's history, and their findings have

been published. They appear under their names in this book.

Wyvern Theatre In 1968, plans were made to provide the town with a new arts centre, with a 600-seat auditorium and suite of rooms that could variously accommodate between 20 and 100 people, and provision for an arts club. It was a time when it was said, 'In Swindon the word art and the word culture are frowned upon with suspicion by the greater part of the population', according to Norman Liddiard, formerly Swindon's social development officer. That year, Ald. A.J. Bown, the then mayor, laid the foundation stone to mark the start of the first phase of Swindon's new Civic Centre, of which the proposed arts centre was a part. He did so with a mallet, presented to him by Sir Hugh Casson, of Casson, Conder & Partners, who were the architects of the scheme, which then comprised a civic hall, a library, and an arts centre. It had been developed with the assistance of J.L. Hodgkinson, the Arts Council's drama director. It was Casson who termed the location of the arts centre as 'Theatre Square', a development of three buildings intended for mixed commercial, office, and civic use. The arts centre, which became the Wyvern Theatre, was the first stage in the construction of the Civic Centre, which included the Islington Street car park. What became the Wyvern Theatre, as well as a few more nearby buildings in the scheme, was designed by Neville Conder of the partnership.

The Wyvern Theatre opened on 7 September 1971 with the first appearance in the UK of the Ukrainian Dance Company. The first-night audience was by invitation only, and each invitee was given a red silk banner printed in gold to mark the occasion.

The artistes then went on to complete a two-week run at the theatre. Thereafter, the theatre featured live performances and showed films. The proposed Civic Centre, of which the theatre was part, was opened by Queen Elizabeth II, accompanied by Prince Philip, in November 1971.

The auditorium of the Wyvern Theatre could seat up to 658 people on seats covered in seven different shades of green and blue-green. The stage was initially thirty feet deep, with a proscenium opening thirty-five feet wide by twenty feet high. The fly tower is sixty feet high, and the total width of stage and wings is seventy-seven feet. The top of the building was equipped as an arts centre with five rooms. There was also a studio room that was used for rehearsals and intimate performances, and another room was taken over by 'The Wyvern Club' members as a place where performers could be met with after the shows. It later became a restaurant. During its heyday, the Club was run by Phil Durber, a retired teacher. He obtained many members by persuasive networking, long before doing so was a fashionable business practice.

The theatre was designed as part of a redevelopment of the area by Casson, Conder & Partners. The buildings they designed around the pedestrianised theatre square as part of the scheme initially housed a sub-Post Office, eleven shops and offices, a techno-centre, a central enquiry and exhibition centre, a public house, and a discotheque. The theatre was run by the Wyvern Arts Trust Limited, set up by Swindon Borough Council, who also subsidised the running of the place and the cost of theatrical productions. The first theatre administrator was Brien Chitty; Mary Morgan was the public relations officer; theatre manager was Alan Knowles; and James Scott was the production manager. On an exterior wall is a twenty-foot-long representation of the mythical beast, part-dragon, part-griffin, after which the theatre is named. In 1979, the Visual Arts Studio, which had been operating in the town hall, relocated to the Wyvern Theatre, and the Jolliffe Visual Arts Studio was established there in 1982. The Wyvern was closed in 2006, following the discovery of asbestos in the roof. It reopened in 2007.

XTC Arguably Swindon's most successful band, XTC was born in 1977 (when they were signed by Virgin Records) of the 'new wave' that followed the emergence of punk in the 1970s. The group comprised John Andrew Partridge (b. 1953); Colin Ivor Moulding (b. Swindon, 1955); Terry Chambers (b. Swindon, 1955); and Barry Andrews (b. West Norwood, London, 1956), who was later replaced by Dave Gregory (b. Swindon 1952). Partridge and Moulding lived at Penhill, met when attending Headlands School, and first played with a band called Clark Kent. XTC was active and recording between 1975 and 2005. In 1979, they hit the pop charts with 'Making Plans For Nigel'. Partridge was born in Malta, but brought up in Swindon, where he has always lived. He was the band's guitarist and song-writer. The cover of the band's 1982 single record 'Ball and Chain' was illustrated with a photograph of a terraced property in Westcott Street, flanked on each side by an empty house, wherein owners Richard and Betty Uzzell, who had won an appeal against compulsory purchase, defied (until 1984) the Borough of Thamesdown's hopes of demolition. XTC ceased touring in 1982, after which Partridge became well

known for the independent recording studio he set up in his garden shed, producing home demo recordings under his Ape House label. The band continued to issue recordings until 2005.

Young, Revd Frederick Rowland (1828-1893) The man who provided Swindon with its original iron church, and the Regent Circus premises that would eventually be the location of the town's first museum, was born in Aldershot, Hampshire. In 1848, he had a daughter, named Annie Juliet, with Olif Wilson (b. Dover, 1827), who was then living in Dial Lane, Ipswich, Suffolk, where her father was a shoemaker and she was occupied as a milliner. The couple married in Ipswich in 1849, and two years later were in Diss, Norfolk, where Olif continued her work as a milliner. Young was described as a Unitarian Baptist Minister, and the family relocated to Adcroft Street, in Trowbridge, Wiltshire, during the 1850s.

In the 1860s, Young met Charles Anthony Wheeler, the Swindon chemist, bookseller, stationer and cigar dealer who, in the 1840s, had built Rose Cottage in Drove Road for himself. The meeting took place in the parish reading room, where the minister handed over a deposit of thirty pounds as a down payment on Rose Cottage, where he then lived until 1879. In 1867, Annie Juliet married Frederick Harber (b.1844) in Islington, London; the couple lived in Peckham, where their daughter Lucy was born in 1870. Frederick died in 1872 and Juliet came back to Swindon to live with her parents. In 1874, she married journalist Robert Stroud Chant (b.1849) at St Mark's church, Swindon, and they went to live at Cranford Lodge, Dartford, Kent.

Young brought faith healers to Swindon,

although lost some credibility when one such, much lauded by the minister, failed to come up to expectations. He also did not enhance his reputation by supporting Daniel Gooch instead of Lord Eliot in the 1866 elections. Although Young established his ministry under the banner of Unitarianism, he did not agree with all of their precepts, and withdrew from the movement in 1875. He was a spiritualist, who in 1870 established and edited *The Christian Spiritualist*, published many religious papers, and held séances of a terrifying nature at his home. He was also a member of the Old Swindon Local Board. Young and his wife Olif remained at 4 Rolleston Street, next to the Free Christian Church he had established, for a few months after he gave up the ministry in 1879, and then went to live at 49 Finsbury Park Road, Hornsey, Middlesex. It was there that he died. Probate was granted to his wife, and to John Harland Appleford, a manager for a company of cigar importers, whose own wife was also named Olif and came from Ipswich, where the Youngs had begun their married life. Afterwards, Olif Young returned to Swindon, where she lived at 28 Hythe Road, with one servant, until her own death in 1907. (See also Free Christian Church; Iron Church; Museums.)

York Place see Regent Circus

Yucca Villa, Bath Road Built of rough coursed limestone with ashlar quoins and dressings, for the Bowly family in 1868, Yucca Villa was always a visually appealing building, with a symmetrical south façade. It is of two storeys with attic, and three bays. The first-floor windows are pairs of square-headed lights divided by stone mullions; to the ground floor are canted bow windows

with cornices flanking a central portico that bears the name of the property. The house was newly built when Elizabeth Bathe Clark came to live there, probably following the death in 1880 of her husband, Jonas Clark, of the family that formerly farmed Wick Farm, Lydiard Tregoze. Elizabeth came to her wedding with Jonas in 1859 as the widow Humphries, but she was born the daughter of Richard Dore King, a relative of the Dore family of Swindon printers and auctioneers who were themselves at the time also living in Bath Road. Elizabeth Clark was blind, and lived at Yucca Villa with her sister Sarah Sheppard King (from 1888), a companion housekeeper, a nurse, and a female servant, until her death, aged 90, in 1903. Sarah King remained there until her death in 1906, aged 87.